SUNDAY MISSAL

2023 – 2024

with Prayers and Hymns

Approved for use in Canada

NOVALIS

©2023 Novalis Publishing Inc.

Novalis Publishing Inc.
1 Eglinton Avenue East, Suite 800
Toronto, ON, M4P 3A1
Canada

Telephone: 1-800-387-7164
Fax: 1-800-204-4140
Email: books@novalis.ca

www.novalis.ca

Since 1936 Novalis has dedicated itself to the development of pastoral resources which assist the People of God in preparing for and participating in the liturgy.

Please write, phone, or visit us for further information on our publications, or visit our website at www.novalis.ca.

For more suggested intentions for the Prayer of the Faithful, please visit: www.livingwithchrist.ca.

Editor: Natalia Kononenko; email: LWC@novalis.ca

Associate Editor: Nancy Keyes

Music: All credits accompany the music texts.

Cover design & layout: Jessica Llewellyn

Cover photo: Bill Wittman

ISBN: 978-2-89830-151-3

ISSN: 0832-5324

Printed in Canada.

We acknowledge the support of the Government of Canada.

Contents

Liturgical Calendar . . . . inside front cover

How to Use this Missal 4

Order of Mass 7

Sunday Readings 73

PRAYER

The Pope's Prayer Intentions for 2023-2024 577

About Prayer 580

Traditional Prayers 581

The Rosary 586

The Way of the Cross 588

Praying with the Eucharist 596

Prayer for Reverence for Life 598

Prayer for Vocations 598

A Prayer for Our Earth 599

Prayer for Peace in the World 600

Inspiration from the Saints 601

Prayers for Cemetery Visits 606

Where Do the Readings at Mass Come From? 609

Prayer in the Morning 613

Prayer in the Evening 617

Celebrating the Sacrament of Reconciliation 621

Prayers for Adoration 625

MUSIC

Eucharistic Chants 627

Hymns 636

Music Index 656

HOW TO USE THIS MISSAL

Missals (and missalettes — the smaller monthly version) were born in the days before Vatican II, when people 'followed' the Latin liturgy using an English translation. Their use in the liturgy immediately after the Council gave people the opportunity to get used to the texts of the newly translated liturgy. However, that often led to a congregation with their noses firmly planted in the missal, almost oblivious to the liturgical action going on around them — not exactly the "full, conscious and active participation" desired by the Council!

So how should we use missals and missalettes? Here are some ideas:

1.   Prepare for the liturgy. Read and meditate on the scriptures and the prayers of the day. Christ is present when the scriptures are being proclaimed. It is Christ who speaks — and part of the reverence we owe the liturgical celebration is to listen attentively at that time.

2.   RCIA catechists and coordinators can give missals and missalettes to inquirers and catechumens to help them through their period of formation.

3.   Musicians who are selecting the music for celebrations will find not only the readings there, but also the prayers of the Roman Missal that can inspire their music selection.

4. Leaders of children's Liturgy of the Word can also use the missal to prepare for their ministry.

5. Often priests and deacons must be away from their parish during the week. Homily and liturgy prep can continue thanks to either a missal or missalette.

6. People who are hard of hearing or unfamiliar with English may need the help of the printed word to support and clarify the spoken word. The same is true if the sound system is failing.

When should we not use missals and missalettes?

1. Certainly not during the proclamation of God's Word, when God is speaking to us through the ministry of the lectors.

2. We should put them down and listen during the Prayer of the Faithful.

3. Missals and missalettes should never replace the Church's liturgical books — the Lectionary or the Roman Missal — in our celebrations. These books, with their beautiful design, add to the dignity of the celebration and speak of the importance of the words and gestures we use.

So once the Mass begins, set aside the missal and focus on the liturgical gestures, actions and words as the ministers bring them to life.

Novalis staff

The Eucharist is the sacrament of love:
it signifies love, it produces love.
The Eucharist is the consummation
of the whole spiritual life.

St. Thomas Aquinas

Order of Mass

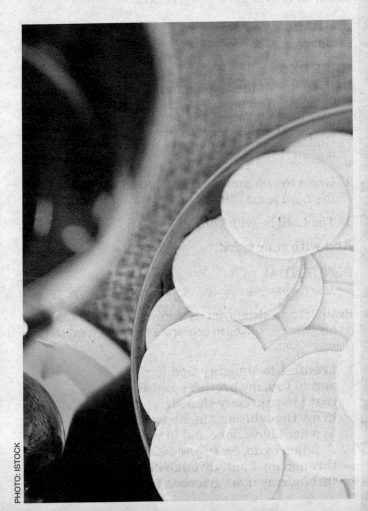

Introductory Rites

ENTRANCE CHANT
(or Entrance Antiphon — ▶ The appropriate day)

GREETING
In the name of the Father, and of the Son, and of the Holy Spirit. **Amen.**

1 The grace of our Lord Jesus Christ, and the love of God, and the communion of the Holy Spirit be with you all.

2 Grace to you and peace from God our Father and the Lord Jesus Christ.

3 The Lord be with you.

And with your spirit.

PENITENTIAL ACT
(or Rite for the Blessing and Sprinkling of Water, p. 10)

Brothers and sisters, let us acknowledge our sins, and so prepare ourselves to celebrate the sacred mysteries. *(Pause)*

1 **I confess to almighty God
and to you, my brothers and sisters,
that I have greatly sinned,
in my thoughts and in my words,
in what I have done and in what I have
     failed to do,** *(striking the breast)*
**through my fault, through my fault,
through my most grievous fault;**

therefore I ask blessed Mary ever-Virgin,
all the Angels and Saints,
and you, my brothers and sisters,
to pray for me to the Lord our God.

May almighty God have mercy on us, forgive us our sins, and bring us to everlasting life. **Amen.**

Lord, have mercy.	**Lord, have mercy.**
or Kyrie, eleison.	**Kyrie, eleison.**
Christ, have mercy.	**Christ, have mercy.**
or Christe, eleison.	**Christe, eleison.**
Lord, have mercy.	**Lord, have mercy.**
or Kyrie, eleison.	**Kyrie, eleison.**

2 Have mercy on us, O Lord.
For we have sinned against you.

Show us, O Lord, your mercy.
And grant us your salvation.

May almighty God have mercy on us, forgive us our sins, and bring us to everlasting life. **Amen.**

Lord, have mercy.	**Lord, have mercy.**
or Kyrie, eleison.	**Kyrie, eleison.**
Christ, have mercy.	**Christ, have mercy.**
or Christe, eleison.	**Christe, eleison.**
Lord, have mercy.	**Lord, have mercy.**
or Kyrie, eleison.	**Kyrie, eleison.**

3 You were sent to heal the contrite of heart:

Lord, have mercy.   **Lord, have mercy.**
or Kyrie, eleison.   **Kyrie, eleison.**

You came to call sinners:

Christ, have mercy.   **Christ, have mercy.**
or Christe, eleison.   **Christe, eleison.**

You are seated at the right hand of the Father to intercede for us:

Lord, have mercy.   **Lord, have mercy.**
or Kyrie, eleison.   **Kyrie, eleison.**

May almighty God have mercy on us, forgive us our sins, and bring us to everlasting life. **Amen.**

(▶ *Glory to God, p. 13*)

RITE FOR THE BLESSING AND SPRINKLING OF WATER

Dear brothers and sisters, let us humbly beseech the Lord our God to bless this water he has created, which will be sprinkled on us as a memorial of our Baptism. May he help us by his grace to remain faithful to the Spirit we have received. *(Pause)*

1 Almighty ever-living God, who willed that through water, the fountain of life and the source of purification, even souls should be cleansed and receive the gift of eternal life; be pleased, we pray, to bless this water, by which we seek protection on this your day, O Lord. Renew the living spring of your grace within us and grant that by this water we may be defended from all ills of spirit and body, and so approach you with hearts made clean and worthily receive your salvation. Through Christ our Lord. **Amen.**

2 Almighty Lord and God, who are the source and origin of all life, whether of body or soul, we ask you to bless this water, which we use in confidence to implore forgiveness for our sins and to obtain the protection of your grace against all illness and every snare of the enemy. Grant, O Lord, in your mercy, that living waters may always spring up for our salvation, and so may we approach you with a pure heart and avoid all danger to body and soul. Through Christ our Lord. **Amen.**

3 *During Easter Time:*
Lord our God, in your mercy be present to your people's prayers, and, for us who recall the wondrous work of our creation and the still greater work of our redemption, graciously bless this water. For you created water to make the fields fruitful and to refresh and cleanse our bodies. You also made water the instrument of your mercy: for through water you freed your people from slavery and quenched their thirst in the desert; through water the Prophets proclaimed the new covenant you were to enter upon with the human race; and last of all, through water, which Christ made holy in the Jordan, you have renewed our corrupted nature in the bath of regeneration. Therefore, may this water be for us a memorial of the Baptism we have received, and grant that we may share in the

gladness of our brothers and sisters who at Easter have received their Baptism. Through Christ our Lord. **Amen.**

Where it is customary to bless salt also, add:

We humbly ask you, almighty God: be pleased in your faithful love to bless this salt you have created, for it was you who commanded the prophet Elisha to cast salt into water, that impure water might be purified. Grant, O Lord, we pray, that, wherever this mixture of salt and water is sprinkled, every attack of the enemy may be repulsed and your Holy Spirit may be present to keep us safe at all times. Through Christ our Lord. **Amen.**

During the sprinkling, an appropriate song may be sung.

May almighty God cleanse us of our sins, and through the celebration of this Eucharist make us worthy to share at the table of his Kingdom. **Amen.**

GLORY TO GOD
Omitted during Advent and Lent.

Glory to God in the highest,
and on earth peace to people of good will.

We praise you,
we bless you,
we adore you,
we glorify you,
we give you thanks for your great glory,
Lord God, heavenly King,
O God, almighty Father.

Lord Jesus Christ, Only Begotten Son,
Lord God, Lamb of God, Son of the Father,
you take away the sins of the world,
    have mercy on us;
you take away the sins of the world,
    receive our prayer;
you are seated at the right hand of the Father,
    have mercy on us.

For you alone are the Holy One,
you alone are the Lord,
you alone are the Most High,
Jesus Christ,
with the Holy Spirit,
in the glory of God the Father.
Amen.

COLLECT (▶ *The appropriate day*)

Liturgy of the Word

READINGS (▶ *The appropriate day*)

HOMILY

PROFESSION OF FAITH

1 Nicene Creed
All bow at the words in italics.

I believe in one God,
the Father almighty,
maker of heaven and earth,
of all things visible and invisible.

I believe in one Lord Jesus Christ,
the Only Begotten Son of God,
born of the Father before all ages.
God from God, Light from Light,
true God from true God,
begotten, not made,
    consubstantial with the Father;
through him all things were made.
For us men and for our salvation
he came down from heaven,
and by the Holy Spirit was incarnate
    of the Virgin Mary,
and became man.
For our sake he was crucified under
    Pontius Pilate,
he suffered death and was buried,
and rose again on the third day
in accordance with the Scriptures.

He ascended into heaven
and is seated at the right hand of the Father.
He will come again in glory
to judge the living and the dead
and his kingdom will have no end.

I believe in the Holy Spirit, the Lord,
    the giver of life,
who proceeds from the Father and the Son,
who with the Father and the Son is adored
    and glorified,
who has spoken through the prophets.

I believe in one, holy, catholic and
    apostolic Church.
I confess one Baptism for the forgiveness
    of sins
and I look forward to the resurrection of
    the dead
and the life of the world to come. Amen.

2 Apostles' Creed

All bow at the words in italics.

I believe in God,
the Father almighty,
Creator of heaven and earth,
and in Jesus Christ, his only Son, our Lord,
who was conceived by the Holy Spirit,
born of the Virgin Mary,
suffered under Pontius Pilate,
was crucified, died and was buried;
he descended into hell;
on the third day he rose again from the dead;
he ascended into heaven,
and is seated at the right hand of God
the Father almighty;
from there he will come to judge
the living and the dead.

I believe in the Holy Spirit,
the holy catholic Church,
the communion of saints,
the forgiveness of sins,
the resurrection of the body,
and life everlasting. Amen.

PRAYER OF THE FAITHFUL (▶ *The appropriate day*)

Liturgy of the Eucharist

PREPARATION OF THE GIFTS

Blessed are you, Lord God of all creation, for through your goodness we have received the bread we offer you: fruit of the earth and work of human hands, it will become for us the bread of life. **Blessed be God for ever.**

By the mystery of this water and wine may we come to share in the divinity of Christ who humbled himself to share in our humanity.

Blessed are you, Lord God of all creation, for through your goodness we have received the wine we offer you: fruit of the vine and work of human hands, it will become our spiritual drink. **Blessed be God for ever.**

With humble spirit and contrite heart may we be accepted by you, O Lord, and may our sacrifice in your sight this day be pleasing to you, Lord God.

Wash me, O Lord, from my iniquity and cleanse me from my sin.

Pray, brothers and sisters, that my sacrifice and yours may be acceptable to God, the almighty Father.

May the Lord accept the sacrifice at your hands for the praise and glory of his name, for our good and the good of all his holy Church.

PRAYER OVER THE OFFERINGS

(The appropriate day)

THE EUCHARISTIC PRAYER

The Lord be with you. **And with your spirit.**
Lift up your hearts. **We lift them up to the Lord.**
Let us give thanks to the Lord our God.
It is right and just.

*The Priest selects an appropriate Preface, which concludes
with the* Holy, Holy.

PREFACE I OF ADVENT

It is truly right and just, our duty and our salvation,
always and everywhere to give you thanks, Lord,
holy Father, almighty and eternal God, through
Christ our Lord.

For he assumed at his first coming the lowliness of
human flesh, and so fulfilled the design you formed
long ago, and opened for us the way to eternal salvation, that, when he comes again in glory and majesty
and all is at last made manifest, we who watch for that
day may inherit the great promise in which now we
dare to hope.

And so, with Angels and Archangels, with Thrones
and Dominions, and with all the hosts and Powers of
heaven, we sing the hymn of your glory, as without end
we acclaim: **Holy, Holy** (*p. 39*)

PREFACE II OF ADVENT

It is truly right and just, our duty and our salvation,
always and everywhere to give you thanks, Lord,
holy Father, almighty and eternal God, through
Christ our Lord.

For all the oracles of the prophets foretold him, the
Virgin Mother longed for him with love beyond all

telling, John the Baptist sang of his coming and proclaimed his presence when he came.

It is by his gift that already we rejoice at the mystery of his Nativity, so that he may find us watchful in prayer and exultant in his praise.

And so, with Angels and Archangels, with Thrones and Dominions, and with all the hosts and Powers of heaven, we sing the hymn of your glory, as without end we acclaim: **Holy, Holy** (*p. 39*)

PREFACE I OF THE NATIVITY OF THE LORD

It is truly right and just, our duty and our salvation, always and everywhere to give you thanks, Lord, holy Father, almighty and eternal God.

For in the mystery of the Word made flesh a new light of your glory has shone upon the eyes of our mind, so that, as we recognize in him God made visible, we may be caught up through him in love of things invisible.

And so, with Angels and Archangels, with Thrones and Dominions, and with all the hosts and Powers of heaven, we sing the hymn of your glory, as without end we acclaim: **Holy, Holy** (*p. 39*)

PREFACE II OF THE NATIVITY OF THE LORD

It is truly right and just, our duty and our salvation, always and everywhere to give you thanks, Lord, holy Father, almighty and eternal God, through Christ our Lord.

For on the feast of this awe-filled mystery, though invisible in his own divine nature, he has appeared visibly in ours; and begotten before all ages, he has begun to exist in time; so that, raising up in himself all that was cast down, he might restore unity to all creation and call straying humanity back to the heavenly Kingdom.

And so, with all the Angels, we praise you, as in joyful celebration we acclaim: **Holy, Holy** *(p. 39)*

PREFACE III OF THE NATIVITY OF THE LORD

It is truly right and just, our duty and our salvation, always and everywhere to give you thanks, Lord, holy Father, almighty and eternal God, through Christ our Lord.

For through him the holy exchange that restores our life has shone forth today in splendour: when our frailty is assumed by your Word not only does human mortality receive unending honour but by this wondrous union we, too, are made eternal.

And so, in company with the choirs of Angels, we praise you, and with joy we proclaim: **Holy, Holy** *(p. 39)*

PREFACE I OF THE BLESSED VIRGIN MARY

It is truly right and just, our duty and our salvation, always and everywhere to give you thanks, Lord, holy Father, almighty and eternal God, and to praise, bless, and glorify your name on the Solemnity of the Motherhood of the Blessed ever-Virgin Mary.

For by the overshadowing of the Holy Spirit she conceived your Only Begotten Son, and without losing the glory of virginity, brought forth into the world the eternal Light, Jesus Christ our Lord.

Through him the Angels praise your majesty, Dominions adore and Powers tremble before you. Heaven and the Virtues of heaven and the blessed

Seraphim worship together with exultation. May our voices, we pray, join with theirs in humble praise, as we acclaim: **Holy, Holy** (*p. 39*)

PREFACE OF THE EPIPHANY OF THE LORD

It is truly right and just, our duty and our salvation, always and everywhere to give you thanks, Lord, holy Father, almighty and eternal God.

For today you have revealed the mystery of our salvation in Christ as a light for the nations, and, when he appeared in our mortal nature, you made us new by the glory of his immortal nature.

And so, with Angels and Archangels, with Thrones and Dominions, and with all the hosts and Powers of heaven, we sing the hymn of your glory, as without end we acclaim: **Holy, Holy** (*p. 39*)

PREFACE I OF LENT

It is truly right and just, our duty and our salvation, always and everywhere to give you thanks, Lord, holy Father, almighty and eternal God, through Christ our Lord.

For by your gracious gift each year your faithful await the sacred paschal feasts with the joy of minds made pure, so that, more eagerly intent on prayer and on the works of charity, and participating in the mysteries by which they have been reborn, they may be led to the fullness of grace that you bestow on your sons and daughters.

And so, with Angels and Archangels, with Thrones and Dominions, and with all the hosts and Powers of heaven, we sing the hymn of your glory, as without end we acclaim: **Holy, Holy** (*p. 39*)

PREFACE II OF LENT

It is truly right and just, our duty and our salvation, always and everywhere to give you thanks, Lord, holy Father, almighty and eternal God.

For you have given your children a sacred time for the renewing and purifying of their hearts, that, freed from disordered affections, they may so deal with the things of this passing world as to hold rather to the things that eternally endure.

And so, with all the Angels and Saints, we praise you, as without end we acclaim: **Holy, Holy** *(p. 39)*

PREFACE III OF LENT

It is truly right and just, our duty and our salvation, always and everywhere to give you thanks, Lord, holy Father, almighty and eternal God.

For you will that our self-denial should give you thanks, humble our sinful pride, contribute to the feeding of the poor, and so help us imitate you in your kindness.

And so we glorify you with countless Angels, as with one voice of praise we acclaim: **Holy, Holy** *(p. 39)*

PREFACE IV OF LENT

It is truly right and just, our duty and our salvation, always and everywhere to give you thanks, Lord, holy Father, almighty and eternal God.

For through bodily fasting you restrain our faults, raise up our minds, and bestow both virtue and its rewards, through Christ our Lord.

Through him the Angels praise your majesty, Dominions adore and Powers tremble before you.

Heaven and the Virtues of heaven and the blessed Seraphim worship together with exultation. May our voices, we pray, join with theirs in humble praise, as we acclaim: **Holy, Holy** *(p. 39)*

PREFACE OF 1ST SUNDAY OF LENT

It is truly right and just, our duty and our salvation, always and everywhere to give you thanks, Lord, holy Father, almighty and eternal God, through Christ our Lord.

By abstaining forty long days from earthly food, he consecrated through his fast the pattern of our Lenten observance and, by overturning all the snares of the ancient serpent, taught us to cast out the leaven of malice, so that, celebrating worthily the Paschal Mystery, we might pass over at last to the eternal paschal feast.

And so, with the company of Angels and Saints, we sing the hymn of your praise, as without end we acclaim: **Holy, Holy** *(p. 39)*

PREFACE OF 2ND SUNDAY OF LENT

It is truly right and just, our duty and our salvation, always and everywhere to give you thanks, Lord, holy Father, almighty and eternal God, through Christ our Lord.

For after he had told the disciples of his coming Death, on the holy mountain he manifested to them his glory, to show, even by the testimony of the law and the prophets, that the Passion leads to the glory of the Resurrection.

And so, with the Powers of heaven, we worship you constantly on earth, and before your majesty without end we acclaim: **Holy, Holy** *(p. 39)*

PREFACE OF 3RD SUNDAY OF LENT

It is truly right and just, our duty and our salvation, always and everywhere to give you thanks, Lord, holy Father, almighty and eternal God, through Christ our Lord.

For when he asked the Samaritan woman for water to drink, he had already created the gift of faith within her and so ardently did he thirst for her faith, that he kindled in her the fire of divine love.

And so we, too, give you thanks and with the Angels praise your mighty deeds, as we acclaim: **Holy, Holy** (p. 39)

PREFACE OF 4TH SUNDAY OF LENT

It is truly right and just, our duty and our salvation, always and everywhere to give you thanks, Lord, holy Father, almighty and eternal God, through Christ our Lord.

By the mystery of the Incarnation, he has led the human race that walked in darkness into the radiance of the faith and has brought those born in slavery to ancient sin through the waters of regeneration to make them your adopted children.

Therefore, all creatures of heaven and earth sing a new song in adoration, and we, with all the host of Angels, cry out, and without end acclaim: **Holy, Holy** (p. 39)

PREFACE OF 5TH SUNDAY OF LENT

It is truly right and just, our duty and our salvation, always and everywhere to give you thanks, Lord, holy Father, almighty and eternal God, through Christ our Lord.

For as true man he wept for Lazarus his friend and as eternal God raised him from the tomb, just as, taking pity on the human race, he leads us by sacred mysteries to new life.

Through him the host of Angels adores your majesty and rejoices in your presence for ever. May our voices, we pray, join with theirs in one chorus of exultant praise, as we acclaim: **Holy, Holy** (p. 39)

PREFACE OF THE PASSION OF THE LORD
(Palm Sunday)

It is truly right and just, our duty and our salvation, always and everywhere to give you thanks, Lord, holy Father, almighty and eternal God, through Christ our Lord.

For, though innocent, he suffered willingly for sinners and accepted unjust condemnation to save the guilty. His Death has washed away our sins, and his Resurrection has purchased our justification.

And so, with all the Angels, we praise you, as in joyful celebration we acclaim: **Holy, Holy** (p. 39)

PREFACE I OF EASTER

It is truly right and just, our duty and our salvation, at all times to acclaim you, O Lord, but

Easter Vigil: on this night
Easter Sunday and Octave: on this day
rest of Easter Time: in this time

above all to laud you yet more gloriously, when Christ our Passover has been sacrificed.

For he is the true Lamb who has taken away the sins of the world; by dying he has destroyed our death, and by rising, restored our life.

Therefore, overcome with paschal joy, every land, every people exults in your praise and even the heavenly Powers, with the angelic hosts, sing together the unending hymn of your glory, as they acclaim: **Holy, Holy** (*p. 39*)

PREFACE II OF EASTER

It is truly right and just, our duty and our salvation, at all times to acclaim you, O Lord, but in this time above all to laud you yet more gloriously, when Christ our Passover has been sacrificed.

Through him the children of light rise to eternal life and the halls of the heavenly Kingdom are thrown open to the faithful; for his Death is our ransom from death, and in his rising the life of all has risen.

Therefore, overcome with paschal joy, every land, every people exults in your praise and even the heavenly Powers, with the angelic hosts, sing together the unending hymn of your glory, as they acclaim: **Holy, Holy** (*p. 39*)

PREFACE III OF EASTER

It is truly right and just, our duty and our salvation, at all times to acclaim you, O Lord, but in this time above all to laud you yet more gloriously, when Christ our Passover has been sacrificed.

He never ceases to offer himself for us but defends us and ever pleads our cause before you: he is the sacrificial Victim who dies no more, the Lamb, once slain, who lives for ever.

Therefore, overcome with paschal joy, every land, every people exults in your praise and even the heavenly Powers, with the angelic hosts, sing together the unending hymn of your glory, as they acclaim: **Holy, Holy** (*p. 39*)

PREFACE IV OF EASTER

It is truly right and just, our duty and our salvation, at all times to acclaim you, O Lord, but in this time above all to laud you yet more gloriously, when Christ our Passover has been sacrificed.

For, with the old order destroyed, a universe cast down is renewed, and integrity of life is restored to us in Christ.

Therefore, overcome with paschal joy, every land, every people exults in your praise and even the heavenly Powers, with the angelic hosts, sing together the unending hymn of your glory, as they acclaim: **Holy, Holy** (*p. 39*)

PREFACE V OF EASTER

It is truly right and just, our duty and our salvation, at all times to acclaim you, O Lord, but in this time above all to laud you yet more gloriously, when Christ our Passover has been sacrificed.

By the oblation of his Body, he brought the sacrifices of old to fulfillment in the reality of the Cross and, by commending himself to you for our salvation, showed himself the Priest, the Altar, and the Lamb of sacrifice.

Therefore, overcome with paschal joy, every land, every people exults in your praise and even the heavenly Powers, with the angelic hosts, sing together the unending hymn of your glory, as they acclaim: **Holy, Holy** (*p. 39*)

PREFACE I OF THE ASCENSION OF THE LORD

It is truly right and just, our duty and our salvation, always and everywhere to give you thanks, Lord, holy Father, almighty and eternal God.

For the Lord Jesus, the King of glory, conqueror of sin and death, ascended (today) to the highest heavens, as the Angels gazed in wonder.

Mediator between God and man, judge of the world and Lord of hosts, he ascended, not to distance himself from our lowly state but that we, his members, might be confident of following where he, our Head and Founder, has gone before.

Therefore, overcome with paschal joy, every land, every people exults in your praise and even the heavenly Powers, with the angelic hosts, sing together the unending hymn of your glory, as they acclaim: **Holy, Holy** (p. 39)

PREFACE II OF THE ASCENSION OF THE LORD

It is truly right and just, our duty and our salvation, always and everywhere to give you thanks, Lord, holy Father, almighty and eternal God, through Christ our Lord.

For after his Resurrection he plainly appeared to all his disciples and was taken up to heaven in their sight, that he might make us sharers in his divinity.

Therefore, overcome with paschal joy, every land, every people exults in your praise and even the heavenly Powers, with the angelic hosts, sing together the unending hymn of your glory, as they acclaim: **Holy, Holy** (p. 39)

PREFACE OF PENTECOST

It is truly right and just, our duty and our salvation, always and everywhere to give you thanks, Lord, holy Father, almighty and eternal God.

For, bringing your Paschal Mystery to completion, you bestowed the Holy Spirit today on those you made your adopted children by uniting them to your Only Begotten Son.

This same Spirit, as the Church came to birth, opened to all peoples the knowledge of God and brought together the many languages of the earth in profession of the one faith.

Therefore, overcome with paschal joy, every land, every people exults in your praise and even the heavenly Powers, with the angelic hosts, sing together the unending hymn of your glory, as they acclaim: **Holy, Holy** (p. 39)

PREFACE OF HOLY TRINITY

It is truly right and just, our duty and our salvation, always and everywhere to give you thanks, Lord, holy Father, almighty and eternal God.

For with your Only Begotten Son and the Holy Spirit you are one God, one Lord: not in the unity of a single person, but in a Trinity of one substance.

For what you have revealed to us of your glory we believe equally of your Son and of the Holy Spirit, so that, in the confessing of the true and eternal Godhead, you might be adored in what is proper to each Person, their unity in substance, and their equality in majesty.

For this is praised by Angels and Archangels, Cherubim, too, and Seraphim, who never cease to cry out each day, as with one voice they acclaim: **Holy, Holy** (p. 39)

PREFACE I OF THE MOST HOLY EUCHARIST

It is truly right and just, our duty and our salvation, always and everywhere to give you thanks, Lord, holy Father, almighty and eternal God, through Christ our Lord.

For he is the true and eternal Priest, who instituted the pattern of an everlasting sacrifice and was the first to offer himself as the saving Victim, commanding us to make this offering as his memorial.

As we eat his flesh that was sacrificed for us, we are made strong, and, as we drink his Blood that was poured out for us, we are washed clean.

And so, with Angels and Archangels, with Thrones and Dominions, and with all the hosts and Powers of heaven, we sing the hymn of your glory, as without end we acclaim: **Holy, Holy** (p. 39)

PREFACE II OF THE MOST HOLY EUCHARIST

It is truly right and just, our duty and our salvation, always and everywhere to give you thanks, Lord, holy Father, almighty and eternal God, through Christ our Lord.

For at the Last Supper with his Apostles, establishing for the ages to come the saving memorial of the Cross, he offered himself to you as the unblemished Lamb, the acceptable gift of perfect praise.

Nourishing your faithful by this sacred mystery, you make them holy, so that the human race, bounded by one world, may be enlightened by one faith and united by one bond of charity.

And so, we approach the table of this wondrous Sacrament, so that, bathed in the sweetness of your grace, we may pass over to the heavenly realities here foreshadowed.

Therefore, all creatures of heaven and earth sing a new song in adoration, and we, with all the host of Angels, cry out, and without end we acclaim: **Holy, Holy** (*p. 39*)

PREFACE OF OUR LORD JESUS CHRIST, KING OF THE UNIVERSE (*Christ the King*)

It is truly right and just, our duty and our salvation, always and everywhere to give you thanks, Lord, holy Father, almighty and eternal God.

For you anointed your Only Begotten Son, our Lord Jesus Christ, with the oil of gladness as eternal Priest and King of all creation, so that, by offering himself on the altar of the Cross as a spotless sacrifice to bring us peace, he might accomplish the mysteries of human redemption and, making all created things subject to his rule, he might present to the immensity of your majesty an eternal and universal kingdom, a kingdom of truth and life, a kingdom of holiness and grace, a kingdom of justice, love and peace.

And so, with Angels and Archangels, with Thrones and Dominions, and with all the hosts and Powers of heaven, we sing the hymn of your glory, as without end we acclaim: **Holy, Holy** (*p. 39*)

PREFACE I OF SUNDAYS IN ORDINARY TIME

It is truly right and just, our duty and our salvation, always and everywhere to give you thanks, Lord, holy Father, almighty and eternal God, through Christ our Lord.

For through his Paschal Mystery, he accomplished the marvellous deed, by which he has freed us from the yoke of sin and death, summoning us to the glory of being now called a chosen race, a royal priesthood, a holy nation, a people for your own possession, to proclaim everywhere your mighty works, for you have called us out of darkness into your own wonderful light.

And so, with Angels and Archangels, with Thrones and Dominions, and with all the hosts and Powers of heaven, we sing the hymn of your glory, as without end we acclaim: **Holy, Holy** *(p. 39)*

PREFACE II OF SUNDAYS IN ORDINARY TIME

It is truly right and just, our duty and our salvation, always and everywhere to give you thanks, Lord, holy Father, almighty and eternal God, through Christ our Lord.

For out of compassion for the waywardness that is ours, he humbled himself and was born of the Virgin; by the passion of the Cross he freed us from unending death, and by rising from the dead he gave us life eternal.

And so, with Angels and Archangels, with Thrones and Dominions, and with all the hosts and Powers of heaven, we sing the hymn of your glory, as without end we acclaim: **Holy, Holy** *(p. 39)*

PREFACE III OF SUNDAYS IN ORDINARY TIME

It is truly right and just, our duty and our salvation, always and everywhere to give you thanks, Lord, holy Father, almighty and eternal God.

For we know it belongs to your boundless glory, that you came to the aid of mortal beings with your divinity and even fashioned for us a remedy out of mortality itself, that the cause of our downfall might become the means of our salvation, through Christ our Lord.

Through him the host of Angels adores your majesty and rejoices in your presence for ever. May our voices, we pray, join with theirs in one chorus of exultant praise, as we acclaim: **Holy, Holy** *(p. 39)*

PREFACE IV OF SUNDAYS IN ORDINARY TIME

It is truly right and just, our duty and our salvation, always and everywhere to give you thanks, Lord, holy Father, almighty and eternal God, through Christ our Lord.

For by his birth he brought renewal to humanity's fallen state, and by his suffering, cancelled out our sins; by his rising from the dead he has opened the way to eternal life, and by ascending to you, O Father, he has unlocked the gates of heaven.

And so, with the company of Angels and Saints, we sing the hymn of your praise, as without end we acclaim: **Holy, Holy** *(p. 39)*

PREFACE V OF SUNDAYS IN ORDINARY TIME

It is truly right and just, our duty and our salvation, always and everywhere to give you thanks, Lord, holy Father, almighty and eternal God.

For you laid the foundations of the world and have arranged the changing of times and seasons; you formed man in your own image and set humanity over the whole world in all its wonder, to rule in your name over all you have made and for ever praise you in your mighty works, through Christ our Lord.

And so, with all the Angels, we praise you, as in joyful celebration we acclaim: **Holy, Holy** *(p. 39)*

PREFACE VI OF SUNDAYS IN ORDINARY TIME

It is truly right and just, our duty and our salvation, always and everywhere to give you thanks, Lord, holy Father, almighty and eternal God.

For in you we live and move and have our being, and while in this body we not only experience the daily effects of your care, but even now possess the pledge of life eternal.

For, having received the first fruits of the Spirit, through whom you raised up Jesus from the dead, we hope for an everlasting share in the Paschal Mystery.

And so, with all the Angels, we praise you, as in joyful celebration we acclaim: **Holy, Holy** *(p. 39)*

PREFACE VII OF SUNDAYS IN ORDINARY TIME

It is truly right and just, our duty and our salvation, always and everywhere to give you thanks, Lord, holy Father, almighty and eternal God.

For you so loved the world that in your mercy you sent us the Redeemer, to live like us in all things but sin, so that you might love in us what you loved in your Son, by whose obedience we have been restored to those gifts of yours that, by sinning, we had lost in disobedience.

And so, Lord, with all the Angels and Saints, we, too, give you thanks, as in exultation we acclaim: **Holy, Holy** *(p. 39)*

PREFACE VIII OF SUNDAYS IN ORDINARY TIME

It is truly right and just, our duty and our salvation, always and everywhere to give you thanks, Lord, holy Father, almighty and eternal God.

For, when your children were scattered afar by sin, through the Blood of your Son and the power of the Spirit, you gathered them again to yourself, that a people, formed as one by the unity of the Trinity, made the body of Christ and the temple of the Holy Spirit, might, to the praise of your manifold wisdom, be manifest as the Church.

And so, in company with the choirs of Angels, we praise you, and with joy we proclaim: **Holy, Holy** (*p. 39*)

PREFACE OF RECONCILIATION I

It is truly right and just that we should always give you thanks, Lord, holy Father, almighty and eternal God.

For you do not cease to spur us on to possess a more abundant life and, being rich in mercy, you constantly offer pardon and call on sinners to trust in your forgiveness alone.

Never did you turn away from us, and, though time and again we have broken your covenant, you have bound the human family to yourself through Jesus your Son, our Redeemer, with a new bond of love so tight that it can never be undone.

Even now you set before your people a time of grace and reconciliation, and, as they turn back to you in spirit, you grant them hope in Christ Jesus and a desire to be of service to all, while they entrust themselves more fully to the Holy Spirit.

And so, filled with wonder, we extol the power of your love, and, proclaiming our joy at the salvation that comes from you, we join in the heavenly hymn of countless hosts, as without end we acclaim: **Holy, Holy** (p. 39)

PREFACE OF RECONCILIATION II

It is truly right and just that we should give you thanks and praise, O God, almighty Father, for all you do in this world, through our Lord Jesus Christ.

For though the human race is divided by dissension and discord, yet we know that by testing us you change our hearts to prepare them for reconciliation.

Even more, by your Spirit you move human hearts that enemies may speak to each other again, adversaries join hands, and peoples seek to meet together.

By the working of your power it comes about, O Lord, that hatred is overcome by love, revenge gives way to forgiveness, and discord is changed to mutual respect.

Therefore, as we give you ceaseless thanks with the choirs of heaven, we cry out to your majesty on earth, and without end we acclaim: **Holy, Holy** (p. 39)

PREFACE OF VARIOUS NEEDS I

It is truly right and just to give you thanks and raise to you a hymn of glory and praise, O Lord, Father of infinite goodness.

For by the word of your Son's Gospel you have brought together one Church from every people, tongue, and nation, and, having filled her with life by the power of your Spirit, you never cease through her to gather the whole human race into one.

Manifesting the covenant of your love, she dispenses without ceasing the blessed hope of your Kingdom and shines bright as the sign of your faithfulness, which in Christ Jesus our Lord you promised would last for eternity.

And so, with all the Powers of heaven, we worship you constantly on earth, while, with all the Church, as one voice we acclaim: **Holy, Holy** (p. 39)

PREFACE OF VARIOUS NEEDS II

It is truly right and just, our duty and our salvation, always and everywhere to give you thanks, Lord, holy Father, creator of the world and source of all life.

For you never forsake the works of your wisdom, but by your providence are even now at work in our midst. With mighty hand and outstretched arm you led your people Israel through the desert. Now, as your Church makes her pilgrim journey in the world, you always accompany her by the power of the Holy Spirit and lead her along the paths of time to the eternal joy of your Kingdom, through Christ our Lord.

And so, with the Angels and Saints, we, too, sing the hymn of your glory, as without end we acclaim: **Holy, Holy** (p. 39)

PREFACE OF VARIOUS NEEDS III

It is truly right and just, our duty and our salvation, always and everywhere to give you thanks, holy Father, Lord of heaven and earth, through Christ our Lord.

For by your Word you created the world and you govern all things in harmony. You gave us the same Word made flesh as Mediator, and he has spoken your words to us and called us to follow him. He is the way that leads us to you, the truth that sets us free, the life that fills us with gladness.

Through your Son you gather men and women, whom you made for the glory of your name, into one family, redeemed by the Blood of his Cross and signed with the seal of the Spirit.

Therefore, now and for ages unending, with all the Angels, we proclaim your glory, as in joyful celebration we acclaim: **Holy, Holy** (p. 39)

PREFACE OF VARIOUS NEEDS IV

It is truly right and just, our duty and our salvation, always and everywhere to give you thanks, Father of mercies and faithful God.

For you have given us Jesus Christ, your Son, as our Lord and Redeemer.

He always showed compassion for children and for the poor, for the sick and for sinners, and he became a neighbour to the oppressed and the afflicted.

By word and deed he announced to the world that you are our Father and that you care for all your sons and daughters.

And so, with all the Angels and Saints, we exalt and bless your name and sing the hymn of your glory, as without end we acclaim: **Holy, Holy** (p. 39)

PREFACE OF EUCHARISTIC PRAYER II

It is truly right and just, our duty and our salvation, always and everywhere to give you thanks, Father most holy, through your beloved Son, Jesus Christ, your Word through whom you made all things, whom you sent as our Saviour and Redeemer, incarnate by the Holy Spirit and born of the Virgin.

Fulfilling your will and gaining for you a holy people, he stretched out his hands as he endured his Passion, so as to break the bonds of death and manifest the resurrection.

And so, with the Angels and all the Saints we declare your glory, as with one voice we acclaim: **Holy, Holy** (*below*)

PREFACE OF EUCHARISTIC PRAYER IV

It is truly right to give you thanks, truly just to give you glory, Father most holy, for you are the one God living and true, existing before all ages and abiding for all eternity, dwelling in unapproachable light; yet you, who alone are good, the source of life, have made all that is, so that you might fill your creatures with blessings and bring joy to many of them by the glory of your light.

And so, in your presence are countless hosts of Angels, who serve you day and night and, gazing upon the glory of your face, glorify you without ceasing.

With them we, too, confess your name in exultation, giving voice to every creature under heaven, as we acclaim:

HOLY, HOLY
Holy, Holy, Holy Lord God of hosts.
Heaven and earth are full of your glory.
Hosanna in the highest.
Blessed is he who comes in the name of the Lord.
Hosanna in the highest.

The Eucharistic Prayer continues:

Eucharistic Prayer I .... *p. 41*
  To you, therefore

Eucharistic Prayer II .... *p. 46*
  You are indeed Holy, O Lord, the fount

Eucharistic Prayer III .... *p. 48*
  You are indeed Holy, O Lord, and all you

Eucharistic Prayer IV .... *p. 51*
  We give you praise

Reconciliation I .... *p. 54*
  You are indeed Holy, O Lord, and from

Reconciliation II .... *p. 56*
  You, therefore, almighty Father

Various Needs I .... *p. 59*
  You are indeed Holy and to be glorified

Various Needs II .... *p. 61*
  You are indeed Holy and to be glorified

Various Needs III .... *p. 64*
  You are indeed Holy and to be glorified

Various Needs IV .... *p. 67*
  You are indeed Holy and to be glorified

EUCHARISTIC PRAYER I

To you, therefore, most merciful Father, we make humble prayer and petition through Jesus Christ, your Son, our Lord: that you accept and bless these gifts, these offerings, these holy and unblemished sacrifices, which we offer you firstly for your holy catholic Church. Be pleased to grant her peace, to guard, unite and govern her throughout the whole world, together with your servant N. our Pope and N. our Bishop, and all those who, holding to the truth, hand on the catholic and apostolic faith.

Remember, Lord, your servants

Christian Initiation (Scrutinies):
who are to present your chosen ones for the holy grace of your Baptism,

N. and N. and all gathered here, whose faith and devotion are known to you. For them, we offer you this sacrifice of praise or they offer it for themselves and all who are dear to them: for the redemption of their souls, in hope of health and well-being, and paying their homage to you, the eternal God, living and true.

Nativity of the Lord and Octave of the Nativity:
Celebrating the most sacred night (day) on which blessed Mary the immaculate Virgin brought forth the Saviour for this world, and

Epiphany of the Lord:
Celebrating the most sacred day on which your Only Begotten Son, eternal with you in your glory, appeared in a human body, truly sharing our flesh, and

Holy Thursday:
Celebrating the most sacred day on which our Lord Jesus
Christ was handed over for our sake, and

Easter Vigil to Second Sunday of Easter:
Celebrating the most sacred night (day) of the Resurrection of our Lord Jesus Christ in the flesh, and

Ascension of the Lord:
Celebrating the most sacred day on which your Only
Begotten Son, our Lord, placed at the right hand of your
glory our weak human nature, which he had united to
himself, and

Pentecost Sunday:
Celebrating the most sacred day of Pentecost, on which
the Holy Spirit appeared to the Apostles in tongues of
fire, and

In communion with those whose memory we vener-
ate, especially the glorious ever-Virgin Mary, Mother
of our God and Lord, Jesus Christ, and blessed Joseph,
her Spouse, your blessed Apostles and Martyrs, Peter
and Paul, Andrew,

James, John, Thomas, James, Philip, Bartholomew, Mat-
thew, Simon and Jude; Linus, Cletus, Clement, Sixtus,
Cornelius, Cyprian, Lawrence, Chrysogonus, John and
Paul, Cosmas and Damian

and all your Saints; we ask that through their merits
and prayers, in all things we may be defended by your
protecting help. (Through Christ our Lord. Amen.)

Therefore, Lord, we pray: graciously accept this
oblation of our service, that of your whole family;

Christian Initiation (Scrutinies):
which we make to you for your servants, whom you have
been pleased to enroll, choose and call for eternal life

and for the blessed gift of your grace. (Through Christ our Lord. Amen.)

Holy Thursday:
which we make to you as we observe the day on which our Lord Jesus Christ handed on the mysteries of his Body and Blood for his disciples to celebrate;

Easter Vigil to Second Sunday of Easter:
which we make to you also for those to whom you have been pleased to give the new birth of water and the Holy Spirit, granting them forgiveness of all their sins;

order our days in your peace, and command that we be delivered from eternal damnation and counted among the flock of those you have chosen. (Through Christ our Lord. Amen.)

Be pleased, O God, we pray, to bless, acknowledge, and approve this offering in every respect; make it spiritual and acceptable, so that it may become for us the Body and Blood of your most beloved Son, our Lord Jesus Christ.

On the day before he was to suffer,

Holy Thursday:
for our salvation and the salvation of all, that is today,

he took bread in his holy and venerable hands, and with eyes raised to heaven to you, O God, his almighty Father, giving you thanks, he said the blessing, broke the bread and gave it to his disciples, saying:

Take this, all of you, and eat of it,
for this is my Body
which will be given up for you.

In a similar way, when supper was ended, he took this precious chalice in his holy and venerable hands, and once more giving you thanks, he said the blessing and gave the chalice to his disciples, saying:

Take this, all of you, and drink from it,
for this is the chalice of my Blood,
the Blood of the new and eternal covenant,
which will be poured out for you and for many
for the forgiveness of sins.
Do this in memory of me.

The mystery of faith.

1 **We proclaim your Death, O Lord, and profess your Resurrection until you come again.**

2 **When we eat this Bread and drink this Cup, we proclaim your Death, O Lord, until you come again.**

3 **Save us, Saviour of the world, for by your Cross and Resurrection you have set us free.**

Therefore, O Lord, as we celebrate the memorial of the blessed Passion, the Resurrection from the dead, and the glorious Ascension into heaven of Christ, your Son, our Lord, we, your servants and your holy people, offer to your glorious majesty from the gifts that you have given us, this pure victim, this holy victim, this spotless victim, the holy Bread of eternal life and the Chalice of everlasting salvation.

Be pleased to look upon these offerings with a serene and kindly countenance, and to accept them, as once you were pleased to accept the gifts of your servant Abel the just, the sacrifice of Abraham, our father in faith, and the offering of your high priest Melchizedek, a holy sacrifice, a spotless victim.

In humble prayer we ask you, almighty God: command that these gifts be borne by the hands of your holy Angel to your altar on high in the sight of your divine majesty, so that all of us, who through this participation at the altar receive the most holy Body and Blood of your Son, may be filled with every grace and heavenly blessing. (Through Christ our Lord. Amen.)

Remember also, Lord, your servants N. and N., who have gone before us with the sign of faith and rest in the sleep of peace. *(Pause)* Grant them, O Lord, we pray, and all who sleep in Christ, a place of refreshment, light and peace. (Through Christ our Lord. Amen.)

To us, also, your servants, who, though sinners, hope in your abundant mercies, graciously grant some share and fellowship with your holy Apostles and Martyrs: with John the Baptist, Stephen, Matthias, Barnabas,

Ignatius, Alexander, Marcellinus, Peter, Felicity, Perpetua, Agatha, Lucy, Agnes, Cecilia, Anastasia

and all your Saints; admit us, we beseech you, into their company, not weighing our merits, but granting us your pardon, through Christ our Lord.

Through whom you continue to make all these good things, O Lord; you sanctify them, fill them with life, bless them, and bestow them upon us.

Through him, and with him, and in him, O God, almighty Father, in the unity of the Holy Spirit, all glory and honour is yours, for ever and ever. **Amen.**

(▶ *Communion Rite, p. 70*)

EUCHARISTIC PRAYER II

You are indeed Holy, O Lord, the fount of all holiness. Make holy, therefore, these gifts, we pray, by sending down your Spirit upon them like the dewfall, so that they may become for us the Body and Blood of our Lord Jesus Christ.

At the time he was betrayed and entered willingly into his Passion, he took bread and, giving thanks, broke it, and gave it to his disciples, saying:

Take this, all of you, and eat of it,
for this is my Body
which will be given up for you.

In a similar way, when supper was ended, he took the chalice and, once more giving thanks, he gave it to his disciples, saying:

Take this, all of you, and drink from it,
for this is the chalice of my Blood,
the Blood of the new and eternal covenant,
which will be poured out for you and for many
for the forgiveness of sins.
Do this in memory of me.

The mystery of faith.

1 **We proclaim your Death, O Lord, and profess your Resurrection until you come again.**

2 **When we eat this Bread and drink this Cup, we proclaim your Death, O Lord, until you come again.**

3 **Save us, Saviour of the world, for by your Cross and Resurrection you have set us free.**

Therefore, as we celebrate the memorial of his Death and Resurrection, we offer you, Lord, the Bread of life and the Chalice of salvation, giving thanks that you have held us worthy to be in your presence and minister to you.

Humbly we pray that, partaking of the Body and Blood of Christ, we may be gathered into one by the Holy Spirit.

Remember, Lord, your Church, spread throughout the world, and bring her to the fullness of charity, together with N. our Pope and N. our Bishop and all the clergy.

Christian Initiation (Scrutinies):
Remember also, Lord, your servants who are to present these chosen ones at the font of rebirth.

Remember also our brothers and sisters who have fallen asleep in the hope of the resurrection, and all who have died in your mercy: welcome them into the light of your face. Have mercy on us all, we pray, that with the Blessed Virgin Mary, Mother of God, with blessed Joseph, her Spouse, with the blessed Apostles, and all the Saints who have pleased you throughout the ages, we may merit to be co-heirs to eternal life, and may praise and glorify you through your Son, Jesus Christ.

Through him, and with him, and in him, O God, almighty Father, in the unity of the Holy Spirit, all glory and honour is yours, for ever and ever. **Amen.**

(▶ *Communion Rite, p. 70*)

EUCHARISTIC PRAYER III

You are indeed Holy, O Lord, and all you have created rightly gives you praise, for through your Son our Lord Jesus Christ, by the power and working of the Holy Spirit, you give life to all things and make them holy, and you never cease to gather a people to yourself, so that from the rising of the sun to its setting a pure sacrifice may be offered to your name.

Therefore, O Lord, we humbly implore you: by the same Spirit graciously make holy these gifts we have brought to you for consecration, that they may become the Body and Blood of your Son our Lord Jesus Christ, at whose command we celebrate these mysteries.

For on the night he was betrayed he himself took bread, and, giving you thanks, he said the blessing, broke the bread and gave it to his disciples, saying:

Take this, all of you, and eat of it,
for this is my Body
which will be given up for you.

In a similar way, when supper was ended, he took the chalice, and, giving you thanks, he said the blessing, and gave the chalice to his disciples, saying:

Take this, all of you, and drink from it,
for this is the chalice of my Blood,
the Blood of the new and eternal covenant,
which will be poured out for you and for many
for the forgiveness of sins.
Do this in memory of me.

The mystery of faith.

1 **We proclaim your Death, O Lord, and profess your Resurrection until you come again.**

2 **When we eat this Bread and drink this Cup, we proclaim your Death, O Lord, until you come again.**

3 **Save us, Saviour of the world, for by your Cross and Resurrection you have set us free.**

Therefore, O Lord, as we celebrate the memorial of the saving Passion of your Son, his wondrous Resurrection and Ascension into heaven, and as we look forward to his second coming, we offer you in thanksgiving this holy and living sacrifice.

Look, we pray, upon the oblation of your Church and, recognizing the sacrificial Victim by whose death you willed to reconcile us to yourself, grant that we, who are nourished by the Body and Blood of your Son and filled with his Holy Spirit, may become one body, one spirit in Christ.

May he make of us an eternal offering to you, so that we may obtain an inheritance with your elect, especially with the most Blessed Virgin Mary, Mother of God, with blessed Joseph, her Spouse, with your blessed Apostles and glorious Martyrs, (with Saint N.) and with all the Saints, on whose constant intercession in your presence we rely for unfailing help.

May this Sacrifice of our reconciliation, we pray, O Lord, advance the peace and salvation of all the world. Be pleased to confirm in faith and charity your pilgrim Church on earth, with your servant N. our Pope and N.

our Bishop, the Order of Bishops, all the clergy, and the entire people you have gained for your own.

Christian Initiation (Scrutinies):
Assist your servants with your grace, O Lord, we pray, that they may lead these chosen ones by word and example to new life in Christ, our Lord.

Listen graciously to the prayers of this family, whom you have summoned before you: in your compassion, O merciful Father, gather to yourself all your children scattered throughout the world. To our departed brothers and sisters and to all who were pleasing to you at their passing from this life, give kind admittance to your kingdom. There we hope to enjoy for ever the fullness of your glory through Christ our Lord, through whom you bestow on the world all that is good.

Through him, and with him, and in him, O God, almighty Father, in the unity of the Holy Spirit, all glory and honour is yours, for ever and ever. **Amen.**

(▶ *Communion Rite, p. 70*)

EUCHARISTIC PRAYER IV

We give you praise, Father most holy, for you are great and you have fashioned all your works in wisdom and in love. You formed man in your own image and entrusted the whole world to his care, so that in serving you alone, the Creator, he might have dominion over all creatures. And when through disobedience he had lost your friendship, you did not abandon him to the domain of death. For you came in mercy to the aid of all, so that those who seek might find you. Time and again you offered them covenants and through the prophets taught them to look forward to salvation.

And you so loved the world, Father most holy, that in the fullness of time you sent your Only Begotten Son to be our Saviour. Made incarnate by the Holy Spirit and born of the Virgin Mary, he shared our human nature in all things but sin. To the poor he proclaimed the good news of salvation, to prisoners, freedom, and to the sorrowful of heart, joy. To accomplish your plan, he gave himself up to death, and, rising from the dead, he destroyed death and restored life.

And that we might live no longer for ourselves but for him who died and rose again for us, he sent the Holy Spirit from you, Father, as the first fruits for those who believe, so that, bringing to perfection his work in the world, he might sanctify creation to the full.

Therefore, O Lord, we pray: may this same Holy Spirit graciously sanctify these offerings, that they may become the Body and Blood of our Lord Jesus Christ for the celebration of this great mystery, which he himself left us as an eternal covenant.

For when the hour had come for him to be glorified by you, Father most holy, having loved his own who were in the world, he loved them to the end: and while they were at supper, he took bread, blessed and broke it, and gave it to his disciples, saying:

Take this, all of you, and eat of it,
for this is my Body
which will be given up for you.

In a similar way, taking the chalice filled with the fruit of the vine, he gave thanks, and gave the chalice to his disciples, saying:

Take this, all of you, and drink from it,
for this is the chalice of my Blood,
the Blood of the new and eternal covenant,
which will be poured out for you and for many
for the forgiveness of sins.
Do this in memory of me.

The mystery of faith.

1 **We proclaim your Death, O Lord, and profess your Resurrection until you come again.**

2 **When we eat this Bread and drink this Cup, we proclaim your Death, O Lord, until you come again.**

3 **Save us, Saviour of the world, for by your Cross and Resurrection you have set us free.**

Therefore, O Lord, as we now celebrate the memorial of our redemption, we remember Christ's Death and his descent to the realm of the dead, we proclaim his Resurrection and his Ascension to your right hand,

and, as we await his coming in glory, we offer you his Body and Blood, the sacrifice acceptable to you which brings salvation to the whole world.

Look, O Lord, upon the Sacrifice which you yourself have provided for your Church, and grant in your loving kindness to all who partake of this one Bread and one Chalice that, gathered into one body by the Holy Spirit, they may truly become a living sacrifice in Christ to the praise of your glory.

Therefore, Lord, remember now all for whom we offer this sacrifice: especially your servant N. our Pope, N. our Bishop, and the whole Order of Bishops, all the clergy, those who take part in this offering, those gathered here before you, your entire people, and all who seek you with a sincere heart.

Remember also those who have died in the peace of your Christ and all the dead, whose faith you alone have known.

To all of us, your children, grant, O merciful Father, that we may enter into a heavenly inheritance with the Blessed Virgin Mary, Mother of God, with blessed Joseph, her Spouse, and with your Apostles and Saints in your kingdom. There, with the whole of creation, freed from the corruption of sin and death, may we glorify you through Christ our Lord, through whom you bestow on the world all that is good.

Through him, and with him, and in him, O God, almighty Father, in the unity of the Holy Spirit, all glory and honour is yours, for ever and ever. **Amen.**

(▶ *Communion Rite, p. 70*)

EUCHARISTIC PRAYER FOR RECONCILIATION I

You are indeed Holy, O Lord, and from the world's beginning are ceaselessly at work, so that the human race may become holy, just as you yourself are holy.

Look, we pray, upon your people's offerings and pour out on them the power of your Spirit, that they may become the Body and Blood of your beloved Son, Jesus Christ, in whom we, too, are your sons and daughters. Indeed, though we once were lost and could not approach you, you loved us with the greatest love: for your Son, who alone is just, handed himself over to death, and did not disdain to be nailed for our sake to the wood of the Cross.

But before his arms were outstretched between heaven and earth, to become the lasting sign of your covenant, he desired to celebrate the Passover with his disciples.

As he ate with them, he took bread and, giving you thanks, he said the blessing, broke the bread and gave it to them, saying:

Take this, all of you, and eat of it,
for this is my Body
which will be given up for you.

In a similar way, when supper was ended, knowing that he was about to reconcile all things in himself through his Blood to be shed on the Cross, he took the chalice, filled with the fruit of the vine, and once more giving you thanks, handed the chalice to his disciples, saying:

Take this, all of you, and drink from it,
for this is the chalice of my Blood,
the Blood of the new and eternal covenant,
which will be poured out for you and for many
for the forgiveness of sins.
Do this in memory of me.

The mystery of faith.

1   **We proclaim your Death, O Lord, and profess your Resurrection until you come again.**

2   **When we eat this Bread and drink this Cup, we proclaim your Death, O Lord, until you come again.**

3   **Save us, Saviour of the world, for by your Cross and Resurrection you have set us free.**

Therefore, as we celebrate the memorial of your Son Jesus Christ, who is our Passover and our surest peace, we celebrate his Death and Resurrection from the dead, and looking forward to his blessed Coming, we offer you, who are our faithful and merciful God, this sacrificial Victim who reconciles to you the human race.

Look kindly, most compassionate Father, on those you unite to yourself by the Sacrifice of your Son, and grant that, by the power of the Holy Spirit, as they partake of this one Bread and one Chalice, they may be gathered into one Body in Christ, who heals every division.

Be pleased to keep us always in communion of mind and heart, together with N. our Pope and N. our Bishop. Help us to work together for the coming of your Kingdom, until the hour when we stand before you, Saints among the Saints in the halls of heaven, with the Blessed Virgin Mary, Mother of God, the blessed Apostles and all the Saints, and with our deceased brothers and sisters, whom we humbly commend to your mercy.

Then, freed at last from the wound of corruption and made fully into a new creation, we shall sing to you with gladness the thanksgiving of Christ, who lives for all eternity.

Through him, and with him, and in him, O God, almighty Father, in the unity of the Holy Spirit, all glory and honour is yours, for ever and ever. **Amen.**

(▶ *Communion Rite, p. 70*)

EUCHARISTIC PRAYER FOR RECONCILIATION II

You, therefore, almighty Father, we bless through Jesus Christ your Son, who comes in your name. He himself is the Word that brings salvation, the hand you extend to sinners, the way by which your peace is offered to us. When we ourselves had turned away from you on account of our sins, you brought us back to be reconciled, O Lord, so that, converted at last to you, we might love one another through your Son, whom for our sake you handed over to death.

And now, celebrating the reconciliation Christ has brought us, we entreat you: sanctify these gifts by the outpouring of your Spirit, that they may become the Body and Blood of your Son, whose command we fulfill when we celebrate these mysteries.

For when about to give his life to set us free, as he reclined at supper, he himself took bread into his hands, and, giving you thanks, he said the blessing, broke the bread and gave it to his disciples, saying:

Take this, all of you, and eat of it,
for this is my Body
which will be given up for you.

In a similar way, on that same evening, he took the chalice of blessing in his hands, confessing your mercy, and gave the chalice to his disciples, saying:

Take this, all of you, and drink from it,
for this is the chalice of my Blood,
the Blood of the new and eternal covenant,
which will be poured out for you and for many
for the forgiveness of sins.
Do this in memory of me.

The mystery of faith.

1 **We proclaim your Death, O Lord, and profess your Resurrection until you come again.**

2 **When we eat this Bread and drink this Cup, we proclaim your Death, O Lord, until you come again.**

3 **Save us, Saviour of the world, for by your Cross and Resurrection you have set us free.**

Celebrating, therefore, the memorial of the Death and Resurrection of your Son, who left us this pledge of his love, we offer you what you have bestowed on us, the Sacrifice of perfect reconciliation.

Holy Father, we humbly beseech you to accept us also, together with your Son, and in this saving banquet graciously to endow us with his very Spirit, who takes away everything that estranges us from one another.

May he make your Church a sign of unity and an instrument of your peace among all people and may he keep us in communion with N. our Pope and N. our Bishop and all the Bishops and your entire people.

Just as you have gathered us now at the table of your Son, so also bring us together, with the glorious Virgin Mary, Mother of God, with your blessed Apostles and all the Saints, with our brothers and sisters and those of every race and tongue who have died in your friendship. Bring us to share with them the unending banquet of unity in a new heaven and a new earth, where the fullness of your peace will shine forth in Christ Jesus our Lord.

Through him, and with him, and in him, O God, almighty Father, in the unity of the Holy Spirit, all glory and honour is yours, for ever and ever. **Amen.**

(▶ *Communion Rite, p. 70*)

EUCHARISTIC PRAYER FOR MASS FOR VARIOUS NEEDS I

The Church on the Path of Unity

You are indeed Holy and to be glorified, O God, who love the human race and who always walk with us on the journey of life. Blessed indeed is your Son, present in our midst when we are gathered by his love, and when, as once for the disciples, so now for us, he opens the Scriptures and breaks the bread.

Therefore, Father most merciful, we ask that you send forth your Holy Spirit to sanctify these gifts of bread and wine, that they may become for us the Body and Blood of our Lord Jesus Christ.

On the day before he was to suffer, on the night of the Last Supper, he took bread and said the blessing, broke the bread and gave it to his disciples, saying:

Take this, all of you, and eat of it,
for this is my Body
which will be given up for you.

In a similar way, when supper was ended, he took the chalice, gave you thanks and gave the chalice to his disciples, saying:

Take this, all of you, and drink from it,
for this is the chalice of my Blood,
the Blood of the new and eternal covenant,
which will be poured out for you and for many
for the forgiveness of sins.
Do this in memory of me.

The mystery of faith.

1 **We proclaim your Death, O Lord, and profess your Resurrection until you come again.**

2 **When we eat this Bread and drink this Cup, we proclaim your Death, O Lord, until you come again.**

3 **Save us, Saviour of the world, for by your Cross and Resurrection you have set us free.**

Therefore, holy Father, as we celebrate the memorial of Christ your Son, our Saviour, whom you led through his Passion and Death on the Cross to the glory of the Resurrection, and whom you have seated at your right hand, we proclaim the work of your love until he comes again and we offer you the Bread of life and the Chalice of blessing.

Look with favour on the oblation of your Church, in which we show forth the paschal Sacrifice of Christ that has been handed on to us, and grant that, by the power of the Spirit of your love, we may be counted now and until the day of eternity among the members of your Son, in whose Body and Blood we have communion.

Lord, renew your Church (which is in N.) by the light of the Gospel. Strengthen the bond of unity between the faithful and the pastors of your people, together with N. our Pope, N. our Bishop, and the whole Order of Bishops, that in a world torn by strife your people may shine forth as a prophetic sign of unity and concord.

Remember our brothers and sisters (N. and N.), who have fallen asleep in the peace of your Christ, and all the dead, whose faith you alone have known.

Admit them to rejoice in the light of your face, and in the resurrection give them the fullness of life.

Grant also to us, when our earthly pilgrimage is done, that we may come to an eternal dwelling place and live with you for ever; there, in communion with the Blessed Virgin Mary, Mother of God, with the Apostles and Martyrs, (with Saint N.) and with all the Saints, we shall praise and exalt you through Jesus Christ, your Son.

Through him, and with him, and in him, O God, almighty Father, in the unity of the Holy Spirit, all glory and honour is yours, for ever and ever. **Amen.**

(▶ *Communion Rite, p. 70*)

EUCHARISTIC PRAYER FOR MASS FOR VARIOUS NEEDS II

God Guides His Church along the Way of Salvation

You are indeed Holy and to be glorified, O God, who love the human race and who always walk with us on the journey of life. Blessed indeed is your Son, present in our midst when we are gathered by his love and when, as once for the disciples, so now for us, he opens the Scriptures and breaks the bread.

Therefore, Father most merciful, we ask that you send forth your Holy Spirit to sanctify these gifts of bread and wine, that they may become for us the Body and Blood of our Lord Jesus Christ.

On the day before he was to suffer, on the night of the Last Supper, he took bread and said the blessing, broke the bread and gave it to his disciples, saying:

Take this, all of you, and eat of it,
for this is my Body
which will be given up for you.

In a similar way, when supper was ended, he took the chalice, gave you thanks and gave the chalice to his disciples, saying:

Take this, all of you, and drink from it,
for this is the chalice of my Blood,
the Blood of the new and eternal covenant,
which will be poured out for you and for many
for the forgiveness of sins.
Do this in memory of me.

The mystery of faith.

1 **We proclaim your Death, O Lord, and profess your Resurrection until you come again.**

2 **When we eat this Bread and drink this Cup, we proclaim your Death, O Lord, until you come again.**

3 **Save us, Saviour of the world, for by your Cross and Resurrection you have set us free.**

Therefore, holy Father, as we celebrate the memorial of Christ your Son, our Saviour, whom you led through his Passion and Death on the Cross to the glory of the Resurrection, and whom you have seated at your right hand, we proclaim the work of your love until he comes again and we offer you the Bread of life and the Chalice of blessing.

Look with favour on the oblation of your Church, in which we show forth the paschal Sacrifice of Christ that has been handed on to us, and grant that, by the power of the Spirit of your love, we may be counted now and until the day of eternity among the members of your Son, in whose Body and Blood we have communion.

And so, having called us to your table, Lord, confirm us in unity, so that, together with N. our Pope and N. our Bishop, with all Bishops, Priests and Deacons, and your entire people, as we walk your ways with faith and hope, we may strive to bring joy and trust into the world.

Remember our brothers and sisters (N. and N.), who have fallen asleep in the peace of your Christ, and all the dead, whose faith you alone have known. Admit them to rejoice in the light of your face, and in the resurrection give them the fullness of life.

Grant also to us, when our earthly pilgrimage is done, that we may come to an eternal dwelling place and live with you for ever; there, in communion with the Blessed Virgin Mary, Mother of God, with the Apostles and Martyrs, (with Saint N.) and with all the Saints, we shall praise and exalt you through Jesus Christ, your Son.

Through him, and with him, and in him, O God, almighty Father, in the unity of the Holy Spirit, all glory and honour is yours, for ever and ever. **Amen.**

(▶ *Communion Rite, p. 70*)

EUCHARISTIC PRAYER FOR MASS FOR VARIOUS NEEDS III

Jesus, the Way to the Father

You are indeed Holy and to be glorified, O God, who love the human race and who always walk with us on the journey of life. Blessed indeed is your Son, present in our midst when we are gathered by his love and when, as once for the disciples, so now for us, he opens the Scriptures and breaks the bread.

Therefore, Father most merciful, we ask that you send forth your Holy Spirit to sanctify these gifts of bread and wine, that they may become for us the Body and Blood of our Lord Jesus Christ.

On the day before he was to suffer, on the night of the Last Supper, he took bread and said the blessing, broke the bread and gave it to his disciples, saying:

Take this, all of you, and eat of it,
for this is my Body
which will be given up for you.

In a similar way, when supper was ended, he took the chalice, gave you thanks and gave the chalice to his disciples, saying:

Take this, all of you, and drink from it,
for this is the chalice of my Blood,
the Blood of the new and eternal covenant,
which will be poured out for you and for many
for the forgiveness of sins.
Do this in memory of me.

The mystery of faith.

1 **We proclaim your Death, O Lord, and profess your Resurrection until you come again.**

2 **When we eat this Bread and drink this Cup, we proclaim your Death, O Lord, until you come again.**

3 **Save us, Saviour of the world, for by your Cross and Resurrection you have set us free.**

Therefore, holy Father, as we celebrate the memorial of Christ your Son, our Saviour, whom you led through his Passion and Death on the Cross to the glory of the Resurrection, and whom you have seated at your right hand, we proclaim the work of your love until he comes again and we offer you the Bread of life and the Chalice of blessing.

Look with favour on the oblation of your Church, in which we show forth the paschal Sacrifice of Christ that has been handed on to us, and grant that, by the power of the Spirit of your love, we may be counted now and until the day of eternity among the members of your Son, in whose Body and Blood we have communion.

By our partaking of this mystery, almighty Father, give us life through your Spirit, grant that we may be conformed to the image of your Son, and confirm us in the bond of communion, together with N. our Pope and N. our Bishop, with all other Bishops, with Priests and Deacons, and with your entire people.

Grant that all the faithful of the Church, looking into the signs of the times by the light of faith, may constantly devote themselves to the service of the Gospel.

Keep us attentive to the needs of all that, sharing their grief and pain, their joy and hope, we may faithfully bring them the good news of salvation and go forward with them along the way of your Kingdom.

Remember our brothers and sisters (N. and N.), who have fallen asleep in the peace of your Christ, and all the dead, whose faith you alone have known. Admit them to rejoice in the light of your face, and in the resurrection give them the fullness of life.

Grant also to us, when our earthly pilgrimage is done, that we may come to an eternal dwelling place and live with you for ever; there, in communion with the Blessed Virgin Mary, Mother of God, with the Apostles and Martyrs, (with Saint N.) and with all the Saints, we shall praise and exalt you through Jesus Christ, your Son.

Through him, and with him, and in him, O God, almighty Father, in the unity of the Holy Spirit, all glory and honour is yours, for ever and ever. **Amen.**

(▶ *Communion Rite, p. 70*)

EUCHARISTIC PRAYER FOR MASS FOR VARIOUS NEEDS IV

Jesus, Who Went About Doing Good

You are indeed Holy and to be glorified, O God, who love the human race and who always walk with us on the journey of life. Blessed indeed is your Son, present in our midst when we are gathered by his love and when, as once for the disciples, so now for us, he opens the Scriptures and breaks the bread.

Therefore, Father most merciful, we ask that you send forth your Holy Spirit to sanctify these gifts of bread and wine, that they may become for us the Body and Blood of our Lord Jesus Christ.

On the day before he was to suffer, on the night of the Last Supper, he took bread and said the blessing, broke the bread and gave it to his disciples, saying:

Take this, all of you, and eat of it,
for this is my Body
which will be given up for you.

In a similar way, when supper was ended, he took the chalice, gave you thanks and gave the chalice to his disciples, saying:

Take this, all of you, and drink from it,
for this is the chalice of my Blood,
the Blood of the new and eternal covenant,
which will be poured out for you and for many
for the forgiveness of sins.
Do this in memory of me.

The mystery of faith.

1 We proclaim your Death, O Lord, and profess your Resurrection until you come again.

2 When we eat this Bread and drink this Cup, we proclaim your Death, O Lord, until you come again.

3 Save us, Saviour of the world, for by your Cross and Resurrection you have set us free.

Therefore, holy Father, as we celebrate the memorial of Christ your Son, our Saviour, whom you led through his Passion and Death on the Cross to the glory of the Resurrection, and whom you have seated at your right hand, we proclaim the work of your love until he comes again and we offer you the Bread of life and the Chalice of blessing.

Look with favour on the oblation of your Church, in which we show forth the paschal Sacrifice of Christ that has been handed on to us, and grant that, by the power of the Spirit of your love, we may be counted now and until the day of eternity among the members of your Son, in whose Body and Blood we have communion.

Bring your Church, O Lord, to perfect faith and charity, together with N. our Pope and N. our Bishop, with all Bishops, Priests and Deacons, and the entire people you have made your own.

Open our eyes to the needs of our brothers and sisters; inspire in us words and actions to comfort those who labour and are burdened. Make us serve them truly, after the example of Christ and at his command. And may your Church stand as a living witness to truth and freedom, to peace and justice, that all people may be raised up to a new hope.

Remember our brothers and sisters (N. and N.), who have fallen asleep in the peace of your Christ, and all the dead, whose faith you alone have known. Admit them to rejoice in the light of your face, and in the resurrection give them the fullness of life.

Grant also to us, when our earthly pilgrimage is done, that we may come to an eternal dwelling place and live with you for ever; there, in communion with the Blessed Virgin Mary, Mother of God, with the Apostles and Martyrs, (with Saint N.) and with all the Saints, we shall praise and exalt you through Jesus Christ, your Son.

Through him, and with him, and in him, O God, almighty Father, in the unity of the Holy Spirit, all glory and honour is yours, for ever and ever. **Amen.**

The Communion Rite

At the Saviour's command and formed by divine teaching, we dare to say:

Our Father, who art in heaven,
hallowed be thy name;
thy kingdom come,
thy will be done
on earth as it is in heaven.
Give us this day our daily bread,
and forgive us our trespasses,
as we forgive those who trespass against us;
and lead us not into temptation,
but deliver us from evil.

Deliver us, Lord, we pray, from every evil, graciously grant peace in our days, that, by the help of your mercy, we may be always free from sin and safe from all distress, as we await the blessed hope and the coming of our Saviour, Jesus Christ.

For the kingdom,
the power and the glory are yours
now and for ever.

Lord Jesus Christ, who said to your Apostles: Peace I leave you, my peace I give you, look not on our sins, but on the faith of your Church, and graciously grant her peace and unity in accordance with your will. Who live and reign for ever and ever. **Amen.**

The peace of the Lord be with you always.
And with your spirit.

Let us offer each other the sign of peace.

> May this mingling of the Body and Blood of our Lord Jesus Christ bring eternal life to us who receive it.

Lamb of God, you take away the sins of the world, have mercy on us.

Lamb of God, you take away the sins of the world, have mercy on us.

Lamb of God, you take away the sins of the world, grant us peace.

1 Lord Jesus Christ, Son of the living God, who, by the will of the Father and the work of the Holy Spirit, through your Death gave life to the world, free me by this, your most holy Body and Blood, from all my sins and from every evil; keep me always faithful to your commandments, and never let me be parted from you.

2 May the receiving of your Body and Blood, Lord Jesus Christ, not bring me to judgment and condemnation, but through your loving mercy be for me protection in mind and body and a healing remedy.

Behold the Lamb of God, behold him who takes away the sins of the world. Blessed are those called to the supper of the Lamb.

Lord, I am not worthy that you should enter under my roof, but only say the word and my soul shall be healed.

> May the Body (Blood) of Christ keep me safe for eternal life.

COMMUNION CHANT
(or Communion Antiphon — ▶ The appropriate day)

What has passed our lips as food, O Lord, may we possess in purity of heart, that what has been given to us in time may be our healing for eternity.

PRAYER AFTER COMMUNION
(▶ The appropriate day)

Concluding Rites

ANNOUNCEMENTS *(Optional)*

BLESSING *(or Solemn Blessing — Optional)*

The Lord be with you.
And with your spirit.
May almighty God bless you,
the Father, and the Son, and the Holy Spirit. **Amen.**

DISMISSAL
During Easter Octave, add the double alleluia.

1 Go forth, the Mass is ended.

2 Go and announce the Gospel of the Lord.

3 Go in peace, glorifying the Lord by your life.

4 Go in peace.

Thanks be to God.

For the Prayer to St. Michael the Archangel (optional), turn to page 583.

Sunday Readings

December Saints' Days

The following saints are traditionally remembered in December in Canada.

Saint Francis Xavier . . . . Dec 3

Saint John Damascene . . . . Dec 4

Saint Nicholas. . . . . Dec 6

Saint Ambrose . . . . Dec 7

The Immaculate Conception of the . . . . Dec 8
    Blessed Virgin Mary

Saint Juan Diego Cuauhtlatoatzin. . . . . Dec 9

Our Lady of Loreto . . . . Dec 10

Saint Damasus I . . . . Dec 11

Our Lady of Guadalupe . . . . Dec 12
Patroness of the Americas

Saint Lucy . . . . Dec 13

Saint John of the Cross . . . . Dec 14

Saint Peter Canisius . . . . Dec 21

Saint John of Kanty . . . . Dec 23

Saint Stephen . . . . Dec 26

Saint John . . . . Dec 27

The Holy Innocents. . . . . Dec 28

Saint Thomas Becket. . . . . Dec 29

Saint Sylvester I . . . . Dec 31

1st Sunday of Advent

Keep awake. Be alert. These words in today's Gospel are clear and direct. But why are they shared with us at the beginning of the Advent season? A time usually associated with preparing for the Christmas season?

It is this question of readiness that is at the heart of the "reason for the season." If God can break into our lives by taking human form, then the season of Advent can challenge us to be on guard for God's coming – both at Christmas and at the end of time. We must be alert in order to answer the call to discipleship we have received, and be ready to account for our actions and decisions at the last judgment.

As we do not know the time or place, let us approach our Advent prayer as an opportunity to reflect on our readiness, remembering that God is gentle and loving. As we see in the first reading, the people felt God had turned his back on them; yet, when they recalled all that God had done for them, they trusted in God's goodness and saving power. Saint Paul reminds us in the second reading that God is faithful and will strengthen us to the end. So let us rejoice and give thanks for this Advent opportunity to reflect on our lives and God's goodness, and stay awake for his coming.

John O'Brien
Oakville, ON

ENTRANCE ANTIPHON *(Cf. Psalm 24.1-3)*
**To you, I lift up my soul, O my God. In you, I have
trusted; let me not be put to shame. Nor let my
enemies exult over me; and let none who hope in
you be put to shame.**

INTRODUCTORY RITES *(p. 8)*

COLLECT
Grant your faithful, we pray, almighty God, the resolve
to run forth to meet your Christ with righteous deeds
at his coming, so that, gathered at his right hand, they
may be worthy to possess the heavenly Kingdom.
Through our Lord Jesus Christ, your Son, who lives
and reigns with you in the unity of the Holy Spirit,
God, for ever and ever. **Amen.**

FIRST READING *(Isaiah 63.16b-17; 64.1, 3-8)*
You, O Lord, are our father;
"Our Redeemer from of old" is your name.
Why, O Lord, do you make us stray from your ways
and harden our heart, so that we do not fear you?
Turn back for the sake of your servants,
for the sake of the tribes that are your heritage.

O that you would tear open the heavens
    and come down,
so that the mountains would quake at your presence.
When you did awesome deeds that we did not expect,
you came down, the mountains quaked
    at your presence.
From ages past no one has heard,
no ear has perceived,

no eye has seen any God besides you,
who works for those who wait for him.

You meet those who gladly do right,
those who remember you in your ways.

But you were angry, and we sinned;
because you hid yourself we transgressed.
We have all become like one who is unclean,
and all our righteous deeds are like a filthy cloth.
We all fade like a leaf,
and our iniquities, like the wind, take us away.
There is no one who calls on your name,
or attempts to take hold of you;
for you have hidden your face from us,
and have delivered us into the hand of our iniquity.

Yet, O Lord, you are our Father;
we are the clay, and you are our potter;
we are all the work of your hand.

The word of the Lord. **Thanks be to God.**

RESPONSORIAL PSALM *(Psalm 80)*

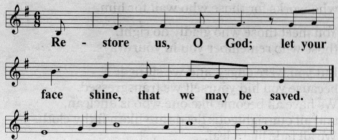

Re - store us, O God; let your face shine, that we may be saved.

R. **Restore us, O God; let your face shine,
that we may be saved.**

Give ear, O Shepherd · **of** Israel,
you who are enthroned upon the cherubim,
    shine · **forth.**
Stir up your · **might,**
and come to · **save_us.** R.

Turn again, O God · **of** hosts;
look down from heaven, and · **see;**
have regard for this · **vine,**
the stock that your right hand has · **planted.** R.

But let your hand be upon the man at · **your** right,
the son of man you have made strong for
    your·-**self.**
Then we will never turn · **back_from_you;**
give us life, and we will call on your · **name.** R.

©2009 Gordon Johnston/Novalis

To hear the Sunday Psalms, visit www.livingwithchrist.ca.

SECOND READING *(1 Corinthians 1.3-9)*
Brothers and sisters: Grace to you and peace from God our Father and the Lord Jesus Christ.

I give thanks to my God always for you because of the grace of God that has been given you in Christ Jesus, for in every way you have been enriched in him, in speech and knowledge of every kind — just as the testimony of Christ has been strengthened among you — so that you are not lacking in any spiritual gift as you wait for the revealing of our Lord Jesus Christ.

He will also strengthen you to the end, so that you may be blameless on the day of our Lord Jesus Christ. God is faithful; by him you were called into fellowship with his Son, Jesus Christ our Lord.

The word of the Lord. **Thanks be to God.**

GOSPEL ACCLAMATION *(Psalm 85.7)*
Alleluia. Alleluia. Show us your steadfast love, O Lord, and grant us your salvation. **Alleluia.**

GOSPEL *(Mark 13.33-37)*
The Lord be with you. **And with your spirit.** A reading from the holy Gospel according to Mark. **Glory to you, O Lord.**

Jesus said to his disciples: "Beware, keep alert; for you do not know when the time will come.

"It is like a man going on a journey, when he leaves home and puts his slaves in charge, each with a particular task, and commands the doorkeeper to be on the watch. Therefore, keep awake — for you do not know when the master of the house will come, in the evening, or at midnight, or at cockcrow, or at dawn, or else he may find you asleep when he comes suddenly.

"And what I say to you I say to all: Keep awake."

The Gospel of the Lord. **Praise to you, Lord Jesus Christ.**

PROFESSION OF FAITH (p. 14)

PRAYER OF THE FAITHFUL

The following intentions are suggestions only.
There are more suggestions at www.livingwithchrist.ca.

R. **Lord, hear our prayer.**

For the Church, eagerly awaiting the fulfillment of the children of God, we pray to the Lord: R.

For the world, longing for its promised salvation, we pray to the Lord: R.

For the sorrowing and despairing, the suffering and alienated, the forgotten and overlooked, we pray to the Lord: R.

For our parish and our diocese, working together as we await the Lord's return in glory, we pray to the Lord: R.

PREPARATION OF THE GIFTS (p. 17)

PRAYER OVER THE OFFERINGS

Accept, we pray, O Lord, these offerings we make, gathered from among your gifts to us, and may what you grant us to celebrate devoutly here below gain for us the prize of eternal redemption. Through Christ our Lord. **Amen.**

PREFACE (Advent I, p. 18)

COMMUNION ANTIPHON *(Psalm 84.13)*
The Lord will bestow his bounty, and our earth shall yield its increase.

PRAYER AFTER COMMUNION
May these mysteries, O Lord, in which we have participated, profit us, we pray, for even now, as we walk amid passing things, you teach us by them to love the things of heaven and hold fast to what endures. Through Christ our Lord. **Amen.**

SOLEMN BLESSING — ADVENT *(Optional)*
Bow down for the blessing.

May the almighty and merciful God, by whose grace you have placed your faith in the First Coming of his Only Begotten Son and yearn for his coming again, sanctify you by the radiance of Christ's Advent and enrich you with his blessing. **Amen.**

As you run the race of this present life, may he make you firm in faith, joyful in hope and active in charity. **Amen.**

So that, rejoicing now with devotion at the Redeemer's coming in the flesh, you may be endowed with the rich reward of eternal life when he comes again in majesty. **Amen.**

And may the blessing of almighty God, the Father, and the Son, and the Holy Spirit, come down on you and remain with you for ever. **Amen.**

DISMISSAL *(p. 72)*

DEC 10

2nd Sunday of Advent

Today's readings extend a hope-filled invitation: Prepare, for the Lord is coming. What is our response to this invitation? Will we listen to the voice speaking truth into the wilderness areas of our lives? Will we speak truth into the wilderness areas of others' lives – offering hope when life is difficult, challenging, pain-filled or exhausting?

When John the Baptist spoke in the wilderness, he carried a message of hope to people facing the challenges of living in those difficult times. He offered them a fresh opportunity to begin their lives anew. People paid attention.

We are called to pay attention with prayer-filled pondering, focusing on the words that touch our minds and hearts. We are offered tender words of comfort, the promise of debt-free forgiveness, the coming of a world filled with righteousness and goodness – all reminders of God's enduring faithfulness. A bold offer: every one of us will find something that brings light into the wilderness areas of our lives. Whatever darkness we are facing, there are life-giving words that offer the light of hope.

This day, as we light the second candle on the Advent wreath, may we hear the voice of truth and respond with our own yes. May we look beyond the wilderness areas in our lives – and see the promises that are before us.

Brenda Merk Hildebrand
Campbell River, BC

ENTRANCE ANTIPHON *(Cf. Isaiah 30.19, 30)*
**O people of Sion, behold, the Lord will come to save
the nations, and the Lord will make the glory of his
voice heard in the joy of your heart.**

INTRODUCTORY RITES *(p. 8)*

COLLECT
Almighty and merciful God, may no earthly undertaking hinder those who set out in haste to meet your
Son, but may our learning of heavenly wisdom gain
us admittance to his company. Who lives and reigns
with you in the unity of the Holy Spirit, God, for ever
and ever. **Amen.**

FIRST READING *(Isaiah 40.1-5, 9-11)*
Comfort, O comfort my people,
says your God.
Speak tenderly to Jerusalem,
and cry to her
that she has served her term,
that her penalty is paid,
that she has received from the Lord's hand
double for all her sins.

A voice cries out:
"In the wilderness prepare the way of the Lord,
make straight in the desert a highway for our God.
Every valley shall be lifted up,
and every mountain and hill be made low;
the uneven ground shall become level,
and the rough places a plain.
Then the glory of the Lord shall be revealed,

and all people shall see it together,
for the mouth of the Lord has spoken."

Get you up to a high mountain,
O Zion, herald of good tidings;
lift up your voice with strength,
O Jerusalem, herald of good tidings,
lift it up, do not fear;
say to the cities of Judah,
"Here is your God!"

See, the Lord God comes with might,
and his arm rules for him;
his reward is with him,
and his recompense before him.
He will feed his flock like a shepherd;
he will gather the lambs in his arms,
and carry them in his bosom,
and gently lead the mother sheep.

The word of the Lord. **Thanks be to God.**

RESPONSORIAL PSALM *(Psalm 85)*

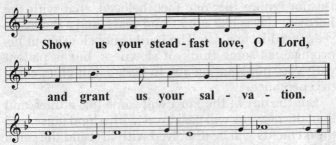

Show us your stead-fast love, O Lord, and grant us your sal-va-tion.

R. **Show us your steadfast love, O Lord,
and grant us your salvation.**

Let me hear what God the Lord will · **speak,**
for he will speak peace to his · **people.**
Surely his salvation is at hand for those
     who · **fear_him,**
that his glory may dwell · **in_our** land. R.

Steadfast love and faithfulness will · **meet;**
righteousness and peace will · **kiss_each_other.**
Faithfulness will spring up from the · **ground,**
and righteousness will look down
     · **from_the** sky. R.

The Lord will give what is · **good,**
and our land will yield its · **increase.**
Righteousness will go be-·-**fore_him,**
and will make a path · **for_his** steps. R.

©2009 Gordon Johnston/Novalis

To hear the Sunday Psalms, visit www.livingwithchrist.ca.

SECOND READING *(2 Peter 3.8-14)*

Do not ignore this one fact, beloved, that with the Lord one day is like a thousand years, and a thousand years are like one day. The Lord is not slow about his promise, as some think of slowness, but is patient with you, not wanting any to perish, but all to come to repentance.

But the day of the Lord will come like a thief, and then the heavens will pass away with a loud noise, and the elements will be dissolved with fire, and the earth and everything that is done on it will be disclosed.

Since all these things are to be dissolved in this way, what sort of persons ought you to be in leading lives of holiness and godliness, waiting for and hastening the coming of the day of God, because of which the heavens will be set ablaze and dissolved, and the elements will melt with fire? But, in accordance with his promise, we wait for new heavens and a new earth, where righteousness is at home.

Therefore, beloved, while you are waiting for these things, strive to be found by him at peace.

The word of the Lord. **Thanks be to God.**

GOSPEL ACCLAMATION *(Luke 3.4, 6)*

Alleluia. Alleluia. Prepare the way of the Lord, make straight his paths: all people shall see the salvation of God. **Alleluia.**

GOSPEL *(Mark 1.1-8)*

The Lord be with you. **And with your spirit.** A reading from the holy Gospel according to Mark. **Glory to you, O Lord.**

The beginning of the good news of Jesus Christ, the Son of God.

As it is written in the Prophet Isaiah, "See, I am sending my messenger ahead of you, who will prepare your way; the voice of one crying out in the wilderness: 'Prepare the way of the Lord, make his paths straight,'" John the Baptist appeared in the wilderness, proclaiming a baptism of repentance for the forgiveness of sins. And people from the whole Judean countryside and all the people of Jerusalem were going out to him, and were baptized by him in the river Jordan, confessing their sins. Now John was clothed with camel's hair, with a leather belt around his waist, and he ate locusts and wild honey. He proclaimed, "The one who is more powerful than I is coming after me; I am not worthy to stoop down and untie the thong of his sandals. I have baptized you with water; but he will baptize you with the Holy Spirit."

The Gospel of the Lord. **Praise to you, Lord Jesus Christ.**

PROFESSION OF FAITH (p. 14)

PRAYER OF THE FAITHFUL

The following intentions are suggestions only.
There are more suggestions at www.livingwithchrist.ca.

R. **Lord, hear our prayer.**

For the Church, courageously open to inner and outer transformation by the Holy Spirit, we pray to the Lord:
R.

For the leaders of nations and communities, striving to build a society of righteousness, peace and justice, we pray to the Lord: R.

For the poor, the weak and the helpless, we pray to the Lord: R.

For this community, open to conversion and forgiveness, we pray to the Lord: R.

PREPARATION OF THE GIFTS *(p. 17)*

PRAYER OVER THE OFFERINGS
Be pleased, O Lord, with our humble prayers and offerings, and, since we have no merits to plead our cause, come, we pray, to our rescue with the protection of your mercy. Through Christ our Lord. **Amen.**

PREFACE *(Advent I, p. 18)*

COMMUNION ANTIPHON *(Baruch 5.5; 4.36)*
Jerusalem, arise and stand upon the heights, and behold the joy which comes to you from God.

PRAYER AFTER COMMUNION
Replenished by the food of spiritual nourishment, we humbly beseech you, O Lord, that, through our partaking in this mystery, you may teach us to judge wisely the things of earth and hold firm to the things of heaven. Through Christ our Lord. **Amen.**

SOLEMN BLESSING AND DISMISSAL *(p. 81)*

3rd Sunday of Advent

In today's Gospel, the priests and Levites challenge John the Baptist, asking: "Who are you? What do you say about yourself?" John confesses he is not the Messiah, but that his life is a testimony to what God has done for us. We too would be wise to consider this all-important question – who are we? What do our lives say about ourselves?

I am Harry, married to Jennifer for nearly forty years. I am a father of six and grandfather of three – so far. I suffer with memory loss, I wear hearing aids and arthritic pain is a frequent companion. Each day I join my suffering with Jesus, who makes it holy. I don't understand how, but I believe.

I recognize the joys and sufferings in this life to be opportunities for God's love and mercy. When I walk with others, whether in celebration or consolation, I am always pointing, like John the Baptist, to Jesus, the reason for my hope.

We who believe must rejoice, as did our Blessed Mother, that we have been chosen, and give thanks in all things. We are called to be witnesses, crying out in the wilderness of our day, testifying so that others might hear and believe. This is the will of God, and it is to this worthy mission that we are called to dedicate our lives and to persevere.

Harry McAvoy
Newmarket, ON

ENTRANCE ANTIPHON *(Philippians 4.4-5)*
**Rejoice in the Lord always; again I say, rejoice.
Indeed, the Lord is near.**

INTRODUCTORY RITES *(p. 8)*

COLLECT
O God, who see how your people faithfully await
the feast of the Lord's Nativity, enable us, we pray, to
attain the joys of so great a salvation and to celebrate
them always with solemn worship and glad rejoicing.
Through our Lord Jesus Christ, your Son, who lives
and reigns with you in the unity of the Holy Spirit,
God, for ever and ever. **Amen.**

FIRST READING *(Isaiah 61.1-2a, 10-11)*
The spirit of the Lord God is upon me,
because the Lord has anointed me;
he has sent me to bring good news to the oppressed,
to bind up the brokenhearted,
to proclaim liberty to the captives,
and release to the prisoners;
to proclaim the year of the Lord's favour.

I will greatly rejoice in the Lord,
my soul shall exult in my God;
for he has clothed me with the garments of salvation,
he has covered me with the robe of righteousness,
as a bridegroom decks himself with a garland,
and as a bride adorns herself with her jewels.

For as the earth brings forth its shoots,
and as a garden causes what is sown in it
    to spring up,

so the Lord God will cause righteousness and praise to spring up before all the nations.

The word of the Lord. **Thanks be to God.**

RESPONSORIAL PSALM *(Luke 1)*

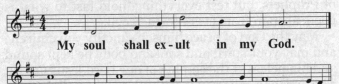

My soul shall ex-ult in my God.

R. **My soul shall exult in my God.**

My soul magnifies the · **Lord**
and my spirit rejoices in God · **my** Saviour,
for he has looked with favour on the lowliness
    of his · **servant.**
Surely, from now on all generations
    will · **call_me** blessed. R.

For the Mighty One has done great things for · **me,**
and holy is · **his** name.
His mercy is for those who · **fear_him**
from generation to · **gener**-ation. R.

The Lord has filled the hungry with · **good_things**
and sent the rich a-·-**way** empty.
He has helped his servant · **Israel,**
in remembrance · **of_his** mercy. R.

©2009 Gordon Johnston/Novalis

To hear the Sunday Psalms, visit www.livingwithchrist.ca.

SECOND READING *(1 Thessalonians 5.16-24)*

Brothers and sisters, rejoice always, pray without ceasing, give thanks in all circumstances; for this is the will of God in Christ Jesus for you.

Do not quench the Spirit. Do not despise the words of Prophets, but test everything; hold fast to what is good; abstain from every form of evil.

May the God of peace himself sanctify you entirely; and may your spirit and soul and body be kept sound and blameless at the coming of our Lord Jesus Christ. The one who calls you is faithful, and he will do this.

The word of the Lord. **Thanks be to God.**

GOSPEL ACCLAMATION *(Luke 4.18 [Isaiah 61.1])*

Alleluia. Alleluia. The Spirit of the Lord is upon me; he has sent me to bring good news to the poor. **Alleluia.**

GOSPEL *(John 1.6-8, 19-28)*

The Lord be with you. **And with your spirit.** A reading from the holy Gospel according to John. **Glory to you, O Lord.**

There was a man sent from God, whose name was John. He came as a witness to testify to the light, so that all might believe through him. He himself was not the light, but he came to testify to the light.

This is the testimony given by John when the Jews sent priests and Levites from Jerusalem to ask him, "Who are you?" He confessed and did not deny it, but confessed, "I am not the Messiah." And they asked him, "What then? Are you Elijah?" He said, "I am not." "Are you the Prophet?" He answered, "No."

Then they said to him, "Who are you? Let us have an answer for those who sent us. What do you say about yourself?" He said, "I am the voice of one crying out in the wilderness, 'Make straight the way of the Lord,'" as the Prophet Isaiah said.

Now they had been sent from the Pharisees. They asked him, "Why then are you baptizing if you are neither the Messiah, nor Elijah, nor the Prophet?" John answered them, "I baptize with water. Among you stands one whom you do not know, the one who is coming after me; I am not worthy to untie the thong of his sandal." This took place in Bethany across the Jordan where John was baptizing.

The Gospel of the Lord. **Praise to you, Lord Jesus Christ.**

PROFESSION OF FAITH (p. 14)

PRAYER OF THE FAITHFUL

The following intentions are suggestions only.
There are more suggestions at www.livingwithchrist.ca.

R. **Lord, hear our prayer.**

For the Church, called to lead humanity to the light of Christ, we pray to the Lord: R.

For civil authorities fulfilling their responsibilities to guide people to a deeper appreciation of all the stages of life, we pray to the Lord: R.

For all who are facing the coming year without hope, we pray to the Lord: R.

For each of us, in our vocation to live the Good News, we pray to the Lord: R.

PREPARATION OF THE GIFTS (p. 17)

PRAYER OVER THE OFFERINGS

May the sacrifice of our worship, Lord, we pray, be offered to you unceasingly, to complete what was begun in sacred mystery and powerfully accomplish for us your saving work. Through Christ our Lord. **Amen.**

PREFACE *(Advent II, p. 18)*

COMMUNION ANTIPHON *(Cf. Isaiah 35.4)*

Say to the faint of heart: Be strong and do not fear. Behold, our God will come, and he will save us.

PRAYER AFTER COMMUNION

We implore your mercy, Lord, that this divine sustenance may cleanse us of our faults and prepare us for the coming feasts. Through Christ our Lord. **Amen.**

SOLEMN BLESSING AND DISMISSAL *(p. 81)*

4th Sunday of Advent

God's plan is filled with surprises that may be different from our own expectations. In today's Gospel, the Angel Gabriel appears to Mary to announce Jesus' birth. The Annunciation is one of these moments in God's plan and Mary's response is a perfect example of how we should welcome God's surprises.

In our first reading, David expected that God's promise would involve an earthly kingdom, but God instead had in mind an everlasting kingdom. His promise to David would be ultimately fulfilled through a humble soul, that of Mary, who trusted completely in the Lord.

Mary is bewildered when she first hears the Angel's message. Gabriel reveals to her that she will bear a son who will be both Son of God and Son of David, the promised Messiah. When reassured that the Angel is God's messenger, Mary responds in faith, with a generous and open heart. Mary is the model believer whose deep faith and trust in God are an example for us all to imitate.

When Mary heard the Angel speak, she heard God's voice in that of his messenger. As we await the birth of our Lord, we are invited to quiet our hearts and listen, as Mary did, for God's voice in our daily lives. Let us walk in her footsteps and be surprised by the ways of God.

Nada Mazzei
Toronto, ON

ENTRANCE ANTIPHON (Cf. Isaiah 45.8)

Drop down dew from above, you heavens, and let the clouds rain down the Just One; let the earth be opened and bring forth a Saviour.

INTRODUCTORY RITES (p. 8)

COLLECT

Pour forth, we beseech you, O Lord, your grace into our hearts, that we, to whom the Incarnation of Christ your Son was made known by the message of an Angel, may by his Passion and Cross be brought to the glory of his Resurrection. Who lives and reigns with you in the unity of the Holy Spirit, God, for ever and ever. **Amen.**

FIRST READING (2 Samuel 7.1-5, 8b-12, 14a, 16)

Now when David, the king, was settled in his house, and the Lord had given him rest from all his enemies around him, the king said to the Prophet Nathan, "See now, I am living in a house of cedar, but the ark of God stays in a tent." Nathan said to the king, "Go, do all that you have in mind, for the Lord is with you."

But that same night the word of the Lord came to Nathan: "Go and tell my servant David: 'Thus says the Lord: Are you the one to build me a house to live in? I took you from the pasture, from following the sheep to be prince over my people Israel: and I have been with you wherever you went, and have cut off all your enemies from before you; and I will make for you a great name, like the name of the great ones of the earth.

"And I will appoint a place for my people Israel and will plant them, so that they may live in their own place, and be disturbed no more; and evildoers shall afflict them no more, as formerly, from the time that I appointed judges over my people Israel; and I will give you rest from all your enemies.

"Moreover the Lord declares to you, David, that the Lord will make you a house. When your days are fulfilled and you lie down with your ancestors, I will raise up your offspring after you, who shall come forth from your body, and I will establish his kingdom.

"I will be a father to him, and he shall be a son to me. Your house and your kingdom shall be made sure forever before me; your throne, David, shall be established forever.'"

The word of the Lord. **Thanks be to God.**

RESPONSORIAL PSALM *(Psalm 89)*

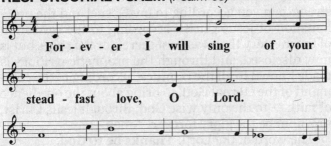

For - ev - er I will sing of your stead - fast love, O Lord.

℟. **Forever I will sing of your steadfast love, O Lord.**

I will sing of your steadfast love, O Lord, for--**ever;**
with my mouth I will proclaim your faithfulness
    to all gener--**ations.**
I declare that your steadfast love is established
    for--**ever;**
your faithfulness is as firm · **as the** heavens. ℟.

You said, "I have made a covenant
  with my · **chosen_one,**
I have sworn to my servant · **David:**
I will establish your descendants for·-**ever,**
and build your throne for all · **gener**-ations." R.

He shall cry to me, "You are my · **Father,**
my God, and the Rock of my sal·-**vation!"**
Forever I will keep my steadfast · **love_for_him,**
and my covenant with him will · **stand** firm. R.

©2009 Gordon Johnston/Novalis

To hear the Sunday Psalms, visit www.livingwithchrist.ca.

SECOND READING *(Romans 16.25-27)*
Brothers and sisters: To the One who is able to
strengthen you according to my Gospel and the proclamation of Jesus Christ, according to the revelation
of the mystery that was kept secret for long ages but is
now disclosed, and through the prophetic writings is
made known to all the Gentiles, according to the command of the eternal God, to bring about the obedience
of faith — to the only wise God, through Jesus Christ,
to whom be the glory forever! Amen.
  The word of the Lord. **Thanks be to God.**

GOSPEL ACCLAMATION *(Luke 1.38)*
Alleluia. Alleluia. Here am I, the servant of the Lord:
let it be done to me according to your word. **Alleluia.**

GOSPEL *(Luke 1.26-38)*
The Lord be with you. **And with your spirit.**
A reading from the holy Gospel according to Luke.
Glory to you, O Lord.

The Angel Gabriel was sent by God to a town in Galilee called Nazareth, to a virgin engaged to a man whose name was Joseph, of the house of David. The virgin's name was Mary.

And he came to her and said, "Hail, full of grace! The Lord is with you." But she was much perplexed by his words and pondered what sort of greeting this might be.

The Angel said to her, "Do not be afraid, Mary, for you have found favour with God. And now, you will conceive in your womb and bear a son, and you will name him Jesus.

"He will be great, and will be called the Son of the Most High, and the Lord God will give to him the throne of his father David. He will reign over the house of Jacob forever, and of his kingdom there will be no end."

Mary said to the Angel, "How can this be, since I am a virgin?" The Angel said to her, "The Holy Spirit will come upon you, and the power of the Most High will overshadow you; therefore the child to be born will be holy; he will be called Son of God.

"And now, your relative Elizabeth in her old age has also conceived a son; and this is the sixth month for her who was said to be barren. For nothing will be impossible with God." Then Mary said, "Here am I, the servant of the Lord; let it be done to me according to your word." Then the Angel departed from her.

The Gospel of the Lord. **Praise to you, Lord Jesus Christ.**

PROFESSION OF FAITH (p. 14)

PRAYER OF THE FAITHFUL

The following intentions are suggestions only.
There are more suggestions at www.livingwithchrist.ca.

R. **Lord, hear our prayer.**

For leaders of the Church, entrusted to be good shepherds of God's people on earth, we pray to the Lord: R.

For those in positions of authority, called to act responsibly, we pray to the Lord: R.

For Christians everywhere, as they prepare to celebrate the birth of Christ, we pray to the Lord: R.

For our community, as we work to heal our relationships with God and with one another, we pray to the Lord: R.

PREPARATION OF THE GIFTS *(p. 17)*

PRAYER OVER THE OFFERINGS

May the Holy Spirit, O Lord, sanctify these gifts laid upon your altar, just as he filled with his power the womb of the Blessed Virgin Mary. Through Christ our Lord. **Amen.**

PREFACE *(Advent II, p. 18)*

COMMUNION ANTIPHON *(Isaiah 7:14)*

Behold, a Virgin shall conceive and bear a son; and his name will be called Emmanuel.

PRAYER AFTER COMMUNION

Having received this pledge of eternal redemption, we pray, almighty God, that, as the feast day of our salvation draws ever nearer, so we may press forward all the more eagerly to the worthy celebration of the mystery of your Son's Nativity. Who lives and reigns for ever and ever. **Amen.**

SOLEMN BLESSING AND DISMISSAL *(p. 81)*

Nativity of the Lord

"How *dare* you mention death – at Christmas?" The indignation at the lyric "Welcoming in love's surrender *death's* dark shadow at his crèche" in my Christmas hymn "In the Darkness Shines the Splendour" (*CBW III, 346*) was palpable.

Therein, however, lies the mystery of Christmas. "God... almighty... maker of heaven and earth, of all things visible and invisible" renounces Godliness for our flesh: flesh that is thrust out of a mother's womb, that suckles at a mother's breast, that pees and poops. Whose cells divide and grow, and whose heart expands in wisdom and understanding. Who learns a trade and accepts a mission. Who embraces human messiness and sinfulness. And then – like every one of us – who dies. To this self-emptying, God's loving response is to raise Jesus on high.

My mind and my heart boggle at the depth and breadth of this mystery. HOW. COULD. GOD. BE. SO. LIKE. ME? LIKE. YOU? SO ONE OF US? Even more: "By this wondrous union we, too, are made eternal." (*Preface III of the Nativity*). Mystery upon mystery.

In response I can only cradle our God, whose flesh today is the refugee child; the homeless young adult searching for a dwelling place; the nurse tending the dying; the parent working three jobs; my limited, sinful self. And join the angels and shepherds in praise and thanks for grace upon grace.

Bernadette Gasslein
Edmonton, AB

MASS DURING THE NIGHT

ENTRANCE ANTIPHON *(Psalm 2.7)*
The Lord said to me: You are my Son. It is I who have begotten you this day.

or

Let us all rejoice in the Lord, for our Saviour has been born in the world. Today true peace has come down to us from heaven.

INTRODUCTORY RITES *(p. 8)*

COLLECT
O God, who have made this most sacred night radiant with the splendour of the true light, grant, we pray, that we, who have known the mysteries of his light on earth, may also delight in his gladness in heaven. Who lives and reigns with you in the unity of the Holy Spirit, God, for ever and ever. **Amen.**

FIRST READING *(Isaiah 9.2-4, 6-7)*
The people who walked in darkness have seen
    a great light;
those who lived in a land of deep darkness —
on them light has shone.
You have multiplied the nation,
you have increased its joy;
they rejoice before you
as with joy at the harvest,
as people exult when dividing plunder.

For the yoke of their burden,
and the bar across their shoulders,

the rod of their oppressor,
you have broken as on the day of Midian.

For a child has been born for us,
a son given to us;
authority rests upon his shoulders;
and he is named
Wonderful Counsellor, Mighty God,
Everlasting Father, Prince of Peace.

His authority shall grow continually,
and there shall be endless peace
for the throne of David and his kingdom.
He will establish and uphold it
with justice and with righteousness
from this time onward and forevermore.
The zeal of the Lord of hosts will do this.

The word of the Lord. **Thanks be to God.**

RESPONSORIAL PSALM *(Psalm 96)*

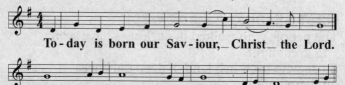

To-day is born our Sav-iour,— Christ— the Lord.

R. **Today is born our Saviour, Christ the Lord.**

O sing to the Lord a · **new** song;
sing to the Lord, · **all_the** earth.
Sing to the Lord, · **bless_his** name;
tell of his salvation from day · **to** day. R.

Declare his glory among · **the** nations,
his marvellous works among all · **the** peoples.
For great is the Lord, and greatly · **to_be** praised;
he is to be revered above · **all** gods. R.

Let the heavens be glad, and let the earth
   · **re**-joice;
let the sea roar, and all · **that** fills_it;
let the field exult, and every·-**thing** in_it.
Then shall all the trees of the forest sing
   · **for** joy. R.

Rejoice before the Lord; for · **he_is** coming,
for he is coming to judge · **the** earth.
He will judge the world · **with** righteousness,
and the peoples · **with_his** truth. R.

©2009 Gordon Johnston/Novalis

To hear the Sunday psalms, visit www.livingwithchrist.ca.

SECOND READING *(Titus 2.11-14)*

Beloved: The grace of God has appeared, bringing salvation to all, training us to renounce impiety and worldly passions, and in the present age to live lives that are self-controlled, upright, and godly, while we wait for the blessed hope and the manifestation of the glory of our great God and Saviour, Jesus Christ.

He it is who gave himself for us that he might redeem us from all iniquity and purify for himself a people of his own who are zealous for good deeds.

The word of the Lord. **Thanks be to God.**

GOSPEL ACCLAMATION *(Luke 2.10-11)*
Alleluia. Alleluia. Good news and great joy to all the world: today is born our Saviour, Christ the Lord. **Alleluia.**

GOSPEL *(Luke 2.1-16)*
The Lord be with you. **And with your spirit.** A reading from the holy Gospel according to Luke. **Glory to you, O Lord.**

In those days a decree went out from Caesar Augustus that all the world should be registered. This was the first registration and was taken while Quirinius was governor of Syria. All went to their own towns to be registered. Joseph also went from the town of Nazareth in Galilee to Judea, to the city of David called Bethlehem, because he was descended from the house and family of David. He went to be registered with Mary, to whom he was engaged and who was expecting a child.

While they were there, the time came for her to deliver her child. And she gave birth to her firstborn son and wrapped him in swaddling clothes, and laid him in a manger, because there was no place for them in the inn.

In that region there were shepherds living in the fields, keeping watch over their flock by night. Then an Angel of the Lord stood before them, and the glory of the Lord shone around them, and they were terrified. But the Angel said to them, "Do not be afraid; for see — I am bringing you good news of great joy for all the people: to you is born this day in the city of David a Saviour, who is the Christ, the Lord. This will be a sign for you: you will find a child wrapped in swaddling clothes and lying in a manger."

And suddenly there was with the Angel a multitude of the heavenly host, praising God and saying, "Glory to God in the highest heaven, and on earth peace among those whom he favours!"

When the Angels had left them and gone into heaven, the shepherds said to one another, "Let us go now to Bethlehem and see this thing that has taken place, which the Lord has made known to us." So they went with haste and found Mary and Joseph, and the child lying in the manger.

The Gospel of the Lord. **Praise to you, Lord Jesus Christ.**

PROFESSION OF FAITH *(Nicene Creed, p. 14. All kneel at the words "and by the Holy Spirit was incarnate.")*

PRAYER OF THE FAITHFUL
The following intentions are suggestions only.
There are more suggestions at www.livingwithchrist.ca.

R. **Lord, hear our prayer.**

For the whole People of God, whose faithful witness brings Jesus into the world each day, we pray to the Lord: R.

For the land where Jesus was born and lived; for reconciliation and mutual respect of the peoples living there, we pray to the Lord: R.

For all whose joy this Christmas is diminished by suffering in mind or body, we pray to the Lord: R.

For ourselves, celebrating the joy of Christmas; and for those around us who, on this very night and day of Christmas, are lonely, we pray to the Lord: R.

PREPARATION OF THE GIFTS *(p. 17)*

PRAYER OVER THE OFFERINGS

May the oblation of this day's feast be pleasing to you,
O Lord, we pray, that through this most holy exchange
we may be found in the likeness of Christ, in whom our
nature is united to you. Who lives and reigns for ever
and ever. **Amen.**

PREFACE *(Nativity, p. 19)*

COMMUNION ANTIPHON *(John 1.14)*
The Word became flesh, and we have seen his glory.

PRAYER AFTER COMMUNION

Grant us, we pray, O Lord our God, that we, who
are gladdened by participation in the feast of our
Redeemer's Nativity, may through an honourable way
of life become worthy of union with him. Who lives
and reigns for ever and ever. **Amen.**

SOLEMN BLESSING — NATIVITY *(Optional)*
Bow down for the blessing.

May the God of infinite goodness, who by the Incarnation of his Son has driven darkness from the world
and by that glorious Birth has illumined this most holy
night (day), drive far from you the darkness of vice and
illumine your hearts with the light of virtue. **Amen.**

May God, who willed that the great joy of his Son's
saving Birth be announced to shepherds by the Angel,
fill your minds with the gladness he gives and make
you heralds of his Gospel. **Amen.**

And may God, who by the Incarnation brought together the earthly and heavenly realm, fill you with the gift of his peace and favour and make you sharers with the Church in heaven. **Amen.**

And may the blessing of almighty God, the Father, and the Son, and the Holy Spirit, come down on you and remain with you for ever. **Amen.**

DISMISSAL *(p. 72)*

MASS AT DAWN

ENTRANCE ANTIPHON *(Cf. Isaiah 9.1, 5; Luke 1.33)*
Today a light will shine upon us, for the Lord is born for us; and he will be called Wondrous God, Prince of peace, Father of future ages: and his reign will be without end.

INTRODUCTORY RITES *(p. 8)*

COLLECT
Grant, we pray, almighty God, that, as we are bathed in the new radiance of your incarnate Word, the light of faith, which illumines our minds, may also shine through in our deeds. Through our Lord Jesus Christ, your Son, who lives and reigns with you in the unity of the Holy Spirit, God, for ever and ever. **Amen.**

FIRST READING *(Isaiah 62.11-12)*

The Lord has proclaimed to the end of the earth:
"Say to daughter Zion,
See, your salvation comes;
his reward is with him,
and his recompense before him.

"They shall be called
'The Holy People,'
'The Redeemed of the Lord';
and you shall be called 'Sought Out,'
'A City Not Forsaken.'"

The word of the Lord. **Thanks be to God.**

RESPONSORIAL PSALM *(Psalm 97)*

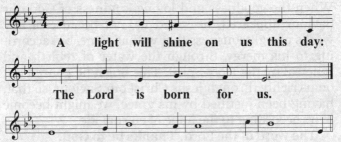

A light will shine on us this day:
The Lord is born for us.

R̸. **A light will shine on us this day:**
The Lord is born for us.

The Lord is king! Let the earth re·**joice;**
let the many coastlands be · **glad!**
Clouds and thick darkness are all a·**round_him;**
righteousness and justice are the foundation
of his · **throne.** R̸.

The mountains melt like wax before the · **Lord,**
before the Lord of all the · **earth.**
The heavens proclaim his · **righteousness;**
and all the peoples behold his · **glory.** R̸.

Light dawns for the · **righteous,**
and joy for the upright in · **heart.**
Rejoice in the Lord, O you · **righteous,**
and give thanks to his holy · **name!** R̸.

©*2009 Gordon Johnston/Novalis*

To hear the Sunday psalms, visit www.livingwithchrist.ca.

SECOND READING *(Titus 3.4-7)*

When the goodness and loving kindness of God our Saviour appeared, he saved us, not because of any works of righteousness that we had done, but according to his mercy, through the water of rebirth and renewal by the Holy Spirit. This Spirit he poured out on us richly through Jesus Christ our Saviour, so that, having been justified by his grace, we might become heirs according to the hope of eternal life.

The word of the Lord. **Thanks be to God.**

GOSPEL ACCLAMATION *(Luke 2.14)*

Alleluia. Alleluia. Glory to God in the highest heaven; peace on earth to people of good will. **Alleluia.**

GOSPEL *(Luke 2.15-20)*

The Lord be with you. **And with your spirit.** A reading from the holy Gospel according to Luke. **Glory to you, O Lord.**

When the Angels had left them and gone into heaven, the shepherds said to one another, "Let us go now to Bethlehem and see this thing that has taken place, which the Lord has made known to us."

So they went with haste and found Mary and Joseph, and the child lying in the manger. When they saw this, they made known what had been told them about this child; and all who heard it were amazed at what the shepherds told them. But Mary treasured all these words and pondered them in her heart. The shepherds returned, glorifying and praising God for all they had heard and seen, as it had been told them.

The Gospel of the Lord. **Praise to you, Lord Jesus Christ.**

PROFESSION OF FAITH *(Nicene Creed, p. 14. All kneel at the words "and by the Holy Spirit was incarnate.")*

PRAYER OF THE FAITHFUL *(p. 107)*

PREPARATION OF THE GIFTS *(p. 17)*

PRAYER OVER THE OFFERINGS
May our offerings be worthy, we pray, O Lord, of the mysteries of the Nativity this day, that, just as Christ was born a man and also shone forth as God, so these earthly gifts may confer on us what is divine. Through Christ our Lord. **Amen.**

PREFACE *(Nativity, p. 19)*

COMMUNION ANTIPHON *(Cf. Zechariah 9.9)*
Rejoice, O Daughter Sion; lift up praise, Daughter Jerusalem: Behold, your King will come, the Holy One and Saviour of the world.

PRAYER AFTER COMMUNION
Grant us, Lord, as we honour with joyful devotion the Nativity of your Son, that we may come to know with fullness of faith the hidden depths of this mystery and to love them ever more and more. Through Christ our Lord. **Amen.**

SOLEMN BLESSING AND DISMISSAL *(p. 108)*

MASS DURING THE DAY

ENTRANCE ANTIPHON (Cf. Isaiah 9.5)
A child is born for us, and a son is given to us; his sceptre of power rests upon his shoulder, and his name will be called Messenger of great counsel.

INTRODUCTORY RITES (p. 8)

COLLECT
O God, who wonderfully created the dignity of human nature and still more wonderfully restored it, grant, we pray, that we may share in the divinity of Christ, who humbled himself to share in our humanity. Who lives and reigns with you in the unity of the Holy Spirit, God, for ever and ever. **Amen.**

FIRST READING (Isaiah 52.7-10)
How beautiful upon the mountains are the feet of the messenger who announces peace, who brings good news, who announces salvation, who says to Zion, "Your God reigns."

Listen! Your watchmen lift up their voices, together they sing for joy; for in plain sight they see the return of the Lord to Zion.

Break forth together into singing, you ruins of Jerusalem; for the Lord has comforted his people, he has redeemed Jerusalem. The Lord has bared his holy arm before the eyes of all the nations; and all the ends of the earth shall see the salvation of our God.

The word of the Lord. **Thanks be to God.**

RESPONSORIAL PSALM (*Psalm 98*)

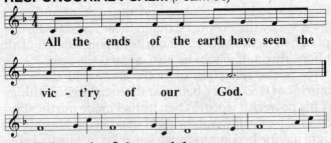

All the ends of the earth have seen the vic-t'ry of our God.

R̥. **All the ends of the earth have seen
the victory of our God.**

O sing to the Lord a · **new** song,
for he has done · **marvellous** things.
His right hand and his holy · **arm**
have brought · **him** victory. R̥.

The Lord has made known · **his** victory;
he has revealed his vindication in the sight
    of · **the** nations.
He has remembered his steadfast love
    and · **faithfulness**
to the house · **of** Israel. R̥.

All the ends of the earth · **have** seen
the victory of · **our** God.
Make a joyful noise to the Lord, all the · **earth;**
break forth into joyous song and · **sing** praises. R̥.

Sing praises to the Lord with · **the** lyre,
with the lyre and the sound · **of** melody.
With trumpets and the sound of the · **horn**
make a joyful noise before the King, · **the** Lord. R̥.

SECOND READING *(Hebrews 1.1-6)*

Long ago God spoke to our ancestors in many and various ways by the Prophets, but in these last days he has spoken to us by the Son, whom he appointed heir of all things, through whom he also created the ages.

He is the reflection of God's glory and the exact imprint of God's very being, and he sustains all things by his powerful word. When he had made purification for sins, he sat down at the right hand of the Majesty on high, having become as much superior to Angels as the name he has inherited is more excellent than theirs.

For to which of the Angels did God ever say, "You are my Son; today I have begotten you"? Or again, "I will be his Father, and he will be my Son"? And again, when he brings the firstborn into the world, he says, "Let all God's Angels worship him."

The word of the Lord. **Thanks be to God.**

GOSPEL ACCLAMATION

Alleluia. Alleluia. A holy day has dawned upon us. Come you nations and adore the Lord. Today a great light has come down upon the earth. **Alleluia.**

GOSPEL *(John 1.1-18)*

For the shorter version, omit the indented parts.

The Lord be with you. **And with your spirit.** A reading from the holy Gospel according to John. **Glory to you, O Lord.**

In the beginning was the Word, and the Word was with God, and the Word was God. He was in the beginning with God. All things came into being through him, and without him not one thing came into being. What has come into being in him was life, and the life was the light of the human race. The light shines in the darkness, and the darkness did not overcome it.

There was a man sent from God, whose name was John. He came as a witness to testify to the light, so that all might believe through him. He himself was not the light, but he came to testify to the light. The true light, which enlightens everyone, was coming into the world. He was in the world, and the world came into being through him; yet the world did not know him. He came to what was his own, and his own people did not accept him. But to all who received him, who believed in his name, he gave power to become children of God, who were born, not of blood or of the will of the flesh or of the will of man, but of God.

And the Word became flesh and lived among us, and we have seen his glory, the glory as of a father's only-begotten son, full of grace and truth. John testified to him and cried out, "This was he of whom I said, 'He who comes after me ranks ahead of me because he was before me.'" From his fullness we have all received, grace upon grace. The law indeed was given through Moses; grace and truth came through Jesus Christ. No one has ever seen God. It is God the only-begotten Son, who is close to the Father's heart, who has made him known.

The Gospel of the Lord. **Praise to you, Lord Jesus Christ.**

PROFESSION OF FAITH (Nicene Creed, p. 14. All kneel at the words "and by the Holy Spirit was incarnate.")

PRAYER OF THE FAITHFUL (p. 107)

PREPARATION OF THE GIFTS (p. 17)

PRAYER OVER THE OFFERINGS

Make acceptable, O Lord, our oblation on this solemn day, when you manifested the reconciliation that makes us wholly pleasing in your sight and inaugurated for us the fullness of divine worship. Through Christ our Lord. **Amen.**

PREFACE (Nativity, p. 19)

COMMUNION ANTIPHON (Cf. Psalm 97.3)
All the ends of the earth have seen the salvation of our God.

PRAYER AFTER COMMUNION

Grant, O merciful God, that, just as the Saviour of the world, born this day, is the author of divine generation for us, so he may be the giver even of immortality. Who lives and reigns for ever and ever. **Amen.**

SOLEMN BLESSING AND DISMISSAL (p. 108)

Holy Family of Jesus, Mary and Joseph

Today's readings have a strong and obvious theme of God's faithfulness. How does this relate to the Feast of the Holy Family? How does this help us understand our own families and our role in them?

I remember one day when my first child had just discovered that game all toddlers love while sitting in their high chair: dropping food and watching Mommy frantically clean up. Grace delighted in dropping bits one by one, even dropping them on me as I was bent over, clearing up. I was getting frustrated; but later, while she was blessedly napping, I reflected on St. Teresa of Kolkata's words about the holiness of little things done with great love.

What is family life but a series of little things, mundane chores, done over and over? It is keeping faithful, staying with the routine: the lunches, drop offs, sign ups, forms, backpacks. The day-in and day-out of family life is not glamorous or exciting but it does call out from each of us a depth of faithfulness that finds its inspiration in God's faithfulness to Abraham, to Simeon and to Anna. These holy ancestors only realized God's presence, the graces of the events, because their "eyes had seen [God's] salvation." Do we have eyes to see the graces in the ordinary, everyday life given to us?

Maureen Wicken
Vancouver, BC

ENTRANCE ANTIPHON *(Luke 2.16)*
**The shepherds went in haste, and found Mary and
Joseph and the Infant lying in a manger.**

INTRODUCTORY RITES *(p. 8)*

COLLECT
O God, who were pleased to give us the shining example of the Holy Family, graciously grant that we may
imitate them in practising the virtues of family life
and in the bonds of charity, and so, in the joy of your
house, delight one day in eternal rewards. Through
our Lord Jesus Christ, your Son, who lives and reigns
with you in the unity of the Holy Spirit, God, for ever
and ever. **Amen.**

Alternate readings can be found on p. 125.

FIRST READING *(Genesis 15.1-6; 17.3b-5, 15-16; 21.1-7)*
The word of the Lord came to Abram in a vision, "Do
not be afraid, Abram, I am your shield; your reward
shall be very great." But Abram said, "O Lord God,
what will you give me, for I continue childless, and the
heir of my house is Eliezer of Damascus?" And Abram
said, "You have given me no offspring, and so a slave
born in my house is to be my heir." But the word of the
Lord came to him, "This man shall not be your heir; no
one but your very own issue shall be your heir."

The Lord brought him outside and said, "Look
toward heaven and count the stars, if you are able
to count them." Then he said to him, "So shall your
descendants be." And he believed the Lord; and the
Lord reckoned it to him as righteousness.

God said to him, "As for me, this is my covenant with you: You shall be the father of a multitude of nations. No longer shall your name be Abram, but your name shall be Abraham; for I have made you the father of a multitude of nations."

God said to Abraham, "As for Sarah your wife, you shall not call her Sarai, but Sarah shall be her name. I will bless her, and moreover I will give you a son by her. I will bless her, and she shall give rise to nations; kings of peoples shall come from her."

The Lord dealt with Sarah as he had said, and the Lord did for Sarah as he had promised. Sarah conceived and bore Abraham a son in his old age, at the time of which God had spoken to him. Abraham gave the name Isaac to his son whom Sarah bore him. And Abraham circumcised his son Isaac when he was eight days old, as God had commanded him. Abraham was a hundred years old when his son Isaac was born to him. Now Sarah said, "God has brought laughter for me; everyone who hears will laugh with me." And she said, "Who would ever have said to Abraham that Sarah would nurse children? Yet I have borne him a son in his old age."

The word of the Lord. **Thanks be to God.**

RESPONSORIAL PSALM *(Psalm 105)*

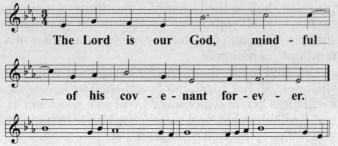

The Lord is our God, mind-ful of his cov-e-nant for-ev-er.

R. **The Lord is our God,
mindful of his covenant forever.**

O give thanks to the Lord, call · **on_his** name,
make known his deeds a-·**mong_the** peoples.
Sing to him, sing · **praises** to him;
tell of all his · **wonderful** works. R.

Glory in his ho-·**ly** name;
let the hearts of those who seek the Lord · **re**-joice.
Seek the Lord · **and** his strength;
seek his presence · **con**-tinually. R.

Remember the wonderful works he · **has** done,
his miracles, and the judgments · **he** uttered,
O offspring of his · **ser**-vant Abraham,
children of Jacob, · **his** chosen_ones. R.

He is mindful of his covenant · **for**-ever,
of the word that he commanded,
for a thousand · **gener**-ations,
the covenant that he · **made** with Abraham,
his sworn promise · **to** Isaac. R.

SECOND READING *(Hebrews 11.8, 11-12, 17-19)*

By faith Abraham obeyed when he was called to set out for a place that he was to receive as an inheritance; and he set out, not knowing where he was going. By faith Sarah herself, though barren, received power to conceive, even when she was too old, because she considered him faithful who had promised.

Therefore from one person, and this one as good as dead, descendants were born, "as many as the stars of heaven and as the innumerable grains of sand by the seashore."

By faith Abraham, when put to the test, offered up Isaac. He who had received the promises was ready to offer up his only-begotten son, of whom he had been told, "It is through Isaac that descendants shall be named for you." Abraham considered the fact that God is able even to raise someone from the dead — and figuratively speaking, he did receive him back.

The word of the Lord. **Thanks be to God.**

GOSPEL ACCLAMATION *(Hebrews 1.1-2)*
Alleluia. Alleluia. Long ago God spoke to our ancestors by the Prophets; in these last days he has spoken to us by the Son. **Alleluia.**

GOSPEL *(Luke 2.22-40)*
For the shorter version, omit the indented parts.
The Lord be with you. **And with your spirit.** A reading from the holy Gospel according to Luke. **Glory to you, O Lord.**

When the time came for their purification according to the law of Moses, Mary and Joseph brought the child Jesus up to Jerusalem to present him to the Lord.

(as it is written in the law of the Lord, "Every first-born male shall be designated as holy to the Lord"), and they offered a sacrifice according to what is stated in the law of the Lord, "a pair of turtledoves or two young pigeons."

Now there was a man in Jerusalem whose name was Simeon; this man was righteous and devout, looking forward to the consolation of Israel, and the Holy Spirit rested on him. It had been revealed to him by the Holy Spirit that he would not see death before he had seen the Christ of the Lord. Guided by the Spirit, Simeon came into the temple; and when the parents brought in the child Jesus, to do for him what was customary under the law,

Simeon took him in his arms and praised God, saying, "Master, now you are dismissing your servant in peace, according to your word; for my eyes have seen your salvation, which you have prepared in the presence of all peoples, a light for revelation to the Gentiles and for glory to your people Israel."

And the child's father and mother were amazed at what was being said about him. Then

Simeon blessed them and said to his mother Mary, "This child is destined for the falling and the rising of many in Israel, and to be a sign that will be opposed so that the inner thoughts of many will be revealed — and a sword will pierce your own soul too."

There was also a Prophet, Anna the daughter of Phanuel, of the tribe of Asher. She was of a great age, having lived with her husband seven years after her marriage, then as a widow to the age of eighty-four. She never left the temple but worshipped there with fasting and prayer night and day. At that moment she came, and began to praise God and to speak about the child to all who were looking for the redemption of Jerusalem.

When Mary and Joseph had finished everything required by the law of the Lord, they returned to Galilee, to their own town of Nazareth. The child grew and became strong, filled with wisdom; and the favour of God was upon him.

The Gospel of the Lord. **Praise to you, Lord Jesus Christ.**

Mass resumes on p. 128.

Alternate readings:

FIRST READING *(Sirach 3.2-6, 12-14)*
The Lord honours a father above his children,
and he confirms a mother's rights over her sons.
Whoever honours their father atones for sins
and gains preservation from them;
when they pray, they will be heard.
Whoever respects their mother
is like one who lays up treasure.
The person who honours their father
will have joy in their own children,
and when they pray they will be heard.
Whoever respects their father will have a long life,
and whoever honours their mother obeys the Lord.

My child, help your father in his old age,
and do not grieve him as long as he lives.
Even if his mind fails, be patient with him;
because you have all your faculties,

do not despise him all the days of his life.
For kindness to your father will not be forgotten,
and will be credited to you against your sins —
a house raised in justice for you.

The word of the Lord. **Thanks be to God.**

RESPONSORIAL PSALM *(Psalm 128)*

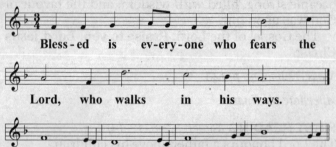

Bless - ed   is   ev-ery-one who   fears   the

Lord,   who   walks   in   his   ways.

R. **Blessed is everyone who fears the Lord.**
or **Blessed is everyone who fears the Lord,**
   who walks in his ways.

Blessed is everyone who fears · **the** Lord,
who walks in · **his** ways.
You shall eat the fruit of the labour
   of · **your** hands;
you shall be happy, and it shall go well
   · **with** you. R.

Your wife will be like a fruit-·**ful** vine
   within · **your** house;
your children will be · **like** olive_shoots
around · **your** table. R.

Thus shall the man be blessed who
　　fears · **the** Lord.
The Lord bless you · **from** Zion.
May you see the prosperity of · **Je**-rusalem
all the days of · **your** life. ℟.

SECOND READING *(Colossians 3.12-21)*
The shorter reading ends at the asterisks.

Brothers and sisters: As God's chosen ones, holy and beloved, clothe yourselves with compassion, kindness, humility, meekness, and patience. Bear with one another and, if anyone has a complaint against another, forgive each other; just as the Lord has forgiven you, so you also must forgive. Above all, clothe yourselves with love, which binds everything together in perfect harmony. And let the peace of Christ rule in your hearts, to which indeed you were called in the one body. And be thankful.

Let the word of Christ dwell in you richly; teach and admonish one another in all wisdom; and with gratitude in your hearts sing Psalms, hymns, and spiritual songs to God. And whatever you do, in word or deed, do everything in the name of the Lord Jesus, giving thanks to God the Father through him.

* * *

Wives, be subject to your husbands, as is fitting in the Lord. Husbands, love your wives and never treat them harshly. Children, obey your parents in everything, for this is your acceptable duty in the Lord. Fathers, do not provoke your children, or they may lose heart.

The word of the Lord. **Thanks be to God.**

For the Gospel: see p. 123.

PROFESSION OF FAITH *(p. 14)*

PRAYER OF THE FAITHFUL

The following intentions are suggestions only.
There are more suggestions at www.livingwithchrist.ca.

R. **Lord, hear our prayer.**

For the Church, beacon of light to the family of nations, we pray to the Lord: R.

For governments throughout the world, in search of peace and understanding among the human family, we pray to the Lord: R.

For peace of mind for all who suffer, we pray to the Lord: R.

For our parish, example of family to all, we pray to the Lord: R.

PREPARATION OF THE GIFTS *(p. 17)*

PRAYER OVER THE OFFERINGS
We offer you, Lord, the sacrifice of conciliation, humbly asking that, through the intercession of the Virgin Mother of God and Saint Joseph, you may establish our families firmly in your grace and your peace. Through Christ our Lord. **Amen.**

PREFACE *(Nativity, p. 19)*

COMMUNION ANTIPHON *(Baruch 3.38)*
Our God has appeared on the earth, and lived among us.

PRAYER AFTER COMMUNION

Bring those you refresh with this heavenly Sacrament, most merciful Father, to imitate constantly the example of the Holy Family, so that, after the trials of this world, we may share their company for ever. Through Christ our Lord. **Amen.**

BLESSING AND DISMISSAL *(p. 72)*

January Saints' Days

The following saints are traditionally remembered in January in Canada.

Solemnity of Mary, the Holy Mother of God .... Jan 1

Saints Basil the Great and Gregory Nazianzen .... Jan 2

Saint André Bessette .... Jan 7

Saint Raymond of Penyafort .... Jan 8

Saint Marguerite Bourgeoys .... Jan 12

Saint Hilary .... Jan 13

Saint Anthony .... Jan 17

Saint Fabian .... Jan 20
Saint Sebastian

Saint Agnes .... Jan 21

Saint Vincent .... Jan 22

Saint Francis de Sales .... Jan 24

Saints Timothy and Titus .... Jan 26

Saint Angela Merici .... Jan 27

Saint Thomas Aquinas .... Jan 28

Saint John Bosco .... Jan 31

Mary, the Holy Mother of God

World Day of Peace

Today is customarily a time for making New Year's resolutions. Would reflecting on the amazing example of our Mother Mary encourage us to engage in new directions throughout 2024?

Mary's faithfulness to God's design was complete. Some medieval preachers suggested that "the angels held their breath" until Mary ("the first believer") said yes at the Annunciation. Such an unlikely pregnancy would not have been well-received in her community – and travelling to Bethlehem in the latter stages was hardly preparation for an easy birth!

Mary is depicted in many ways and in many cultures. When I lived in Nicaragua, *La Purissima* celebrations made December 8 (Immaculate Conception) a bigger event than Christmas. And in Mexico on December 12, pilgrimages to revere *La Guadalupana* are celebrated by huge crowds at the largest shrine in all the Americas. What depictions of Mary inspire you the most?

For me, Mary's nobility of soul epitomizes the feminine humanity of faith. Her commitment to the Visitation of her pregnant cousin and her commitment to justice as recounted in the Magnificat both suggest a woman who lived a love story rather than an imposed code of conduct. Here indeed is a loving mother, for us and for the Church, whose example we can all treasure and ponder in our hearts.

Joe Gunn, Ottawa, ON

ENTRANCE ANTIPHON

Hail, Holy Mother, who gave birth to the King who rules heaven and earth for ever.

or (Cf. Isaiah 9.1, 5; Luke 1.33)

Today a light will shine upon us, for the Lord is born for us; and he will be called Wondrous God, Prince of peace, Father of future ages: and his reign will be without end.

INTRODUCTORY RITES *(p. 8)*

COLLECT

O God, who through the fruitful virginity of Blessed Mary bestowed on the human race the grace of eternal salvation, grant, we pray, that we may experience the intercession of her, through whom we were found worthy to receive the author of life, our Lord Jesus Christ, your Son. Who lives and reigns with you in the unity of the Holy Spirit, God, for ever and ever. **Amen.**

FIRST READING *(Numbers 6.22-27)*

The Lord spoke to Moses: Speak to Aaron and his sons, saying, Thus you shall bless the children of Israel: You shall say to them,

The Lord bless you and keep you;
the Lord make his face to shine upon you,
and be gracious to you;
the Lord lift up his countenance upon you,
and give you peace.

So they shall put my name on the children of Israel, and I will bless them.

The word of the Lord. **Thanks be to God.**

RESPONSORIAL PSALM *(Psalm 67)*

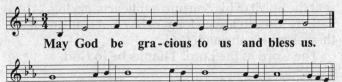

May God be gra-cious to us and bless us.

R. **May God be gracious to us and bless us.**

May God be gracious to us · **and** bless_us
and make his face to shine · **up**-on_us,
that your way may be known up--**on** earth,
your saving power a--**mong** all nations. R.

Let the nations be glad and sing · **for** joy,
for you judge the peoples with equity and guide
    the nations up--**on** earth.
Let the peoples praise you, · **O** God;
let all the · **peo**-ples praise_you. R.

The earth has yielded · **its** increase;
God, our God, · **has** blessed_us.
May God continue · **to** bless_us;
let all the ends of the · **earth** re-vere_him. R.

©2009 *Gordon Johnston/Novalis*

To hear the Sunday Psalms, visit www.livingwithchrist.ca.

SECOND READING *(Galatians 4.4-7)*
Brothers and sisters: When the fullness of time had
come, God sent his Son, born of a woman, born under
the law, in order to redeem those who were under the
law, so that we might receive adoption to sonship.

And because you are sons and daughters, God has sent the Spirit of his Son into our hearts, crying, "Abba! Father!" So you are no longer slave but son, and if son then also heir, through God.

The word of the Lord. **Thanks be to God.**

GOSPEL ACCLAMATION *(Hebrews 1.1-2)*
Alleluia. Alleluia. Long ago God spoke to our ancestors by the Prophets; in these last days he has spoken to us by the Son. **Alleluia.**

GOSPEL *(Luke 2.16-21)*
The Lord be with you. **And with your spirit.** A reading from the holy Gospel according to Luke. **Glory to you, O Lord.**

The shepherds went with haste to Bethlehem and found Mary and Joseph, and the child lying in the manger. When they saw this, they made known what had been told them about this child; and all who heard it were amazed at what the shepherds told them.

But Mary treasured all these words and pondered them in her heart.

The shepherds returned, glorifying and praising God for all they had heard and seen, as it had been told them.

After eight days had passed, it was time to circumcise the child; and he was called Jesus, the name given by the Angel before he was conceived in the womb.

The Gospel of the Lord. **Praise to you, Lord Jesus Christ.**

PROFESSION OF FAITH *(p. 14)*

PRAYER OF THE FAITHFUL

The following intentions are suggestions only.
There are more suggestions at www.livingwithchrist.ca.

R. **Lord, hear our prayer.**

For the Church, called to celebrate God's peace in the world, we pray to the Lord: R.

For all nations longing for God's kingdom of peace, we pray to the Lord: R.

For the Spirit of peace wherever there is fear, anxiety or anger, we pray to the Lord: R.

For this eucharistic community gathered around God's table of peace, we pray to the Lord: R.

PREPARATION OF THE GIFTS *(p. 17)*

PRAYER OVER THE OFFERINGS
O God, who in your kindness begin all good things and bring them to fulfillment, grant to us, who find joy in the Solemnity of the holy Mother of God, that, just as we glory in the beginnings of your grace, so one day we may rejoice in its completion. Through Christ our Lord. **Amen.**

PREFACE *(Blessed Virgin Mary, p. 20)*

COMMUNION ANTIPHON *(Hebrews 13.8)*
Jesus Christ is the same yesterday, today, and for ever.

PRAYER AFTER COMMUNION
We have received this heavenly Sacrament with joy, O Lord: grant, we pray, that it may lead us to eternal

life, for we rejoice to proclaim the blessed ever-Virgin Mary Mother of your Son and Mother of the Church. Through Christ our Lord. **Amen.**

SOLEMN BLESSING — NEW YEAR *(Optional)*
Bow down for the blessing.

May God, the source and origin of all blessing, grant you grace, pour out his blessing in abundance, and keep you safe from harm throughout the year. **Amen.**

May he give you integrity in the faith, endurance in hope, and perseverance in charity with holy patience to the end. **Amen.**

May he order your days and your deeds in his peace, grant your prayers in this and in every place, and lead you happily to eternal life. **Amen.**

And may the blessing of almighty God, the Father, and the Son, and the Holy Spirit, come down on you and remain with you for ever. **Amen.**

DISMISSAL *(p. 72)*

Epiphany of the Lord

Today's Gospel tells of the wise men journeying to meet the infant king. We are told they were following a star and when they found Jesus, they rejoiced and responded with worship and gifts. We can do the same in our lives today.

We must notice the star – the call from God that beckons us – and respond as they did. These wise men no doubt had busy and demanding lives, but they dropped everything and followed a star to something, to someone, beyond their imagining. At the beginning, they could not have known what the journey would hold for them, only that they should follow wholeheartedly. They must have made space in their hearts, to respond so fully. In the season of Advent, we were called to make space for Jesus to come. Not that Jesus was not already present, but to brush away the clutter and make space again for what – for who – is most important.

Once Jesus has arrived in the space we have made in our hearts, how do we respond to his arrival? To this new awareness? Are we overwhelmed with joy as the wise men were? Can we too respond by sharing our time, our attentive presence and our gifts? What is God calling us to do and to share? Can we respond as the wise men did, with hope and without reservation?

Kelly Bourke
Regina, SK

ENTRANCE ANTIPHON *(Cf. Mal 3.1; 1 Chr 29.12)*
Behold, the Lord, the Mighty One, has come; and kingship is in his grasp, and power and dominion.

INTRODUCTORY RITES *(p. 8)*

COLLECT
O God, who on this day revealed your Only Begotten Son to the nations by the guidance of a star, grant in your mercy that we, who know you already by faith, may be brought to behold the beauty of your sublime glory. Through our Lord Jesus Christ, your Son, who lives and reigns with you in the unity of the Holy Spirit, God, for ever and ever. **Amen.**

FIRST READING *(Isaiah 60.1-6)*
Arise, shine, for your light has come,
and the glory of the Lord has risen upon you!
For darkness shall cover the earth,
and thick darkness the peoples;
but the Lord will arise upon you,
and his glory will appear over you.
Nations shall come to your light,
and kings to the brightness of your dawn.
Lift up your eyes and look around;
they all gather together, they come to you;
your sons shall come from far away,
and your daughters shall be carried
    on their nurses' arms.
Then you shall see and be radiant;
your heart shall thrill and rejoice,
because the abundance of the sea shall be brought
    to you,

the wealth of the nations shall come to you.
A multitude of camels shall cover you,
the young camels of Midian and Ephah;
all those from Sheba shall come.
They shall bring gold and frankincense,
and shall proclaim the praise of the Lord.

The word of the Lord. **Thanks be to God.**

RESPONSORIAL PSALM *(Psalm 72)*

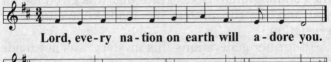

Lord, eve-ry na-tion on earth will a-dore you.

R. **Lord, every nation on earth will adore you.**

Give the king your justice, O · **God,**
and your righteousness to a king's · **son.**
May he judge your · **people** with righteousness,
and your · **poor** with justice. R.

In his days may righteousness · **flourish**
and peace abound, until the moon is no · **more.**
May he have dominion from · **sea** to sea,
and from the River to the · **ends_of** the earth. R.

May the kings of Tarshish and of the isles render
    him · **tribute,**
may the kings of Sheba and Seba bring · **gifts.**
May all kings fall · **down** be-fore_him,
all nations · **give** him service. R.

For he delivers the needy one who · **calls,**
the poor and the one who has no · **helper.**
He has pity on the · **weak_and** the needy,
and saves the · **lives_of** the needy. R.

To hear the Sunday Psalms, visit www.livingwithchrist.ca.

SECOND READING *(Ephesians 3.2-3a, 5-6)*

Brothers and sisters: Surely you have already heard of
the commission of God's grace that was given me for
you, and how the mystery was made known to me by
revelation.

In former generations this mystery was not made
known to humankind as it has now been revealed to
his holy Apostles and Prophets by the Spirit: that is,
the Gentiles have become fellow heirs, members of the
same body, and sharers in the promise in Christ Jesus
through the Gospel.

The word of the Lord. **Thanks be to God.**

GOSPEL ACCLAMATION *(See Matthew 2.2)*

Alleluia. Alleluia. We observed his star at its rising,
and have come to pay homage to the Lord. **Alleluia.**

GOSPEL *(Matthew 2.1-12)*

The Lord be with you. **And with your spirit.**
A reading from the holy Gospel according to Matthew.
Glory to you, O Lord.

In the time of King Herod, after Jesus was born in
Bethlehem of Judea, wise men from the East came to
Jerusalem, asking, "Where is the child who has been
born king of the Jews? For we observed his star at its
rising, and have come to pay him homage."

When King Herod heard this, he was frightened, and all Jerusalem with him; and calling together all the chief priests and scribes of the people, he inquired of them where the Messiah was to be born. They told him, "In Bethlehem of Judea; for so it has been written by the Prophet: 'And you, Bethlehem, in the land of Judah, are by no means least among the rulers of Judah; for from you shall come a ruler who is to shepherd my people Israel.'"

Then Herod secretly called for the wise men and learned from them the exact time when the star had appeared. Then he sent them to Bethlehem, saying, "Go and search diligently for the child; and when you have found him, bring me word so that I may also go and pay him homage."

When they had heard the king, they set out; and there, ahead of them, went the star that they had seen at its rising, until it stopped over the place where the child was. When they saw that the star had stopped, they were overwhelmed with joy.

On entering the house, they saw the child with Mary his mother; and they knelt down and paid him homage. Then, opening their treasure chests, they offered him gifts of gold, frankincense, and myrrh.

And having been warned in a dream not to return to Herod, they left for their own country by another road.

The Gospel of the Lord. **Praise to you, Lord Jesus Christ.**

PROFESSION OF FAITH *(p. 14)*

PRAYER OF THE FAITHFUL

The following intentions are suggestions only.
There are more suggestions at www.livingwithchrist.ca.

R. **Lord, hear our prayer.**

For the Church, light of the nations, witness to the gospel of Christ Jesus, we pray to the Lord: R.

For the members of all faith communities working in mutual respect and acceptance, we pray to the Lord: R.

For those who seek food at our table and a place in our community, we pray to the Lord: R.

For ourselves, God's people, yearning to follow the Light of Christ, we pray to the Lord: R.

PREPARATION OF THE GIFTS *(p. 17)*

PRAYER OVER THE OFFERINGS
Look with favour, Lord, we pray, on these gifts of your Church, in which are offered now not gold or frankincense or myrrh, but he who by them is proclaimed, sacrificed and received, Jesus Christ. Who lives and reigns for ever and ever. **Amen.**

PREFACE *(Epiphany, p. 21)*

COMMUNION ANTIPHON *(Cf. Matthew 2.2)*
We have seen his star in the East, and have come with gifts to adore the Lord.

PRAYER AFTER COMMUNION

Go before us with heavenly light, O Lord, always and everywhere, that we may perceive with clear sight and revere with true affection the mystery in which you have willed us to participate. Through Christ our Lord. **Amen.**

SOLEMN BLESSING — EPIPHANY *(Optional)*

Bow down for the blessing.

May God, who has called you out of darkness into his wonderful light, pour out in kindness his blessing upon you and make your hearts firm in faith, hope and charity. **Amen.**

And since in all confidence you follow Christ, who today appeared in the world as a light shining in darkness, may God make you, too, a light for your brothers and sisters. **Amen.**

And so when your pilgrimage is ended, may you come to him whom the Magi sought as they followed the star and whom they found with great joy, the Light from Light, who is Christ the Lord. **Amen.**

And may the blessing of almighty God, the Father, and the Son, and the Holy Spirit, come down on you and remain with you for ever. **Amen.**

DISMISSAL *(p. 72)*

2nd Sunday in Ordinary Time

Today's Gospel recounts the story of Jesus calling his first disciples. After spending a day with Jesus, Andrew immediately tells his brother Simon about the Messiah. Have you shared about your encounter with Christ with a friend or family member lately? Too often we keep these experiences to ourselves, worried what other people may think of us, or afraid we won't say the right words. Andrew's example is simple: he shares with a loved one the joyful news of finding the Messiah.

Next, Andrew brings Simon to Jesus. He gives him the opportunity to meet the Lord and experience for himself the love of God. There are many ways we can bring others to Christ. Extending invitations to Holy Mass, adoration or Bible study can encourage people to meet Jesus in the Eucharist and in the Word.

These two simple yet life-changing acts undertaken by Andrew – telling Simon about the Messiah and inviting him to meet the Lord – had a meaningful impact not only on Simon's life, but also on the entire Church. Through that invitation, Simon (now called Peter) was able to respond to his call to be a great leader among the early Christians, and ultimately became our first pope. Never underestimate what marvels God can work through our openness to share him with others!

Myriam Fernandes
Etobicoke, ON

ENTRANCE ANTIPHON *(Psalm 65.4)*

All the earth shall bow down before you, O God, and shall sing to you, shall sing to your name, O Most High!

INTRODUCTORY RITES *(p. 8)*

COLLECT

Almighty ever-living God, who govern all things, both in heaven and on earth, mercifully hear the pleading of your people and bestow your peace on our times. Through our Lord Jesus Christ, your Son, who lives and reigns with you in the unity of the Holy Spirit, God, for ever and ever. **Amen.**

FIRST READING *(1 Samuel 3.3b-10, 19)*

Samuel was lying down in the temple of the Lord, where the ark of God was. Then the Lord called, "Samuel! Samuel!" and he said, "Here I am!" Samuel ran to Eli, and said, "Here I am, for you called me." But Eli said, "I did not call; lie down again." So he went and lay down.

The Lord called again, "Samuel!" Samuel got up and went to Eli, and said, "Here I am, for you called me." But he said, "I did not call, my son; lie down again." Now Samuel did not yet know the Lord, and the word of the Lord had not yet been revealed to him.

The Lord called Samuel again, a third time. And he got up and went to Eli, and said, "Here I am, for you called me." Then Eli perceived that the Lord was calling the boy. Therefore Eli said to Samuel, "Go, lie down; and if he calls you, you shall say, 'Speak, Lord, for your servant is listening.'" So Samuel went and lay down in his place.

Now the Lord came and stood there, calling as before, "Samuel! Samuel!" And Samuel said, "Speak, for your servant is listening."

As Samuel grew up, the Lord was with him and let none of his words fall to the ground.

The word of the Lord. **Thanks be to God.**

RESPONSORIAL PSALM *(Psalm 40)*

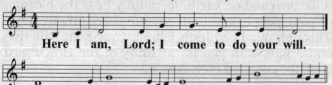

Here I am, Lord; I come to do your will.

R. **Here I am, Lord; I come to do your will.**

I waited patiently for the · **Lord;**
he inclined to me and · **heard** my cry.
He put a new song in · **my** mouth,
a song of praise · **to** our God. R.

Sacrifice and offering you do not de--**sire,**
but you have given me an · **o**-pen ear.
Burnt offering · **and** sin_offering
you have · **not** re-quired. R.

Then I said, "Here I · **am;**
In the scroll of the book it is · **written** of me.
I delight to do your will, O · **my** God;
your law is with--**in** my heart." R.

I have told the glad news of de-·**liverance**
in the great · **con**-gre-gation;
see, I have not restrained · **my** lips,
as you · **know,** O Lord. R.

©2009 Gordon Johnston/Novalis

To hear the Sunday Psalms, visit www.livingwithchrist.ca.

SECOND READING *(1 Corinthians 6.13c-15a, 17-20)*
Brothers and sisters: The body is meant not for fornication but for the Lord, and the Lord for the body. And God raised the Lord and will also raise us by his power.

Do you not know that your bodies are members of Christ? But anyone united to the Lord becomes one spirit with him. Shun fornication! Every sin that a person commits is outside the body; but the fornicator sins against the body itself.

Or do you not know that your body is a temple of the Holy Spirit within you, which you have from God, and that you are not your own? For you were bought with a price; therefore glorify God in your body.

The word of the Lord. **Thanks be to God.**

GOSPEL ACCLAMATION *(See John 1.41, 17)*
Alleluia. Alleluia. We have found the Messiah: Jesus Christ, who brings us grace and truth. **Alleluia.**

GOSPEL *(John 1.35-42)*
The Lord be with you. **And with your spirit.**
A reading from the holy Gospel according to John.
Glory to you, O Lord.

John was standing with two of his disciples, and as he watched Jesus walk by, he exclaimed, "Look, here is the Lamb of God!" The two disciples heard him say this, and they followed Jesus.

When Jesus turned and saw them following, he said to them, "What are you looking for?" They said to him, "Rabbi" (which translated means Teacher), "where are you staying?" He said to them, "Come and see." They came and saw where he was staying, and they remained with him that day. It was about four o'clock in the afternoon.

One of the two who heard John speak and followed him was Andrew, Simon Peter's brother. He first found his brother Simon and said to him, "We have found the Messiah" (which is translated the Christ). He brought Simon to Jesus, who looked at him and said, "You are Simon son of John. You are to be called Cephas" (which is translated Peter).

The Gospel of the Lord. **Praise to you, Lord Jesus Christ.**

PROFESSION OF FAITH (p. 14)

PRAYER OF THE FAITHFUL

The following intentions are suggestions only.
There are more suggestions at www.livingwithchrist.ca.

R. **Lord, hear our prayer.**

For the Church, hearing and proclaiming God's call to holiness, we pray to the Lord: R.

For world leaders, working for a lasting peace, we pray to the Lord: R.

For those who hunger for food, for understanding and for companionship, we pray to the Lord: R.

For ourselves, gathered to share the gifts of faith, hope and love, we pray to the Lord: ℟.

PREPARATION OF THE GIFTS *(p. 17)*

PRAYER OVER THE OFFERINGS
Grant us, O Lord, we pray, that we may participate worthily in these mysteries, for whenever the memorial of this sacrifice is celebrated the work of our redemption is accomplished. Through Christ our Lord. **Amen.**

PREFACE *(Sundays in Ordinary Time, p. 31)*

COMMUNION ANTIPHON *(Cf. Psalm 22.5)*
You have prepared a table before me, and how precious is the chalice that quenches my thirst.

or (1 John 4.16)
We have come to know and to believe in the love that God has for us.

PRAYER AFTER COMMUNION
Pour on us, O Lord, the Spirit of your love, and in your kindness make those you have nourished by this one heavenly Bread one in mind and heart. Through Christ our Lord. **Amen.**

BLESSING AND DISMISSAL *(p. 72)*

3rd Sunday in Ordinary Time

Sunday of the Word of God
Week of Prayer for Christian Unity

It my late teens, I read William Thomas Walsh's *Our Lady of Fatima*. It prompted me to quit a job that was lacking some ethics. Afterward, I was in a spiritual fog. I went for one of those long walks in an attempt to reconnect with the Lord. At an intersection I saw a yellow Volkswagen with these words boldly painted on it: *Pray the Rosary, Fatima 1917.*

In today's Gospel, we hear the familiar story of how Jesus called his first disciples to be fishers of people. If we fast forward today's Gospel into the present day, we can imagine Jesus walking through an office complex and asking us to leave our desks. Do we drop everything and go?

The response from the apostles was immediate. There was an expectation of the coming of the Messiah, so perhaps they were ready. And Jesus chose humble people whose hearts, he knew, were receptive to the call.

Through the sacraments, prayer, and Scripture we seek the Lord and anticipate his call. God can also speak via a billboard, a bumper sticker, a song, a conversation and even a yellow Volkswagen. This is the all-powerful voice of Love that spoke creation into existence. We are prudent to seek it, listen for it and trust that it indeed will come in the manner God chooses for us.

Denis Grady, OFS
Calgary, AB

ENTRANCE ANTIPHON *(Cf. Psalm 95.1, 6)*
**O sing a new song to the Lord; sing to the Lord, all
the earth. In his presence are majesty and splendour, strength and honour in his holy place.**

INTRODUCTORY RITES *(p. 8)*

COLLECT
Almighty ever-living God, direct our actions according to your good pleasure, that in the name of your
beloved Son we may abound in good works. Through
our Lord Jesus Christ, your Son, who lives and reigns
with you in the unity of the Holy Spirit, God, for ever
and ever. **Amen.**

FIRST READING *(Jonah 3.1-5, 10)*
The word of the Lord came to Jonah, saying, "Get up,
go to Nineveh, that great city, and proclaim to it the
message that I tell you." So Jonah set out and went to
Nineveh, according to the word of the Lord.

Now Nineveh was an exceedingly large city, a three
days' walk across. Jonah began to go into the city, going
a day's walk. And he cried out, "Forty days more, and
Nineveh shall be overthrown!"

And the people of Nineveh believed God; they proclaimed a fast, and everyone, great and small, put on
sackcloth.

When God saw what they did, how they turned
from their evil ways, God changed his mind about the
calamity that he had said he would bring upon them;
and he did not do it.

The word of the Lord. **Thanks be to God.**

RESPONSORIAL PSALM *(Psalm 25)*

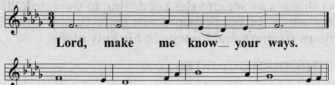

Lord, make me know your ways.

R. **Lord, make me know your ways.**

Make me to know your ways, O · **Lord;**
teach me · **your** paths.
Lead me in your truth, and · **teach_me,**
for you are the God of my · **sal**-vation. R.

Be mindful of your mercy, O Lord,
   and of your steadfast · **love,**
for they have been from · **of** old.
According to your steadfast love re-·**member_me,**
for the sake of your goodness, · **O** Lord! R.

Good and upright is the · **Lord;**
therefore he instructs sinners in · **the** way.
He leads the humble in what is · **right,**
and teaches the humble · **his** way. R.

To hear the Sunday Psalms, visit www.livingwithchrist.ca.

SECOND READING *(1 Corinthians 7.29-31)*

Brothers and sisters, the appointed time has grown short; from now on, let even those who have wives be as though they had none, and those who mourn as though they were not mourning, and those who rejoice as though they were not rejoicing, and those who buy as though they had no possessions, and those who deal with the world as though they had no dealings with it. For the present form of this world is passing away.

The word of the Lord. **Thanks be to God.**

GOSPEL ACCLAMATION *(Mark 1.15)*
Alleluia. Alleluia. The kingdom of God has come near: repent and believe the good news! **Alleluia.**

GOSPEL *(Mark 1.14-20)*
The Lord be with you. **And with your spirit.** A reading from the holy Gospel according to Mark. **Glory to you, O Lord.**

After John was arrested, Jesus came to Galilee, proclaiming the good news of God, and saying, "The time is fulfilled, and the kingdom of God has come near; repent, and believe in the good news."

As Jesus passed along the Sea of Galilee, he saw Simon and his brother Andrew casting a net into the sea — for they were fishermen. And Jesus said to them, "Come follow me and I will make you fishers of people." And immediately they left their nets and followed him.

As Jesus went a little farther, he saw James son of Zebedee and his brother John, who were in their boat mending the nets. Immediately he called them; and they left their father Zebedee in the boat with the hired men, and followed him.

The Gospel of the Lord. **Praise to you, Lord Jesus Christ.**

PROFESSION OF FAITH *(p. 14)*

PRAYER OF THE FAITHFUL

The following intentions are suggestions only.
There are more suggestions at www.livingwithchrist.ca.

℟. **Lord, hear our prayer.**

For unity among Christians across the country and around the world, we pray to the Lord: ℟.

For peace in our world, our churches, our schools and our families, we pray to the Lord: ℟.

For all who are lonely, isolated or grieving, we pray to the Lord: ℟.

For ourselves gathered here, messengers of the Good News of Jesus Christ, we pray to the Lord: ℟.

PREPARATION OF THE GIFTS *(p. 17)*

PRAYER OVER THE OFFERINGS

Accept our offerings, O Lord, we pray, and in sanctifying them grant that they may profit us for salvation. Through Christ our Lord. **Amen.**

PREFACE *(Sundays in Ordinary Time, p. 31)*

COMMUNION ANTIPHON *(Cf. Psalm 33.6)*

Look toward the Lord and be radiant; let your faces not be abashed.

or (John 8.12)

I am the light of the world, says the Lord; whoever follows me will not walk in darkness, but will have the light of life.

PRAYER AFTER COMMUNION

Grant, we pray, almighty God, that, receiving the grace by which you bring us to new life, we may always glory in your gift. Through Christ our Lord. **Amen.**

BLESSING AND DISMISSAL (p. 72)

4th Sunday in Ordinary Time

When I moved to the Maritimes, I planned to spend one of my first Sundays relaxing on a beach after Mass. However, not knowing where such a beach was, I sat in my parked car looking at a map. Thunk! Someone leaving Mass had backed into my vehicle. "No problem," I thought. "I'm at church; this process will be painless." I had had a previous car mishap in a secular context which turned into quite an ordeal.

My expectations of ease and that adversity would not reach into the church parking lot were false – our fallen humanity follows us everywhere. Thankfully, our faith ought not depend on anyone or anything apart from Jesus. No wickedness can snatch us from either his gaze or his hand; someone's sins or poor choices do not affect that.

In today's Gospel we hear how there was "in their synagogue a man with an unclean spirit" who was crying out. Evil manifested itself in the holy place of God. And Jesus handled it.

When we experience disappointing behaviour amongst the faithful or are even faced with larger scandals involving those in leadership, we need not lose our faith in Jesus. Such circumstances do not reflect Jesus' authenticity, nor do they question his authority. Instead, we turn to the One who silences the voice of evil and casts it out.

Nicole Snook
Halifax, NS

ENTRANCE ANTIPHON *(Psalm 105.47)*

Save us, O Lord our God! And gather us from the nations, to give thanks to your holy name, and make it our glory to praise you.

INTRODUCTORY RITES *(p. 8)*

COLLECT

Grant us, Lord our God, that we may honour you with all our mind, and love everyone in truth of heart. Through our Lord Jesus Christ, your Son, who lives and reigns with you in the unity of the Holy Spirit, God, for ever and ever. **Amen.**

FIRST READING *(Deuteronomy 18.15-20)*

Moses spoke to the people; he said: "The Lord your God will raise up for you a Prophet like me from among your own kin; you shall heed such a Prophet. This is what you requested of the Lord your God at Horeb on the day of the assembly when you said: 'Let me not hear the voice of the Lord my God any more, or ever again see this great fire, lest I die.'

"Then the Lord replied to me: 'They are right in what they have said. I will raise up for them a Prophet like you from among their own kin; I will put my words in his mouth, and he shall speak to them everything that I command him.

"'Anyone who does not heed the words that he shall speak in my name, I myself will hold him accountable. But any Prophet who speaks in the name of other gods, or who presumes to speak in my name a word that I have not commanded him to speak — that Prophet shall die.'"

The word of the Lord. **Thanks be to God.**

RESPONSORIAL PSALM *(Psalm 95)*

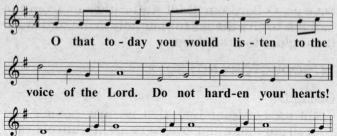

O that to-day you would lis-ten to the voice of the Lord. Do not hard-en your hearts!

℟. **O that today you would listen to the voice of the Lord. Do not harden your hearts!**

O come, let us sing to · **the** Lord.
Let us make a joyful noise to the rock
  of our · **sal**-vation!
Let us come into his presence with · **thanks**-giving;
let us make a joyful noise to him
  with songs · **of** praise! ℟.

O come, let us worship and · **bow** down,
let us kneel before the Lord, · **our** Maker!
For he is our God, and we are the people
  of · **his** pasture,
and the sheep of · **his** hand. ℟.

O that today you would listen to · **his** voice!
Do not harden your hearts, as at Meribah,
  as on the day at Massah in · **the** wilderness,
when your ancestors tested me,
  and put me to · **the** proof,
though they had seen · **my** work. ℟.

SECOND READING *(1 Corinthians 7.32-35)*
Brothers and sisters, I want you to be free from anxieties. The unmarried man is anxious about the affairs of the Lord, how to please the Lord; but the married man is anxious about the affairs of the world, how to please his wife, and his interests are divided.

The unmarried woman and the virgin are concerned about the affairs of the Lord, so that they may be holy in body and spirit; but the married woman is concerned about the affairs of the world, how to please her husband.

I say this for your own benefit, not to put any restraint upon you, but to promote good order and unhindered devotion to the Lord.

The word of the Lord. **Thanks be to God.**

GOSPEL ACCLAMATION *(Matthew 4.16)*
Alleluia. Alleluia. The people who sat in darkness have seen a great light, and for those who sat in the region and shadow of death, light has dawned. **Alleluia.**

GOSPEL *(Mark 1.21-28)*
The Lord be with you. **And with your spirit.**
A reading from the holy Gospel according to Mark.
Glory to you, O Lord.

The disciples went to Capernaum; and when the Sabbath came, Jesus entered the synagogue and taught. They were astounded at his teaching, for he taught them as one having authority, and not as the scribes. Just then there was in their synagogue a man with an unclean spirit, and he cried out, "What have you to do with us, Jesus of Nazareth? Have you come to destroy us? I know who you are, the Holy One of God."

But Jesus rebuked him, saying, "Be silent, and come out of him!" And the unclean spirit, convulsing the man and crying with a loud voice, came out of him. They were all amazed, and they kept on asking one another, "What is this? A new teaching — with authority! He commands even the unclean spirits, and they obey him."

At once Jesus' fame began to spread throughout the surrounding region of Galilee.

The Gospel of the Lord. **Praise to you, Lord Jesus Christ.**

PROFESSION OF FAITH (p. 14)

PRAYER OF THE FAITHFUL

The following intentions are suggestions only.
There are more suggestions at www.livingwithchrist.ca.

R. **Lord, hear our prayer.**

For the Church, speaking with God's loving authority, we pray to the Lord: R.

For world leaders to act with integrity, we pray to the Lord. R.

For all who face the future with fear or uncertainty, we pray to the Lord: R.

For ourselves, gathered to hear and put into action God's healing love, we pray to the Lord: R.

PREPARATION OF THE GIFTS (p. 17)

PRAYER OVER THE OFFERINGS

O Lord, we bring to your altar these offerings of our service: be pleased to receive them, we pray, and transform them into the Sacrament of our redemption. Through Christ our Lord. **Amen.**

PREFACE *(Sundays in Ordinary Time, p. 31)*

COMMUNION ANTIPHON *(Cf. Psalm 30.17-18)*

Let your face shine on your servant. Save me in your merciful love. O Lord, let me never be put to shame, for I call on you.

or (Matthew 5.3-4)

Blessed are the poor in spirit, for theirs is the Kingdom of Heaven. Blessed are the meek, for they shall possess the land.

PRAYER AFTER COMMUNION

Nourished by these redeeming gifts, we pray, O Lord, that through this help to eternal salvation true faith may ever increase. Through Christ our Lord. **Amen.**

BLESSING AND DISMISSAL *(p. 72)*

February Saints' Days

The following saints are traditionally remembered in February in Canada.

Saint Blaise . . . . Feb 3
Saint Ansgar

Saint Agatha . . . . Feb 5

Saint Paul Miki and Companions . . . . Feb 6

Saint Jerome Emiliani . . . . Feb 8
Saint Josephine Bakhita

Saint Scholastica . . . . Feb 10

Our Lady of Lourdes . . . . Feb 11

Saints Cyril and Methodius . . . . Feb 14

The Seven Holy Founders . . . . Feb 17
   of the Servite Order

Saint Peter Damian . . . . Feb 21

Saint Polycarp . . . . Feb 23

Saint Gregory of Narek . . . . Feb 27

5th Sunday in Ordinary Time

The readings today hint both that the kingdom is not yet here and the kingdom is here! On the one hand, Job and Paul give us a bleak version of reality, one filled with weakness, suffering and exhaustion. On the other hand, we have Jesus, in whom heaven and earth come together.

Jesus knows what it is like for us: what it is to be human, and how demanding people can be. He sees the hurt, pain and suffering we endure. We have the Incarnate Jesus: he brings healing and hope to all humanity. He comes to us, sharing in our humanity and offers healing, friendship and joy – all avenues to transform our suffering into blessings.

There is a crucial line in Mark's Gospel that tells us how we can do this: "In the morning, while it was still very dark, Jesus got up and went out to a deserted place and there he prayed." No audience or crowds: Jesus alone in the dark in prayer with the Father.

We gather around the table of the Lord, where past and present meet, to encounter Jesus in the Eucharist. Let us quiet ourselves to be with the One who sees us, understands us, heals us and sends us forth, to bring the kingdom wherever we are needed.

Adriana Rerecich
Hamilton, ON

ENTRANCE ANTIPHON *(Psalm 94.6-7)*
O come, let us worship God and bow low before the God who made us, for he is the Lord our God.

INTRODUCTORY RITES *(p. 8)*

COLLECT
Keep your family safe, O Lord, with unfailing care, that, relying solely on the hope of heavenly grace, they may be defended always by your protection. Through our Lord Jesus Christ, your Son, who lives and reigns with you in the unity of the Holy Spirit, God, for ever and ever. **Amen.**

FIRST READING *(Job 7.1-4, 6-7)*
Job spoke to his friends: "Does not the human being have a hard service on earth, and are not their days like the days of a labourer? Like a slave who longs for the shadow, and like a labourer who looks for their wages, so I am allotted months of emptiness, and nights of misery are apportioned to me.

"When I lie down I say, 'When shall I rise?' But the night is long, and I am full of tossing until dawn.

"My days are swifter than a weaver's shuttle, and come to their end without hope. Remember that my life is a breath; my eye will never again see good."

The word of the Lord. **Thanks be to God.**

RESPONSORIAL PSALM *(Psalm 147)*

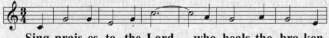

Sing prais-es to the Lord___ who heals the bro-ken

heart - ed.

R̠. **Sing praises to the Lord
who heals the broken-hearted.**
or **Alleluia!**

How good it is to sing praises · **to** our God;
for he is gracious, and a song of · **praise** is fitting.
The Lord builds · **up** Je-rusalem;
he gathers the · **outcasts** of Israel. R̠.

The Lord heals the · **bro**-ken-hearted,
and binds · **up** their wounds.
He determines the · **number** of the stars;
he gives to all of · **them** their names. R̠.

Great is our Lord, and a-·**bundant** in power;
his understanding · **is be**-yond measure.
The Lord lifts · **up** the downtrodden;
he casts the wicked · **to** the ground. R̠.

©2009 Gordon Johnston/Novalis

To hear the Sunday Psalms, visit www.livingwithchrist.ca.

SECOND READING *(1 Corinthians 9.16-19, 22-23)*

Brothers and sisters: If I proclaim the Gospel, this gives
me no ground for boasting, for an obligation is laid on
me, and woe to me if I do not proclaim the Gospel! For
if I do this of my own will, I have a reward; but if not of

my own will, I am entrusted with a commission. What then is my reward? Just this: that in my proclamation I may make the Gospel free of charge, so as not to make full use of my rights in the Gospel.

For though I am free with respect to all, I have made myself a slave to all, so that I might win more of them.

To the weak I became weak, so that I might win the weak. I have become all things to all people, that I might by all means save some. I do it all for the sake of the Gospel, so that I may share in its blessings.

The word of the Lord. **Thanks be to God.**

GOSPEL ACCLAMATION (Matthew 8.17)
Alleluia. Alleluia. Christ took our infirmities, and bore our diseases. **Alleluia.**

GOSPEL (Mark 1.29-39)
The Lord be with you. **And with your spirit.** A reading from the holy Gospel according to Mark. **Glory to you, O Lord.**

As soon as Jesus and his disciples left the synagogue, they entered the house of Simon and Andrew, with James and John. Now Simon's mother-in-law was in bed with a fever, and they told Jesus about her at once. He came and took her by the hand and lifted her up. Then the fever left her, and she began to serve them.

That evening, at sunset, they brought to Jesus all who were sick or possessed with demons. And the whole city was gathered around the door. And he cured many who were sick with various diseases, and cast out many demons; and he would not permit the demons to speak, because they knew him.

In the morning, while it was still very dark, Jesus got up and went out to a deserted place, and there he prayed. And Simon and his companions hunted for him. When they found him, they said to him, "Everyone is searching for you."

He answered, "Let us go on to the neighbouring towns, so that I may proclaim the message there also; for that is what I came out to do." And Jesus went throughout Galilee, proclaiming the message in their synagogues and casting out demons.

The Gospel of the Lord. **Praise to you, Lord Jesus Christ.**

PROFESSION OF FAITH (p. 14)

PRAYER OF THE FAITHFUL

The following intentions are suggestions only.
There are more suggestions at www.livingwithchrist.ca.

R. **Lord, hear our prayer.**

For all witnesses to the Gospel, called to proclaim the Good News of God's love, we pray to the Lord: R.

For leaders of nations, called to respond to suffering in our world, we pray to the Lord: R.

For all who work in healing professions, called to alleviate suffering, we pray to the Lord: R.

For ourselves, the People of God, called to follow Christ in service, prayer and witness, we pray to the Lord: R.

PREPARATION OF THE GIFTS (p. 17)

PRAYER OVER THE OFFERINGS

O Lord our God, who once established these created things to sustain us in our frailty, grant, we pray, that they may become for us now the Sacrament of eternal life. Through Christ our Lord. **Amen.**

PREFACE *(Sundays in Ordinary Time, p. 31)*

COMMUNION ANTIPHON *(Cf. Psalm 106.8-9)*
Let them thank the Lord for his mercy, his wonders for the children of men, for he satisfies the thirsty soul, and the hungry he fills with good things.

or (Matthew 5.5-6)
Blessed are those who mourn, for they shall be consoled. Blessed are those who hunger and thirst for righteousness, for they shall have their fill.

PRAYER AFTER COMMUNION

O God, who have willed that we be partakers in the one Bread and the one Chalice, grant us, we pray, so to live that, made one in Christ, we may joyfully bear fruit for the salvation of the world. Through Christ our Lord. **Amen.**

BLESSING AND DISMISSAL *(p. 72)*

6th Sunday in Ordinary Time

World Day of the Sick

Last year, something happened to a friend of mine in a place where some 60 people were present. Over the next few weeks, people who had heard about it (including strangers and those from other parts of the city) approached me with questions. Word had spread so far and fast, yet all it took was the sharing of a few witnesses!

On display here is our natural desire to share news and stories. Just imagine what might happen if this enthusiasm were to be applied to the sharing of Jesus, the Good News, with others? Today's Gospel displays the impact.

A humble leper approaches Jesus with faith; Jesus heals the man. Jesus then warns him not to tell others because, at this point, such sharing would impede Jesus' ability to minister openly in certain areas. Yet, the leper's life is so changed that he cannot contain himself. His witness moves others to run to Jesus in droves.

Jesus' invitation to us now is unlike the exhortation made to the leper: we are called to witness freely. God's will is for many to draw close to him. So it is that when Mass ends, we are sent to witness to the gospel by our life. May our eucharistic Lord fill us with all the grace we need to share the good news of Jesus with others.

Alison Endrizzi
North York, ON

ENTRANCE ANTIPHON *(Cf. Psalm 30.3-4)*
Be my protector, O God, a mighty stronghold to save me. For you are my rock, my stronghold! Lead me, guide me, for the sake of your name.

INTRODUCTORY RITES *(p. 8)*

COLLECT
O God, who teach us that you abide in hearts that are just and true, grant that we may be so fashioned by your grace as to become a dwelling pleasing to you. Through our Lord Jesus Christ, your Son, who lives and reigns with you in the unity of the Holy Spirit, God, for ever and ever. **Amen.**

FIRST READING *(Leviticus 13.1-2, 45-46)*
The Lord spoke to Moses and Aaron, saying: "When someone has on the skin of their body a swelling or an eruption or a spot, and it turns into a leprous disease on the skin of their body, that person shall be brought to Aaron the priest or to one of his sons the priests.

"Anyone who has the leprous disease shall wear torn clothes and let the hair of their head be dishevelled and shall cover their upper lip and cry out, 'Unclean, unclean.' That person shall remain unclean as long as the disease persists; and being unclean, such a one shall live alone with their dwelling outside the camp."

The word of the Lord. **Thanks be to God.**

RESPONSORIAL PSALM *(Psalm 32)*

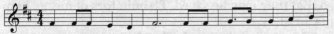

You are my ref-uge, Lord; with de-liv-er-ance you sur-

round me.

℟. **You are my refuge, Lord;**
with deliverance you surround me.

Blessed is the one whose transgression is
for··**given,**
whose sin is · **covered.**
Blessed is the one to whom the Lord imputes
no in··**iquity,**
and in whose spirit there is no de··**ceit.** ℟.

I acknowledged my sin to · **you,**
and I did not hide my in··**iquity;**
I said, "I will confess my transgressions
to the · **Lord,"**
and you forgave the guilt of my · **sin.** ℟.

1 · Be glad in the Lord and rejoice, O · **righteous,**
4 · and shout for joy, all you upright in · **heart.** ℟.

©2009 Gordon Johnston/Novalis

To hear the Sunday Psalms, visit www.livingwithchrist.ca.

SECOND READING *(1 Corinthians 10.31 – 11.1)*

Brothers and sisters: Whether you eat or drink, or
whatever you do, do everything for the glory of God.
Give no offence to Jews or to Greeks or to the Church
of God, just as I try to please everyone in everything I

do, not seeking my own advantage, but that of many, so that they may be saved. Be imitators of me, as I am of Christ.

The word of the Lord. **Thanks be to God.**

GOSPEL ACCLAMATION *(Luke 7.16)*
Alleluia. Alleluia. A great Prophet has risen among us; God has looked favourably on his people. **Alleluia.**

GOSPEL *(Mark 1.40-45)*
The Lord be with you. **And with your spirit.** A reading from the holy Gospel according to Mark. **Glory to you, O Lord.**

A man with leprosy came to Jesus begging him, and kneeling said to Jesus, "If you choose, you can make me clean." Moved with pity, Jesus stretched out his hand and touched him, and said to him, "I do choose. Be made clean!" Immediately the leprosy left him, and he was made clean.

After sternly warning him Jesus sent him away at once, saying to him, "See that you say nothing to anyone; but go, show yourself to the priest, and offer for your cleansing what Moses commanded, as a testimony to them."

But the man went out and began to proclaim it freely, and to spread the word, so that Jesus could no longer go into a town openly, but stayed out in the country; and people came to Jesus from every quarter.

The Gospel of the Lord. **Praise to you, Lord Jesus Christ.**

PROFESSION OF FAITH *(p. 14)*

PRAYER OF THE FAITHFUL

The following intentions are suggestions only.
There are more suggestions at www.livingwithchrist.ca.

R̩. Lord, hear our prayer.

For the Church, communicating Jesus' healing presence to the world, we pray to the Lord: R̩.

For world leaders, called to lead all nations in harmony, we pray to the Lord: R̩.

For the sick and those who minister to them, we pray to the Lord: R̩.

For us here today, united in faith and love, we pray to the Lord: R̩.

PREPARATION OF THE GIFTS *(p. 17)*

PRAYER OVER THE OFFERINGS

May this oblation, O Lord, we pray, cleanse and renew us and may it become for those who do your will the source of eternal reward. Through Christ our Lord. **Amen.**

PREFACE *(Sundays in Ordinary Time, p. 31)*

COMMUNION ANTIPHON *(Cf. Psalm 77.29-30)*
They ate and had their fill, and what they craved the Lord gave them; they were not disappointed in what they craved.

or (John 3.16)
God so loved the world that he gave his Only Begotten Son, so that all who believe in him may not perish, but may have eternal life.

PRAYER AFTER COMMUNION

Having fed upon these heavenly delights, we pray, O Lord, that we may always long for that food by which we truly live. Through Christ our Lord. **Amen.**

BLESSING AND DISMISSAL *(p. 72)*

Ash Wednesday

Today we are invited to allow the ashes that we receive to serve as a kind of alarm bell, reminding us of the shortness and preciousness of life, of the great sacrifice that Jesus made for us, and of the invitation, once again this Lent, to be renewed in our spiritual life.

After cautioning us against showing off our generosity, Jesus, in the three main paragraphs of today's Gospel, instructs us as to the way we should engage in the three familiar Lenten practices that are meant to lead to our spiritual renewal – praying, fasting and the sharing of our resources with those in need. Jesus tells us we are to do these quietly, privately and not with the ulterior motive of seeking the admiration of others. We can be just as prone to the latter temptation as the synagogue-goers of Jesus' day. To help us in that regard, today's readings include the very beautiful Psalm 51, the prayer for a clean heart and right spirit. It is a psalm well worth memorizing.

Ultimately, for each of us, our relationship with our loving and forgiving God is intensely private. The fruitfulness of our Lenten practices will be manifest in the clean and joyful heart with which we will be able to celebrate Easter.

Beth Porter
Richmond Hill, ON

ENTRANCE ANTIPHON *(Wisdom 11.24, 25, 27)*
You are merciful to all, O Lord, and despise nothing that you have made. You overlook people's sins, to bring them to repentance, and you spare them, for you are the Lord our God.

GREETING *(p. 8)*
The Penitential Act *and the* Glory to God *are omitted today.*

COLLECT
Grant, O Lord, that we may begin with holy fasting this campaign of Christian service, so that, as we take up battle against spiritual evils, we may be armed with weapons of self-restraint. Through our Lord Jesus Christ, your Son, who lives and reigns with you in the unity of the Holy Spirit, God, for ever and ever. **Amen.**

FIRST READING *(Joel 2.12-18)*
Even now, says the Lord, return to me with all your heart, with fasting, with weeping, and with mourning; rend your hearts and not your clothing.

Return to the Lord, your God, for he is gracious and merciful, slow to anger, and abounding in steadfast love, and relents from punishing.

Who knows whether the Lord will not turn and relent, and leave a blessing behind him: a grain offering and a drink offering to be presented to the Lord, your God?

Blow the trumpet in Zion; sanctify a fast; call a solemn assembly; gather the people. Sanctify the congregation; assemble the aged; gather the children, even infants at the breast. Let the bridegroom leave his room, and the bride her canopy.

Between the vestibule and the altar let the priests, the ministers of the Lord, weep. Let them say, "Spare your people, O Lord, and do not make your heritage a mockery, a byword among the nations. Why should it be said among the peoples, 'Where is their God?'"

Then the Lord became jealous for his land, and had pity on his people.

The word of the Lord. **Thanks be to God.**

RESPONSORIAL PSALM *(Psalm 51)*

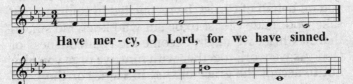

R̸. **Have mercy, O Lord, for we have sinned.**

Have mercy on me, O God, according
    to your steadfast · **love;**
according to your abundant mercy blot out
    my trans-·**gressions.**
Wash me thoroughly from my in-·**iquity,**
and cleanse me from my · **sin.** R̸.

For I know my trans-·**gressions,**
and my sin is ever be-·**fore_me.**
Against you, you alone, have I · **sinned,**
and done what is evil in your · **sight.** R̸.

Create in me a clean heart, O · **God,**
and put a new and right spirit with-·**in_me.**
Do not cast me away from your · **presence,**
and do not take your holy spirit from · **me.** R̸.

Restore to me the joy of your sal·-**vation,**
and sustain in me a willing · **spirit.**
O Lord, open my · **lips,**
and my mouth will declare your · **praise.** R.

©2009 Gordon Johnston/Novalis

To hear the Sunday Psalms, visit www.livingwithchrist.ca.

SECOND READING *(2 Corinthians 5.20 – 6.2)*

Brothers and sisters: We are ambassadors for Christ, since God is making his appeal through us; we entreat you on behalf of Christ, be reconciled to God. For our sake God made Christ to be sin who knew no sin, so that in Christ we might become the righteousness of God. As we work together with him, we urge you also not to accept the grace of God in vain. For the Lord says, "At an acceptable time I have listened to you, and on a day of salvation I have helped you." See, now is the acceptable time; see, now is the day of salvation!

The word of the Lord. **Thanks be to God.**

GOSPEL ACCLAMATION *(Psalm 95.7-8)*

Praise and honour to you, Lord Jesus Christ! Today, do not harden your hearts, but listen to the voice of the Lord. **Praise and honour to you, Lord Jesus Christ!**

GOSPEL *(Matthew 6.1-6, 16-18)*

The Lord be with you. **And with your spirit.**
A reading from the holy Gospel according to Matthew. **Glory to you, O Lord.**

Jesus said to the disciples: "Beware of practising your piety before people in order to be seen by them; for then you have no reward from your Father in heaven.

"So whenever you give alms, do not sound a trumpet before you, as the hypocrites do in the synagogues and in the streets, so that they may be praised by others. Truly I tell you, they have received their reward. But when you give alms, do not let your left hand know what your right hand is doing, so that your alms may be done in secret; and your Father who sees in secret will reward you.

"And whenever you pray, do not be like the hypocrites; for they love to stand and pray in the synagogues and at the street corners, so that they may be seen by others. Truly I tell you, they have received their reward. But whenever you pray, go into your room and shut the door and pray to your Father who is in secret; and your Father who sees in secret will reward you.

"And whenever you fast, do not look dismal, like the hypocrites, for they disfigure their faces so as to show others that they are fasting. Truly I tell you, they have received their reward. But when you fast, put oil on your head and wash your face, so that your fasting may be seen not by others but by your Father who is in secret; and your Father who sees in secret will reward you."

The Gospel of the Lord. **Praise to you, Lord Jesus Christ.**

BLESSING AND DISTRIBUTION OF ASHES

Dear brothers and sisters, let us humbly ask God our Father that he be pleased to bless with the abundance of his grace these ashes, which we will put on our heads in penitence. *(Pause)*

1 O God, who are moved by acts of humility and respond with forgiveness to works of penance, lend your merciful ear to our prayers and in your kindness pour out the grace of your blessing on your servants who are marked with these ashes, that, as they follow the Lenten observances, they may be worthy to come with minds made pure to celebrate the Paschal Mystery of your Son. Through Christ our Lord. **Amen.**

2 O God, who desire not the death of sinners, but their conversion, mercifully hear our prayers and in your kindness be pleased to bless these ashes, which we intend to receive upon our heads, that we, who acknowledge we are but ashes and shall return to dust, may, through a steadfast observance of Lent, gain pardon for sins and newness of life after the likeness of your Risen Son. Who lives and reigns for ever and ever. **Amen.**

While the faithful come forward to receive ashes, an appropriate song may be sung.

1 Repent, and believe in the Gospel.
2 Remember that you are dust, and to dust you shall return.

PRAYER OF THE FAITHFUL

The following intentions are suggestions only.
There are more suggestions at www.livingwithchrist.ca.

R̶. **Lord, hear our prayer.**

For the Church, proclaiming renewal in the ashes both distributed and received, we pray to the Lord: R̶.

For leaders in the world community, called to creative action towards life beyond the ashes of violence and war, we pray to the Lord: R.

For all who taste dust and ashes in their own personal experience, we pray to the Lord: R.

For the members of this assembly, accepting Lenten ashes as an invitation to fullness of life, we pray to the Lord: R.

* *Ash Wednesday Service: When ashes are blessed outside Mass, the ceremony concludes with the* Prayer over the People *and the* Blessing (p. 182).

PREPARATION OF THE GIFTS *(p. 17)*

PRAYER OVER THE OFFERINGS
As we solemnly offer the annual sacrifice for the beginning of Lent, we entreat you, O Lord, that, through works of penance and charity, we may turn away from harmful pleasures and, cleansed from our sins, may become worthy to celebrate devoutly the Passion of your Son. Who lives and reigns for ever and ever. **Amen.**

PREFACE *(Lent III-IV, p. 21)*

COMMUNION ANTIPHON *(Cf. Psalm 1.2-3)*
He who ponders the law of the Lord day and night will yield fruit in due season.

PRAYER AFTER COMMUNION

May the Sacrament we have received sustain us, O Lord, that our Lenten fast may be pleasing to you and be for us a healing remedy. Through Christ our Lord. **Amen.**

PRAYER OVER THE PEOPLE

Pour out a spirit of compunction, O God, on those who bow before your majesty, and by your mercy may they merit the rewards you promise to those who do penance. Through Christ our Lord. **Amen.**

BLESSING AND DISMISSAL (p. 72)

1st Sunday of Lent

The theme of 40 days comes up repeatedly in Scripture. Noah sent the raven out 40 days after the flood abated (Gn 8). Moses fasted 40 days on Mount Sinai (Ex 34). Goliath taunts the Israelite army for 40 days until his battle with David (1 Sm 17). In today's Gospel Jesus fasts for 40 days and nights prior to being tempted by the Devil. And there are other examples.

Each case involves a period of penance and sacrifice, leading to transformation and fulfillment. God cleanses the earth of evil during the flood, and then establishes a new Covenant. Moses' fast is followed by the Ten Commandments and Mosaic Law. After 40 days of humiliation, David emerges to slay Goliath and the Israelites vanquish their enemies. Jesus' fast and temptation in the desert prepare him to begin his public ministry, culminating in his death and resurrection.

Every year Our Lord invites us to join him in his redemptive suffering through 40 days of prayer and sacrifice. This Lent, may the Holy Spirit cleanse us of our worldly and sinful attachments and bring us closer to Jesus. Let us give ourselves fully to the Divine Mercy of Jesus in the Sacrament of Confession. Our Heavenly Father will forgive us, and we too shall be renewed and made whole. The promise of Easter awaits.

Connor Brownrigg
Ottawa, ON

Parishes engaged in the Rite of Christian Initiation of Adults (RCIA) *may celebrate the* Rite of Election *today.*

ENTRANCE ANTIPHON *(Cf. Psalm 90.15-16)*
When he calls on me, I will answer him; I will deliver him and give him glory, I will grant him length of days.

Rite of Election (Cf. Psalm 104.3-4):
Let the hearts that seek the Lord rejoice; turn to the Lord and his strength; constantly seek his face.

INTRODUCTORY RITES *(p. 8)*

COLLECT
Grant, almighty God, through the yearly observances of holy Lent, that we may grow in understanding of the riches hidden in Christ and by worthy conduct pursue their effects. Through our Lord Jesus Christ, your Son, who lives and reigns with you in the unity of the Holy Spirit, God, for ever and ever. **Amen.**

Rite of Election:
O God, who though you are ever the cause of the salvation of the human race now gladden your people with grace in still greater measure, look mercifully, we pray, upon your chosen ones, that your compassionate and protecting help may defend both those yet to be born anew and those already reborn. Through our Lord Jesus Christ, your Son, who lives and reigns with you in the unity of the Holy Spirit, God, for ever and ever. **Amen.**

FIRST READING (*Genesis 9.8-15*)

God said to Noah and to his sons with him, "As for me, I am establishing my covenant with you and your descendants after you, and with every living creature that is with you, the birds, the domestic animals, and every animal of the earth with you, as many as came out of the ark. I establish my covenant with you, that never again shall all flesh be cut off by the waters of a flood, and never again shall there be a flood to destroy the earth."

God said, "This is the sign of the covenant that I make between me and you and every living creature that is with you, for all future generations: I have set my bow in the clouds, and it shall be a sign of the covenant between me and the earth. When I bring clouds over the earth and the bow is seen in the clouds, I will remember my covenant that is between me and you and every living creature of all flesh; and the waters shall never again become a flood to destroy all flesh."

The word of the Lord. **Thanks be to God.**

RESPONSORIAL PSALM *(Psalm 25)*

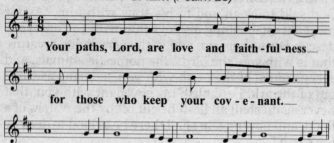

Your paths, Lord, are love and faith-ful-ness for those who keep your cov-e-nant.

R̲. **Your paths, Lord, are love and faithfulness**
for those who keep your covenant.

Make me to know your ways, · **O** Lord;
teach · **me** your paths.
Lead me in your · **truth,** and teach_me,
for you are the God of · **my** sal-vation. R̲.

Be mindful of your mercy, O Lord,
    and of your stead--**fast** love,
for they have been · **from** of old.
According to your steadfast · **love** re-member_me,
for the sake of your · **goodness,** O Lord! R̲.

Good and upright · **is_the** Lord;
therefore he instructs sinners · **in** the way.
He leads the humble in · **what** is right,
and teaches the · **humble** his way. R̲.

To hear the Sunday Psalms, visit www.livingwithchrist.ca.

SECOND READING *(1 Peter 3.18-22)*

Beloved: Christ suffered for sins once for all, the righteous for the unrighteous, in order to bring you to God. He was put to death in the flesh, but made alive in the spirit, in which also he went and made a proclamation to the spirits in prison. In former times these did not obey, when God waited patiently in the days of Noah, during the building of the ark, in which a few, that is, eight persons, were saved through water.

Baptism, which this prefigured, now saves you — not as a removal of dirt from the body, but as an appeal to God for a good conscience through the resurrection of Jesus Christ, who has gone into heaven and is at the right hand of God, with Angels, Authorities, and Powers made subject to him.

The word of the Lord. **Thanks be to God.**

GOSPEL ACCLAMATION *(Matthew 4.4)*

Praise and honour to you, Lord Jesus Christ! Man does not live by bread alone, but by every word that comes from the mouth of God. **Praise and honour to you, Lord Jesus Christ!**

GOSPEL *(Mark 1.12-15)*

The Lord be with you. **And with your spirit.** A reading from the holy Gospel according to Mark. **Glory to you, O Lord.**

After Jesus was baptized, the Spirit drove him out into the wilderness. He was in the wilderness forty days, tempted by Satan; and he was with the wild beasts; and the Angels waited on him.

Now after John was arrested, Jesus came to Galilee, proclaiming the good news of God, and saying, "The time is fulfilled, and the kingdom of God has come near; repent, and believe in the good news."

The Gospel of the Lord. **Praise to you, Lord Jesus Christ.**

For parishes engaged in the RCIA, *the* Rite of Election *takes place now.*

PROFESSION OF FAITH *(p. 14)*

PRAYER OF THE FAITHFUL

The following intentions are suggestions only.
There are more suggestions at www.livingwithchrist.ca.

R. **Lord, hear our prayer.**

For the Church, called to transformation in the spirit of Lent, we pray to the Lord: R.

For all who exercise authority over others, we pray to the Lord: R.

For all who dwell in the darkness of poverty, injustice, war or disease, we pray to the Lord: R.

For this community, called to be Good News for all we encounter, we pray to the Lord: R.

PREPARATION OF THE GIFTS *(p. 17)*

PRAYER OVER THE OFFERINGS

Give us the right dispositions, O Lord, we pray, to make these offerings, for with them we celebrate the beginning of this venerable and sacred time. Through Christ our Lord. **Amen.**

Rite of Election:
Almighty ever-living God, who restore us by the Sacrament of Baptism to eternal life as we confess

your name, receive, we beseech you, the offerings
and prayers of your servants and command that
those who hope in you may have their desires fulfilled and their sins cancelled out. Through Christ
our Lord. **Amen.**

PREFACE *(1st Sunday of Lent, p. 23)*

COMMUNION ANTIPHON *(Matthew 4.4)*
**One does not live by bread alone, but by every word
that comes forth from the mouth of God.**

or (Cf. Psalm 90.4)
**The Lord will conceal you with his pinions, and
under his wings you will trust.**

Rite of Election (Ephesians 1.7):
**In Christ, we have redemption by his Blood and
forgiveness of our sins, in accord with the riches
of his grace.**

PRAYER AFTER COMMUNION
Renewed now with heavenly bread, by which faith
is nourished, hope increased, and charity strengthened, we pray, O Lord, that we may learn to hunger
for Christ, the true and living Bread, and strive to
live by every word which proceeds from your mouth.
Through Christ our Lord. **Amen.**

Rite of Election:
May this Sacrament we have received purify us,
we pray, O Lord, and grant your servants freedom
from all blame, that those bound by a guilty conscience may glory in the fullness of heavenly remedy. Through Christ our Lord. **Amen.**

PRAYER OVER THE PEOPLE

May bountiful blessing, O Lord, we pray, come down upon your people, that hope may grow in tribulation, virtue be strengthened in temptation, and eternal redemption be assured. Through Christ our Lord. **Amen.**

BLESSING AND DISMISSAL (p. 72)

2nd Sunday of Lent

In Scripture, mountains are places of encounter with God. As such, they are also often places of incomprehension. We can only imagine the anguish behind Abraham's answer to young Isaac's innocent question about the missing lamb. Abraham did not know how God was going to resolve this quandary, but he knew that God was good and so he trusted.

In today's Gospel, we find more confusion in the mountains. In the Transfiguration, Jesus' divinity is revealed before the disciples in a way that does not clarify, but baffles. Poor Peter doesn't know what to say. This perplexity is compounded when Jesus tells them to keep silent about their experience until after his resurrection. Like Abraham before them, the disciples have only a glimpse of God's saving plan. They must trust God and wait for further understanding.

And what do we learn when we trust and wait? This mysterious God, who appears incredibly demanding, is in fact always providing. He seems to ask everything, but the goal of such asking is to open our hearts so that we can receive what he is offering. It's not easy to believe that it is in giving that we receive. Paul applies the same phrase to God – who is for us, not against us – that Genesis uses for Abraham: he "did not withhold his own Son." What am I withholding?

Brett Salkeld
Regina, SK

ENTRANCE ANTIPHON (Cf. Psalm 26.8-9)

Of you my heart has spoken: Seek his face. It is your face, O Lord, that I seek; hide not your face from me.

or (Cf. Psalm 24.6, 2, 22)

Remember your compassion, O Lord, and your merciful love, for they are from of old. Let not our enemies exult over us. Redeem us, O God of Israel, from all our distress.

INTRODUCTORY RITES (p. 8)

COLLECT

O God, who have commanded us to listen to your beloved Son, be pleased, we pray, to nourish us inwardly by your word, that, with spiritual sight made pure, we may rejoice to behold your glory. Through our Lord Jesus Christ, your Son, who lives and reigns with you in the unity of the Holy Spirit, God, for ever and ever. **Amen.**

FIRST READING (Genesis 22.1-2, 9-13, 15-18)

God tested Abraham. He said to him, "Abraham!" And Abraham said, "Here I am."

God said, "Take your son, your only son Isaac, whom you love, and go to the land of Moriah, and offer him there as a burnt offering on one of the mountains that I shall show you."

When Abraham and Isaac came to the place that God had shown him, Abraham built an altar there and laid the wood in order. He bound his son Isaac, and laid him on the altar, on top of the wood. Then Abraham reached out his hand and took the knife to kill his son.

But the Angel of the Lord called to him from heaven, and said, "Abraham, Abraham!" And he said, "Here I am." The Angel said, "Do not lay your hand on the boy or do anything to him; for now I know that you fear God, since you have not withheld your son, your only son, from me."

Abraham looked up and saw a ram, caught in a thicket by its horns. Abraham went and took the ram and offered it up as a burnt offering instead of his son.

The Angel of the Lord called to Abraham a second time from heaven, and said, "By myself I have sworn, says the Lord: Because you have done this, and have not withheld your son, your only son, I will indeed bless you, and I will make your offspring as numerous as the stars of heaven and as the sand that is on the seashore. And your offspring shall possess the gate of their enemies, and by your offspring shall all the nations of the earth gain blessing for themselves, because you have obeyed my voice."

The word of the Lord. **Thanks be to God.**

RESPONSORIAL PSALM *(Psalm 116)*

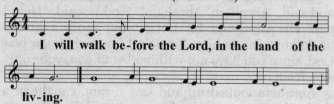

I will walk be-fore the Lord, in the land of the liv-ing.

R. **I will walk before the Lord,
in the land of the living.**

I kept my faith, even when I · **said,**
"I am greatly · **af**-flicted."
Precious in the sight of the · **Lord**
is the death of · **his** faithful_ones. **R.**

O Lord, I am your · **servant.**
You have loosed · **my** bonds.
I will offer to you a thanksgiving · **sacrifice**
and call on the name of · **the** Lord. **R.**

I will pay my vows to the · **Lord**
in the presence of all · **his** people,
in the courts of the house of the · **Lord,**
in your midst, O · **Je**-rusalem. **R.**

©2009 Gordon Johnston/Novalis

To hear the Sunday Psalms, visit www.livingwithchrist.ca.

SECOND READING *(Romans 8.31b-35, 37)*
Brothers and sisters: If God is for us, who is against us? He who did not withhold his own Son, but gave him up for all of us, will he not with him also give us everything else?

Who will bring any charge against God's elect? It is God who justifies. Who is to condemn?

It is Christ Jesus, who died, yes, who was raised, who is at the right hand of God, who indeed intercedes for us.

Who will separate us from the love of Christ? Will hardship, or distress, or persecution, or famine, or nakedness, or peril, or sword?

No, in all these things we are more than conquerors through him who loved us.

The word of the Lord. **Thanks be to God.**

GOSPEL ACCLAMATION *(See Luke 9.35)*

Praise and honour to you, Lord Jesus Christ! From the bright cloud the Father's voice is heard: This is my Son, the Beloved, listen to him. **Praise and honour to you, Lord Jesus Christ!**

GOSPEL *(Mark 9.2-10)*

The Lord be with you. **And with your spirit.** A reading from the holy Gospel according to Mark. **Glory to you, O Lord.**

Jesus took with him Peter and James and John, and led them up a high mountain apart, by themselves. And he was transfigured before them, and his clothes became dazzling white, such as no one on earth could bleach them.

And there appeared to them Elijah and Moses, who were talking with Jesus. Then Peter said to Jesus, "Rabbi, it is good for us to be here; let us make three dwellings, one for you, one for Moses, and one for Elijah." Peter did not know what to say, for they were terrified.

Then a cloud overshadowed them, and from the cloud there came a voice, "This is my Son, the Beloved; listen to him!" Suddenly when they looked around, they saw no one with them any more, but only Jesus.

As they were coming down the mountain, he ordered them to tell no one about what they had seen, until after the Son of Man had risen from the dead. So they kept the matter to themselves, questioning what this rising from the dead could mean.

The Gospel of the Lord. **Praise to you, Lord Jesus Christ.**

PROFESSION OF FAITH (p. 14)

PRAYER OF THE FAITHFUL

The following intentions are suggestions only.
There are more suggestions at www.livingwithchrist.ca.

R. **Lord, hear our prayer.**

For the family of God, faithful to Jesus' call to repent and believe the Good News, we pray to the Lord: R.

For world leaders, called to govern with justice and compassion, we pray to the Lord: R.

For all who suffer illness, discomfort and pain, we pray to the Lord: R.

For our community, ever striving to be true followers of Jesus, we pray to the Lord: R.

PREPARATION OF THE GIFTS (p. 17)

PRAYER OVER THE OFFERINGS

May this sacrifice, O Lord, we pray, cleanse us of our faults and sanctify your faithful in body and mind for the celebration of the paschal festivities. Through Christ our Lord. **Amen.**

PREFACE *(2nd Sunday of Lent, p. 23)*

COMMUNION ANTIPHON *(Matthew 17.5)*

This is my beloved Son, with whom I am well pleased; listen to him.

PRAYER AFTER COMMUNION

As we receive these glorious mysteries, we make thanksgiving to you, O Lord, for allowing us while still on earth to be partakers even now of the things of heaven. Through Christ our Lord. **Amen.**

PRAYER OVER THE PEOPLE

Bless your faithful, we pray, O Lord, with a blessing that endures for ever, and keep them faithful to the Gospel of your Only Begotten Son, so that they may always desire and at last attain that glory whose beauty he showed in his own Body, to the amazement of his Apostles. Through Christ our Lord. **Amen.**

BLESSING AND DISMISSAL *(p. 72)*

March Saints' Days

The following saints are traditionally remembered in March in Canada.

Saint Casimir . . . . Mar 4

Saints Perpetua and Felicity . . . . Mar 7

Saint John of God. . . . . Mar 8

Saint Frances of Rome . . . . Mar 9

Saint Patrick. . . . . Mar 17

Saint Cyril of Jerusalem . . . . Mar 18

Saint Joseph. . . . . Mar 19
Principal Patron of Canada

Saint Turibius of Mogrovejo . . . . Mar 23

3rd Sunday of Lent

The image in today's Gospel of Jesus over-turning tables is in forceful contrast to the gentle images of our Lord with children and healing the sick. In the temple Jesus witnesses the injustice taking place in his Father's house and is moved to take a stand. Animals for sacrifice are being sold to travellers for unfair prices. Money changers are making a profit off those who travelled from afar. The temple was no longer a holy place where one could encounter God.

While jarring, this Gospel reminds us of the new life that is found only in Jesus. Through Jesus' life, death and resurrection, all people may now encounter the love of the living God. Through baptism, we as Christians welcome Christ to dwell within us. We meet God not only in bricks-and-mortar churches: an encounter with God is just a breath – a heartbeat – away.

Like the merchants in the Gospel today, we can lose sight of the peace that comes from simply being in the all-loving presence of God. As we continue our Lenten journey towards the resurrection, may we cleanse our hearts of the greed, gluttony, and selfishness that form a barrier between us and the true love of God. May our hearts be converted to love, peace and new life.

Elizabeth Chesley-Jewell
Toronto, ON

Parishes engaged in the Rite of Christian Initiation of Adults (RCIA) *may celebrate the* 1st Scrutiny *today (p. 206).*

ENTRANCE ANTIPHON *(Cf. Psalm 24.15-16)*

My eyes are always on the Lord, for he rescues my feet from the snare. Turn to me and have mercy on me, for I am alone and poor.

or (Cf. Ezekiel 36.23-26)

When I prove my holiness among you, I will gather you from all the foreign lands; and I will pour clean water upon you and cleanse you from all your impurities, and I will give you a new spirit, says the Lord.

INTRODUCTORY RITES *(p. 8)*

COLLECT

O God, author of every mercy and of all goodness, who in fasting, prayer and almsgiving have shown us a remedy for sin, look graciously on this confession of our lowliness, that we, who are bowed down by our conscience, may always be lifted up by your mercy. Through our Lord Jesus Christ, your Son, who lives and reigns with you in the unity of the Holy Spirit, God, for ever and ever. **Amen.**

FIRST READING *(Exodus 20.1-17)*

For the shorter version, omit the indented parts.

God spoke all these words: I am the Lord your God, who brought you out of the land of Egypt, out of the house of slavery; you shall have no other gods before me.

You shall not make for yourself an idol, whether in the form of anything that is in heaven above, or that is on the earth beneath, or that is in the water under the earth. You shall not bow down to them or worship them; for I the Lord your God am a jealous God, punishing children for the iniquity of parents, to the third and the fourth generation of those who reject me, but showing steadfast love to the thousandth generation of those who love me and keep my commandments.

You shall not make wrongful use of the name of the Lord your God, for the Lord will not acquit anyone who misuses his name. Remember the Sabbath day, and keep it holy.

Six days you shall labour and do all your work. But the seventh day is a Sabbath to the Lord your God; you shall not do any work — you, your son or your daughter, your male or female slave, your livestock, or the alien resident in your towns. For in six days the Lord made heaven and earth, the sea, and all that is in them, but rested the seventh day; therefore the Lord blessed the Sabbath day and consecrated it.

Honour your father and your mother, so that your days may be long in the land that the Lord your God is giving you.

You shall not murder. You shall not commit adultery. You shall not steal. You shall not bear false witness against your neighbour. You shall not covet your neighbour's house; you shall not covet your neighbour's wife, or male or female slave, or ox, or donkey, or anything that belongs to your neighbour.

The word of the Lord. **Thanks be to God.**

RESPONSORIAL PSALM *(Psalm 19)*

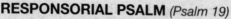

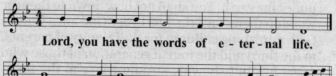

℟. **Lord, you have the words of eternal life.**

The law of the Lord is · **perfect,**
reviving the · **soul;**
the decrees of the Lord are · **sure,**
making · **wise** the simple. ℟.

The precepts of the Lord are · **right,**
rejoicing the · **heart;**
the commandment of the Lord is · **clear,**
en--**lightening** the eyes. ℟.

The fear of the Lord is · **pure,**
enduring for--**ever;**
the ordinances of the Lord are · **true**
and righteous · **al**-to-gether. ℟.

More to be desired are they than · **gold,**
even much fine · **gold;**
sweeter also than · **honey,**
and drippings · **of** the honeycomb. ℟.

©2009 Gordon Johnston/Novalis

SECOND READING *(1 Corinthians 1.18, 22-25)*
Brothers and sisters: The message about the Cross is
foolishness to those who are perishing, but to us who
are being saved it is the power of God.

For Jews demand signs and Greeks desire wisdom, but we proclaim Christ crucified, a stumbling block to Jews and foolishness to Gentiles, but to those who are the called, both Jews and Greeks, Christ the power of God and the wisdom of God.

For God's foolishness is wiser than human wisdom, and God's weakness is stronger than human strength.

The word of the Lord. **Thanks be to God.**

GOSPEL ACCLAMATION *(John 3.16)*

Praise and honour to you, Lord Jesus Christ! God so loved the world that he gave his only Son, that everyone who believes in him may have eternal life. **Praise and honour to you, Lord Jesus Christ!**

GOSPEL *(John 2.13-25)*

The Lord be with you. **And with your spirit.** A reading from the holy Gospel according to John. **Glory to you, O Lord.**

The Passover of the Jews was near, and Jesus went up to Jerusalem. In the temple he found people selling cattle, sheep, and doves, and the money changers seated at their tables. Making a whip of cords, he drove all of them out of the temple, both the sheep and the cattle. He also poured out the coins of the money changers and overturned their tables. He told those who were selling the doves, "Take these things out of here! Stop making my Father's house a marketplace!"

His disciples remembered that it was written, "Zeal for your house will consume me."

The Jews then said to him, "What sign can you show us for doing this?" Jesus answered them, "Destroy this temple, and in three days I will raise it up." They then said, "This temple has been under construction for forty-six years, and will you raise it up in three days?" But Jesus was speaking of the temple of his body.

After he was raised from the dead, his disciples remembered that he had said this; and they believed the Scripture and the word that Jesus had spoken.

When he was in Jerusalem during the Passover festival, many believed in his name because they saw the signs that he was doing. But Jesus on his part would not entrust himself to them, because he knew all people and needed no one to testify about human nature, for he himself knew what was within the human person.

The Gospel of the Lord. **Praise to you, Lord Jesus Christ.**

PROFESSION OF FAITH (p. 14)

PRAYER OF THE FAITHFUL

The following intentions are suggestions only.
There are more suggestions at www.livingwithchrist.ca.

R. **Lord, hear our prayer.**

For Church leaders who teach with the wisdom, courage and zeal that come from the Holy Spirit, we pray to the Lord: R.

For peaceful discernment in the hearts of those called to positions of leadership, we pray to the Lord: R.

For all who desire freedom from oppression in their lives, we pray to the Lord: R.

For ourselves, called to live the message of Jesus, we pray to the Lord: R.

PREPARATION OF THE GIFTS (p. 17)

PRAYER OVER THE OFFERINGS
Be pleased, O Lord, with these sacrificial offerings, and grant that we who beseech pardon for our own sins may take care to forgive our neighbour. Through Christ our Lord. **Amen.**

PREFACE (Lent I-II, p. 21)

COMMUNION ANTIPHON (Cf. Psalm 83.4-5)
The sparrow finds a home, and the swallow a nest for her young: by your altars, O Lord of hosts, my King and my God. Blessed are they who dwell in your house, for ever singing your praise.

PRAYER AFTER COMMUNION
As we receive the pledge of things yet hidden in heaven and are nourished while still on earth with the Bread that comes from on high, we humbly entreat you, O Lord, that what is being brought about in us in mystery may come to true completion. Through Christ our Lord. **Amen.**

PRAYER OVER THE PEOPLE
Direct, O Lord, we pray, the hearts of your faithful, and in your kindness grant your servants this grace: that, abiding in the love of you and their neighbour, they may fulfill the whole of your commands. Through Christ our Lord. **Amen.**

BLESSING AND DISMISSAL (p. 72)

CHRISTIAN INITIATION: 1ST SCRUTINY

ENTRANCE ANTIPHON *(Ezekiel 36.23-26)*
When I prove my holiness among you, I will gather you from all the foreign lands and I will pour clean water upon you and cleanse you from all your impurities, and I will give you a new spirit, says the Lord.

or (Cf. Isaiah 55.1)
Come to the waters, you who are thirsty, says the Lord; you who have no money, come and drink joyfully.

INTRODUCTORY RITES *(p. 8)*

COLLECT
Grant, we pray, O Lord, that these chosen ones may come worthily and wisely to the confession of your praise, so that in accordance with that first dignity which they lost by original sin they may be fashioned anew through your glory. Through our Lord Jesus Christ, your Son, who lives and reigns with you in the unity of the Holy Spirit, God, for ever and ever. **Amen.**

FIRST READING *(Exodus 17.3-7)*
In the wilderness the people thirsted for water; and the people complained against Moses and said, "Why did you bring us out of Egypt, to kill us and our children and livestock with thirst?" So Moses cried out to the Lord, "What shall I do with this people? They are almost ready to stone me."

The Lord said to Moses, "Go on ahead of the people, and take some of the elders of Israel with you; take in your hand the staff with which you struck the Nile, and go. I will be standing there in front of you on the rock at Horeb. Strike the rock, and water will come out of it, so that the people may drink." Moses did so, in the sight of the elders of Israel.

He called the place Massah and Meribah, because the children of Israel quarrelled and tested the Lord, saying, "Is the Lord among us or not?"

The word of the Lord. **Thanks be to God.**

RESPONSORIAL PSALM *(Psalm 95)*

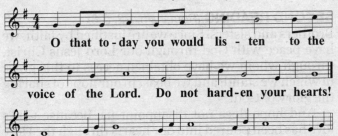

O that to-day you would lis-ten to the voice of the Lord. Do not hard-en your hearts!

R. **O that today you would listen to the voice of the Lord. Do not harden your hearts!**

O come, let us sing to · **the** Lord;
let us make a joyful noise to the rock of our
    · **sal**-vation!
Let us come into his presence with · **thanks**-giving;
let us make a joyful noise to him with songs
    · **of** praise! R.

O come, let us worship and · **bow** down,
let us kneel before the Lord, · **our** Maker!
For he is our God, and we are the people of
    · **his** pasture,
and the sheep of · **his** hand. R.

O that today you would listen to · **his** voice!
Do not harden your hearts, as at Meribah, as on
    the day at Massah in · **the** wilderness,
when your ancestors tested me, and put me to
    · **the** proof,
though they had seen · **my** work. R̲

To hear the Sunday Psalms, visit www.livingwithchrist.ca.

SECOND READING *(Romans 5.1-2, 5-8)*
Brothers and sisters: Since we are justified by faith, we have peace with God through our Lord Jesus Christ, through whom we have obtained access to this grace in which we stand; and we boast in our hope of sharing the glory of God.

And hope does not disappoint us, because God's love has been poured into our hearts through the Holy Spirit that has been given to us. For while we were still weak, at the right time Christ died for the ungodly. Indeed, rarely will anyone die for a righteous person — though perhaps for a good person someone might actually dare to die. But God proves his love for us in that while we still were sinners Christ died for us.

The word of the Lord. **Thanks be to God.**

GOSPEL ACCLAMATION *(John 4.42, 15)*
Praise and honour to you, Lord Jesus Christ! Lord, you are truly the Saviour of the world; give me living water, that I may never be thirsty. **Praise and honour to you, Lord Jesus Christ!**

GOSPEL (John 4.5-42)

For the shorter reading, omit the indented parts.

The Lord be with you. **And with your spirit.**

A reading from the holy Gospel according to John. **Glory to you, O Lord.**

Jesus came to a Samaritan city called Sychar, near the plot of ground that Jacob had given to his son Joseph. Jacob's well was there, and Jesus, tired out by his journey, was sitting by the well. It was about noon.

A Samaritan woman came to draw water, and Jesus said to her, "Give me a drink." (His disciples had gone to the city to buy food.)

The Samaritan woman said to him, "How is it that you, a Jew, ask a drink of me, a woman of Samaria?" (Jews do not share things in common with Samaritans.) Jesus answered her, "If you knew the gift of God, and who it is that is saying to you, 'Give me a drink,' you would have asked him, and he would have given you living water."

The woman said to him, "Sir, you have no bucket, and the well is deep. Where do you get that living water? Are you greater than our father Jacob, who gave us the well, and with his children and his flocks drank from it?" Jesus said to her, "Everyone who drinks of this water will be thirsty again, but the one who drinks of the water that I will give will never be thirsty. The water that I will give him will become in him a spring of water gushing up to eternal life." The woman said to him, "Sir, give me this water, so that I may never be thirsty or have to keep coming here to draw water."

Jesus said to her, "Go, call your husband, and come back." The woman answered him, "I have no husband." Jesus said to her, "You are right in saying, 'I have no husband'; for you have had five husbands, and the one you have now is not your husband. What you have said is true!" The woman said to him, "Sir,

"I see that you are a Prophet. Our ancestors worshipped on this mountain, but you say that the place where people must worship is in Jerusalem."

Jesus said to her, "Woman, believe me, the hour is coming when you will worship the Father neither on this mountain nor in Jerusalem. You worship what you do not know; we worship what we know, for salvation is from the Jews. But the hour is coming, and is now here, when the true worshippers will worship the Father in spirit and truth, for the Father seeks such as these to worship him. God is spirit, and those who worship him must worship in spirit and truth."

The woman said to him, "I know that the Messiah is coming" (who is called the Christ). "When he comes, he will proclaim all things to us." Jesus said to her, "I am he, the one who is speaking to you."

Just then his disciples came. They were astonished that he was speaking with a woman, but no one said, "What do you want?" or, "Why are you speaking with her?" Then the woman left her water jar and went back to the city. She said to the people, "Come and see a man who told me everything I have ever done! He cannot be the Messiah, can he?" They left the city and were on their way to him. Meanwhile the disciples were urging him, "Rabbi, eat something." But he said to them, "I have food to eat that you do not know about." So the disciples said to one another, "Surely no one has brought him something to eat?" Jesus said to them, "My food is to do the will of him who sent me and to complete his work. Do you not say, 'Four months more, then comes the harvest'? But I tell you, look around you, and see how the fields are ripe for harvesting. The reaper is already receiving wages and is gathering fruit for eternal life, so that sower and reaper may rejoice together. For here the saying holds true, 'One sows and another reaps.' I sent you to reap that for which you did not labour. Others have laboured, and you have entered into their labour."

Many Samaritans from that city believed in Jesus.
because of the woman's testimony, "He told me everything I have ever done."

So when they [the Samaritans] came to him, they asked him to stay with them; and he stayed there two days. And many more believed because of his word. They said to the woman, "It is no longer because of what you said that we believe, for we have heard for ourselves, and we know that this is truly the Saviour of the world."

The Gospel of the Lord. **Praise to you, Lord Jesus Christ.**

PROFESSION OF FAITH *(p. 14)*

PRAYER OF THE FAITHFUL *(p. 204)*

PREPARATION OF THE GIFTS *(p. 17)*

PRAYER OVER THE OFFERINGS

May your merciful grace prepare your servants, O Lord, for the worthy celebration of these mysteries and lead them to it by a devout way of life. Through Christ our Lord. **Amen.**

PREFACE *(3rd Sunday of Lent, p. 24)*

COMMUNION ANTIPHON *(Cf. John 4.14)*
For anyone who drinks it, says the Lord, the water I shall give will become in him a spring welling up to eternal life.

PRAYER AFTER COMMUNION

Give help, O Lord, we pray, by the grace of your redemption and be pleased to protect and prepare those you are to initiate through the Sacraments of eternal life. Through Christ our Lord. **Amen.**

PRAYER OVER THE PEOPLE

Direct, O Lord, we pray, the hearts of your faithful, and in your kindness grant your servants this grace: that, abiding in the love of you and their neighbour, they may fulfill the whole of your commands. Through Christ our Lord. **Amen.**

BLESSING AND DISMISSAL *(p. 72)*

4th Sunday of Lent

That God loved the world so much as to send the Only-Begotten Son to save and not condemn the world is not as easy a message to receive as it appears. If it were, would not everyone by now have embraced such a loving offer of salvation, wholeness and quality of life?

Testimony about the steadfast love of God, such as we hear in today's first reading, and about the extent and results of the saving mercy of God that Paul's letter to the Ephesians describes, is certainly helpful, but the Gospel reading encourages us to be even more personally engaged. Nothing short of a life-altering encounter with Jesus, involving honesty and repentance – and the cross – will do. Such an encounter is difficult, because seeing our lives in the light of Jesus and his self-sacrificial love reveals the truth of who we are, and requires of us a life-determining choice to become who we were meant to be.

We know that to accept Jesus as the gift of God who gives all for the sake of our salvation is life-giving beyond our imagination. We ask for the grace to receive this gift wholeheartedly. We give thanks, too, for the Scriptures, each other, the Eucharist, and all the means by which we encounter and remember Christ. May the lives we live make it easier for others to meet and follow him.

Christine Mader
Waverly, NS

Parishes engaged in the Rite of Christian Initiation of Adults (RCIA) *may celebrate the* 2nd Scrutiny *today (p. 220).*

ENTRANCE ANTIPHON *(Cf. Isaiah 66.10-11)*
Rejoice, Jerusalem, and all who love her. Be joyful, all who were in mourning; exult and be satisfied at her consoling breast.

INTRODUCTORY RITES *(p. 8)*

COLLECT
O God, who through your Word reconcile the human race to yourself in a wonderful way, grant, we pray, that with prompt devotion and eager faith the Christian people may hasten toward the solemn celebrations to come. Through our Lord Jesus Christ, your Son, who lives and reigns with you in the unity of the Holy Spirit, God, for ever and ever. **Amen.**

FIRST READING *(2 Chronicles 36.14-17a, 19-23)*
All the leading priests and the people were exceedingly unfaithful, following all the abominations of the nations; and they polluted the house of the Lord that he had consecrated in Jerusalem.

The Lord, the God of their ancestors, persistently sent his messengers to them, because he had compassion on his people and on his dwelling place; but they kept mocking the messengers of God, despising his words, and scoffing at his Prophets, until the wrath of the Lord against his people became so great that there was no remedy.

Therefore the Lord brought up against them the king of the Chaldeans, who burned the house of God, broke down the wall of Jerusalem, burned all its palaces with fire, and destroyed all its precious vessels. The king took into exile in Babylon those who had escaped from the sword, and they became servants to him and to his sons until the establishment of the kingdom of Persia, to fulfill the word of the Lord by the mouth of Jeremiah, until the land had made up for its Sabbaths. All the days that it lay desolate it kept Sabbath, to fulfill seventy years.

In the first year of King Cyrus of Persia, in fulfillment of the word of the Lord spoken by Jeremiah, the Lord stirred up the spirit of King Cyrus of Persia so that he sent a herald throughout all his kingdom and also declared in a written edict: "Thus says King Cyrus of Persia: The Lord, the God of heaven, has given me all the kingdoms of the earth, and he has charged me to build him a house at Jerusalem, which is in Judah. Whoever is among you of all his people, may the Lord his God be with him! Let him go up."

The word of the Lord. **Thanks be to God.**

RESPONSORIAL PSALM *(Psalm 137)*

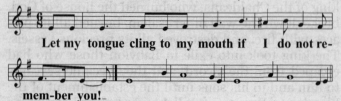

Let my tongue cling to my mouth if I do not re-mem-ber you!_

R. **Let my tongue cling to my mouth
if I do not remember you!**

By the rivers of · **Babylon —**
there we sat down and there · **we** wept
when we remembered · **Zion.**
On the willows there we hung up · **our** harps. R.

For there our · **captors**
asked us · **for** songs,
and our tormentors asked for · **mirth,_saying,**
"Sing us one of the songs · **of** Zion!" R.

How could we sing the Lord's · **song**
in a for--**eign** land?
If I forget you, O Je--**rusalem,**
let my right · **hand** wither! R.

Let my tongue cling to the roof of my · **mouth,**
if I do not · **re**-member_you,
if I do not set Je--**rusalem**
above my high--**est** joy. R.

To hear the Sunday Psalms, visit www.livingwithchrist.ca.

SECOND READING *(Ephesians 2.4-10)*

God, who is rich in mercy, out of the great love with which he loved us even when we were dead through our trespasses, made us alive together with Christ — for it is by grace you have been saved.

And God raised us up with Christ and seated us with him in the heavenly places in Christ Jesus, so that in the ages to come God might show the immeasurable riches of his grace in kindness toward us in Christ Jesus.

For by grace you have been saved through faith, and this is not your own doing; it is the gift of God. This is not the result of works, so that no one may boast. For we are what he has made us, created in Christ Jesus for good works, which God prepared beforehand to be our way of life.

The word of the Lord. **Thanks be to God.**

GOSPEL ACCLAMATION *(John 3.16)*

Praise and honour to you, Lord Jesus Christ! God so loved the world that he gave his only Son, that everyone who believes in him may have eternal life. **Praise and honour to you, Lord Jesus Christ!**

GOSPEL *(John 3.14-21)*

The Lord be with you. **And with your spirit.** A reading from the holy Gospel according to John. **Glory to you, O Lord.**

Jesus said to Nicodemus: "Just as Moses lifted up the serpent in the wilderness, so must the Son of Man be lifted up, that whoever believes in him may have eternal life. For God so loved the world that he gave his only-begotten Son, so that everyone who believes in him may not perish but may have eternal life.

"Indeed, God did not send the Son into the world to condemn the world, but in order that the world might be saved through him. The one who believes in him is not condemned; but the one who does not believe is condemned already, for not having believed in the name of the only-begotten Son of God.

"And this is the judgment, that the light has come into the world, and people loved darkness rather than light because their deeds were evil. For all who do evil hate the light and do not come to the light, so that their deeds may not be exposed. But those who do what is true come to the light, so that it may be clearly seen that their deeds have been done in God."

The Gospel of the Lord. **Praise to you, Lord Jesus Christ.**

PROFESSION OF FAITH (p. 14)

PRAYER OF THE FAITHFUL

The following intentions are suggestions only.
There are more suggestions at www.livingwithchrist.ca.

R. **Lord, hear our prayer.**

For the Church, called to submit humbly to the searching light of Christ, we pray to the Lord: R.

For leaders with courage, wisdom and compassion, we pray to the Lord: R.

For people weighed down by poverty, despair or infirmity, we pray to the Lord: R.

In thanksgiving for the witness of all catechumens, we pray to the Lord: R.

PREPARATION OF THE GIFTS (p. 17)

PRAYER OVER THE OFFERINGS

We place before you with joy these offerings, which bring eternal remedy, O Lord, praying that we may both faithfully revere them and present them to you, as is fitting, for the salvation of all the world. Through Christ our Lord. **Amen.**

PREFACE (Lent I-II, p. 21)

COMMUNION ANTIPHON (Cf. Psalm 121.3-4)

Jerusalem is built as a city bonded as one together. It is there that the tribes go up, the tribes of the Lord, to praise the name of the Lord.

PRAYER AFTER COMMUNION

O God, who enlighten everyone who comes into this world, illuminate our hearts, we pray, with the splendour of your grace, that we may always ponder what is worthy and pleasing to your majesty and love you in all sincerity. Through Christ our Lord. **Amen.**

PRAYER OVER THE PEOPLE

Look upon those who call to you, O Lord, and sustain the weak; give life by your unfailing light to those who walk in the shadow of death, and bring those rescued by your mercy from every evil to reach the highest good. Through Christ our Lord. **Amen.**

BLESSING AND DISMISSAL (p. 72)

CHRISTIAN INITIATION: 2ND SCRUTINY

ENTRANCE ANTIPHON *(Cf. Psalm 24.15-16)*
My eyes are always on the Lord, for he rescues my feet from the snare. Turn to me and have mercy on me, for I am alone and poor.

INTRODUCTORY RITES *(p. 8)*

COLLECT
Almighty ever-living God, give to your Church an increase in spiritual joy, so that those once born of earth may be reborn as citizens of heaven. Through our Lord Jesus Christ, your Son, who lives and reigns with you in the unity of the Holy Spirit, God, for ever and ever. **Amen.**

FIRST READING *(1 Samuel 16.1b, 6-7, 10-13)*
The Lord said to Samuel, "Fill your horn with oil and set out; I will send you to Jesse of Bethlehem, for I have provided for myself a king among his sons."

When the sons of Jesse came, Samuel looked on Eliab and thought, "Surely the Lord's anointed is now before the Lord." But the Lord said to Samuel, "Do not look on his appearance or on the height of his stature, because I have rejected him; for the Lord does not see as the human sees; the human looks on the outward appearance, but the Lord looks on the heart."

Jesse made seven of his sons pass before Samuel, and Samuel said to Jesse, "The Lord has not chosen any of these." Samuel said to Jesse, "Are all your sons here?" And he said, "There remains yet the youngest, but he is keeping the sheep." And Samuel said to

Jesse, "Send and bring him; for we will not sit down until he comes here." Jesse sent and brought David in. Now he was ruddy, and had beautiful eyes, and was handsome. The Lord said, "Rise and anoint him; for this is the one."

Then Samuel took the horn of oil, and anointed him in the presence of his brothers; and the spirit of the Lord came mightily upon David from that day forward.

The word of the Lord. **Thanks be to God.**

or

FIRST READING *(Exodus 13.21-22)*
The Lord went in front of them in a pillar of cloud by day, to lead them along the way, and in a pillar of fire by night, to give them light, so that they might travel by day and by night. Neither the pillar of cloud by day nor the pillar of fire by night left its place in front of the people.

The word of the Lord. **Thanks be to God.**

RESPONSORIAL PSALM *(Psalm 23)*

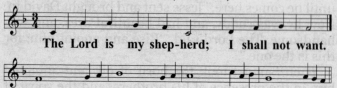

The Lord is my shep-herd; I shall not want.

R. **The Lord is my shepherd; I shall not want.**

The Lord is my shepherd, I shall · **not** want.
He makes me lie down in · **green** pastures;
he leads me be-·**side** still waters;
he re-·**stores** my soul. R.

He leads me in right paths for his · **name's** sake.
Even though I walk through the darkest valley,
    I fear · **no** evil;
for · **you** are with me;
your rod and your · **staff** — they comfort me. R.

You prepare a table · **be**-fore me
in the presence · **of my** enemies;
you anoint my · **head** with oil;
my · **cup** over-flows. R.

Surely goodness and mercy · **shall** follow me
all the days of · **my** life,
and I shall dwell in the · **house of** the Lord
my · **whole** life long. R.

©2009 Gordon Johnston/Novalis

To hear the Sunday Psalms, visit www.livingwithchrist.ca.

SECOND READING (Ephesians 5.8-14)

Brothers and sisters: Once you were darkness, but now in the Lord you are light. Live as children of light — for the fruit of the light is found in all that is good and right and true.

Try to find out what is pleasing to the Lord. Take no part in the unfruitful works of darkness, but instead expose them. For it is shameful even to mention what such people do secretly; but everything exposed by the light becomes visible, for everything that becomes visible is light. Therefore it is said, "Sleeper, awake! Rise from the dead, and Christ will shine on you."

The word of the Lord. **Thanks be to God.**

GOSPEL ACCLAMATION (John 8.12)

Praise and honour to you, Lord Jesus Christ! I am the light of the world, says the Lord; whoever follows me will have the light of life. **Praise and honour to you, Lord Jesus Christ!**

GOSPEL (John 9.1-41)

For the shorter version, omit the indented parts.

The Lord be with you. **And with your spirit.**

A reading from the holy Gospel according to John. **Glory to you, O Lord.**

As Jesus walked along, he saw a man blind from birth. His disciples asked him, "Rabbi, who sinned, this man or his parents, that he was born blind?" Jesus answered, "Neither this man nor his parents sinned; he was born blind so that God's works might be revealed in him. We must work the works of him who sent me while it is day; night is coming

when no one can work. As long as I am in the world,
I am the light of the world." When he had said this,
He spat on the ground and made mud with the saliva
and spread the mud on the man's eyes, saying to him,
"Go, wash in the pool of Siloam" (which means Sent).

Then the man who was blind went and washed,
and came back able to see. The neighbours and those
who had seen him before as a beggar began to ask,
"Is this not the man who used to sit and beg?" Some
were saying, "It is he." Others were saying, "No, but it
is someone like him." He kept saying, "I am the man."
But they kept asking him, "Then how were your
eyes opened?" He answered, "The man called Jesus
made mud, spread it on my eyes, and said to me,
'Go to Siloam and wash.' Then I went and washed
and received my sight." They said to him, "Where
is he?" He said, "I do not know."

They brought to the Pharisees the man who had formerly been blind. Now it was a Sabbath day when
Jesus made the mud and opened his eyes. Then the
Pharisees also began to ask him how he had received
his sight. He said to them, "He put mud on my eyes.
Then I washed, and now I see." Some of the Pharisees said, "This man is not from God, for he does not
observe the Sabbath." But others said, "How can a man
who is a sinner perform such signs?" And they were
divided. So they said again to the blind man, "What do
you say about him? It was your eyes he opened." He
said, "He is a Prophet."

They did not believe that he had been blind and
had received his sight until they called the parents
of the man who had received his sight and asked

them, "Is this your son, who you say was born blind? How then does he now see?" His parents answered, "We know that this is our son, and that he was born blind; but we do not know how it is that now he sees, nor do we know who opened his eyes. Ask him; he is of age. He will speak for himself." His parents said this because they were afraid of the Jewish authorities, who had already agreed that anyone who confessed Jesus to be the Messiah would be put out of the synagogue. Therefore his parents said, "He is of age; ask him."

So for the second time they called the man who had been blind, and they said to him, "Give glory to God! We know that this man is a sinner." He answered, "I do not know whether he is a sinner. One thing I do know, that though I was blind, now I see." They said to him, "What did he do to you? How did he open your eyes?" He answered them, "I have told you already, and you would not listen. Why do you want to hear it again? Do you also want to become his disciples?" Then they reviled him, saying, "You are his disciple, but we are disciples of Moses. We know that God has spoken to Moses, but as for this man, we do not know where he comes from." The man answered, "Here is an astonishing thing! You do not know where he comes from, and yet he opened my eyes. We know that God does not listen to sinners, but he does listen to one who worships him and obeys his will. Never since the world began has it been heard that anyone opened the eyes of a person born blind. If this man were not from God, he could do nothing."

They answered him, "You were born entirely in sins, and are you trying to teach us?" And they drove him out.

Jesus heard that they had driven him out, and when he found him, he said, "Do you believe in the Son of Man?" He answered, "And who is he, sir? Tell me, so that I may believe in him." Jesus said to him, "You have seen him, and the one speaking with you is he." He said, "Lord, I believe." And he worshipped him.

Jesus said, "I came into this world for judgment so that those who do not see may see, and those who do see may become blind." Some of the Pharisees near him heard this and said to him, "Surely we are not blind, are we?" Jesus said to them, "If you were blind, you would have no sin. But now that you say, 'We see,' your sin remains."

The Gospel of the Lord. **Praise to you, Lord Jesus Christ.**

PROFESSION OF FAITH (p. 14)

PRAYER OF THE FAITHFUL (p. 218)

PREPARATION OF THE GIFTS (p. 17)

PRAYER OVER THE OFFERINGS

We place before you with joy these offerings, which bring eternal remedy, O Lord, praying that we may both faithfully revere them and present them to you, as is fitting, for those who seek salvation. Through Christ our Lord. **Amen.**

PREFACE (4th Sunday of Lent, p. 24)

COMMUNION ANTIPHON *(Cf. John 9.11, 38)*
The Lord anointed my eyes; I went, I washed, I saw and I believed in God.

PRAYER AFTER COMMUNION
Sustain your family always in your kindness, O Lord, we pray, correct them, set them in order, graciously protect them under your rule, and in your unfailing goodness direct them along the way of salvation. Through Christ our Lord. **Amen.**

PRAYER OVER THE PEOPLE
Look upon those who call to you, O Lord, and sustain the weak; give life by your unfailing light to those who walk in the shadow of death, and bring those rescued by your mercy from every evil to reach the highest good. Through Christ our Lord. **Amen.**

BLESSING AND DISMISSAL *(p. 72)*

5th Sunday of Lent

Exercise and taking care of our health is good for our mind and body, and it's the same with our faith. We know we need to keep up a nutritious diet, maintain an active lifestyle and keep our mind sharp throughout life; likewise, we know that we should be praying more, frequenting the sacraments, imitating Christ and growing in our faith. However, our human weakness fails us and we regularly get off track.

It often takes reminders to start exercising and eating healthy again, and sometimes a shocking television ad is what motivates us to get back into a healthy lifestyle. Likewise, God sometimes speaks in a loud thundering voice to get our attention, like in today's Gospel. That thundering voice could come in many forms, whether through the death of a loved one, a natural disaster or a starving child. It reminds us of our own mortality and need for salvation, urging us to get back on the right path.

Fortunately, virtue like fitness increases with practice. We grow in strength and endurance the more we exercise it. We can see Jesus who leads by example. He is constantly encouraging us and is there when we fall.

We give thanks for the Lord's mercy, compassion, and patience because, although we fail so often, he seeks us out and does not reject a contrite heart.

Sarah Escobar
Ottawa, ON

National Collection for Development & Peace

Parishes engaged in the Rite of Christian Initiation of Adults (RCIA) *may celebrate the* 3rd Scrutiny *today (p. 235).*

ENTRANCE ANTIPHON *(Cf. Psalm 42.1-2)*
Give me justice, O God, and plead my cause against a nation that is faithless. From the deceitful and cunning rescue me, for you, O God, are my strength.

INTRODUCTORY RITES *(p. 8)*

COLLECT
By your help, we beseech you, Lord our God, may we walk eagerly in that same charity with which, out of love for the world, your Son handed himself over to death. Through our Lord Jesus Christ, your Son, who lives and reigns with you in the unity of the Holy Spirit, God, for ever and ever. **Amen.**

FIRST READING *(Jeremiah 31.31-34)*
The days are surely coming, says the Lord,
when I will make a new covenant
with the house of Israel and the house of Judah.
It will not be like the covenant that I made with
    their fathers
when I took them by the hand
to bring them out of the land of Egypt —
a covenant that they broke,
though I was their husband,
says the Lord.

But this is the covenant
that I will make with the house of Israel after
    those days,
says the Lord:

I will put my law within them,
and I will write it on their hearts;
and I will be their God, and they shall be my people.
No longer shall they teach one another, or say
   to each other,
"Know the Lord,"
for they shall all know me,
from the least of them to the greatest, says the Lord;
for I will forgive their iniquity,
and remember their sin no more.

The word of the Lord. **Thanks be to God.**

RESPONSORIAL PSALM *(Psalm 51)*

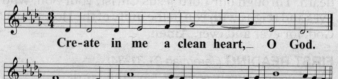

Cre-ate in me a clean heart,— O God.

℟. **Create in me a clean heart, O God.**

Have mercy on me, O God,
   according to your stead-·**fast** love;
according to your abundant mercy blot out
   my · **trans**-gressions.
Wash me thoroughly from my · **in**-iquity,
and cleanse me · **from** my sin. ℟.

Create in me a clean heart, · **O** God,
and put a new and right spirit · **with**-in_me.
Do not cast me away from · **your** presence,
and do not take your holy · **spirit** from me. ℟.

Restore to me the joy of your · **sal**-vation,
and sustain in me a will-·**ing** spirit.
Then I will teach transgressors · **your** ways,
and sinners will re-·**turn** to you. R̥

©2009 Gordon Johnston/Novalis

To hear the Sunday Psalms, visit www.livingwithchrist.ca.

SECOND READING *(Hebrews 5.7-9)*

In the days of his flesh, Jesus offered up prayers and supplications, with loud cries and tears, to the one who was able to save him from death, and he was heard because of his reverent submission. Although he was a Son, he learned obedience through what he suffered; and having been made perfect, he became the source of eternal salvation for all who obey him.

The word of the Lord. **Thanks be to God.**

GOSPEL ACCLAMATION *(John 12.26)*

Praise and honour to you, Lord Jesus Christ! Whoever serves me must follow me, says the Lord; where I am, there will my servant be also. **Praise and honour to you, Lord Jesus Christ!**

GOSPEL *(John 12.20-33)*

The Lord be with you. **And with your spirit.** A reading from the holy Gospel according to John. **Glory to you, O Lord.**

Among those who went up to worship at the festival were some Greeks. They came to Philip, who was from Bethsaida in Galilee, and said to him, "Sir, we wish to see Jesus." Philip went and told Andrew; then Andrew and Philip went and told Jesus. Jesus answered them,

"The hour has come for the Son of Man to be glorified. Very truly, I tell you, unless a grain of wheat falls into the earth and dies, it remains just a single grain; but if it dies, it bears much fruit. The person who loves their life loses it, and the person who hates their life in this world will keep it for eternal life.

"Whoever serves me must follow me, and where I am, there will my servant be also. Whoever serves me, the Father will honour.

"Now my soul is troubled. And what should I say — 'Father, save me from this hour'? No, it is for this reason that I have come to this hour. Father, glorify your name."

Then a voice came from heaven, "I have glorified it, and I will glorify it again."

The crowd standing there heard it and said that it was thunder. Others said, "An Angel has spoken to him." Jesus answered, "This voice has come for your sake, not for mine. Now is the judgment of this world; now the ruler of this world will be driven out. And I, when I am lifted up from the earth, will draw all people to myself."

Jesus said this to indicate the kind of death he was to die.

The Gospel of the Lord. **Praise to you, Lord Jesus Christ.**

PROFESSION OF FAITH (p. 14)

PRAYER OF THE FAITHFUL

The following intentions are suggestions only.
There are more suggestions at www.livingwithchrist.ca.

R. Lord, hear our prayer.

For the Church, as we reflect and act upon the words of Jesus today, we pray to the Lord: **R.**

For governments, responsible for ensuring a life of dignity for all, we pray to the Lord: **R.**

For the women, men and children throughout the world who struggle through each day, we pray to the Lord: **R.**

For our community, thirsting for justice and the courage to express our solidarity with the poor this Lent, we pray to the Lord: **R.**

PREPARATION OF THE GIFTS *(p. 17)*

PRAYER OVER THE OFFERINGS

Hear us, almighty God, and, having instilled in your servants the teachings of the Christian faith, graciously purify them by the working of this sacrifice. Through Christ our Lord. **Amen.**

PREFACE *(Lent I-II, p. 21)*

COMMUNION ANTIPHON *(John 12.24)*

Amen, Amen I say to you: Unless a grain of wheat falls to the ground and dies, it remains a single grain. But if it dies, it bears much fruit.

PRAYER AFTER COMMUNION

We pray, almighty God, that we may always be counted among the members of Christ, in whose Body and Blood we have communion. Who lives and reigns for ever and ever. **Amen.**

PRAYER OVER THE PEOPLE

Bless, O Lord, your people, who long for the gift of your mercy, and grant that what, at your prompting, they desire they may receive by your generous gift. Through Christ our Lord. **Amen.**

BLESSING AND DISMISSAL (p. 72)

CHRISTIAN INITIATION: 3RD SCRUTINY

ENTRANCE ANTIPHON *(Cf. Psalm 17.5-7)*
The waves of death rose about me; the pains of the netherworld surrounded me. In my anguish I called to the Lord; and from his holy temple he heard my voice.

INTRODUCTORY RITES *(p. 8)*

COLLECT
Grant, O Lord, to these chosen ones that, instructed in the holy mysteries, they may receive new life at the font of Baptism and be numbered among the members of your Church. Through our Lord Jesus Christ, your Son, who lives and reigns with you in the unity of the Holy Spirit, God, for ever and ever. **Amen.**

FIRST READING *(Ezekiel 37.12-14)*
Thus says the Lord God: "I am going to open your graves, and bring you up from your graves, O my people; and I will bring you back to the land of Israel. And you shall know that I am the Lord, when I open your graves, and bring you up from your graves, O my people.

"I will put my spirit within you, and you shall live, and I will place you on your own soil; then you shall know that I, the Lord, have spoken and will act," says the Lord.

The word of the Lord. **Thanks be to God.**

RESPONSORIAL PSALM *(Psalm 130)*

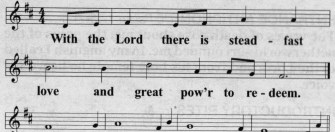

With the Lord there is stead - fast love and great pow'r to re - deem.

R̥. **With the Lord there is steadfast love**
  and great power to redeem.

Out of the depths I cry to you, O · **Lord.**
Lord, hear · **my** voice!
Let your ears be at·-**tentive**
to the voice of my sup·-**pli**-cations! **R̥.**

If you, O Lord, should mark in·-**iquities,**
Lord, who · **could** stand?
But there is forgiveness with · **you,**
so that you may be · **re**-vered. **R̥.**

I wait for the · **Lord,**
my soul waits, and in his word · **I** hope;
my soul waits for the · **Lord**
more than watchmen for · **the** morning. **R̥.**

For with the Lord there is steadfast · **love,**
and with him is great power to · **re**-deem.
It is he who will redeem · **Israel**
from all its · **in**-iquities. **R̥.**

To hear the Sunday Psalms, visit www.livingwithchrist.ca.

SECOND READING *(Romans 8.8-11)*

Brothers and sisters: Those who are in the flesh cannot please God. But you are not in the flesh; you are in the Spirit, since the Spirit of God dwells in you. Anyone who does not have the Spirit of Christ does not belong to him.

But if Christ is in you, though the body is dead because of sin, the Spirit is life because of righteousness.

If the Spirit of God who raised Jesus from the dead dwells in you, he who raised Christ from the dead will give life to your mortal bodies also through his Spirit that dwells in you.

The word of the Lord. **Thanks be to God.**

GOSPEL ACCLAMATION *(John 11.25, 26)*

Praise and honour to you, Lord Jesus Christ! I am the resurrection and the life, says the Lord; whoever believes in me will never die. **Praise and honour to you, Lord Jesus Christ!**

GOSPEL *(John 11.1-45)*

For the shorter version, omit the indented parts.

The Lord be with you. **And with your spirit.**

A reading from the holy Gospel according to John. **Glory to you, O Lord.**

Now a certain man, Lazarus, was ill. He was from Bethany, the village of Mary and her sister Martha. Mary was the one who anointed the Lord with perfume and wiped his feet with her hair; her brother Lazarus was ill. So

The sisters [of Lazarus] sent a message to Jesus, "Lord, he whom you love is ill." But when Jesus heard this, he said, "This illness does not lead to death; rather it is for God's glory, so that the Son of God may be glorified through it." Accordingly, though Jesus loved Martha and her sister and Lazarus, after having heard that Lazarus was ill, he stayed two days longer in the place where he was. Then after this he said to the disciples, "Let us go to Judea again."

The disciples said to him, "Rabbi, the people there were just now trying to stone you, and are you going there again?" Jesus answered, "Are there not twelve hours of daylight? Those who walk during the day do not stumble, because they see the light of this world. But those who walk at night stumble, because the light is not in them." After saying this, he told them, "Our friend Lazarus has fallen asleep, but I am going there to awaken him." The disciples said to him, "Lord, if he has fallen asleep, he will be all right." Jesus, however, had been speaking about his death, but they thought that he was referring merely to sleep. Then Jesus told them plainly, "Lazarus is dead. For your sake I am glad I was not there, so that you may believe. But let us go to him." Thomas, who was called the Twin, said to his fellow disciples, "Let us also go, that we may die with him." When Jesus arrived, he found that Lazarus had already been in the tomb four days.

Now Bethany was near Jerusalem, some two miles away, and many Jews had come to Martha and Mary to console them about their brother. When Martha heard that Jesus was coming, she went and met him, while Mary stayed at home. Martha said to Jesus, "Lord, if you had been here, my brother would not have died. But even now I know that God will give you whatever you ask of him." Jesus said to her, "Your brother will rise again." Martha said to him, "I know that he will rise again in the resurrection on the last day." Jesus said to her, "I am the resurrection and the life. Whoever believes in me, even though they die, will live, and everyone who lives and believes in me will never die. Do you believe this?" She said to him, "Yes, Lord, I believe that you are the Christ, the Son of God, the one coming into the world."

When she had said this, she went back and called her sister Mary, and told her privately, "The Teacher is here and is calling for you." And when Mary heard it, she got up quickly and went to him. Now Jesus had not yet come to the village, but was still at the place where Martha had met him. The Jews who were with her in the house, consoling her, saw Mary get up quickly and go out. They followed her because they thought that she was going to the tomb to weep there. When Mary came where Jesus was and saw him, she knelt at his feet and said to him, "Lord, if you had been here, my brother would not have died." When Jesus saw her weeping, and the Jews who came with her also weeping, he [Jesus] was greatly disturbed in spirit and deeply moved. He said, "Where have you laid him?" They said to him, "Lord, come and see." Jesus began to weep. So the Jews said, "See how he loved him!" But some of them said, "Could not he who opened the eyes of the blind man have kept this man from dying?"

Then Jesus, again greatly disturbed, came to the tomb. It was a cave, and a stone was lying against it. Jesus said, "Take away the stone." Martha, the sister of the dead man, said to him, "Lord, already there is a stench because he has been dead four days." Jesus said to her, "Did I not tell you that if you believed, you would see the glory of God?" So they took away the stone. And Jesus looked upward and said, "Father, I thank you for having heard me. I knew that you always hear me, but I have said this for the sake of the crowd standing here, so that they may believe that you sent me."

When he had said this, he cried with a loud voice, "Lazarus, come out!" The dead man came out, his hands and feet bound with strips of cloth, and his face wrapped in a cloth. Jesus said to them, "Unbind him, and let him go."

Many of the Jews therefore, who had come with Mary and had seen what Jesus did, believed in him.

The Gospel of the Lord. **Praise to you, Lord Jesus Christ.**

PROFESSION OF FAITH (p. 14)

PRAYER OF THE FAITHFUL (p. 233)

PREPARATION OF THE GIFTS (p. 17)

PRAYER OVER THE OFFERINGS

Hear us, almighty God, and, having instilled in your servants the first fruits of the Christian faith, graciously purify them by the working of this sacrifice. Through Christ our Lord. **Amen.**

PREFACE (5th Sunday of Lent, p. 24)

COMMUNION ANTIPHON (Cf. John 11.26)

Everyone who lives and believes in me will not die for ever, says the Lord.

PRAYER AFTER COMMUNION

May your people be at one, O Lord, we pray, and in wholehearted submission to you may they obtain this grace: that, safe from all distress, they may readily live out their joy at being saved and remember in loving prayer those to be reborn. Through Christ our Lord. **Amen.**

PRAYER OVER THE PEOPLE

Bless, O Lord, your people, who long for the gift of your mercy, and grant that what, at your prompting, they desire they may receive by your generous gift. Through Christ our Lord. **Amen.**

BLESSING AND DISMISSAL (p. 72)

**MAR
24**

Passion (Palm) Sunday

A triumphant entry into Jerusalem marked a double departure for Jesus and his three-year public ministry. The arrival at Jerusalem was both a precursor to his pending crucifixion and a deviation from a ministry in which Jesus had been content to travel the countryside on foot, attracting little fanfare. This time, he sent disciples ahead to fetch a colt for an arrival that included shouts of Hosanna from a local throng spreading cloaks and branches along the mucky road.

During his public ministry, Jesus performed many healings and miracles but often told those healed not to publicize what had happened. Arriving in Jerusalem to complete his earthly mission, Jesus embraced the publicity and reverence he had previously downplayed.

Jesus' triumphant arrival in Jerusalem was greeted both by those who accepted him as a saviour and others who erroneously saw Jesus as a leader who would overthrow Roman rule. The latter group's shouts of Hosanna would soon be supplanted by cries to crucify him when Jesus didn't fulfill their worldly wishes.

On this solemn day, as we begin Holy Week, let us dig deep and rekindle our own profession of life-giving faith enkindled by Jesus' arrival at Jerusalem. May our voices join with those who cry, "Hosanna! Blessed is the one who comes in the name of the Lord!"

*Francis Campbell
Enfield, NS*

COMMEMORATION OF THE LORD'S ENTRANCE INTO JERUSALEM

FIRST FORM: The Procession

INTRODUCTION

The people, carrying palm branches, gather in a suitable place distinct from the church to which the procession will move. The assembly may sing Hosanna! or another suitable hymn.

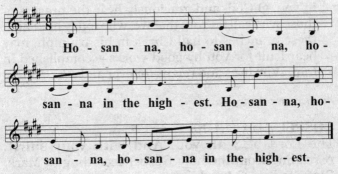

Ho - san - na, ho - san - na, ho - san - na in the high - est. Ho - san - na, ho - san - na, ho - san - na in the high - est.

© Michel Guimont

GREETING *(p. 8)*

Dear brothers and sisters, since the beginning of Lent until now we have prepared our hearts by penance and charitable works. Today we gather together to herald with the whole Church the beginning of the celebration of our Lord's Paschal Mystery, that is to say, of his Passion and Resurrection. For it was to accomplish this mystery that he entered his own city of Jerusalem. Therefore, with all faith and devotion, let us commemorate the Lord's entry into the city for our salvation, following in his footsteps, so that, being made by his grace partakers of the Cross, we may have a share also in his Resurrection and in his life.

Let us pray.

1 Almighty ever-living God, sanctify these branches with your blessing, that we, who follow Christ the King in exultation, may reach the eternal Jerusalem through him. Who lives and reigns for ever and ever. **Amen.**

2 Increase the faith of those who place their hope in you, O God, and graciously hear the prayers of those who call on you, that we, who today hold high these branches to hail Christ in his triumph, may bear fruit for you by good works accomplished in him. Who lives and reigns for ever and ever. **Amen.**

An alternate reading follows.

GOSPEL *(Mark 11.1-10)*
The Lord be with you. **And with your spirit.**
A reading from the holy Gospel according to Mark. **Glory to you, O Lord.**

When they were approaching Jerusalem, at Beth-phage and Bethany, near the Mount of Olives, Jesus sent two of his disciples and said to them, "Go into the village ahead of you, and immediately as you enter it, you will find tied there a colt that has never been ridden; untie it and bring it. If anyone says to you, 'Why are you doing this?' just say this, 'The Lord needs it and will send it back here immediately.'"

They went away and found a colt tied near a door, outside in the street. As they were untying it, some of the bystanders said to them, "What are you doing, untying the colt?" The disciples told them what Jesus had said; and they allowed them to take it.

Then they brought the colt to Jesus and threw their cloaks on it; and he sat on it. Many people spread their cloaks on the road, and others spread leafy branches that they had cut in the fields.

Then those who went ahead and those who followed were shouting, "Hosanna! Blessed is the one who comes in the name of the Lord! Blessed is the coming kingdom of our father David! Hosanna in the highest heaven!"

The Gospel of the Lord. **Praise to you, Lord Jesus Christ.**

or

GOSPEL (John 12.12-16)
The Lord be with you. **And with your spirit.** A reading from the holy Gospel according to John. **Glory to you, O Lord.**

The great crowd that had come to the festival heard that Jesus was coming to Jerusalem. So they took branches of palm trees and went out to meet him, shouting, "Hosanna! Blessed is the one who comes in the name of the Lord — the King of Israel!"

Jesus found a young donkey and sat on it; as it is written: "Do not be afraid, daughter of Zion. Look, your king is coming, sitting on a donkey's colt!"

His disciples did not understand these things at first; but when Jesus was glorified, then they remembered that these things had been written of him and had been done to him.

The Gospel of the Lord. **Praise to you, Lord Jesus Christ.**

PROCESSION

1 Dear brothers and sisters, like the crowds who
   acclaimed Jesus in Jerusalem, let us go forth in
   peace.
2 Let us go forth in peace. **In the name of Christ.
   Amen.**

*All process to the church singing a hymn in honour of Christ the King.
Mass continues with the* Collect *(p. 247).*

SECOND FORM: The Solemn Entrance

*The blessing of branches and proclamation of the Gospel take place, as
above, but in the church. After the Gospel, the priest moves solemnly
through the church to the sanctuary, while all sing. Mass continues with
the* Collect *(p. 247).*

THIRD FORM: The Simple Entrance

*The people gather in the church as usual. While the priest goes to the
altar, the following* Entrance Antiphon *or a suitable hymn is sung.*

ENTRANCE ANTIPHON *(Cf. Jn 12.1, 12-13; Ps 23.9-10)*
**Six days before the Passover, when the Lord came
into the city of Jerusalem, the children ran to meet
him; in their hands they carried palm branches and
with a loud voice cried out:**

**Hosanna in the highest!
Blessed are you, who have come
    in your abundant mercy!**

**O gates, lift high your heads;
grow higher, ancient doors.
Let him enter, the king of glory!
Who is this king of glory?
He, the Lord of hosts, he is the king of glory.**

Hosanna in the highest!
Blessed are you, who have come
in your abundant mercy!

INTRODUCTORY RITES *(p. 8)*

COLLECT

Almighty ever-living God, who as an example of humility for the human race to follow caused our Saviour to take flesh and submit to the Cross, graciously grant that we may heed his lesson of patient suffering and so merit a share in his Resurrection. Who lives and reigns with you in the unity of the Holy Spirit, God, for ever and ever. **Amen.**

FIRST READING *(Isaiah 50.4-7)*

The servant of the Lord said: "The Lord God has given me the tongue of a teacher, that I may know how to sustain the weary with a word. Morning by morning he wakens — wakens my ear to listen as those who are taught. The Lord God has opened my ear, and I was not rebellious, I did not turn backward.

"I gave my back to those who struck me, and my cheeks to those who pulled out the beard; I did not hide my face from insult and spitting.

"The Lord God helps me; therefore I have not been disgraced; therefore I have set my face like flint, and I know that I shall not be put to shame."

The word of the Lord. **Thanks be to God.**

RESPONSORIAL PSALM *(Psalm 22)*

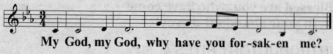

My God, my God, why have you for-sak-en me?

℟. **My God, my God, why have you forsaken me?**

All who see me · **mock_at_me;**
they make mouths at me,
    they shake · **their** heads;
"Commit your cause to the Lord;
    let him de·-**liver;**
let him rescue the one in whom he · **de**-lights!" ℟.

For dogs are all a·-**round_me;**
a company of evildoers · **en**-circles_me.
My hands and feet have · **shrivelled;**
I can count all · **my** bones. ℟.

They divide my clothes a·-**mong_themselves,**
and for my clothing they · **cast** lots.
But you, O Lord, do not be far a·-**way!**
O my help, come quickly · **to_my** aid! ℟.

I will tell of your name to my brothers and
    sisters; in the midst of the congregation
    I will · **praise_you:**
You who fear the · **Lord,** praise_him!
All you offspring of Jacob, · **glorify_him;**
stand in awe of him, all you offspring · **of** Israel! ℟.

To hear the Sunday Psalms, visit www.livingwithchrist.ca.

SECOND READING *(Philippians 2.6-11)*

Christ Jesus, though he was in the form of God, did not regard equality with God as something to be exploited, but emptied himself, taking the form of a slave, being born in human likeness. And being found in human form, he humbled himself and became obedient to the point of death — even death on a cross.

Therefore God highly exalted him and gave him the name that is above every name, so that at the name of Jesus every knee should bend, in heaven and on earth and under the earth, and every tongue should confess that Jesus Christ is Lord, to the glory of God the Father.

The word of the Lord. **Thanks be to God.**

GOSPEL ACCLAMATION *(Philippians 2.8-9)*

Praise and honour to you, Lord Jesus Christ! Christ became obedient for us to death, even death on a Cross. Therefore God exalted him and gave him the name above every name. **Praise and honour to you, Lord Jesus Christ!**

GOSPEL *(Mark 14.1 – 15.47)*

Several readers may proclaim the passion narrative today. N indicates the narrator, J the words of Jesus, and S the words of other speakers.

N The Passion of our Lord Jesus Christ according to Mark.

It was two days before the Passover and the festival of Unleavened Bread. The chief priests and the scribes were looking for a way to arrest Jesus by stealth and kill him; for they said,

S *Not during the festival, or there may be a riot among the people.*

N   While Jesus was at Bethany in the house of Simon the leper, as he sat at the table, a woman came with an alabaster jar of very costly ointment of nard, and she broke open the jar and poured the ointment on his head. But some were there who said to one another in anger,

S   *Why was the ointment wasted in this way? For this ointment could have been sold for more than three hundred denarii, and the money given to the poor.*

N   And they scolded her. But Jesus said,

J   **Let her alone; why do you trouble her? She has performed a good service for me. For you always have the poor with you, and you can show kindness to them whenever you wish; but you will not always have me. She has done what she could; she has anointed my body beforehand for its burial. Truly I tell you, wherever the good news is proclaimed in the whole world, what she has done will be told in remembrance of her.**

N   Then Judas Iscariot, who was one of the twelve, went to the chief priests in order to betray him to them. When they heard it, they were greatly pleased, and promised to give him money. So he began to look for an opportunity to betray him.

On the first day of Unleavened Bread, when the Passover lamb is sacrificed, the disciples said to Jesus,

S   *Where do you want us to go and make the preparations for you to eat the Passover?*

N   So he sent two of his disciples, saying to them,

J   **Go into the city, and a man carrying a jar of water will meet you; follow him, and wherever he enters, say to the owner of the house, "The**

Teacher asks, 'Where is my guest room where I may eat the Passover with my disciples?'" He will show you a large room upstairs, furnished and ready. Make preparations for us there.

N So the disciples set out and went to the city, and found everything as he had told them; and they prepared the Passover meal.

When it was evening, Jesus came with the twelve. And when they had taken their places and were eating, Jesus said,

J **Truly I tell you, one of you will betray me, one who is eating with me.**

N They began to be distressed and to say to him one after another,

S *Surely, not I?*

J **It is one of the twelve, one who is dipping bread into the bowl with me. For the Son of Man goes as it is written of him, but woe to that one by whom the Son of Man is betrayed! It would have been better for that one not to have been born.**

N While they were eating, he took a loaf of bread, and after blessing it he broke it, gave it to them, and said,

J **Take; this is my Body.**

N Then he took a cup, and after giving thanks he gave it to them, and all of them drank from it. He said to them,

J **This is my Blood of the covenant, which is poured out for many. Truly I tell you, I will never again drink of the fruit of the vine until that day when I drink it new in the kingdom of God.**

N When they had sung the hymn, they went out to the Mount of Olives. And Jesus said to them,

J **You will all become deserters; for it is written, "I will strike the shepherd, and the sheep will be scattered." But after I am raised up, I will go before you to Galilee.**

N Peter said to him,

S *Even though all become deserters, I will not.*

J **Truly I tell you, this day, this very night, before the cock crows twice, you will deny me three times.**

N But he said vehemently,

S *Even though I must die with you, I will not deny you.*

N And all of them said the same.

*At this point all may join in singing
an appropriate acclamation.*

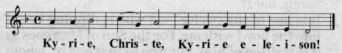

Ky - ri - e,   Chris - te,   Ky - ri - e   e - le - i - son!

Text: Didier Rimaud, © *CNPL*. **Music:** Jacques Berthier
Source: © *Éditions Musicales Studio SM*, 060794-2

N They went to a place called Gethsemane; and Jesus said to his disciples,

J **Sit here while I pray.**

N He took with him Peter and James and John, and began to be distressed and agitated. And he said to them,

J **I am deeply grieved, even to death; remain here, and keep awake.**

N And going a little farther, he threw himself on the ground and prayed that, if it were possible, the hour might pass from him.

J **Abba, Father, for you all things are possible; remove this cup from me; yet, not what I want, but what you want.**

N Jesus came and found them sleeping; and he said to Peter,

J **Simon, are you asleep? Could you not keep awake one hour? Keep awake and pray that you may not come into temptation; the spirit indeed is willing, but the flesh is weak.**

N And again he went away and prayed, saying the same words. And once more he came and found them sleeping, for their eyes were very heavy; and they did not know what to say to him.

He came a third time and said to them,

J **Are you still sleeping and taking your rest? Enough! The hour has come; the Son of Man is betrayed into the hands of sinners. Get up, let us be going. See, my betrayer is at hand.**

N Immediately, while he was still speaking, Judas, one of the twelve, arrived; and with him there was a crowd with swords and clubs, from the chief priests, the scribes, and the elders. Now the betrayer had given them a sign, saying,

S *The one I will kiss is the man; arrest him and lead him away under guard.*

N So when he came, he went up to Jesus at once and said,

S *"Rabbi!"*

N and kissed him. Then they laid hands on him and arrested him. But one of those who stood near drew his sword and struck the slave of the high priest, cutting off his ear. Then Jesus said to them,

J   Have you come out with swords and clubs to arrest me as though I were a bandit? Day after day I was with you in the temple teaching, and you did not arrest me. But let the Scriptures be fulfilled.

N   All of them deserted him and fled.

A certain young man was following Jesus, wearing nothing but a linen cloth. They caught hold of him, but he left the linen cloth and ran off naked.

They took Jesus to the high priest; and all the chief priests, the elders, and the scribes were assembled.

Peter had followed him at a distance, right into the courtyard of the high priest; and he was sitting with the guards, warming himself at the fire.

Now the chief priests and the whole council were looking for testimony against Jesus to put him to death; but they found none. For many gave false testimony against him, and their testimony did not agree. Some stood up and gave false testimony against him, saying,

S   *We heard him say, "I will destroy this temple that is made with hands, and in three days I will build another, not made with hands."*

N   But even on this point their testimony did not agree. Then the high priest stood up before them and asked Jesus,

S   *Have you no answer? What is it that they testify against you?*

N   But he was silent and did not answer. Again the high priest asked him,

S   *Are you the Christ, the Son of the Blessed One?*

J I am; and "you will see the Son of Man seated at the right hand of the Power," and "coming with the clouds of heaven."

N Then the high priest tore his clothes and said,

S *Why do we still need witnesses? You have heard his blasphemy! What is your decision?*

N All of them condemned him as deserving death. Some began to spit on him, to blindfold him, and to strike him, saying to him,

S *Prophesy!*

N The guards also took him over and beat him.

   While Peter was below in the courtyard, one of the servant girls of the high priest came by. When she saw Peter warming himself, she stared at him and said,

S *You also were with Jesus, the man from Nazareth.*

N But he denied it, saying,

S *I do not know or understand what you are talking about.*

N And he went out into the forecourt. Then the cock crowed. And the servant girl, on seeing him, began again to say to the bystanders,

S *This man is one of them.*

N But again he denied it. Then after a little while the bystanders again said to Peter,

S *Certainly you are one of them; for you are a Galilean.*

N But he began to curse, and he swore an oath,

S *I do not know this man you are talking about.*

N At that moment the cock crowed for the second time. Then Peter remembered that Jesus had said to him, "Before the cock crows twice, you will deny me three times." And he broke down and wept.

*At this point all may join in singing
an appropriate acclamation.*

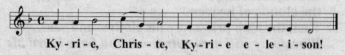

Ky - ri - e,   Chris - te,   Ky - ri - e   e - le - i - son!

Text: Didier Rimaud, © *CNPL.* **Music:** Jacques Berthier
Source: © *Éditions Musicales Studio SM,* 060794-2

N As soon as it was morning, the chief priests held a consultation with the elders and scribes and the whole council. They bound Jesus, led him away, and handed him over to Pilate. Pilate asked him,

S *Are you the King of the Jews?*

J **You say so.**

N Then the chief priests accused him of many things. Pilate asked him again,

S *Have you no answer? See how many charges they bring against you.*

N But Jesus made no further reply, so that Pilate was amazed.

Now at the festival Pilate used to release a prisoner for them, anyone for whom they asked. Now a man called Barabbas was in prison with the rebels who had committed murder during the insurrection. So the crowd came and began to ask Pilate to do for them according to his custom. Then he answered them,

S *Do you want me to release for you the King of the Jews?*

N For he realized that it was out of jealousy that the chief priests had handed him over. But the chief priests stirred up the crowd to have him release

Barabbas for them instead. Pilate spoke to them again,

S *Then what do you wish me to do with the man you call the King of the Jews?*

N They shouted back,

S *Crucify him!*

N Pilate asked them,

S *Why, what evil has he done?*

N But they shouted all the more,

S *Crucify him!*

N So Pilate, wishing to satisfy the crowd, released Barabbas for them; and after flogging Jesus, he handed him over to be crucified. Then the soldiers led him into the courtyard of the palace, (that is, the governor's headquarters); and they called together the whole cohort. And they clothed him in a purple cloak; and after twisting some thorns into a crown, they put it on him. And they began saluting him,

S *Hail, King of the Jews!*

N They struck his head with a reed, spat upon him, and knelt down in homage to him. After mocking him, they stripped him of the purple cloak and put his own clothes on him. Then they led him out to crucify him.

They compelled a passer-by, who was coming in from the country, to carry his Cross; it was Simon of Cyrene, the father of Alexander and Rufus. Then they brought Jesus to the place called Golgotha, (which means the Place of a Skull). And they offered him wine mixed with myrrh; but he did not take it. And they crucified him, and divided his clothes among them, casting lots to decide what each should take.

It was nine o'clock in the morning when they crucified him. The inscription of the charge against him read, "The King of the Jews." And with him they crucified two bandits, one on his right and one on his left. Those who passed by derided him, shaking their heads and saying,

S *Aha! You would destroy the temple and build it in three days; save yourself, and come down from the Cross!*

N In the same way the chief priests, along with the scribes, were also mocking him among themselves and saying,

S *He saved others; he cannot save himself. Let the Christ, the King of Israel, come down from the Cross now, so that we may see and believe.*

N Those who were crucified with him also taunted him.

When it was noon, darkness came over the whole land until three in the afternoon. At three o'clock Jesus cried out with a loud voice,

J **Eloi, Eloi, lema sabachthani?**

N which means, "My God, my God, why have you forsaken me?" When some of the bystanders heard it, they said,

S *Listen, he is calling for Elijah.*

N And someone ran, filled a sponge with sour wine, put it on a stick, and gave it to him to drink, saying,

S *Wait, let us see whether Elijah will come to take him down.*

N Then Jesus gave a loud cry and breathed his last.

Here all kneel and pause for a short time.

N And the curtain of the temple was torn in two, from top to bottom. Now when the centurion, who stood facing him, saw that in this way he breathed his last, he said,

S ***Truly this man was God's Son!***

N There were also women looking on from a distance; among them were Mary Magdalene, and Mary the mother of James the younger and of Joses, and Salome. These used to follow him and provided for him when he was in Galilee; and there were many other women who had come up with him to Jerusalem.

When evening had come, and since it was the day of Preparation, that is, the day before the Sabbath, Joseph of Arimathea, a respected member of the council, who was also himself waiting expectantly for the kingdom of God, went boldly to Pilate and asked for the body of Jesus. Then Pilate wondered if he were already dead; and summoning the centurion, he asked him whether he had been dead for some time. When he learned from the centurion that Jesus was dead, he granted the body to Joseph.

Then Joseph bought a linen cloth, and taking down the body, wrapped it in the linen cloth, and laid it in a tomb that had been hewn out of the rock. He then rolled a stone against the door of the tomb. Mary Magdalene and Mary the mother of Joses saw where the body was laid.

At this point the readers return to their places in silence.

PROFESSION OF FAITH (p. 14)

PRAYER OF THE FAITHFUL
The following intentions are suggestions only.
There are more suggestions at www.livingwithchrist.ca.

R. **Lord, hear our prayer.**

For the Church, living presence of God's compassion, we pray to the Lord: R.

For civic and world leaders, builders of a just society, we pray to the Lord: R.

For the special needs of all who suffer in any way this day, we pray to the Lord: R.

For the community of faith gathered today, we pray to the Lord: R.

PREPARATION OF THE GIFTS (p. 17)

PRAYER OVER THE OFFERINGS
Through the Passion of your Only Begotten Son, O Lord, may our reconciliation with you be near at hand, so that, though we do not merit it by our own deeds, yet by this sacrifice made once for all, we may feel already the effects of your mercy. Through Christ our Lord. **Amen.**

PREFACE (Passion [Palm] Sunday, p. 25)

COMMUNION ANTIPHON (Matthew 26.42)
Father, if this chalice cannot pass without my drinking it, your will be done.

PRAYER AFTER COMMUNION

Nourished with these sacred gifts, we humbly beseech you, O Lord, that, just as through the death of your Son you have brought us to hope for what we believe, so by his Resurrection you may lead us to where you call. Through Christ our Lord. **Amen.**

PRAYER OVER THE PEOPLE

Look, we pray, O Lord, on this your family, for whom our Lord Jesus Christ did not hesitate to be delivered into the hands of the wicked and submit to the agony of the Cross. Who lives and reigns for ever and ever. **Amen.**

SOLEMN BLESSING — PASSION OF THE LORD

(Optional)

Bow down for the blessing.

May God, the Father of mercies, who has given you an example of love in the Passion of his Only Begotten Son, grant that, by serving God and your neighbour, you may lay hold of the wondrous gift of his blessing. **Amen.**

So that you may receive the reward of everlasting life from him, through whose earthly Death you believe that you escape eternal death. **Amen.**

And by following the example of his self-abasement, may you possess a share in his Resurrection. **Amen.**

And may the blessing of almighty God, the Father, and the Son, and the Holy Spirit, come down on you and remain with you for ever. **Amen.**

DISMISSAL *(p. 72)*

Holy Thursday

Mass of the Lord's Supper

"If you cannot find Christ in the beggar at the church door," said St. John Chrysostom, "you will not find him in the chalice." On this Holy Thursday evening, we celebrate Christ's miraculous, abiding and real presence in eucharistic bread and wine. And we celebrate also Christ's very real presence in our neighbour.

Before his death, Jesus invited his closest friends (and at least one enemy) to share a meal with him. It wasn't just any meal: it was the Passover. All present would have remembered the night, long ago, when the Angel of Death passed them over. They would have known that God's answer to the cry of the slave, then and evermore, is "Freedom!" They would have recalled that being liberated from slavery, they must never again enslave or oppress. They would have relished in being the beloved people of God – divinely chosen. It was in this context that Jesus shared bread and wine and commanded them to "Do this in remembrance of me."

At the same meal Christ gave another command. Do THIS in memory of me. And he bent down and washed the feet of his companions. At the celebration of freedom from servitude, Christ freely became a servant. Our faith in Christ's eucharistic presence is, thus, forever bound to our service of Christ in our neighbour.

Christine Way Skinner
Newmarket, ON

ENTRANCE ANTIPHON (Cf. Galatians 6.14)
We should glory in the Cross of our Lord Jesus Christ, in whom is our salvation, life and resurrection, through whom we are saved and delivered.

INTRODUCTORY RITES (p. 8)

COLLECT
O God, who have called us to participate in this most sacred Supper, in which your Only Begotten Son, when about to hand himself over to death, entrusted to the Church a sacrifice new for all eternity, the banquet of his love, grant, we pray, that we may draw from so great a mystery, the fullness of charity and of life. Through our Lord Jesus Christ, your Son, who lives and reigns with you in the unity of the Holy Spirit, God, for ever and ever. **Amen.**

FIRST READING (Exodus 12.1-8, 11-14)
The Lord said to Moses and Aaron in the land of Egypt: This month shall mark for you the beginning of months; it shall be the first month of the year for you. Tell the whole congregation of Israel that on the tenth of this month they are to take a lamb for each family, a lamb for each household. If a household is too small for a whole lamb, it shall join its closest neighbour in obtaining one; the lamb shall be divided in proportion to the number of people who eat of it.

Your lamb shall be without blemish, a year-old male; you may take it from the sheep or from the goats. You shall keep it until the fourteenth day of this month; then the whole assembled congregation of Israel shall slaughter it at twilight. They shall take some of the blood and put it on the two doorposts and the lintel of the houses in which they eat it. They shall eat the lamb that same night; they shall eat it roasted over the fire with unleavened bread and bitter herbs.

This is how you shall eat it: your loins girded, your sandals on your feet, and your staff in your hand; and you shall eat it hurriedly. It is the Passover of the Lord. For I will pass through the land of Egypt that night, and I will strike down every firstborn in the land of Egypt, both human beings and animals; on all the gods of Egypt I will execute judgments: I am the Lord.

The blood shall be a sign for you on the houses where you live: when I see the blood, I will pass over you, and no plague shall destroy you when I strike the land of Egypt.

This day shall be a day of remembrance for you. You shall celebrate it as a festival to the Lord; throughout your generations you shall observe it as a perpetual ordinance.

The word of the Lord. **Thanks be to God.**

RESPONSORIAL PSALM *(Psalm 116)*

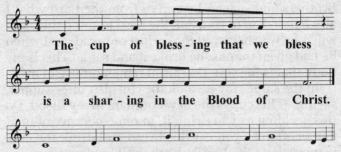

The cup of bless-ing that we bless
is a shar-ing in the Blood of Christ.

R̷. **The cup of blessing that we bless
is a sharing in the Blood of Christ.**

What shall I return to the · **Lord**
for all his bounty to · **me?**
I will lift up the cup of sal·-**vation**
and call on the name · **of_the** Lord. R̷.

Precious in the sight of the · **Lord**
is the death of his · **faithful_ones.**
I am your servant, the son
of your · **serving_girl.**
You have loosed · **my** bonds. R̷.

I will offer to you a thanksgiving · **sacrifice**
and call on the name of the · **Lord.**
I will pay my vows to the · **Lord**
in the presence of all · **his** people. R̷.

©2009 Gordon Johnston/Novalis

To hear the Sunday Psalms, visit www.livingwithchrist.ca.

SECOND READING *(1 Corinthians 11.23-26)*

Brothers and sisters: I received from the Lord what I also handed on to you, that the Lord Jesus on the night when he was betrayed took a loaf of bread, and when he had given thanks, he broke it and said, "This is my Body that is for you. Do this in remembrance of me."

In the same way he took the cup also, after supper, saying, "This cup is the new covenant in my Blood. Do this, as often as you drink it, in remembrance of me." For as often as you eat this bread and drink the cup, you proclaim the Lord's death until he comes.

The word of the Lord. **Thanks be to God.**

GOSPEL ACCLAMATION *(John 13.34)*

Praise and honour to you, Lord Jesus Christ! I give you a new commandment: love one another as I have loved you. **Praise and honour to you, Lord Jesus Christ!**

GOSPEL *(John 13.1-15)*

The Lord be with you. **And with your spirit.** A reading from the holy Gospel according to John. **Glory to you, O Lord.**

Before the festival of the Passover, Jesus knew that his hour had come to depart from this world and go to the Father. Having loved his own who were in the world, he loved them to the end.

The devil had already put it into the heart of Judas, son of Simon Iscariot, to betray him. And during supper Jesus, knowing that the Father had given all things into his hands, and that he had come from God and was going to God, got up from the table, took off his outer robe, and tied a towel around himself. Then he poured water into a basin and began to wash the disciples' feet and to wipe them with the towel that was tied around him.

He came to Simon Peter, who said to him, "Lord, are you going to wash my feet?" Jesus answered, "You do not know now what I am doing, but later you will understand." Peter said to him, "You will never wash my feet." Jesus answered, "Unless I wash you, you have no share with me." Simon Peter said to him, "Lord, not my feet only but also my hands and my head!" Jesus said to him, "One who has bathed does not need to wash, except for the feet, but is entirely clean. And you are clean, though not all of you." For he knew who was to betray him; for this reason he said, "Not all of you are clean."

After he had washed their feet, put on his robe, and returned to the table, Jesus said to them, "Do you know what I have done to you? You call me Teacher and Lord — and you are right, for that is what I am. So if I, your Lord and Teacher, have washed your feet, you also ought to wash one another's feet. For I have set you an example, that you also should do as I have done to you."

The Gospel of the Lord. **Praise to you, Lord Jesus Christ.**

The Profession of Faith *is omitted.*

THE WASHING OF FEET (Optional)

During the washing of feet, an appropriate song may be sung.

PRAYER OF THE FAITHFUL

The following intentions are suggestions only.
There are more suggestions at www.livingwithchrist.ca.

R. **Lord, hear our prayer.**

For the healing of divisions in the Christian Church, we pray to the Lord: R.

For world leaders who listen to those who cry out for peace and justice, we pray to the Lord: R.

For all who have died and for those who mourn their loss, we pray to the Lord: R.

For those in our community who are suffering, and for those who reach out to ease their suffering, we pray to the Lord: R.

PREPARATION OF THE GIFTS *(p. 17)*

PRAYER OVER THE OFFERINGS

Grant us, O Lord, we pray, that we may participate worthily in these mysteries, for whenever the memorial of this sacrifice is celebrated, the work of our redemption is accomplished. Through Christ our Lord. **Amen.**

PREFACE *(Holy Eucharist I, p. 30)*

COMMUNION ANTIPHON *(1 Corinthians 11.24-25)*
This is the Body that will be given up for you; this is the Chalice of the new covenant in my Blood, says the Lord; do this, whenever you receive it, in memory of me.

PRAYER AFTER COMMUNION

Grant, almighty God, that, just as we are renewed by the Supper of your Son in this present age, so we may enjoy his banquet for all eternity. Who lives and reigns for ever and ever. **Amen.**

TRANSFER OF THE HOLY EUCHARIST

The Blessed Sacrament is carried through the church to the place of repose. During the procession, the hymn Pange Lingua *(p. 270, stanzas 1-4) or another eucharistic song is sung. At the place of repose, the presider incenses the Blessed Sacrament, while* Tantum ergo Sacramentum (Pange Lingua, *stanzas 5-6) or another eucharistic song is sung. The tabernacle of repose is then closed.*

After a period of silent adoration, the priests and ministers of the altar retire. The faithful are encouraged to continue adoration before the Blessed Sacrament for a suitable period of time. There should be no solemn adoration after midnight.

HAIL OUR SAVIOUR'S GLORIOUS BODY
(Pange Lingua)

Hail our Sa-viour's glo-rious Bo - dy,

Which his Vir - gin Mo - ther bore;

Hail the Blood which, shed for sin - ners,

Did a bro-ken world re - store;

Hail the sac - ra - ment most ho - ly,

Flesh and Blood of Christ a-dore. A - men.

2. To the Virgin, for our healing,
   His own Son the Father sends;
   From the Father's love proceeding
   Sower, seed and word descends;
   Wondrous life of Word incarnate
   With his greatest wonder ends.

3. On that paschal evening see him
   With the chosen twelve recline,
   To the old law still obedient
   In its feast of love divine;
   Love divine, the new law giving,
   Gives himself as Bread and Wine.

4. By his word the Word almighty
   Makes of bread his flesh indeed;
   Wine becomes his very life-blood;
   Faith God's living Word must heed!
   Faith alone may safely guide us
   Where the senses cannot lead!

At the incensing of the Blessed Sacrament:

5. Come, adore this wondrous presence;
   Bow to Christ, the source of grace!
   Here is kept the ancient promise
   Of God's earthly dwelling place!
   Sight is blind before God's glory,
   Faith alone may see God's face.

6. Glory be to God the Father,
   Praise to his co-equal Son,
   Adoration to the Spirit,
   Bond of love in God-head one!
   Blest be God by all creation
   Joyously while ages run! Amen.

Text: *Pange Lingua*, Thomas Aquinas, 1227-74; tr. James Quinn, SJ (1919-2010). Used by permission of Oregon Catholic Press. **Tune:** PANGE LINGUA, 87.87.87. **Music:** CBW II 583; CBW III 381

**MAR
29**

Good Friday
Celebration of the Passion of the Lord

Step by painful step, people making the Spiritual Exercises of St. Ignatius go through the brutality of Jesus' Passion. Ignatius tells them to ask for "grief and confusion." These come easily as they watch an innocent man get mutilated by compromised people caught in broken systems.

Earlier in the Exercises, retreatants also ask for confusion. There they go step by painful step through the history of their own sins. The point is not to generate self-hatred. We all have that in spades. The focus on sin helps us see the extent of God's love. Joy then enters the confusion. I feel but can't understand how much God loves me, faults and all.

This also happens when I contemplate the corporate sins at play in the Passion. I mustn't stop at the blood and gore, but push through to the love that survives them. I know "God so loved the world." I feel it, however, when I see what Jesus did for the world's sake.

Knowing I'm loved strengthens me to make changes in my life fitting with God's regard. Changes to our systemic lives – caught in cutthroat capitalism and ecological crimes – flow from our experience of God's creative love for us and our common home. The Passion, even as it confuses, empowers us to live up to God's hope for the world.

*Greg Kennedy
Guelph, ON*

National Collection for the Church in the Holy Land

PRAYER

1 Remember your mercies, O Lord, and with your eternal protection sanctify your servants, for whom Christ your Son, by the shedding of his Blood, established the Paschal Mystery. Who lives and reigns for ever and ever. **Amen.**

2 O God, who by the Passion of Christ your Son, our Lord, abolished the death inherited from ancient sin by every succeeding generation, grant that just as, being conformed to him, we have borne by the law of nature the image of the man of earth, so by the sanctification of grace we may bear the image of the Man of heaven. Through Christ our Lord. **Amen.**

LITURGY OF THE WORD

FIRST READING (Isaiah 52.13 – 53.12)

See, my servant shall prosper; he shall be exalted and lifted up, and shall be very high.

Just as there were many who were astonished at him — so marred was his appearance, beyond human semblance, and his form beyond that of the sons of man — so he shall startle many nations; kings shall shut their mouths because of him; for that which had not been told them they shall see, and that which they had not heard they shall contemplate. Who has believed what we have heard? And to whom has the arm of the Lord been revealed?

For he grew up before the Lord like a young plant, and like a root out of dry ground; he had no form or majesty that we should look at him, nothing in his appearance that we should desire him. He was despised and rejected by men; a man of suffering and acquainted with infirmity; and as one from whom others hide their faces he was despised, and we held him of no account.

Surely he has borne our infirmities and carried our diseases; yet we accounted him stricken, struck down by God, and afflicted. But he was wounded for our transgressions, crushed for our iniquities; upon him was the punishment that made us whole, and by his bruises we are healed.

All we like sheep have gone astray; each has turned to their own way and the Lord has laid on him the iniquity of us all.

He was oppressed, and he was afflicted, yet he did not open his mouth; like a lamb that is led to the slaughter, and like a sheep that before its shearers is silent, so he did not open his mouth.

By a perversion of justice he was taken away. Who could have imagined his future? For he was cut off from the land of the living, stricken for the transgression of my people. They made his grave with the wicked and his tomb with the rich, although he had done no violence, and there was no deceit in his mouth.

Yet it was the will of the Lord to crush him with pain. When you make his life an offering for sin, he shall see his offspring, and shall prolong his days; through him the will of the Lord shall prosper. Out of his anguish he shall see light; he shall find satisfaction through his knowledge. The righteous one, my servant, shall make many righteous, and he shall bear their iniquities.

Therefore I will allot him a portion with the great, and he shall divide the spoil with the strong; because he poured out himself to death, and was numbered with the transgressors; yet he bore the sin of many, and made intercession for the transgressors.

The word of the Lord. **Thanks be to God.**

RESPONSORIAL PSALM *(Psalm 31)*

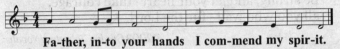

Fa-ther, in-to your hands I com-mend my spir-it.

℟. **Father, into your hands I commend my spirit.**

In you, O Lord, I seek refuge;
 do not let me ever be put · **to** shame;
in your righteousness · **de**-liver_me.
Into your hand I commit · **my** spirit;
you have redeemed me,
 O Lord, · **faith**-ful God. ℟.

I am the scorn of all my adversaries,
 a horror to my neighbours,
 an object of dread to my · **ac**-quaintances.
Those who see me in the · **street** flee_from_me.
I have passed out of mind like one
 who · **is** dead;
I have become like a · **bro**-ken vessel. ℟.

But I trust in you, · **O** Lord;
I say, "You are · **my** God."
My times are in · **your** hand;
deliver me from the hand
    of my · **enemies** and persecutors. R.

Let your face shine upon · **your** servant;
save me in your stead-·**fast** love.
Be strong, and let your heart · **take** courage,
all you who wait · **for** the Lord. R.

©2009 Gordon Johnston/Novalis

To hear the Sunday Psalms, visit www.livingwithchrist.ca.

SECOND READING *(Hebrews 4.14-16; 5.7-9)*

Brothers and sisters: Since we have a great high priest who has passed through the heavens, Jesus, the Son of God, let us hold fast to our confession. For we do not have a high priest who is unable to sympathize with our weaknesses, but we have one who in every respect has been tested as we are, yet without sin. Let us therefore approach the throne of grace with boldness, so that we may receive mercy and find grace to help in time of need.

In the days of his flesh, Jesus offered up prayers and supplications, with loud cries and tears, to the one who was able to save him from death, and he was heard because of his reverent submission. Although he was a Son, he learned obedience through what he suffered; and having been made perfect, he became the source of eternal salvation for all who obey him.

The word of the Lord. **Thanks be to God.**

GOSPEL ACCLAMATION *(Philippians 2.8-9)*
Praise and honour to you, Lord Jesus Christ! Christ became obedient for us to death, even death on a Cross. Therefore God exalted him and gave him the name above every name. **Praise and honour to you, Lord Jesus Christ!**

GOSPEL *(John 18.1 – 19.42)*

Several readers may proclaim the passion narrative today. N indicates the narrator, J the words of Jesus, and S the words of other speakers.

N   The Passion of our Lord Jesus Christ according to John.

    After they had eaten the supper, Jesus went out with his disciples across the Kidron valley to a place where there was a garden, which he and his disciples entered. Now Judas, who betrayed him, also knew the place, because Jesus often met there with his disciples. So Judas brought a detachment of soldiers together with police from the chief priests and the Pharisees, and they came there with lanterns and torches and weapons.

    Then Jesus, knowing all that was to happen to him, came forward and asked them,

J   **Whom are you looking for?**

N   They answered,

S   *Jesus of Nazareth.*

J   **I am he.**

N   Judas, who betrayed him, was standing with them. When Jesus said to them, "I am he," they stepped back and fell to the ground. Again he asked them,

J   **Whom are you looking for?**

S   *Jesus of Nazareth.*

J **I told you that I am he. So if you are looking for me, let these men go.**

N This was to fulfill the word that he had spoken, "I did not lose a single one of those whom you gave me."

    Then Simon Peter, who had a sword, drew it, struck the high priest's slave, and cut off his right ear. The slave's name was Malchus. Jesus said to Peter,

J **Put your sword back into its sheath. Am I not to drink the cup that the Father has given me?**

N So the soldiers, their officer, and the Jewish police arrested Jesus and bound him. First they took him to Annas, who was the father-in-law of Caiaphas, the high priest that year. Caiaphas was the one who had advised the Jews that it was better to have one person die for the people.

    Simon Peter and another disciple followed Jesus. Since that disciple was known to the high priest, he went with Jesus into the courtyard of the high priest, but Peter was standing outside at the gate. So the other disciple, who was known to the high priest, went out, spoke to the woman who guarded the gate, and brought Peter in. The woman said to Peter,

S *You are not also one of this man's disciples, are you?*

N Peter said,

S *I am not.*

N Now the slaves and the police had made a charcoal fire because it was cold, and they were standing around it and warming themselves. Peter also was standing with them and warming himself.

    Then the high priest questioned Jesus about his disciples and about his teaching. Jesus answered,

J I have spoken openly to the world; I have always taught in synagogues and in the temple, where all the Jews come together. I have said nothing in secret. Why do you ask me? Ask those who heard what I said to them; they know what I said.

N When he had said this, one of the police standing nearby struck Jesus on the face, saying,

S *Is that how you answer the high priest?*

J If I have spoken wrongly, testify to the wrong. But if I have spoken rightly, why do you strike me?

N Then Annas sent him bound to Caiaphas the high priest.

   Now Simon Peter was standing and warming himself. They asked him,

S *You are not also one of his disciples, are you?*

N He denied it and said,

S *I am not.*

N One of the slaves of the high priest, a relative of the man whose ear Peter had cut off, asked,

S *Did I not see you in the garden with him?*

N Again Peter denied it, and at that moment the cock crowed.

*At this point all may join in singing
an appropriate acclamation.*

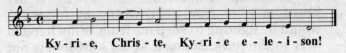

Ky - ri - e, Chris - te, Ky - ri - e e - le - i - son!

Text: Didier Rimaud, © *CNPL*. **Music:** Jacques Berthier
Source: © *Éditions Musicales Studio SM*, 060794-2

N Then they took Jesus from Caiaphas to Pilate's headquarters. It was early in the morning. They themselves did not enter the headquarters, so as to avoid ritual defilement and to be able to eat the Passover. So Pilate went out to them and said,

S *What accusation do you bring against this man?*

N They answered,

S *If this man were not a criminal, we would not have handed him over to you.*

N Pilate said to them,

S *Take him yourselves and judge him according to your law.*

N They replied,

S *We are not permitted to put anyone to death.*

N This was to fulfill what Jesus had said when he indicated the kind of death he was to die.

Then Pilate entered the headquarters again, summoned Jesus, and asked him,

S *Are you the King of the Jews?*

J Do you ask this on your own, or did others tell you about me?

S *I am not a Jew, am I? Your own nation and the chief priests have handed you over to me. What have you done?*

J My kingdom is not from this world. If my kingdom were from this world, my followers would be fighting to keep me from being handed over to the Jews. But as it is, my kingdom is not from here.

S *So you are a king?*

J You say that I am a king. For this I was born, and for this I came into the world, to testify to the

truth. Everyone who belongs to the truth listens to my voice.

S *What is truth?*

N After he had said this, Pilate went out to the Jews again and told them,

S *I find no case against him. But you have a custom that I release someone for you at the Passover. Do you want me to release for you the King of the Jews?*

N They shouted in reply,

S *Not this man, but Barabbas!*

N Now Barabbas was a bandit. Then Pilate took Jesus and had him flogged. And the soldiers wove a crown of thorns and put it on his head, and they dressed him in a purple robe. They kept coming up to him, saying,

S *"Hail, King of the Jews!"*

N and they struck him on the face. Pilate went out again and said to them,

S *Look, I am bringing him out to you to let you know that I find no case against him.*

N So Jesus came out, wearing the crown of thorns and the purple robe. Pilate said to them,

S *Here is the man!*

N When the chief priests and the police saw him, they shouted,

S *Crucify him! Crucify him!*

N Pilate said to them,

S *Take him yourselves and crucify him; I find no case against him.*

N They answered him,

S *We have a law, and according to that law he ought to die because he has claimed to be the Son of God.*

N Now when Pilate heard this, he was more afraid than ever. He entered his headquarters again and asked Jesus,

S *Where are you from?*

N But Jesus gave him no answer. Pilate therefore said to him,

S *Do you refuse to speak to me? Do you not know that I have power to release you, and power to crucify you?*

J **You would have no power over me unless it had been given you from above; therefore the one who handed me over to you is guilty of a greater sin.**

N From then on Pilate tried to release him, but the Jews cried out,

S *If you release this man, you are no friend of the emperor. Everyone who claims to be a king sets himself against the emperor.*

N When Pilate heard these words, he brought Jesus outside and sat on the judge's bench at a place called "The Stone Pavement," or in Hebrew "Gabbatha."

Now it was the day of Preparation for the Passover; and it was about noon. Pilate said to the Jews,

S *Here is your King!*

N They cried out,

S *Away with him! Away with him! Crucify him!*

N Pilate asked them,

S *Shall I crucify your King?*

N The chief priests answered,

S *We have no king but the emperor.*

*At this point all may join in singing
an appropriate acclamation.*

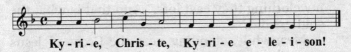

Ky - ri - e,   Chris - te,   Ky - ri - e   e - le - i - son!

Text: Didier Rimaud, © *CNPL*. **Music:** Jacques Berthier
Source: © *Éditions Musicales Studio SM,* 060794-2

N   Then Pilate handed Jesus over to them to be crucified. So they took Jesus; and carrying the Cross by
himself, he went out to what is called The Place
of the Skull, which in Hebrew is called Golgotha.
There they crucified him, and with him two others,
one on either side, with Jesus between them.

   Pilate also had an inscription written and put
on the Cross. It read, "Jesus of Nazareth, the King
of the Jews." Many of the people read this inscription, because the place where Jesus was crucified
was near the city; and it was written in Hebrew, in
Latin, and in Greek. Then the chief priests of the
Jews said to Pilate,

S   *Do not write, "The King of the Jews," but, "This man
said, I am King of the Jews."*

N   Pilate answered,

S   *What I have written I have written.*

N   When the soldiers had crucified Jesus, they took his
clothes and divided them into four parts, one for
each soldier. They also took his tunic; now the tunic
was seamless, woven in one piece from the top. So
they said to one another,

S   *Let us not tear it, but cast lots for it to see who will
get it.*

N This was to fulfill what the Scripture says, "They divided my clothes among themselves, and for my clothing they cast lots." And that is what the soldiers did.

Meanwhile, standing near the Cross of Jesus were his mother, and his mother's sister, Mary the wife of Clopas, and Mary Magdalene. When Jesus saw his mother and the disciple whom he loved standing beside her, he said to his mother,

J **Woman, here is your son.**

N Then he said to the disciple,

J **Here is your mother.**

N And from that hour the disciple took her into his own home.

After this, when Jesus knew that all was now finished, in order to fulfill the Scripture, he said,

J **I am thirsty.**

N A jar full of sour wine was standing there. So they put a sponge full of the wine on a branch of hyssop and held it to his mouth.

When Jesus had received the wine, he said,

J **It is finished.**

N Then he bowed his head and gave up his spirit.

Here all kneel and pause for a short time.

N Since it was the day of Preparation, the Jews did not want the bodies left on the cross during the Sabbath, especially because that Sabbath was a day of great Solemnity. So they asked Pilate to have the legs of the crucified men broken and the bodies removed. Then the soldiers came and broke the legs of the first and of the other who had been crucified with him. But when they came to Jesus and saw that he was already dead, they did not break his legs. Instead, one of the soldiers pierced his side with a spear, and at once blood and water came out.

(He who saw this has testified so that you also may believe. His testimony is true, and he knows that he tells the truth.) These things occurred so that the Scripture might be fulfilled, "None of his bones shall be broken." And again another passage of Scripture says, "They will look on the one whom they have pierced."

After these things, Joseph of Arimathea, who was a disciple of Jesus, though a secret one because of his fear of the Jews, asked Pilate to let him take away the body of Jesus. Pilate gave him permission; so he came and removed his body.

Nicodemus, who had at first come to Jesus by night, also came, bringing a mixture of myrrh and aloes, weighing about a hundredweight. They took the body of Jesus and wrapped it with the spices in linen cloths, according to the burial custom of the Jews. Now there was a garden in the place where he was crucified, and in the garden there was a new tomb in which no one had ever been laid. And so, because it was the Jewish day of Preparation, and the tomb was nearby, they laid Jesus there.

The readers return to their places in silence.

THE SOLEMN INTERCESSIONS

For Holy Church

Let us pray, dearly beloved, for the holy Church of God, that our God and Lord be pleased to give her peace, to guard her and to unite her throughout the whole world and grant that, leading our life in tranquillity and quiet, we may glorify God the Father almighty. *(Pause)*

Almighty ever-living God, who in Christ revealed your glory to all the nations, watch over the works of your mercy, that your Church, spread throughout all the world, may persevere with steadfast faith in confessing your name. Through Christ our Lord. **Amen.**

For the Pope

Let us pray also for our most Holy Father Pope N., that our God and Lord, who chose him for the Order of Bishops, may keep him safe and unharmed for the Lord's holy Church, to govern the holy People of God. *(Pause)*

Almighty ever-living God, by whose decree all things are founded, look with favour on our prayers and in your kindness protect the Pope chosen for us, that, under him, the Christian people, governed by you their maker, may grow in merit by reason of their faith. Through Christ our Lord. **Amen.**

For all orders and degrees of the faithful

Let us pray also for our Bishop N., for all Bishops, Priests, and Deacons of the Church and for the whole of the faithful people. *(Pause)*

Almighty ever-living God, by whose Spirit the whole body of the Church is sanctified and governed, hear our humble prayer for your ministers, that, by the gift of your grace, all may serve you faithfully. Through Christ our Lord. **Amen.**

For catechumens

Let us pray also for (our) catechumens, that our God and Lord may open wide the ears of their inmost hearts and unlock the gates of his mercy, that, having received forgiveness of all their sins through the waters of rebirth, they, too, may be one with Christ Jesus our Lord. *(Pause)*

Almighty ever-living God, who make your Church ever fruitful with new offspring, increase the faith and understanding of (our) catechumens, that, reborn in the font of Baptism, they may be added to the number of your adopted children. Through Christ our Lord. **Amen.**

For the unity of Christians

Let us pray also for all our brothers and sisters who believe in Christ, that our God and Lord may be pleased, as they live the truth, to gather them together and keep them in his one Church. *(Pause)*

Almighty ever-living God, who gather what is scattered and keep together what you have gathered, look kindly on the flock of your Son, that those whom one Baptism has consecrated may be joined together by integrity of faith and united in the bond of charity. Through Christ our Lord. **Amen.**

For the Jewish people
Let us pray also for the Jewish people, to whom the Lord our God spoke first, that he may grant them to advance in love of his name and in faithfulness to his covenant. *(Pause)*

Almighty ever-living God, who bestowed your promises on Abraham and his descendants, graciously hear the prayers of your Church, that the people you first made your own may attain the fullness of redemption. Through Christ our Lord. **Amen.**

For those who do not believe in Christ
Let us pray also for those who do not believe in Christ, that, enlightened by the Holy Spirit, they, too, may enter on the way of salvation. *(Pause)*

Almighty ever-living God, grant to those who do not confess Christ that, by walking before you with a sincere heart, they may find the truth and that we ourselves, being constant in mutual love and striving to understand more fully the mystery of your life, may be made more perfect witnesses to your love in the world. Through Christ our Lord. **Amen.**

For those who do not believe in God
Let us pray also for those who do not acknowledge God, that, following what is right in sincerity of heart, they may find the way to God himself. *(Pause)*

Almighty ever-living God, who created all people to seek you always by desiring you and, by finding you, come to rest, grant, we pray, that, despite every harmful obstacle, all may recognize the signs of your fatherly love and the witness of the good works done by those who believe in you, and so in gladness confess you, the one true God and Father of our human race. Through Christ our Lord. **Amen.**

For those in public office
Let us pray also for those in public office, that our God and Lord may direct their minds and hearts according to his will for the true peace and freedom of all. *(Pause)*

Almighty ever-living God, in whose hand lies every human heart and the rights of peoples, look with favour, we pray, on those who govern with authority over us, that throughout the whole world, the prosperity of peoples, the assurance of peace, and freedom of religion may through your gift be made secure. Through Christ our Lord. **Amen.**

For those in tribulation
Let us pray, dearly beloved, to God the Father almighty, that he may cleanse the world of all errors, banish disease, drive out hunger, unlock prisons, loosen fetters, granting to travellers safety, to pilgrims return, health to the sick, and salvation to the dying. *(Pause)*

Almighty ever-living God, comfort of mourners, strength of all who toil, may the prayers of those who cry out in any tribulation come before you, that all may rejoice, because in their hour of need your mercy was at hand. Through Christ our Lord. **Amen.**

ADORATION OF THE HOLY CROSS

Three times the priest or deacon invites the assembly to proclaim its faith:

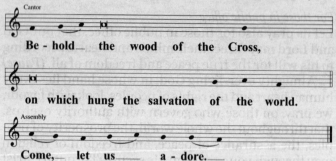

Cantor

Be - hold __ the wood of the Cross,

on which hung the salvation of the world.

Assembly

Come, __ let us __ a - dore. __

Behold the wood of the Cross, on which hung the salvation of the world. **Come, let us adore.**

After each response all adore the Cross briefly in silence. After the third response, the Cross and the candles are placed at the entrance to the sanctuary and the people approach, moving as in procession, to adore the Cross. They may make a simple genuflection or perform some other appropriate sign of reverence according to local custom.

During the adoration, suitable songs may be sung. All who have already adored the Cross remain seated. Where large numbers of people make individual adoration difficult, the priest may raise the Cross briefly for all to adore in silence.

HOLY COMMUNION

LORD'S PRAYER *(p. 70)*

PRAYER AFTER COMMUNION

Almighty ever-living God, who have restored us to life by the blessed Death and Resurrection of your Christ, preserve in us the work of your mercy, that, by partaking of this mystery, we may have a life unceasingly devoted to you. Through Christ our Lord. **Amen.**

PRAYER OVER THE PEOPLE AND DISMISSAL

Bow down for the blessing.

May abundant blessing, O Lord, we pray, descend upon your people, who have honoured the Death of your Son in the hope of their resurrection: may pardon come, comfort be given, holy faith increase, and everlasting redemption be made secure. Through Christ our Lord. **Amen.**

All genuflect to the Cross, then depart in silence.

Easter Vigil

Resurrection of the Lord

Such sadness! What happens in your heart when you receive overwhelming news, such as the violent death of a friend? Do you freeze? Are you numb? Do you eat, sleep or pray? I like to think I make healthy choices, but not always. The women in tonight's Gospel turned to their traditions, heading to the tomb to anoint the body of their friend. Theirs is a story of continued hardship and God's ongoing intervention. They were quite practical in their actions. "Who will roll away the stone?" The experiences these past days were unfathomable. The suffering and death of their friend was earth-shattering. The traditions of the time, the duties of the people, took them to the tomb.

With more unexpected twists and turns, in their wonderment, they are comforted by a stranger, the young man: "Do not be afraid." Whatever our response, we do not walk this journey alone. With more information, they and we are commissioned and sent forth with a loud and clear "Go."

What is our response? Like the women in the Gospel, are we initially kept by fear from sharing the amazing news of the resurrection? Does a stone block our desire, our zeal to offer witness? Or do we find friends and others with whom we share the Good News? It is no small task, but a life-giving one.

Sr. Susan Kidd, CND
Charlottetown, PE

SOLEMN BEGINNING OF THE VIGIL
(Lucernarium)

GREETING

The priest and the ministers, one of whom carries the unlit paschal candle, approach the fire.

In the name of the Father, and of the Son, and of the Holy Spirit. **Amen.**

1 The grace of our Lord Jesus Christ, and the love of God, and the communion of the Holy Spirit be with you all.

2 Grace to you and peace from God our Father and the Lord Jesus Christ.

3 The Lord be with you.

And with your spirit.

BLESSING OF THE FIRE

Dear brothers and sisters, on this most sacred night, in which our Lord Jesus Christ passed over from death to life, the Church calls upon her sons and daughters, scattered throughout the world, to come together to watch and pray. If we keep the memorial of the Lord's paschal solemnity in this way, listening to his word and celebrating his mysteries, then we shall have the sure hope of sharing his triumph over death and living with him in God.

Let us pray. O God, who through your Son bestowed upon the faithful the fire of your glory, sanctify this new fire, we pray, and grant that, by these paschal celebrations, we may be so inflamed with heavenly desires, that with minds made pure we may attain festivities of unending splendour. Through Christ our Lord. **Amen.**

PREPARATION AND LIGHTING OF THE CANDLE

*The priest cuts a cross in the paschal candle and traces the Greek letters
alpha (A) and omega (z) and the numerals 2024, saying:*

Christ yesterday and today, the Beginning and the
End, the Alpha and the Omega. All time belongs to
him, and all the ages. To him be glory and power,
through every age and for ever. Amen.

*When the marks have been made, the priest may insert five grains of
incense into the candle in the form of a cross, saying:*

By his holy and glorious wounds, may Christ our Lord
guard us and protect us. Amen.

The priest lights the paschal candle from the new fire, saying:

May the light of Christ rising in glory dispel the darkness of our hearts and minds.

PROCESSION WITH THE PASCHAL CANDLE

*The deacon or another suitable minister holds the paschal candle and,
three times during the procession to the altar, lifts it high and sings.*

Deacon/Cantor   Assembly

The Light of Christ.   Thanks be to God.

The Light of Christ. **Thanks be to God.**

*After the first response, the priest lights his candle from the paschal
candle.*

*After the second response, all the people light their candles from the
flame of the paschal candle.*

*After the third response, all the lights in the church are lit, except for the
altar candles.*

EASTER PROCLAMATION *(Exsultet)*

For the shorter version, omit the indented parts.

Exult, let them exult, the hosts of heaven,
exult, let Angel ministers of God exult,
let the trumpet of salvation
sound aloud our mighty King's triumph!
Be glad, let earth be glad, as glory floods her,
ablaze with light from her eternal King,
let all corners of the earth be glad,
knowing an end to gloom and darkness.
Rejoice, let Mother Church also rejoice,
arrayed with the lightning of his glory,
let this holy building shake with joy,
filled with the mighty voices of the peoples.

(Therefore, dearest friends,
standing in the awesome glory of this holy light,
invoke with me, I ask you,
the mercy of God almighty,
that he, who has been pleased to number me,
though unworthy, among the Levites,
may pour into me his light unshadowed,
that I may sing this candle's perfect praises.)

(The Lord be with you. **And with your spirit.**)
Lift up your hearts. **We lift them up to the Lord.**
Let us give thanks to the Lord our God. **It is right
and just.**

It is truly right and just,
with ardent love of mind and heart
and with devoted service of our voice,
to acclaim our God invisible, the almighty Father,
and Jesus Christ, our Lord, his Son, his Only Begotten.

Who for our sake paid Adam's debt to the eternal Father,
and, pouring out his own dear Blood,
wiped clean the record of our ancient sinfulness.
These, then, are the feasts of Passover,
in which is slain the Lamb, the one true Lamb,
whose Blood anoints the doorposts of believers.

This is the night
when once you led our forebears, Israel's children,
from slavery in Egypt
and made them pass dry-shod through the Red Sea.
This is the night
that with a pillar of fire
banished the darkness of sin.
This is the night
that even now, throughout the world,
sets Christian believers apart from worldly vices
and from the gloom of sin,
leading them to grace
and joining them to his holy ones.
This is the night
when Christ broke the prison-bars of death
and rose victorious from the underworld.

Our birth would have been no gain,
had we not been redeemed.

O wonder of your humble care for us!
O love, O charity beyond all telling,
to ransom a slave you gave away your Son!
O truly necessary sin of Adam,
destroyed completely by the Death of Christ!
O happy fault
that earned so great, so glorious a Redeemer!

longer version:

O truly blessed night, worthy alone to know the time and hour when Christ rose from the underworld!

This is the night of which it is written: The night shall be as bright as day, dazzling is the night for me, and full of gladness.

The sanctifying power of this night dispels wickedness, washes faults away, restores innocence to the fallen, and joy to mourners, drives out hatred, fosters concord, and brings down the mighty.

On this, your night of grace, O holy Father, accept this candle, a solemn offering, the work of bees and of your servants' hands, an evening sacrifice of praise, this gift from your most holy Church.

shorter version:

The sanctifying power of this night dispels wickedness, washes faults away, restores innocence to the fallen, and joy to mourners.

O truly blessed night, when things of heaven are wed to those of earth and divine to the human.

On this, your night of grace, O holy Father, accept this candle, a solemn offering, the work of bees and of your servants' hands, an evening sacrifice of praise, this gift from your most holy Church.

But now we know the
praises of this pillar,
which glowing fire
ignites for God's
honour, a fire into
many flames divided,
yet never dimmed by
sharing of its light,
for it is fed by melting
wax, drawn out by
mother bees to build
a torch so precious.

O truly blessed night,
when things of heaven
are wed to those of
earth, and divine to
the human.

Therefore, O Lord,
we pray you that this candle,
hallowed to the honour of your name,
may persevere undimmed,
to overcome the darkness of this night.
Receive it as a pleasing fragrance,
and let it mingle with the lights of heaven.
May this flame be found still burning
by the Morning Star:
the one Morning Star who never sets,
Christ your Son,
who, coming back from death's domain,
has shed his peaceful light on humanity,
and lives and reigns for ever and ever. **Amen.**

LITURGY OF THE WORD

Dear brothers and sisters, now that we have begun our solemn Vigil, let us listen with quiet hearts to the Word of God. Let us meditate on how God in times past saved his people and in these, the last days, has sent us his Son as our Redeemer. Let us pray that our God may complete this paschal work of salvation by the fullness of redemption.

FIRST READING (Genesis 1.1 – 2.2)

For the shorter version, omit the indented parts.

In the beginning when God created the heavens and the earth,

> the earth was a formless void and darkness covered the face of the deep, while the spirit of God swept over the face of the waters. Then God said, "Let there be light"; and there was light. And God saw that the light was good; and God separated the light from the darkness. God called the light "Day," and the darkness he called "Night." And there was evening and there was morning, the first day.
>
> And God said, "Let there be a dome in the midst of the waters, and let it separate the waters from the waters." So God made the dome and separated the waters that were under the dome from the waters that were above the dome. And it was so. God called the dome "Sky." And there was evening and there was morning, the second day.
>
> And God said, "Let the waters under the sky be gathered together into one place, and let the dry land appear." And it was so. God called the dry land

"Earth," and the waters that were gathered together he called "Seas." And God saw that it was good.

Then God said, "Let the earth put forth vegetation: plants yielding seed, and fruit trees of every kind on earth that bear fruit with the seed in it." And it was so. The earth brought forth vegetation: plants yielding seed of every kind, and trees of every kind bearing fruit with the seed in it. And God saw that it was good. And there was evening and there was morning, the third day.

And God said, "Let there be lights in the dome of the sky to separate the day from the night; and let them be for signs and for seasons and for days and years, and let them be lights in the dome of the sky to give light upon the earth." And it was so.

God made the two great lights — the greater light to rule the day and the lesser light to rule the night — and the stars. God set them in the dome of the sky to give light upon the earth, to rule over the day and over the night, and to separate the light from the darkness. And God saw that it was good. And there was evening and there was morning, the fourth day.

And God said, "Let the waters bring forth swarms of living creatures, and let birds fly above the earth across the dome of the sky." So God created the great sea monsters and every living creature that moves, of every kind, with which the waters swarm, and every winged bird of every kind. And God saw that it was good. God blessed them, saying, "Be fruitful and multiply and fill the waters in the seas, and let birds multiply on the earth." And there was evening and there was morning, the fifth day.

And God said, "Let the earth bring forth living creatures of every kind: cattle and creeping things and wild animals of the earth of every kind." And it was so. God made the wild animals of the earth of every kind, and the cattle of every kind, and everything that creeps upon the ground of every kind. And God saw that it was good. Then God said, "Let us make man in our image, according to our likeness; and let them have dominion over the fish of the sea, and over the birds of the air, and over the cattle, and over all the wild animals of the earth, and over every creeping thing that creeps upon the earth." So God created man in his image, in the image of God he created him; male and female he created them.

God blessed them, and God said to them, "Be fruitful and multiply, and fill the earth and subdue it; and have dominion over the fish of the sea and over the birds of the air and over every living thing that moves upon the earth."

God said, "See, I have given you every plant yielding seed that is upon the face of all the earth, and every tree with seed in its fruit; you shall have them for food. And to every beast of the earth, and to every bird of the air, and to everything that creeps on the earth, everything that has the breath of life, I have given every green plant for food." And it was so.

God saw everything that he had made, and indeed, it was very good. And there was evening and there was morning, the sixth day.

Thus the heavens and the earth were finished, and all their multitude. And on the seventh day God finished the work that he had done, and he rested on the seventh day from all the work that he had done. The word of the Lord. **Thanks be to God.**

An alternate psalm follows.

RESPONSORIAL PSALM *(Psalm 104)*

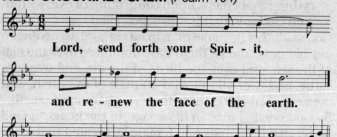

Lord, send forth your Spir-it, and re-new the face of the earth.

R. **Lord, send forth your Spirit,**
and renew the face of the earth.

Bless the Lord, O · **my** soul.
O Lord my God, you are very · **great.**
You are clothed with · **honour** and majesty,
wrapped in light as with · **a** garment. R.

You set the earth on its · **foun**-dations,
so that it shall never be · **shaken.**
You cover it with the deep as · **with** a garment;
the waters stood above · **the** mountains. R.

You make springs gush forth in · **the** valleys;
they flow between the · **hills.**
By the streams the birds of the air
    have their · **ha**-bi-tation;
they sing among · **the** branches. R.

From your lofty abode you water · **the** mountains;
the earth is satisfied with the fruit of your · **work.**
You cause the grass to · **grow_for** the cattle,
and plants for people to use,
    to bring forth food from · **the** earth. R.

O Lord, how manifold are · **your** works!
In wisdom you have made them · **all;**
the earth is · **full_of** your creatures.
Bless the Lord, O · **my** soul. R.

©2009 Gordon Johnston/Novalis

or

RESPONSORIAL PSALM *(Psalm 33)*

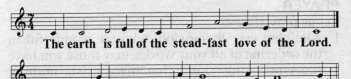

The earth is full of the stead-fast love of the Lord.

R. **The earth is full of the steadfast love of the Lord.**

The word of the Lord · **is** upright,
and all his work is done · **in** faithfulness.
He loves righteousness · **and** justice;
the earth is full of the steadfast love of · **the** Lord. R.

By the word of the Lord
    the heavens · **were** made,
and all their host by the breath of · **his** mouth.
He gathered the waters of the sea
    as in · **a** bottle;
he put the deeps · **in** storehouses. R.

Blessed is the nation whose God is · **the** Lord,
the people whom he has chosen
    as · **his** heritage.
The Lord looks down · **from** heaven;
he sees all · **human** beings. R.

Our soul waits for · **the** Lord;
he is our help · **and** shield.
Let your steadfast love, O Lord, be · **up**-on_us,
even as we hope · **in** you. R.

©2009 Gordon Johnston/Novalis

To hear the Sunday Psalms, visit www.livingwithchrist.ca.

PRAYER

Let us pray. *(Pause)*

1 Almighty ever-living God, who are wonderful in
the ordering of all your works, may those you have
redeemed understand that there exists nothing
more marvellous than the world's creation in the
beginning except that, at the end of the ages, Christ
our Passover has been sacrificed. Who lives and
reigns for ever and ever. **Amen.**

2 O God, who wonderfully created human nature
and still more wonderfully redeemed it, grant us,
we pray, to set our minds against the enticements
of sin, that we may merit to attain eternal joys.
Through Christ our Lord. **Amen.**

SECOND READING *(Genesis 22.1-18)*

For the shorter version, omit the indented parts.

God tested Abraham. He said to him, "Abraham!" And
Abraham said, "Here I am." God said, "Take your son,

your only son Isaac, whom you love, and go to the land of Moriah, and offer him there as a burnt offering on one of the mountains that I shall show you."

So Abraham rose early in the morning, saddled his donkey, and took two of his young men with him, and his son Isaac; he cut the wood for the burnt offering, and set out and went to the place in the distance that God had shown him.

On the third day Abraham looked up and saw the place far away. Then Abraham said to his young men, "Stay here with the donkey; the boy and I will go over there; we will worship, and then we will come back to you." Abraham took the wood of the burnt offering and laid it on his son Isaac, and he himself carried the fire and the knife. So the two of them walked on together.

Isaac said to his father Abraham, "Father!" And Abraham said, "Here I am, my son." Isaac said, "The fire and the wood are here, but where is the lamb for a burnt offering?" Abraham said, "God himself will provide the lamb for a burnt offering, my son." So the two of them walked on together.

When Abraham and Isaac came to the place that God had shown him, Abraham built an altar there and laid the wood in order. He bound his son Isaac, and laid him on the altar, on top of the wood. Then Abraham reached out his hand and took the knife to kill his son.

But the Angel of the Lord called to him from heaven, and said, "Abraham, Abraham!" And he said, "Here I am." The Angel said, "Do not lay your hand on the boy or do anything to him; for now I know that you fear God, since you have not withheld your son, your only son, from me." And Abraham looked up and saw a ram, caught in a thicket by its horns. Abraham went and took the ram and offered it up as a burnt offering instead of his son.

So Abraham called that place "The Lord will provide"; as it is said to this day, "On the mount of the Lord it shall be provided."

The Angel of the Lord called to Abraham a second time from heaven, and said, "By myself I have sworn, says the Lord: Because you have done this, and have not withheld your son, your only son, I will indeed bless you, and I will make your offspring as numerous as the stars of heaven and as the sand that is on the seashore. And your offspring shall possess the gate of their enemies, and by your offspring shall all the nations of the earth gain blessing for themselves, because you have obeyed my voice."

The word of the Lord. **Thanks be to God.**

RESPONSORIAL PSALM (Psalm 16)

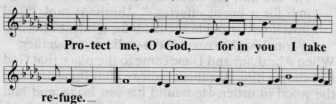

Pro-tect me, O God, for in you I take refuge.

R. **Protect me, O God, for in you I take refuge.**

The Lord is my chosen portion · **and_my** cup;
  you hold · **my** lot.
I keep the Lord always · **be**-fore_me;
because he is at my right hand,
  I shall · **not** be moved. R.

Therefore my heart is glad,
   and my soul · **re**-joices;
my body also rests · **se**-cure.
For you do not give me up · **to** Sheol,
or let your faithful one · **see** the Pit. R.

You show me the path · **of** life.
In your presence there is fullness · **of** joy;
in your right hand · **are** pleasures
for--**ev**-er-more. R.

©2009 Gordon Johnston/Novalis

PRAYER

Let us pray. *(Pause)* O God, supreme Father of the faithful, who increase the children of your promise by pouring out the grace of adoption throughout the whole world and who through the Paschal Mystery make your servant Abraham father of nations, as once you swore, grant, we pray, that your peoples may enter worthily into the grace to which you call them. Through Christ our Lord. **Amen.**

THIRD READING *(Exodus 14.15-31; 15.20, 1)*

The Lord said to Moses, "Why do you cry out to me? Tell the children of Israel to go forward. But you, lift up your staff, and stretch out your hand over the sea and divide it, that the children of Israel may go into the sea on dry ground. Then I will harden the hearts of the Egyptians so that they will go in after them; and so I will gain glory for myself over Pharaoh and all his army, his chariots, and his chariot drivers. And the Egyptians shall know that I am the Lord, when I have gained glory for myself over Pharaoh, his chariots, and his chariot drivers."

The Angel of God who was going before the Israelite army moved and went behind them; and the pillar of cloud moved from in front of them and took its place behind them. It came between the army of Egypt and the army of Israel. And so the cloud was there with the darkness, and it lit up the night; one did not come near the other all night. Then Moses stretched out his hand over the sea. The Lord drove the sea back by a strong east wind all night, and turned the sea into dry land; and the waters were divided. The children of Israel went into the sea on dry ground, the waters forming a wall for them on their right and on their left.

The Egyptians pursued, and went into the sea after them, all of Pharaoh's horses, chariots, and chariot drivers. At the morning watch, the Lord in the pillar of fire and cloud looked down upon the Egyptian army, and threw the Egyptian army into panic. He clogged their chariot wheels so that they turned with difficulty. The Egyptians said, "Let us flee from the children of Israel, for the Lord is fighting for them against Egypt."

Then the Lord said to Moses, "Stretch out your hand over the sea, so that the water may come back upon the Egyptians, upon their chariots and chariot drivers." So Moses stretched out his hand over the sea, and at dawn the sea returned to its normal depth. As the Egyptians fled before it, the Lord tossed the Egyptians into the sea. The waters returned and covered the chariots and the chariot drivers, the entire army of Pharaoh that had followed them into the sea; not one of them remained.

But the children of Israel walked on dry ground through the sea, the waters forming a wall for them on their right and on their left. Thus the Lord saved

Israel that day from the Egyptians; and Israel saw the Egyptians dead on the seashore. Israel saw the great work that the Lord did against the Egyptians. So the people feared the Lord and believed in the Lord and in his servant Moses.

The Prophet Miriam, Aaron's sister, took a tambourine in her hand; and all the women went out after her with tambourines and with dancing. Moses and the children of Israel sang this song to the Lord:

RESPONSORIAL PSALM *(Exodus 15)*

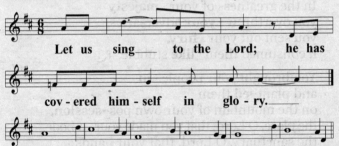

Let us sing to the Lord; he has covered himself in glory.

R. **Let us sing to the Lord;**
   he has covered himself in glory.

I will sing to the Lord,
      for he has triumphed · **gloriously;**
horse and rider he has thrown into · **the** sea.
The Lord is my strength and my · **might,**
and he has become my · **sal**-vation;
this is my God, and I will · **praise_him,**
my father's God, and I will · **ex-alt_him.**   R.

The Lord is a · **warrior;**
the Lord is · **his** name.
Pharaoh's chariots and his army
   he cast into the · **sea;**
his picked officers were sunk in the · **Red** Sea.
The floods · **covered_them;**
they went down into the depths
   · **like_a** stone. ℟.

Your right hand, O Lord, glorious in · **power;**
your right hand, O Lord, shattered · **the** enemy.
In the greatness of your · **majesty**
you overthrew · **your** adversaries;
you sent out your · **fury,**
it consumed them · **like** stubble. ℟.

You brought your people · **in**
and plant·-**ed** them
on the mountain of your own pos·-**session,**
the place, O Lord, that you made your · **a**-bode,
the sanctuary, O Lord, that your hands
   have es·-**tablished.**
The Lord will reign forever · **and** ever. ℟.

©2009 Gordon Johnston/Novalis

PRAYER

Let us pray. *(Pause)*

1 O God, whose ancient wonders remain undimmed in splendour even in our day, for what you once bestowed on a single people, freeing them from Pharaoh's persecution by the power of your right hand, now you bring about as the salvation of the nations through the waters of rebirth, grant, we

pray, that the whole world may become children of Abraham and inherit the dignity of Israel's birthright. Through Christ our Lord. **Amen.**

2 O God, who by the light of the New Testament have unlocked the meaning of wonders worked in former times, so that the Red Sea prefigures the sacred font and the nation delivered from slavery foreshadows the Christian people, grant, we pray, that all nations, obtaining the privilege of Israel by merit of faith, may be reborn by partaking of your Spirit. Through Christ our Lord. **Amen.**

FOURTH READING *(Isaiah 54.5-14)*

Thus says the Lord, the God of hosts. Your Maker is your husband, the Lord of hosts is his name; the Holy One of Israel is your Redeemer, the God of the whole earth he is called. For the Lord has called you like a wife forsaken and grieved in spirit, like the wife of a man's youth when she is cast off, says your God.

For a brief moment I abandoned you, but with great compassion I will gather you. In overflowing wrath for a moment I hid my face from you, but with everlasting love I will have compassion on you, says the Lord, your Redeemer.

This is like the days of Noah to me: Just as I swore that the waters of Noah would never again go over the earth, so I have sworn that I will not be angry with you and will not rebuke you. For the mountains may depart and the hills be removed, but my steadfast love shall not depart from you, and my covenant of peace shall not be removed, says the Lord, who has compassion on you.

O afflicted one, storm-tossed, and not comforted, I am about to set your stones in antimony, and lay your foundations with sapphires. I will make your pinnacles of rubies, your gates of jewels, and all your walls of precious stones.

All your children shall be taught by the Lord, and great shall be the prosperity of your children. In righteousness you shall be established; you shall be far from oppression, for you shall not fear; and from terror, for it shall not come near you.

The word of the Lord. **Thanks be to God.**

RESPONSORIAL PSALM *(Psalm 30)*

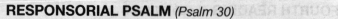

I will ex-tol you, Lord, for you have raised me up.

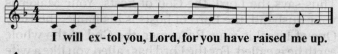

R. **I will extol you, Lord, for you have raised me up.**

I will extol you, O Lord, for you have drawn me · **up,**
and did not let my foes rejoice · **over_me.**
O Lord, you brought up my soul from · **Sheol,**
restored me to life from among those gone
    down · **to_the** Pit. R.

Sing praises to the Lord, O you his · **faithful_ones,**
and give thanks to his holy · **name.**
For his anger is but for a moment;
    his favour is for a · **lifetime.**
Weeping may linger for the night,
    but joy comes · **with_the** morning. R.

Hear, O Lord, and be gracious to · **me!**
O Lord, be my · **helper!**
You have turned my mourning into · **dancing.**
O Lord my God, I will give thanks
    to you · **for-**ever. R.

©2009 Gordon Johnston/Novalis

To hear the Sunday Psalms, visit www.livingwithchrist.ca.

PRAYER

Let us pray. *(Pause)* Almighty ever-living God, surpass, for the honour of your name, what you pledged to the Patriarchs by reason of their faith, and through sacred adoption increase the children of your promise, so that what the Saints of old never doubted would come to pass your Church may now see in great part fulfilled. Through Christ our Lord. **Amen.**

FIFTH READING *(Isaiah 55.1-11)*

Thus says the Lord: "Everyone who thirsts, come to the waters; and you that have no money, come, buy and eat! Come, buy wine and milk without money and without price. Why do you spend your money for that which is not bread, and your labour for that which does not satisfy? Listen carefully to me, and eat what is good, and delight yourselves in rich food. Incline your ear, and come to me; listen, so that you may live. I will make with you an everlasting covenant, my steadfast, sure love for David.

"See, I made him a witness to the peoples, a leader and commander for the peoples. See, you shall call nations that you do not know, and nations that do not know you shall run to you, because of the Lord your God, the Holy One of Israel, for he has glorified you.

"Seek the Lord while he may be found, call upon him while he is near; let the wicked person forsake their way, and the unrighteous person their thoughts; let that person return to the Lord that he may have mercy on them, and to our God, for he will abundantly pardon.

"For my thoughts are not your thoughts, nor are your ways my ways, says the Lord. For as the heavens are higher than the earth, so are my ways higher than your ways and my thoughts than your thoughts. For as the rain and the snow come down from heaven, and do not return there until they have watered the earth, making it bring forth and sprout, giving seed to the sower and bread to the one who eats, so shall my word be that goes out from my mouth; it shall not return to me empty, but it shall accomplish that which I purpose, and succeed in the thing for which I sent it."

The word of the Lord. **Thanks be to God.**

RESPONSORIAL PSALM *(Isaiah 12)*

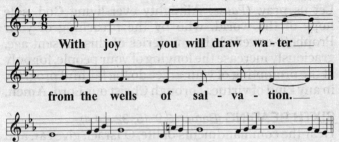

With joy you will draw water from the wells of sal-va-tion.

R. **With joy you will draw water**
from the wells of salvation.

Surely God is my salvation;
 I will trust, and will not · **be** a-fraid,
for the Lord God is my strength and my might;
 he has be-·**come_my** sal-vation.
With joy · **you_will** draw water
from the wells · **of** sal-vation. R.

Give thanks · **to** the Lord,
call · **on** his name;
make known his deeds a-·**mong** the nations;
proclaim that his · **name_is** ex-alted. R.

Sing praises to the Lord,
 for he · **has** done gloriously;
let this be known in · **all** the earth.
Shout aloud and sing for joy, O · **roy**-al Zion,
for great in your midst
 is the Holy · **One** of Israel. R.

To hear the Sunday Psalms, visit www.livingwithchrist.ca.

PRAYER

Let us pray. *(Pause)* Almighty ever-living God, sole hope of the world, who by the preaching of your Prophets unveiled the mysteries of this present age, graciously increase the longing of your people, for only at the prompting of your grace do the faithful progress in any kind of virtue. Through Christ our Lord. **Amen.**

SIXTH READING *(Baruch 3.9-15, 32 – 4.4)*

Hear the commandments of life, O Israel; give ear, and learn wisdom! Why is it, O Israel, why is it that you are in the land of your enemies, that you are growing old in a foreign country, that you are defiled with the dead, that you are counted among those in Hades? You have forsaken the fountain of wisdom. If you had walked in the way of God, you would be living in peace forever.

Learn where there is wisdom, where there is strength, where there is understanding, so that you may at the same time discern where there is length of days, and life, where there is light for the eyes, and peace. Who has found her place? And who has entered her storehouses?

But the one who knows all things knows her, he found her by his understanding. The one who prepared the earth for all time filled it with four-footed creatures; the one who sends forth the light, and it goes; he called it, and it obeyed him, trembling; the stars shone in their watches, and were glad; he called them, and they said, "Here we are!" They shone with gladness for him who made them.

This is our God; no other can be compared to him. He found the whole way to knowledge, and gave her to his servant Jacob and to Israel, whom he loved. Afterward she appeared on earth and lived with humanity. She is the book of the commandments of God, the law that endures forever. All who hold her fast will live, and those who forsake her will die. Turn, O Jacob, and take her; walk toward the shining of her light. Do not give your glory to another, or your advantages to an alien people.

Happy are we, O Israel, for we know what is pleasing to God.

The word of the Lord. **Thanks be to God.**

RESPONSORIAL PSALM *(Psalm 19)*

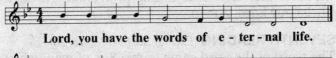

Lord, you have the words of e - ter - nal life.

R. **Lord, you have the words of eternal life.**

The law of the Lord is · **perfect,**
reviving the · **soul;**
the decrees of the Lord are · **sure,**
making · **wise** the simple. R.

The precepts of the Lord are · **right,**
rejoicing the · **heart;**
the commandment of the Lord is · **clear,**
en-**lightening** the eyes. R.

The fear of the Lord is · **pure,**
enduring for-**ever;**
the ordinances of the Lord are · **true**
and righteous · **al**-to-gether. R.

More to be desired are they than · **gold,**
even much fine · **gold;**
sweeter also than · **honey,**
and drippings · **of** the honeycomb. R̰.

©2009 Gordon Johnston/Novalis

To hear the Sunday Psalms, visit www.livingwithchrist.ca.

PRAYER

Let us pray. *(Pause)* O God, who constantly increase your Church by your call to the nations, graciously grant to those you wash clean in the waters of Baptism the assurance of your unfailing protection. Through Christ our Lord. **Amen.**

SEVENTH READING *(Ezekiel 36.16-17a, 18-28)*

The word of the Lord came to me: Son of man, when the house of Israel lived on their own soil, they defiled it with their ways and their deeds; their conduct in my sight was unclean. So I poured out my wrath upon them for the blood that they had shed upon the land, and for the idols with which they had defiled it. I scattered them among the nations, and they were dispersed through the countries; in accordance with their conduct and their deeds I judged them.

But when they came to the nations, wherever they came, they profaned my holy name, in that it was said of them, "These are the people of the Lord, and yet they had to go out of his land."

But I had concern for my holy name, which the house of Israel had profaned among the nations to which they came. Therefore say to the house of Israel, Thus says the Lord God: It is not for your sake, O house of Israel, that I am about to act, but for the sake of my holy name, which you have profaned among the nations to which you came.

I will sanctify my great name, which has been profaned among the nations, and which you have profaned among them; and the nations shall know that I am the Lord, says the Lord God, when through you I display my holiness before their eyes.

I will take you from the nations, and gather you from all the countries, and bring you into your own land.

I will sprinkle clean water upon you, and you shall be clean from all your uncleanness, and from all your idols I will cleanse you.

A new heart I will give you, and a new spirit I will put within you; and I will remove from your body the heart of stone and give you a heart of flesh. I will put my spirit within you, and make you follow my statutes and be careful to observe my ordinances. Then you shall live in the land that I gave to your ancestors; and you shall be my people, and I will be your God.

The word of the Lord. **Thanks be to God.**

An alternate psalm follows. When baptism is celebrated, sing Isaiah 12 (p. 315).

RESPONSORIAL PSALM *(Psalm 42; 43)*

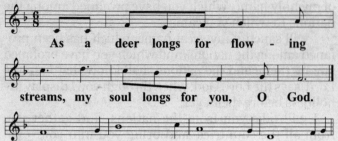

As a deer longs for flow - ing streams, my soul longs for you, O God.

℟. **As a deer longs for flowing streams,
my soul longs for you, O God.**

My soul thirsts for · **God,**
for the living · **God.**
When shall I · **come**
and behold the face · **of** God? ℟.

I went with the · **throng,**
and led them in procession to the house of · **God,**
with glad shouts and songs of · **thanksgiving,**
a multitude · **keeping** festival. ℟.

O send out your light and your · **truth;**
let them · **lead_me;**
let them bring me to your holy · **mountain**
and to · **your** dwelling. ℟.

Then I will go to the altar of · **God,**
to God my exceeding · **joy;**
and I will praise you with the · **harp,**
O God, · **my** God. ℟.

or

RESPONSORIAL PSALM *(Psalm 51)*

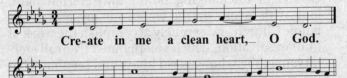

Cre-ate in me a clean heart,__ O God.

℟. **Create in me a clean heart, O God.**

Create in me a clean heart, · **O** God,
and put a new and right spirit · **with**-in_me.
Do not cast me away from · **your** presence,
and do not take your holy · **spirit** from me. ℟.

Restore to me the joy of your · **sal**-vation,
and sustain in me a will-**ing** spirit.
Then I will teach transgressors · **your** ways,
and sinners will re--**turn** to you. ℟.

For you have no delight · **in** sacrifice;
if I were to give a burnt offering,
    you would not · **be** pleased.
The sacrifice acceptable to God
    is a bro--**ken** spirit;
a broken and contrite heart, O God,
    you will · **not** des-pise. ℟.

©2009 Gordon Johnston/Novalis

To hear the Sunday Psalms, visit www.livingwithchrist.ca.

PRAYER

Let us pray. *(Pause)*

1 O God of unchanging power and eternal light, look with favour on the wondrous mystery of the whole Church and serenely accomplish the work of human salvation, which you planned from all eternity; may the whole world know and see that what was cast down is raised up, what had become old is made new, and all things are restored to integrity through Christ, just as by him they came into being. Who lives and reigns for ever and ever. **Amen**.

2 O God, who by the pages of both Testaments instruct and prepare us to celebrate the Paschal Mystery, grant that we may comprehend your mercy, so that the gifts we receive from you this night may confirm our hope of the gifts to come. Through Christ our Lord. **Amen.**

GLORY TO GOD *(p. 13)*

COLLECT

Let us pray. O God, who make this most sacred night radiant with the glory of the Lord's Resurrection, stir up in your Church a spirit of adoption, so that, renewed in body and mind, we may render you undivided service. Through our Lord Jesus Christ, your Son, who lives and reigns with you in the unity of the Holy Spirit, God, for ever and ever. **Amen.**

EPISTLE *(Romans 6.3-11)*

Brothers and sisters: Do you not know that all of us who have been baptized into Christ Jesus were baptized into his death? Therefore we have been buried with him by baptism into death, so that, just as Christ was raised from the dead by the glory of the Father, so we too might walk in newness of life. For if we have been united with him in a death like his, we will certainly be united with him in a resurrection like his.

We know that our old self was crucified with him so that the body of sin might be destroyed, and we might no longer be enslaved to sin. For whoever has died is freed from sin. But if we have died with Christ, we believe that we will also live with him.

We know that Christ, being raised from the dead, will never die again; death no longer has dominion over him. The death he died, he died to sin, once for all; but the life he lives, he lives to God. So you also must consider yourselves dead to sin and alive to God in Christ Jesus.

The word of the Lord. **Thanks be to God.**

SOLEMN ALLELUIA *(Psalm 118)*

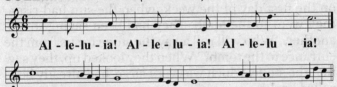

Al - le-lu - ia! Al - le - lu - ia! Al - le-lu - ia!

R. **Alleluia! Alleluia! Alleluia!**

O give thanks to the Lord, for · **he** is good;
his steadfast love en-·**dures** for-ever.
Let Is-·**rael** say,
"His steadfast love en-·**dures** for-ever." R.

"The right hand of the Lord · **is** ex-alted;
the right hand of the · **Lord** does valiantly."
I shall not die, but · **I_shall** live,
and recount the · **deeds_of** the Lord. R.

The stone that the · **builders** re-jected
has become · **the** chief cornerstone.
This is the · **Lord's** doing;
it is marvellous · **in** our eyes. R.

©2009 Gordon Johnston/Novalis

To hear the Sunday Psalms, visit www.livingwithchrist.ca.

GOSPEL *(Mark 16.1-8)*

The Lord be with you. **And with your spirit.**
A reading from the holy Gospel according to Mark.
Glory to you, O Lord.

When the Sabbath was over, Mary Magdalene, and
Mary the Mother of James, and Salome bought spices,
so that they might go and anoint Jesus. And very early
on the first day of the week, when the sun had risen,
they went to the tomb. They had been saying to one
another, "Who will roll away the stone for us from the
entrance to the tomb?" When they looked up, they saw
that the stone, which was very large, had already been
rolled back.

As they entered the tomb, they saw a young man,
dressed in a white robe, sitting on the right side; and
they were alarmed. But he said to them, "Do not be
alarmed; you are looking for Jesus of Nazareth, who
was crucified. He has been raised; he is not here. Look,
there is the place they laid him.

"But go, tell his disciples and Peter that he is going ahead of you to Galilee; there you will see him, just as he told you." So they went out and fled from the tomb, for terror and amazement had seized them; and they said nothing to anyone, for they were afraid.

The Gospel of the Lord. **Praise to you, Lord Jesus Christ.**

BAPTISMAL LITURGY

This celebration combines text from the Roman Missal *(2011), the* Rite of Christian Initiation of Adults *(1987) and the* Rite of Confirmation *(2016), where appropriate.*

INTRODUCTION

1 *If there are candidates for baptism:*
   Dearly beloved, with one heart and one soul, let us by our prayers come to the aid of these our brothers and sisters in their blessed hope, so that, as they approach the font of rebirth, the almighty Father may bestow on them all his merciful help.

2 *If there are no candidates for baptism:*
   Dearly beloved, let us humbly invoke upon this font the grace of God the almighty Father, that those who from it are born anew may be numbered among the children of adoption in Christ.

3 *If there are no candidates for baptism and the font is not to be blessed, proceed to the* Blessing of Water, *p. 333.*

LITANY OF THE SAINTS

Lord, have mer - cy.   Lord, have mer - cy.

Lord, have mercy. **Lord, have mercy.**
Christ, have mercy. **Christ, have mercy.**
Lord, have mercy. **Lord, have mercy.**

Holy Mary, Mother of God,   pray_ for us.

Holy Mary, Mother of God, **pray for us.**
Saint Michael,
Holy Angels of God,
Saint John the Baptist,
Saint Joseph,
Saint Peter and Saint Paul,
Saint Andrew,
Saint John,
Saint Mary Magdalene,
Saint Stephen,
Saint Ignatius of Antioch,
Saint Lawrence,
Saint Perpetua and Saint Felicity,
Saint Agnes,
Saint Gregory,
Saint Augustine,
Saint Athanasius,
Saint Basil,
Saint Martin,
Saint Benedict,

Saint Francis and Saint Dominic,
Saint Francis Xavier,
Saint John Vianney,
Saint Catherine of Siena,
Saint Teresa of Jesus,
(other saints)
All holy men and women, Saints of God,

Lord, be mer - ci - ful, Lord, de - liv - er us, we pray.

Lord, be merciful, **Lord, deliver us, we pray.**
From all evil,
From every sin,
From everlasting death,
By your Incarnation,
By your Death and Resurrection,
By the outpouring of the Holy Spirit,

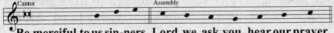

Be merciful to us sin-ners, Lord, we ask you, hear our prayer.

Be merciful to us sinners,
Lord, we ask you, hear our prayer.
1 *If there are candidates for baptism:*
   Bring these chosen ones to new birth through the
   grace of Baptism,
   Lord, we ask you, hear our prayer.
2 *If there are no candidates for baptism:*
   Make this font holy by your grace for the new
   birth of your children,
   Lord, we ask you, hear our prayer.

Jesus, Son of the living God,
Lord, we ask you, hear our prayer.

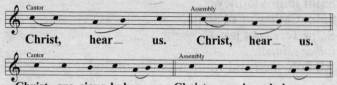

Christ, hear us.
Christ, hear us.
Christ, graciously hear us.
Christ, graciously hear us.

If there are candidates for baptism, the priest prays:
Almighty ever-living God, be present by the mysteries of your great love and send forth the spirit of adoption to create the new peoples brought to birth for you in the font of Baptism, so that what is to be carried out by our humble service may be brought to fulfillment by your mighty power. Through Christ our Lord. **Amen.**

BLESSING OF BAPTISMAL WATER

O God, who by invisible power accomplish a wondrous effect through sacramental signs and who in many ways have prepared water, your creation, to show forth the grace of Baptism;

O God, whose Spirit in the first moments of the world's creation hovered over the waters, so that the very substance of water would even then take to itself the power to sanctify;

O God, who by the outpouring of the flood foreshadowed regeneration, so that from the mystery of one and the same element of water would come an end to vice and a beginning of virtue;

O God, who caused the children of Abraham to pass dry-shod through the Red Sea, so that the chosen people, set free from slavery to Pharaoh, would prefigure the people of the baptized;

O God, whose Son, baptized by John in the waters of the Jordan, was anointed with the Holy Spirit, and, as he hung upon the Cross, gave forth water from his side along with blood, and after his Resurrection, commanded his disciples: "Go forth, teach all nations, baptizing them in the name of the Father and of the Son and of the Holy Spirit," look now, we pray, upon the face of your Church and graciously unseal for her the fountain of Baptism. May this water receive by the Holy Spirit the grace of your Only Begotten Son, so that human nature, created in your image and washed clean through the Sacrament of Baptism from all the squalor of the life of old, may be found worthy to rise to the life of newborn children through water and the Holy Spirit.

May the power of the Holy Spirit, O Lord, we pray, come down through your Son into the fullness of this font, so that all who have been buried with Christ by Baptism into death may rise again to life with him. Who lives and reigns with you in the unity of the Holy Spirit, God, for ever and ever. **Amen.**

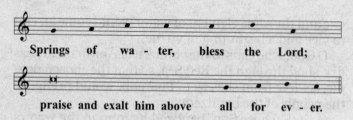

Springs of water, bless the Lord;
praise and exalt him above all for ever.

Springs of water, bless the Lord;
praise and exalt him above all for ever.

RENUNCIATION OF SIN

Using one of the following formularies, the priest questions all the candidates together or individually.

1 Do you reject sin so as to live in the freedom of God's children? **I do.**
Do you reject the glamour of evil, and refuse to be mastered by sin? **I do.**
Do you reject Satan, father of sin and prince of darkness? **I do.**

2 Do you reject Satan, and all his works, and all his empty promises? **I do.**

3 Do you reject Satan? **I do.**
And all his works? **I do.**
And all his empty promises? **I do.**

Adult candidates may now be anointed with the Oil of Catechumens.
We anoint you with the oil of salvation in the name of Christ our Saviour. May he strengthen you with his power. **Amen.**

PROFESSION OF FAITH

N., do you believe in God, the Father almighty, creator of heaven and earth? **I do.**

Do you believe in Jesus Christ, his only Son, our Lord, who was born of the Virgin Mary, was crucified, died, and was buried, rose from the dead, and is now seated at the right hand of the Father? **I do.**

Do you believe in the Holy Spirit, the holy catholic Church, the communion of saints, the forgiveness of sins, the resurrection of the body, and the life everlasting? **I do.**

BAPTISM

The priest baptizes each candidate either by immersion or by the pouring of water.

N., I baptize you in the name of the Father, and of the Son, and of the Holy Spirit.

ANOINTING AFTER BAPTISM

Any newly baptized infants are anointed now with chrism.

The God of power and Father of our Lord Jesus Christ has freed you from sin and brought you to new life through water and the Holy Spirit.

He now anoints you with the chrism of salvation, so that, united with his people, you may remain for ever a member of Christ who is Priest, Prophet, and King. **Amen.**

CLOTHING WITH A BAPTISMAL GARMENT

All the newly baptized receive a white garment.

N. and N., you have become a new creation and have clothed yourselves in Christ. Receive this baptismal garment and bring it unstained to the judgment seat of our Lord Jesus Christ, so that you may have everlasting life. **Amen.**

PRESENTATION OF A LIGHTED CANDLE

Godparents, please come forward to give to the newly baptized the light of Christ.

A godparent of each of the newly baptized lights a candle from the paschal candle and presents it to the newly baptized.

You have been enlightened by Christ. Walk always as children of the light and keep the flame of faith alive in your hearts. When the Lord comes, may you go out to meet him with all the saints in the heavenly kingdom. **Amen.**

CONFIRMATION OF ADULTS

The newly baptized adults with their godparents stand before the priest.

My dear candidates for confirmation, by your baptism you have been born again in Christ and you have become members of Christ and of his priestly people. Now you are to share in the outpouring of the Holy Spirit among us, the Spirit sent by the Lord upon his apostles at Pentecost and given by them and their successors to the baptized.

The promised strength of the Holy Spirit, which you are to receive, will make you more like Christ and help you to be witnesses to his suffering, death, and resurrection. It will strengthen you to be active members of the Church and to build up the Body of Christ in faith and love.

My dear friends, let us pray to God our Father, that he will pour out the Holy Spirit on these candidates for confirmation to strengthen them with his gifts and anoint them to be more like Christ, the Son of God.

LAYING ON OF HANDS

Dearly beloved, let us pray to God the almighty Father, for these, his adopted sons and daughters, already born again to eternal life in Baptism, that he will graciously pour out the Holy Spirit upon them to confirm them with his abundant gifts, and through his anointing conform them more fully to Christ, the Son of God. *(Pause)*

Almighty God, Father of our Lord Jesus Christ, who brought these your servants to new birth by water and the Holy Spirit, freeing them from sin: send upon them, O Lord, the Holy Spirit, the Paraclete; give them the spirit of wisdom and understanding, the spirit of counsel and fortitude, the spirit of knowledge and piety; fill them with the spirit of the fear of the Lord. Through Christ our Lord. **Amen.**

ANOINTING WITH CHRISM

During the conferral of the sacrament an appropriate song may be sung.
N., be sealed with the Gift of the Holy Spirit. **Amen.**
Peace be with you. **And with your spirit.**

BLESSING OF WATER
(when no one is to be baptized)

Dear brothers and sisters, let us humbly beseech the Lord our God to bless this water he has created, which will be sprinkled upon us as a memorial of our Baptism. May he graciously renew us, that we may remain faithful to the Spirit whom we have received. *(Pause)*

Lord our God, in your mercy be present to your people who keep vigil on this most sacred night, and, for us who recall the wondrous work of our creation and the still greater work of our redemption, graciously bless this water. For you created water to make the fields fruitful and to refresh and cleanse our bodies. You also made water the instrument of your mercy: for through water you freed your people from slavery and quenched their thirst in the desert; through water the Prophets proclaimed the new covenant you were to enter upon with the human race; and last of all, through water, which Christ made holy in the Jordan, you have renewed our corrupted nature in the bath of regeneration.

Therefore, may this water be for us a memorial of the Baptism we have received, and grant that we may share in the gladness of our brothers and sisters, who at Easter have received their Baptism. Through Christ our Lord. **Amen.**

RENEWAL OF BAPTISMAL PROMISES

While holding lit candles, the entire community renews its baptismal promises, if it has not already done so.

Dear brothers and sisters, through the Paschal Mystery we have been buried with Christ in Baptism, so that we may walk with him in newness of life. And so, now that our Lenten observance is concluded, let us renew the promises of Holy Baptism, by which we once renounced Satan and his works and promised to serve God in the holy Catholic Church.

And so I ask you:

1   Do you renounce Satan? **I do.**
    And all his works? **I do.**
    And all his empty show? **I do.**

2 Do you renounce sin, so as to live in the freedom of the children of God? **I do.**
Do you renounce the lure of evil, so that sin may have no mastery over you? **I do.**
Do you renounce Satan, the author and prince of sin? **I do.**

3 Do you reject sin so as to live in the freedom of God's children? **I do.**
Do you reject the glamour of evil, and refuse to be mastered by sin? **I do.**
Do you reject Satan, father of sin and prince of darkness? **I do.**

The community professes its faith:

Do you believe in God, the Father almighty, Creator of heaven and earth? **I do.**

Do you believe in Jesus Christ, his only Son, our Lord, who was born of the Virgin Mary, suffered death and was buried, rose again from the dead and is seated at the right hand of the Father? **I do.**

Do you believe in the Holy Spirit, the holy catholic Church, the communion of saints, the forgiveness of sins, the resurrection of the body, and life everlasting? **I do.**

And may almighty God, the Father of our Lord Jesus Christ, who has given us new birth by water and the Holy Spirit and bestowed on us forgiveness of our sins, keep us by his grace, in Christ Jesus our Lord, for eternal life. **Amen.**

The priest sprinkles the people with blessed water, while an appropriate song is sung.

PRAYER OF THE FAITHFUL

The following intentions are suggestions only.
There are more suggestions at www.livingwithchrist.ca.

R. **Lord, hear our prayer.**

For the Church, proclaiming the Resurrection in word and in deed, we pray to the Lord: R.

For world leaders making wise choices to safeguard all of God's creation, we pray to the Lord: R.

For those baptized this night into Christ's death and resurrection, we pray to the Lord: R.

For all of us gathered here, living witnesses to the truth of the Resurrection, we pray to the Lord: R.

LITURGY OF THE EUCHARIST

PREPARATION OF THE GIFTS *(p. 17)*

PRAYER OVER THE OFFERINGS
Accept, we ask, O Lord, the prayers of your people with the sacrificial offerings, that what has begun in the paschal mysteries may, by the working of your power, bring us to the healing of eternity. Through Christ our Lord. **Amen.**

PREFACE *(Easter I, p. 25)*

COMMUNION ANTIPHON *(1 Corinthians 5.7-8)*
Christ our Passover has been sacrificed; therefore let us keep the feast with the unleavened bread of purity and truth, alleluia.

PRAYER AFTER COMMUNION

Pour out on us, O Lord, the Spirit of your love, and in your kindness make those you have nourished by this paschal Sacrament one in mind and heart. Through Christ our Lord. **Amen.**

SOLEMN BLESSING — EASTER

Bow down for the blessing.

May almighty God bless you through today's Easter Solemnity and, in his compassion, defend you from every assault of sin. **Amen.**

And may he, who restores you to eternal life in the Resurrection of his Only Begotten, endow you with the prize of immortality. **Amen.**

Now that the days of the Lord's Passion have drawn to a close, may you who celebrate the gladness of the Paschal Feast come with Christ's help, and exulting in spirit, to those feasts that are celebrated in eternal joy. **Amen.**

And may the blessing of almighty God, the Father, and the Son, and the Holy Spirit, come down on you and remain with you for ever. **Amen.**

DISMISSAL

1 Go forth, the Mass is ended, alleluia, alleluia!
2 Go in peace, alleluia, alleluia!

Thanks be to God, al-le-lu-ia, al-le - lu - ia!

R. **Thanks be to God, alleluia, alleluia!**

Easter Sunday
Resurrection of the Lord

In the Gospel for the Easter Vigil, we see a few faithful women set out before dawn on Easter morning. The heaviness in their hearts was stifling. Who would roll away the stone so they could anoint the body of Jesus?

It looked like death, but really it was life! The sun was up; the Son was raised. That morning the beauty of the Son of Man, who was the Son of God, gradually came to life in the hearts of his followers. "Do not be alarmed," the angel said. "You are looking for Jesus... He has been raised!" What joy! What peace!

Two millennia after the resurrection, how often do we, too, feel locked into temporal tragedies of death and despair? But, like those listening to Peter in today's first reading, we know about the great event that took place. Like Mary Magdalene in the Gospel for Easter Sunday, when we are weeping beside our empty tombs of experience, we have only to listen to hear our name being called by the Lord and raise the eyes of our heart to behold the glory of Christ Jesus, the Risen One.

This Easter season, let each of us who have been raised with Christ through baptism remember that, though "it" might look like death, really it is life – by the power and purpose of God our Father. Alleluia!

Beverly Illauq
Kemptville, ON

ENTRANCE ANTIPHON (Cf. Psalm 138.18, 5-6)

I have risen, and I am with you still, alleluia. You have laid your hand upon me, alleluia. Too wonderful for me, this knowledge, alleluia, alleluia.

or (Luke 24.34; cf. Revelation 1.6)

The Lord is truly risen, alleluia. To him be glory and power for all the ages of eternity, alleluia, alleluia.

INTRODUCTORY RITES (p. 8)

COLLECT

O God, who on this day, through your Only Begotten Son, have conquered death and unlocked for us the path to eternity, grant, we pray, that we who keep the solemnity of the Lord's Resurrection may, through the renewal brought by your Spirit, rise up in the light of life. Through our Lord Jesus Christ, your Son, who lives and reigns with you in the unity of the Holy Spirit, God, for ever and ever. **Amen.**

FIRST READING (Acts 10.34a, 37-43)

Peter began to speak: "You know the message that spread throughout Judea, beginning in Galilee after the baptism that John announced: how God anointed Jesus of Nazareth with the Holy Spirit and with power; how he went about doing good and healing all who were oppressed by the devil, for God was with him.

"We are witnesses to all that he did both in Judea and in Jerusalem. They put him to death by hanging him on a tree; but God raised him on the third day and allowed him to appear, not to all the people but to us who were chosen by God as witnesses, and who ate and drank with him after he rose from the dead.

"He commanded us to preach to the people and to testify that he is the one ordained by God as judge of the living and the dead. All the Prophets testify about him that everyone who believes in him receives forgiveness of sins through his name."

The word of the Lord. **Thanks be to God.**

RESPONSORIAL PSALM *(Psalm 118)*

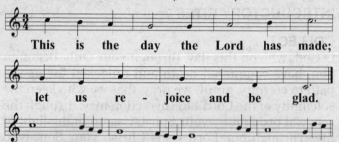

℟. **This is the day the Lord has made;**
   let us rejoice and be glad.
or **Alleluia! Alleluia! Alleluia!**

O give thanks to the Lord, for · **he** is good;
his steadfast love en·-**dures** for-ever.
Let Is·-**rael** say,
"His steadfast love en·-**dures** for-ever." ℟.

"The right hand of the Lord · **is** ex-alted;
the right hand of the · **Lord** does valiantly."
I shall not die, but · **I shall** live,
and recount the · **deeds of** the Lord. ℟.

The stone that the · **builders** re-jected
has become · **the** chief cornerstone.
This is the · **Lord's** doing;
it is marvellous · **in** our eyes. R.

©2009 Gordon Johnston/Novalis

To hear the Sunday Psalms, visit www.livingwithchrist.ca.

An alternate reading follows.

SECOND READING *(Colossians 3.1-4)*
Brothers and sisters: If you have been raised with Christ, seek the things that are above, where Christ is, seated at the right hand of God. Set your minds on things that are above, not on things that are on earth, for you have died, and your life is hidden with Christ in God. When Christ who is your life is revealed, then you also will be revealed with him in glory.

The word of the Lord. **Thanks be to God.**

or

SECOND READING *(1 Corinthians 5.6b-8)*
Do you not know that a little yeast leavens the whole batch of dough? Clean out the old yeast so that you may be a new batch, as you really are unleavened. For our paschal lamb, Christ, has been sacrificed. Therefore, let us celebrate the festival, not with the old yeast, the yeast of malice and evil, but with the unleavened bread of sincerity and truth.

The word of the Lord. **Thanks be to God.**

EASTER SEQUENCE

On this day the following sequence is sung. An earlier version can be found at CBW II 202.

1. Christians, praise the paschal victim!
   Offer thankful sacrifice!

2. Christ the Lamb has saved the sheep,
   Christ the just one paid the price,
   Reconciling sinners to the Father.

3. Death and life fought bitterly
   For this wondrous victory;
   The Lord of life who died reigns glorified!

4. "O Mary, come and say
   what you saw at break of day."

5. "The empty tomb of my living Lord!
   I saw Christ Jesus risen and adored!

6. "Bright Angels testified,
   Shroud and grave clothes side by side!

7. "Yes, Christ my hope rose gloriously.
   He goes before you into Galilee."

8. Share the Good News, sing joyfully:
   His death is victory!
   Lord Jesus, Victor King, show us mercy.

Text: *Victimae Paschali Laudes;* tr. © 1983 *Peter J. Scagnelli.*
Tune: VICTIMAE PASCHALI LAUDES. **Music:** *CBW III 690*

GOSPEL ACCLAMATION *(1 Corinthians 5.7-8)*
Alleluia. Alleluia. Christ, our Paschal Lamb, has been sacrificed; let us feast with joy in the Lord. **Alleluia.**

The Gospel from the Easter Vigil (p. 324) may be read instead.
For an afternoon or evening Mass, see p. 344.

GOSPEL *(John 20.1-18)*
The shorter version ends at the asterisks.
The Lord be with you. **And with your spirit.** A reading from the holy Gospel according to John. **Glory to you, O Lord.**

Early on the first day of the week, while it was still dark, Mary Magdalene came to the tomb and saw that the stone had been removed from the tomb. So she ran and went to Simon Peter and the other disciple, the one whom Jesus loved, and said to them, "They have taken the Lord out of the tomb, and we do not know where they have laid him."

Then Peter and the other disciple set out and went toward the tomb. The two were running together, but the other disciple outran Peter and reached the tomb first. He bent down to look in and saw the linen wrappings lying there, but he did not go in.

Then Simon Peter came, following him, and went into the tomb. He saw the linen wrappings lying there, and the cloth that had been on Jesus' head, not lying with the linen wrappings but rolled up in a place by itself. Then the other disciple, who reached the tomb first, also went in, and he saw and believed; for as yet they did not understand the Scripture, that he must rise from the dead.

* * *

Then the disciples returned to their homes. But Mary Magdalene stood weeping outside the tomb. As she wept, she bent over to look into the tomb; and she saw two Angels in white, sitting where the body of Jesus had been lying, one at the head and the other at the feet. They said to her, "Woman, why are you weeping?" She said to them, "They have taken away my Lord, and I do not know where they have laid him."

When she had said this, she turned around and saw Jesus standing there, but she did not know that it was Jesus. Jesus said to her, "Woman, why are you weeping? Whom are you looking for?" Supposing him to be the gardener, she said to him, "Sir, if you have carried him away, tell me where you have laid him, and I will take him away."

Jesus said to her, "Mary!" She turned and said to him in Hebrew, "Rabbouni!" which means Teacher. Jesus said to her, "Do not hold on to me, because I have not yet ascended to the Father. But go to my brothers and say to them, 'I am ascending to my Father and your Father, to my God and your God.'"

Mary Magdalene went and announced to the disciples, "I have seen the Lord," and she told them that he had said these things to her.

The Gospel of the Lord. **Praise to you, Lord Jesus Christ.**

Alternate Gospel for an afternoon or evening Mass:

GOSPEL *(Luke 24.13-35)*
The Lord be with you. **And with your spirit.**
A reading from the holy Gospel according to Luke. **Glory to you, O Lord.**

On the first day of the week, two of the disciples were going to a village called Emmaus, about eleven kilometres from Jerusalem, and talking with each other about all these things that had happened. While they were talking and discussing, Jesus himself came near and went with them, but their eyes were kept from recognizing him.

And he said to them, "What are you discussing with each other while you walk along?" They stood still, looking sad. Then one of them, whose name was Cleopas, answered him, "Are you the only stranger in Jerusalem who does not know the things that have taken place there in these days?" He asked them, "What things?" They replied, "The things about Jesus of Nazareth, who was a Prophet mighty in deed and word before God and all the people, and how our chief priests and leaders handed him over to be condemned to death and crucified him. But we had hoped that he was the one to redeem Israel. Yes, and besides all this, it is now the third day since these things took place. Moreover, some women of our group astounded us. They were at the tomb early this morning, and when they did not find his body there, they came back and told us that they had indeed seen a vision of Angels who said that he was alive. Some of those who were with us went to the tomb and found it just as the women had said; but they did not see him."

Then he said to them, "Oh, how foolish you are, and how slow of heart to believe all that the Prophets have declared! Was it not necessary that the Christ should suffer these things and then enter into his glory?"

Then beginning with Moses and all the Prophets, he interpreted to them the things about himself in all the Scriptures. As they came near the village to which they were going, he walked ahead as if he were going on. But they urged him strongly, saying, "Stay with us, because it is almost evening and the day is now nearly over." So he went in to stay with them.

When he was at the table with them, he took bread, blessed and broke it, and gave it to them. Then their eyes were opened, and they recognized him; and he vanished from their sight.

They said to each other, "Were not our hearts burning within us while he was talking to us on the road, while he was opening the Scriptures to us?"

That same hour they got up and returned to Jerusalem; and they found the eleven and their companions gathered together. These were saying, "The Lord has risen indeed, and he has appeared to Simon!"

Then they told what had happened on the road, and how he had been made known to them in the breaking of the bread.

The Gospel of the Lord. **Praise to you, Lord Jesus Christ.**

RENEWAL OF BAPTISMAL PROMISES *(p. 334)*

PRAYER OF THE FAITHFUL

The following intentions are suggestions only.
There are more suggestions at www.livingwithchrist.ca.

R. **Lord, hear our prayer.**

For the Church, sign of Christ's continuing presence among us, we pray to the Lord: R.

For peace and reconciliation in the world, we pray to the Lord: R.

For those who have no hope, we pray to the Lord: R.

For all of us here today, called to proclaim Jesus' Resurrection, we pray to the Lord: R.

PREPARATION OF THE GIFTS *(p. 17)*

PRAYER OVER THE OFFERINGS
Exultant with paschal gladness, O Lord, we offer the sacrifice by which your Church is wondrously reborn and nourished. Through Christ our Lord. **Amen.**

PREFACE *(Easter I, p. 25)*

COMMUNION ANTIPHON *(1 Corinthians 5.7-8)*
Christ our Passover has been sacrificed, alleluia; therefore let us keep the feast with the unleavened bread of purity and truth, alleluia, Alleluia.

PRAYER AFTER COMMUNION
Look upon your Church, O God, with unfailing love and favour, so that, renewed by the paschal mysteries, she may come to the glory of the resurrection. Through Christ our Lord. **Amen.**

SOLEMN BLESSING *(Optional)*
AND DISMISSAL *(p. 337)*

April Saints' Days

The following saints are traditionally remembered in April in Canada.

Saint Francis of Paola .... Apr 2

Saint Isidore .... Apr 4

Saint Vincent Ferrer .... Apr 5

Saint John Baptist de la Salle .... Apr 7

Saint Stanislaus .... Apr 11

Saint Martin I .... Apr 13

Saint Kateri Tekakwitha .... Apr 17

Blessed Marie-Anne Blondin .... Apr 18

Saint Anselm .... Apr 21

Saint George .... Apr 23
Saint Adalbert

Saint Fidelis of Sigmaringen .... Apr 24

Saint Mark .... Apr 25

Our Lady of Good Counsel .... Apr 26

Saint Peter Chanel .... Apr 28
Saint Louis Grignion de Montfort

Saint Catherine of Siena .... Apr 29

Saint Marie of the Incarnation .... Apr 30

2nd Sunday of Easter

Divine Mercy Sunday

St. Thomas has gotten a bad rap. Too often labelled "doubting Thomas," he was actually the first apostle to worship Jesus as "my Lord and my God." "Have you believed because you have seen me?" Jesus asked him. The others were silent the previous Sunday when they had first seen the risen Jesus.

What is believing? John's Gospel uses terms such as "to believe" and "believing" about forty times, always as a verb, never a noun. Believing is not an intellectual process but rather dynamic action. Earlier in the Gospel, when Jesus announced he would go to Bethany where Lazarus had just died, Thomas said, "Let us also go that we may die with [Jesus]." No doubter, Thomas was a bulwark of faith in Jesus. He was ready to give his life for Jesus; he worshipped Jesus when others were tentative.

Believing is discipleship. Thomas was open to the Spirit – the Spirit who came by the water and blood of the crucified Lord, as Saint John tells us in the second reading. The Spirit guided Thomas, in his believing, to the truth.

Thomas did not defend his reluctance to believe in the resurrection until he could put his hand in Jesus' wounds. Instead, he saw, he changed and he worshipped. May we also be so forthright.

Glen Argan
Edmonton, AB

ENTRANCE ANTIPHON *(1 Peter 2.2)*
Like newborn infants, you must long for the pure, spiritual milk, that in him you may grow to salvation, alleluia.

or (4 Esdras 2.36-37)
Receive the joy of your glory, giving thanks to God, who has called you into the heavenly kingdom, alleluia.

INTRODUCTORY RITES *(p. 8)*

COLLECT
God of everlasting mercy, who in the very recurrence of the paschal feast kindle the faith of the people you have made your own, increase, we pray, the grace you have bestowed, that all may grasp and rightly understand in what font they have been washed, by whose Spirit they have been reborn, by whose Blood they have been redeemed. Through our Lord Jesus Christ, your Son, who lives and reigns with you in the unity of the Holy Spirit, God, for ever and ever. **Amen.**

FIRST READING *(Acts 4.32-35)*
The whole group of those who believed were of one heart and soul, and no one claimed private ownership of any possessions, but everything they owned was held in common.

With great power the Apostles gave their testimony to the resurrection of the Lord Jesus, and great grace was upon them all.

There was not a needy person among them, for as many as owned lands or houses sold them and brought the proceeds of what was sold. They laid it at the Apostles' feet, and it was distributed to each as any had need.

The word of the Lord. **Thanks be to God.**

RESPONSORIAL PSALM (Psalm 118)

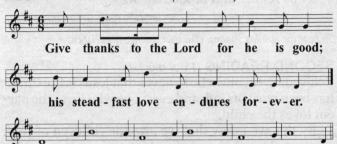

Give thanks to the Lord for he is good;
his stead-fast love en-dures for-ev-er.

R̶. **Give thanks to the Lord, for he is good;
his steadfast love endures forever.**
or **Alleluia!**

Let Israel · **say,**
"His steadfast love endures for-·**ever.**"
Let the house of Aaron · **say,**
"His steadfast love endures for-·**ever.**"
Let those who fear the Lord · **say,**
"His steadfast love endures for-·**ever.**" R̶.

"The right hand of the Lord is ex-·**alted;**
the right hand of the Lord does · **valiantly.**"
I shall not die, but I shall · **live,**
and recount the deeds of the · **Lord.**
The Lord has punished me se-·**verely,**
but he did not give me over to · **death.** R̶.

The stone that the builders re-·**jected**
has become the chief · **cornerstone.**
This is the Lord's · **doing;**
it is marvellous in our · **eyes.**
This is the day that the Lord has · **made;**
let us rejoice and be glad in · **it.** R.

©2009 Gordon Johnston/Novalis

To hear the Sunday Psalms, visit www.livingwithchrist.ca.

SECOND READING *(1 John 5.1-6)*
Beloved: Everyone who believes that Jesus is the Christ
has been born of God, and everyone who loves the parent loves the child.

By this we know that we love the children of God,
when we love God and obey his commandments. For
the love of God is this, that we obey his commandments. And his commandments are not burdensome,
for whatever is born of God conquers the world. And
this is the victory that conquers the world, our faith.

Who is it that conquers the world but the one who
believes that Jesus is the Son of God? This is the one
who came by water and blood, Jesus Christ, not with
the water only but with the water and the blood. And
the Spirit is the one that testifies, for the Spirit is the
truth.

The word of the Lord. **Thanks be to God.**

GOSPEL ACCLAMATION *(See John 20.29)*
Alleluia. Alleluia. You believed, Thomas, because you
have seen me; blessed are those who have not seen and
yet believe. **Alleluia.**

GOSPEL (*John 20.19-31*)

The Lord be with you. **And with your spirit.**
A reading from the holy Gospel according to John.
Glory to you, O Lord.

It was evening on the day Jesus rose from the dead, the first day of the week, and the doors of the house where the disciples had met were locked for fear of the Jews. Jesus came and stood among them and said, "Peace be with you." After he said this, he showed them his hands and his side. Then the disciples rejoiced when they saw the Lord.

Jesus said to them again, "Peace be with you. As the Father has sent me, so I send you." When he had said this, he breathed on them and said to them, "Receive the Holy Spirit. If you forgive the sins of any, they are forgiven them; if you retain the sins of any, they are retained."

But Thomas, who was called the Twin, one of the twelve, was not with them when Jesus came. So the other disciples told him, "We have seen the Lord." But he said to them, "Unless I see the mark of the nails in his hands, and put my finger in the mark of the nails and my hand in his side, I will not believe."

After eight days his disciples were again in the house, and Thomas was with them. Although the doors were shut, Jesus came and stood among them and said, "Peace be with you." Then he said to Thomas, "Put your finger here and see my hands. Reach out your hand and put it in my side. Do not doubt but believe." Thomas answered him, "My Lord and my God!"

Jesus said to him, "Have you believed because you have seen me? Blessed are those who have not seen and yet have come to believe."

Now Jesus did many other signs in the presence of his disciples, which are not written in this book. But these are written so that you may come to believe that Jesus is the Christ, the Son of God, and that through believing you may have life in his name.

The Gospel of the Lord. **Praise to you, Lord Jesus Christ.**

PROFESSION OF FAITH *(p. 14)*

PRAYER OF THE FAITHFUL

The following intentions are suggestions only.
There are more suggestions at www.livingwithchrist.ca.

R. **Lord, hear our prayer.**

For the Church, called to be a sign of God's forgiveness and love, we pray to the Lord: R.

For leaders of governments, dedicated to exercising wisdom for the well-being of all, we pray to the Lord: R.

For those among us who struggle with fears, regrets and doubts, we pray to the Lord: R.

For ourselves during this Easter season, invited to enter into the grace of the Resurrection, we pray to the Lord: R.

PREPARATION OF THE GIFTS *(p. 17)*

PRAYER OVER THE OFFERINGS

Accept, O Lord, we pray, the oblations of your people (and of those you have brought to new birth), that, renewed by confession of your name and by Baptism, they may attain unending happiness. Through Christ our Lord. **Amen.**

PREFACE (Easter I, p. 25)

COMMUNION ANTIPHON (Cf. John 20.27)

Bring your hand and feel the place of the nails, and do not be unbelieving but believing, alleluia.

PRAYER AFTER COMMUNION

Grant, we pray, almighty God, that our reception of this paschal Sacrament may have a continuing effect in our minds and hearts. Through Christ our Lord. **Amen.**

SOLEMN BLESSING — EASTER TIME (Optional)

Bow down for the blessing.

May God, who by the Resurrection of his Only Begotten Son was pleased to confer on you the gift of redemption and of adoption, give you gladness by his blessing. **Amen.**

May he, by whose redeeming work you have received the gift of everlasting freedom, make you heirs to an eternal inheritance. **Amen.**

And may you, who have already risen with Christ in Baptism through faith, by living in a right manner on this earth, be united with him in the homeland of heaven. **Amen.**

And may the blessing of almighty God, the Father, and the Son, and the Holy Spirit, come down on you and remain with you for ever. **Amen.**

DISMISSAL

1   Go forth, the Mass is ended, alleluia, alleluia!
2   Go in peace, alleluia, alleluia!

Thanks be to God, al-le-lu - ia,   al - le -   lu - ia!

R̠. **Thanks be to God, alleluia, alleluia!**

3rd Sunday of Easter

Our Claretian mission team set out from Santo Tomas de Castillo, Guatemala early one morning. The long *cayuco*, a dugout canoe, held all seven of us as we glided over the quiet waters of the Bay of Amatique. With a skilled hand at the tiller, we found the mouth of a small river, then motored up it as far as it could be navigated. Our guide, machete in hand, cut a path for us through – to my eyes – impenetrable rainforest undergrowth towards a settlement of simple farmer's huts.

Villagers eagerly awaited. A Franciscan nurse improvised a clinic. We all had assigned tasks. A Mass would be celebrated. Afterwards, the small community gathered around rough tables set up under a thatched roofed *champa*. We shared a chicken and yuca broth with corn tortillas. What little they had, they shared gladly.

Like the apostles in today's Gospel, we met Jesus there in the sharing of a meal, the breaking of bread. How could we not see him in those villagers? His peace was with us. Listening to his words opens the path to repentance and forgiveness of our sins. The commandments serve to keep us on a path that may seem as bewildering as ours was through that rainforest. A gathering storm hastened our departure. We knew we had nothing to fear.

Michael Dougherty
Whitehorse, YT

ENTRANCE ANTIPHON (Cf. Psalm 65.1-2)
Cry out with joy to God, all the earth; O sing to the glory of his name. O render him glorious praise, alleluia.

INTRODUCTORY RITES (p. 8)

COLLECT
May your people exult for ever, O God, in renewed youthfulness of spirit, so that, rejoicing now in the restored glory of our adoption, we may look forward in confident hope to the rejoicing of the day of resurrection. Through our Lord Jesus Christ, your Son, who lives and reigns with you in the unity of the Holy Spirit, God, for ever and ever. **Amen.**

FIRST READING (Acts 3.13-15, 17-19)
At the temple gate, Peter addressed the people: "The God of Abraham, the God of Isaac, and the God of Jacob, the God of our fathers has glorified his servant Jesus, whom you handed over and rejected in the presence of Pilate, though he had decided to release him.

"But you rejected the Holy and Righteous One and asked to have a murderer given to you, and you killed the Author of life, whom God raised from the dead. To this we are witnesses.

"And now, brothers and sisters, I know that you acted in ignorance, as did also your rulers. In this way God fulfilled what he had foretold through all the Prophets, that his Christ would suffer.

"Repent therefore, and turn to God so that your sins may be wiped out."

The word of the Lord. **Thanks be to God.**

RESPONSORIAL PSALM *(Psalm 4)*

Let the light of your face shine on us, O Lord.

℟. **Let the light of your face shine on us, O Lord.**
or **Alleluia!**

Answer me when I call, O God of · **my** right!
You gave me room when I was in · **dis**-tress.
Be gracious to me, and · **hear** my prayer. ℟.

But know that the Lord has set · **a**-part
the faithful for · **him**-self;
the Lord hears when I · **call** to him. ℟.

There are many · **who** say,
"O that we might see · **some** good!
Let the light of your face shine on · **us**, O Lord!" ℟.

I will both lie down and sleep · **in** peace;
for you alone, · **O** Lord,
make me lie · **down** in safety. ℟.

©2009 Gordon Johnston/Novalis

To hear the Sunday Psalms, visit www.livingwithchrist.ca.

SECOND READING *(1 John 2.1-5)*

My little children, I am writing these things to you so that you may not sin. But if anyone does sin, we have an advocate with the Father, Jesus Christ the righteous; and he is the atoning sacrifice for our sins, and not for ours only but also for the sins of the whole world.

Now by this we may be sure that we know him, if we obey his commandments. Whoever says, "I have come to know him," but does not obey his commandments, is a liar, and in such a person the truth does not exist; but whoever obeys his word, truly in this person the love of God has reached perfection. By this we may be sure that we are in him.

The word of the Lord. **Thanks be to God.**

GOSPEL ACCLAMATION *(See Luke 24.32)*
Alleluia. Alleluia. Lord Jesus, open the Scriptures to us: make our hearts burn with love when you speak. **Alleluia.**

GOSPEL *(Luke 24.35-48)*
The Lord be with you. **And with your spirit.** A reading from the holy Gospel according to Luke. **Glory to you, O Lord.**

The two disciples told the eleven and their companions what had happened on the road to Emmaus, and how Jesus had been made known to them in the breaking of the bread.

While they were talking about this, Jesus himself stood among them and said to them, "Peace be with you." They were startled and terrified, and thought that they were seeing a ghost. He said to them, "Why are you frightened, and why do doubts arise in your hearts? Look at my hands and my feet; see that it is I myself. Touch me and see; for a ghost does not have flesh and bones as you see that I have."

And when he had said this, he showed them his hands and his feet. While in their joy they were disbelieving and still wondering, he said to them, "Have you anything here to eat?" They gave him a piece of broiled fish, and he took it and ate in their presence.

Then he said to them, "These are my words that I spoke to you while I was still with you — that everything written about me in the Law of Moses, the Prophets, and the Psalms must be fulfilled." Then he opened their minds to understand the Scriptures, and he said to them, "Thus it is written, that the Christ is to suffer and to rise from the dead on the third day, and that repentance and forgiveness of sins is to be proclaimed in his name to all nations, beginning from Jerusalem. You are witnesses of these things."

The Gospel of the Lord. **Praise to you, Lord Jesus Christ.**

PROFESSION OF FAITH *(p. 14)*

PRAYER OF THE FAITHFUL

The following intentions are suggestions only.
There are more suggestions at www.livingwithchrist.ca.

R. **Lord, hear our prayer.**

For the Church during this Easter season, calling us to see Jesus in our brothers and sisters everywhere, we pray to the Lord: R.

For world leaders working together to find solutions to our common global problems, we pray to the Lord: R.

For all who call out in their need and for those who respond, we pray to the Lord: R.

For all the members of this community, working to be faithful followers of Jesus, we pray to the Lord: R.

PREPARATION OF THE GIFTS (p. 17)

PRAYER OVER THE OFFERINGS
Receive, O Lord, we pray, these offerings of your exultant Church, and, as you have given her cause for such great gladness, grant also that the gifts we bring may bear fruit in perpetual happiness. Through Christ our Lord. **Amen.**

PREFACE (Easter, p. 25)

COMMUNION ANTIPHON (Luke 24.35)
The disciples recognized the Lord Jesus in the breaking of the bread, alleluia.

or (Luke 24.46-47)
The Christ had to suffer and on the third day rise from the dead; in his name repentance and remission of sins must be preached to all the nations, alleluia.

PRAYER AFTER COMMUNION
Look with kindness upon your people, O Lord, and grant, we pray, that those you were pleased to renew by eternal mysteries may attain in their flesh the incorruptible glory of the resurrection. Through Christ our Lord. **Amen.**

SOLEMN BLESSING (Optional, p. 355)

DISMISSAL (p. 72)

4th Sunday of Easter

World Day of Prayer for Vocations

APR 21

See what love the Father has given us, that we should be called children of God. (1 Jn 3.1)

Have you ever deeply pondered on the fact that you are a child of God? If we allow it, this mystery can ignite a mystical journey from this moment forward.

Letting the reality of our true identity settle into our hearts is a magnificent grace – one that can free and empower us. It can remind us that God doesn't make junk – and that, as his children, we are precious.

Nestling into the relationship as a child of his, we'll be called to snuggle up to him, listen to him, praise him, thank him, take refuge in him, rejoice in him, run to him for help. And yes, take commands from him. Jesus knows us and we know him.

You see, Jesus is the Good Shepherd and not a hired hand. He gave his life for us. We've heard the story of the Good Shepherd hundreds of times. What does it mean? When Jesus sees evil or hard times befalling us, he does not run away. He is there with us in battle. A hired hand may run away because a hired hand might not care. Jesus the Son of God cares deeply. In fact, Jesus loves us! Will we lay down our lives for him?

Dorothy Pilarski
Mississauga, ON

ENTRANCE ANTIPHON *(Cf. Psalm 32.5-6)*
The merciful love of the Lord fills the earth; by the word of the Lord the heavens were made, alleluia.

INTRODUCTORY RITES *(p. 8)*

COLLECT
Almighty ever-living God, lead us to a share in the joys of heaven, so that the humble flock may reach where the brave Shepherd has gone before. Who lives and reigns with you in the unity of the Holy Spirit, God, for ever and ever. **Amen.**

FIRST READING *(Acts 4.7-12)*
While Peter and John were speaking to the people about the resurrection of Jesus, the captain of the temple arrested them and placed them in custody.

The next day the rulers, elders and scribes assembled. When they had made the prisoners stand in their midst, they inquired, "By what power or by what name did you do this?" Then Peter, filled with the Holy Spirit, said to them, "Rulers of the people and elders, if we are questioned today because of a good deed done to someone who was sick and are asked how this man has been healed, let it be known to all of you, and to all the people of Israel, that this man is standing before you in good health by the name of Jesus Christ of Nazareth, whom you crucified, whom God raised from the dead. This Jesus is 'the stone that was rejected by you, the builders; it has become the cornerstone.' There is salvation in no one else, for there is no other name under heaven given among human beings by which we must be saved."

The word of the Lord. **Thanks be to God.**

RESPONSORIAL PSALM *(Psalm 118)*

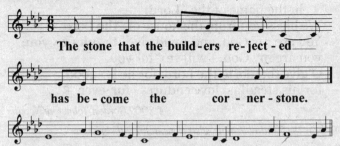

The stone that the build-ers re-ject-ed
has be-come the cor-ner-stone.

R. **The stone that the builders rejected
has become the cornerstone.**
or **Alleluia!**

O give thanks to the Lord, for he is · **good;**
his steadfast love endures · **for**-ever!
It is better to take refuge in the · **Lord**
than to put confidence · **in** humans.
It is better to take refuge in the · **Lord**
than to put confidence · **in** princes. R.

I thank you that you have · **answered_me**
and have become my · **sal**-vation.
The stone that the builders re-·**jected**
has become the · **chief** cornerstone.
This is the Lord's · **doing;**
it is marvellous in · **our** eyes. R.

Blessed is the one who comes
    in the name of the · **Lord.**
We bless you from the house of · **the** Lord.
You are my God, and I will give · **thanks_to_you;**
you are my God, I will · **ex**-tol_you.
O give thanks to the Lord, for he is · **good,**
for his steadfast love endures · **for**-ever. R.

To hear the Sunday Psalms, visit www.livingwithchrist.ca.

SECOND READING *(1 John 3.1-2)*

Beloved: See what love the Father has given us, that
we should be called children of God; and that is what
we are. The reason the world does not know us is that
it did not know him.

    Beloved, we are God's children now; what we will
be has not yet been revealed. What we do know is this:
when he is revealed, we will be like him, for we will
see him as he is.

    The word of the Lord. **Thanks be to God.**

GOSPEL ACCLAMATION *(John 10.14)*

Alleluia. Alleluia. I am the good shepherd, says the
Lord; I know my own, and my own know me. **Alleluia.**

GOSPEL *(John 10.11-18)*

The Lord be with you. **And with your spirit.**
A reading from the holy Gospel according to John.
Glory to you, O Lord.

    Jesus said: "I am the good shepherd. The good shep-
herd lays down his life for the sheep. The hired hand,
who is not the shepherd and does not own the sheep,

sees the wolf coming and leaves the sheep and runs away — and the wolf snatches them and scatters them. The hired hand runs away because a hired hand does not care for the sheep.

"I am the good shepherd. I know my own and my own know me, just as the Father knows me and I know the Father. And I lay down my life for the sheep. I have other sheep that do not belong to this fold. I must bring them also, and they will listen to my voice. So there will be one flock, one shepherd.

"For this reason the Father loves me, because I lay down my life in order to take it up again. No one takes it from me, but I lay it down of my own accord. I have power to lay it down, and I have power to take it up again. I have received this command from my Father."

The Gospel of the Lord. **Praise to you, Lord Jesus Christ.**

PROFESSION OF FAITH (p. 14)

PRAYER OF THE FAITHFUL

The following intentions are suggestions only.
There are more suggestions at www.livingwithchrist.ca.

R. **Lord, hear our prayer.**

For all who bring the Spirit of God to us each day, we pray to the Lord: R.

For the world as it continues to struggle to find peace, we pray to the Lord: R.

In gratitude for all the special people in our lives who have acted as mentors and guides, we pray to the Lord: R.

For this flock, called together by the Good Shepherd, we pray to the Lord: R.

PREPARATION OF THE GIFTS *(p. 17)*

PRAYER OVER THE OFFERINGS
Grant, we pray, O Lord, that we may always find delight in these paschal mysteries, so that the renewal constantly at work within us may be the cause of our unending joy. Through Christ our Lord. **Amen.**

PREFACE *(Easter, p. 25)*

COMMUNION ANTIPHON
The Good Shepherd has risen, who laid down his life for his sheep and willingly died for his flock, alleluia.

PRAYER AFTER COMMUNION
Look upon your flock, kind Shepherd, and be pleased to settle in eternal pastures the sheep you have redeemed by the Precious Blood of your Son. Who lives and reigns for ever and ever. **Amen.**

SOLEMN BLESSING *(Optional, p. 355)*

DISMISSAL *(p. 72)*

5th Sunday of Easter

Just about everyone has experienced a power outage at some time in their life. With our modern dependence on electricity, when it fails we can find ourselves at a loss, uncertain how to accomplish even the most ordinary tasks. We resort to substitutes, such as batteries, generators, candles. Depending on how long the outage lasts, we begin to alter our patterns. Life just isn't the same when we lose our connection to the power supply.

And so it is with the spiritual life. If we lose our connection to Christ, the source of all spiritual life, we become spiritually disoriented. In those moments we can find ourselves searching for substitutes that will give us at least a temporary security but that ultimately will fail us and increase our loneliness. The difference is that the power of Christ's love is never turned off. Rather, we sometimes unplug ourselves.

If we are not tapped into the source of spiritual life – into Christ, the true vine – if we are not fed by the sap of Christ's love, our spirit withers and dies, just as our bodies wither and die if we do not receive sufficient nourishment to sustain them.

As we pray this week, let us ask for the grace to remain connected to our God, because apart from him we can do nothing.

Rev. Leonard Altilia, SJ
Montréal, QC

ENTRANCE ANTIPHON *(Cf. Psalm 97.1-2)*
O sing a new song to the Lord, for he has worked wonders; in the sight of the nations he has shown his deliverance, alleluia.

INTRODUCTORY RITES *(p. 8)*

COLLECT
Almighty ever-living God, constantly accomplish the Paschal Mystery within us, that those you were pleased to make new in Holy Baptism may, under your protective care, bear much fruit and come to the joys of life eternal. Through our Lord Jesus Christ, your Son, who lives and reigns with you in the unity of the Holy Spirit, God, for ever and ever. **Amen.**

FIRST READING *(Acts 9.26-31)*
When Saul had come to Jerusalem, he attempted to join the disciples; and they were all afraid of him, for they did not believe that he was a disciple. But Barnabas took him, brought him to the Apostles, and described for them how on the road he had seen the Lord, who had spoken to him, and how in Damascus Saul had spoken boldly in the name of Jesus. So Saul went in and out among them in Jerusalem, speaking boldly in the name of the Lord. He spoke and argued with the Hellenists; but they were attempting to kill him. When the believers learned of it, they brought Saul down to Caesarea and sent him off to Tarsus. Meanwhile the Church throughout Judea, Galilee, and Samaria had peace and was built up. Living in the fear of the Lord and in the comfort of the Holy Spirit, it increased in numbers.
    The word of the Lord. **Thanks be to God.**

RESPONSORIAL PSALM *(Psalm 22)*

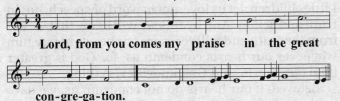

Lord, from you comes my praise in the great con-gre-ga-tion.

℞. **Lord, from you comes my praise**
in the great congregation.
or **Alleluia!**

My vows I will pay before those who · **fear_him.**
The poor shall eat · **and** be satisfied;
those who seek him shall · **praise** the Lord.
May your hearts live · **for**-ever. ℞.

All the ends of the earth shall remember
 and turn to the · **Lord;**
and all the families of the nations shall
 wor-·**ship** be-fore_him.
To him, indeed, shall all who sleep in the · **earth**
 bow down;
before him shall bow all who go down
 to · **the** dust. ℞.

I shall live for him. Posterity will · **serve_him;**
future generations will be told a-·**bout** the Lord,
and proclaim his deliverance to a people
 · **yet** un-born,
saying that he · **has** done_it. ℞.

To hear the Sunday Psalms, visit www.livingwithchrist.ca.

SECOND READING *(1 John 3.18-24)*

Little children, let us love, not in word or speech, but in truth and action. And by this we will know that we are from the truth and will reassure our hearts before him whenever our hearts condemn us; for God is greater than our hearts, and God knows everything.

Beloved, if our hearts do not condemn us, we have boldness before God; and we receive from him whatever we ask, because we obey his commandments and do what pleases him.

And this is his commandment, that we should believe in the name of his Son Jesus Christ and love one another, just as he has commanded us. Whoever obeys his commandments abides in him, and he abides in them. And by this we know that he abides in us, by the Spirit that he has given us.

The word of the Lord. **Thanks be to God.**

GOSPEL ACCLAMATION *(John 15.4, 5)*

Alleluia. Alleluia. Abide in me as I abide in you, says the Lord; my branches bear much fruit. **Alleluia.**

GOSPEL *(John 15.1-8)*

The Lord be with you. **And with your spirit.** A reading from the holy Gospel according to John. **Glory to you, O Lord.**

Jesus said to his disciples: "I am the true vine, and my Father is the vinegrower. He removes every branch in me that bears no fruit. Every branch that bears fruit he prunes to make it bear more fruit. You have already been cleansed by the word that I have spoken to you.

"Abide in me as I abide in you. Just as the branch cannot bear fruit by itself unless it abides in the vine, neither can you unless you abide in me. I am the vine, you are the branches. Whoever abides in me and I in them bears much fruit, because apart from me you can do nothing.

"Whoever does not abide in me is thrown away like a branch and withers; such branches are gathered, thrown into the fire, and burned.

"If you abide in me, and my words abide in you, ask for whatever you wish, and it will be done for you. My Father is glorified by this, that you bear much fruit and become my disciples."

The Gospel of the Lord. **Praise to you, Lord Jesus Christ.**

PROFESSION OF FAITH *(p. 14)*

PRAYER OF THE FAITHFUL

The following intentions are suggestions only.
There are more suggestions at www.livingwithchrist.ca.

R. **Lord, hear our prayer.**

For the Church, striving to share the Good News of the Resurrection, we pray to the Lord: R.

For all who make decisions that affect the lives of others, we pray to the Lord: R.

For all who remain entombed in darkness and for all who seek to liberate them, we pray to the Lord: R.

For Easter hope in our eucharistic community, we pray to the Lord: R.

PREPARATION OF THE GIFTS *(p. 17)*

PRAYER OVER THE OFFERINGS
O God, who by the wonderful exchange effected in this sacrifice have made us partakers of the one supreme Godhead, grant, we pray, that, as we have come to know your truth, we may make it ours by a worthy way of life. Through Christ our Lord. **Amen.**

PREFACE *(Easter, p. 25)*

COMMUNION ANTIPHON *(Cf. John 15.1, 5)*
I am the true vine and you are the branches, says the Lord. Whoever remains in me, and I in him, bears fruit in plenty, alleluia.

PRAYER AFTER COMMUNION
Graciously be present to your people, we pray, O Lord, and lead those you have imbued with heavenly mysteries to pass from former ways to newness of life. Through Christ our Lord. **Amen.**

SOLEMN BLESSING *(Optional, p. 355)*

DISMISSAL *(p. 72)*

May Saints' Days

The following saints are traditionally remembered in May in Canada.

Saint Joseph the Worker . . . . May 1
Saint Pius V

Saint Athanasius . . . . May 2

Saints Philip and James . . . . May 3

Blessed Marie-Léonie Paradis . . . . May 4

Saint François de Laval . . . . May 6

Blessed Catherine of Saint Augustine . . . . May 8

Saint John of Avila . . . . May 10

Saints Nereus and Achilleus . . . . May 12
Saint Pancras

Our Lady of Fatima . . . . May 13

Saint Matthias . . . . May 14

Saint John I . . . . May 18

Saint Bernardine of Siena . . . . May 20

Saint Christopher Magallanes . . . . May 21
  and Companions
Saint Eugène de Mazenod

Saint Rita of Cascia . . . . May 22

Blessed Louis-Zéphirin Moreau . . . . May 24

Saint Bede the Venerable . . . . May 25
Saint Gregory VII
Saint Mary Magdalene de' Pazzi

Saint Philip Neri . . . . May 26

Saint Augustine of Canterbury . . . . May 27

Saint Paul VI . . . . May 29

6th Sunday of Easter

A beautiful aspect of creation is the congruence of spiritual law and natural law. It is as though God uses the the created world to deepen our understanding of the spiritual order. And so it is with love, as Jesus teaches us in today's Gospel.

Jesus says we are to abide in his love, as he abides in the love of the Father, and that in order to do so, we must love others. As with forgiveness or mercy or grace, we will only receive in the measure we extend these gifts to others. As a cistern can only receive the flow of fresh water when there is an outlet from it, if we are to be immersed in the stream of God's love, then love must flow through us freely to the people around us.

Jesus tells us an abundant outpouring of God's love is available to us, his friends, and yet so many of us don't experience the blessing or the fruit of that in full measure. The Gospel today would point us to the outlet valve as the first place to look for a remedy to this.

Fear, pride, hurt, criticisms, selfishness are impediments to love. Let us pray for the grace of humility, that we might see one another through the eyes of Christ and serve freely in love.

Kathleen Giffin
Hinton, AB

National Collection for the Pope's Pastoral Works

ENTRANCE ANTIPHON *(Cf. Isaiah 48.20)*
Proclaim a joyful sound and let it be heard; proclaim to the ends of the earth: The Lord has freed his people, alleluia.

INTRODUCTORY RITES *(p. 8)*

COLLECT
Grant, almighty God, that we may celebrate with heartfelt devotion these days of joy, which we keep in honour of the risen Lord, and that what we relive in remembrance we may always hold to in what we do. Through our Lord Jesus Christ, your Son, who lives and reigns with you in the unity of the Holy Spirit, God, for ever and ever. **Amen.**

FIRST READING *(Acts 10.25-26, 34-35, 44-48)*
On Peter's arrival, Cornelius, a centurion of the Italian cohort, met him, and falling at his feet, worshipped him. But Peter made him get up, saying, "Stand up; I am only a man."

Then Peter began to speak, "I truly understand that God shows no partiality, but in every nation anyone who fears him and does what is right is acceptable to him."

While Peter was still speaking, the Holy Spirit fell upon all who heard the word. The circumcised believers who had come with Peter were astounded that the gift of the Holy Spirit had been poured out even on the Gentiles, for they heard them speaking in tongues and extolling God.

Then Peter said, "Can anyone withhold the water for baptizing these people who have received the Holy Spirit just as we have?" So he ordered them to be baptized in the name of Jesus Christ. Then they invited him to stay for several days.

The word of the Lord. **Thanks be to God.**

RESPONSORIAL PSALM *(Psalm 98)*

R. **The Lord has revealed his victory**
in the sight of the nations.
or **Alleluia!**

O sing to the Lord · **a** new song,
for he has done · **marvel**-lous things.
His right hand and his · **ho**-ly arm
have · **brought** him victory. R.

The Lord has made · **known** his victory;
he has revealed his vindication
    in the · **sight_of** the nations.
He has remembered his · **stead**-fast love
and faithfulness to the · **house** of Israel. R.

All the ends of the · **earth** have seen
the victory · **of** our God.
Make a joyful noise to the Lord, · **all** the earth;
break forth into joyous · **song_and** sing praises. R.

SECOND READING *(1 John 4.7-10)*
Beloved, let us love one another, because love is from God; everyone who loves is born of God and knows God. Whoever does not love does not know God, for God is love.

God's love was revealed among us in this way: God sent his only-begotten Son into the world so that we might live through him. In this is love, not that we loved God but that he loved us and sent his Son to be the atoning sacrifice for our sins.

The word of the Lord. **Thanks be to God.**

GOSPEL ACCLAMATION *(John 14.23)*
Alleluia. Alleluia. Those who love me will keep my word, and my Father will love them, and we will come to them. **Alleluia.**

GOSPEL *(John 15.9-17)*
The Lord be with you. **And with your spirit.** A reading from the holy Gospel according to John. **Glory to you, O Lord.**

Jesus said to his disciples: "As the Father has loved me, so I have loved you; abide in my love. If you keep my commandments, you will abide in my love, just as I have kept my Father's commandments and abide in his love.

"I have said these things to you so that my joy may be in you, and that your joy may be complete. This is my commandment, that you love one another as I have loved you. No one has greater love than this, to lay down one's life for one's friends.

"You are my friends if you do what I command you. I do not call you servants any longer, because the servant does not know what the master is doing; but I have called you friends, because I have made known to you everything that I have heard from my Father.

"You did not choose me but I chose you. And I appointed you to go and bear fruit, fruit that will last, so that the Father will give you whatever you ask him in my name. I am giving you these commands so that you may love one another."

The Gospel of the Lord. **Praise to you, Lord Jesus Christ.**

PROFESSION OF FAITH (p. 14)

PRAYER OF THE FAITHFUL

The following intentions are suggestions only.
There are more suggestions at www.livingwithchrist.ca.

R. **Lord, hear our prayer.**

For the Church, witness to the saving life, death and Resurrection of Jesus, we pray to the Lord: R.

For just and sound stewardship of God's creation, we pray to the Lord: R.

For those among us who suffer silently, we pray to the Lord: R.

For the special needs of this community gathered here today, we pray to the Lord: R.

PREPARATION OF THE GIFTS (p. 17)

PRAYER OVER THE OFFERINGS

May our prayers rise up to you, O Lord, together with the sacrificial offerings, so that, purified by your graciousness, we may be conformed to the mysteries of your mighty love. Through Christ our Lord. **Amen.**

PREFACE (Easter, p. 25)

COMMUNION ANTIPHON (John 14.15-16)

If you love me, keep my commandments, says the Lord, and I will ask the Father and he will send you another Paraclete, to abide with you for ever, alleluia.

PRAYER AFTER COMMUNION

Almighty ever-living God, who restore us to eternal life in the Resurrection of Christ, increase in us, we pray, the fruits of this paschal Sacrament and pour into our hearts the strength of this saving food. Through Christ our Lord. **Amen.**

SOLEMN BLESSING (Optional, p. 355)

DISMISSAL (p. 72)

Ascension of the Lord
World Communications Day
Canada Health Day

When we were children, we were happy and felt safe when we believed that our loved ones were protecting us, especially if our sense of security had not been shaken previously. Jesus promises that if we believe and are baptized, we will be saved. Through the Holy Spirit, we will be able to do great things: we will have an unshaken sense of security.

When we experience hardship, our faith can be tested. Does this mean that our faith is not deep enough? We know what Jesus promised; and yet we doubt, sometimes even despair. Is the Holy Spirit in our hearts? Do we seek his guidance? Do we reach out to God to deepen our faith through Scripture and daily prayer? This will fortify us, helping us to see the workings of the Holy Spirit and maintaining our faith and the sense of security that we had as children. Hardship is inevitable, but through prayer we gain wisdom and understanding.

On Ascension Sunday, let us pray for the Holy Spirit to guide us on our journey. May God reveal to us the gift of wisdom and revelation of which Paul writes in the second reading. Praise God with great joy and share the good news – Jesus, through his death, resurrection and ascension, is still with us. God is good!

Ildiko O'Dacre
Cambridge, ON

ENTRANCE ANTIPHON *(Acts 1.11)*
**Men of Galilee, why gaze in wonder at the heavens?
This Jesus whom you saw ascending into heaven
will return as you saw him go, alleluia.**

INTRODUCTORY RITES *(p. 8)*

COLLECT
Gladden us with holy joys, almighty God, and make us
rejoice with devout thanksgiving, for the Ascension of
Christ your Son is our exaltation, and, where the Head
has gone before in glory, the Body is called to follow in
hope. Through our Lord Jesus Christ, your Son, who
lives and reigns with you in the unity of the Holy Spirit,
God, for ever and ever. **Amen.**

or

Grant, we pray, almighty God, that we, who believe
that your Only Begotten Son, our Redeemer, ascended
this day to the heavens, may in spirit dwell already in
heavenly realms. Who lives and reigns with you in the
unity of the Holy Spirit, God, for ever and ever. **Amen.**

FIRST READING *(Acts 1.1-11)*
In the first book, Theophilus, I wrote about all that
Jesus did and taught from the beginning until the day
when he was taken up to heaven, after giving instruc-
tions through the Holy Spirit to the Apostles whom he
had chosen. After his suffering he presented himself
alive to them by many convincing proofs, appearing
to them during forty days and speaking about the
kingdom of God.

While staying with them, he ordered them not to
leave Jerusalem, but to wait there for the promise of the

Father. "This," he said, "is what you have heard from me; for John baptized with water, but you will be baptized with the Holy Spirit not many days from now."

So when they had come together, they asked him, "Lord, is this the time when you will restore the kingdom to Israel?" He replied, "It is not for you to know the times or periods that the Father has set by his own authority. But you will receive power when the Holy Spirit has come upon you; and you will be my witnesses in Jerusalem, in all Judea and Samaria, and to the ends of the earth."

When he had said this, as they were watching, he was lifted up, and a cloud took him out of their sight. While he was going and they were gazing up toward heaven, suddenly two men in white robes stood by them. They said, "Men of Galilee, why do you stand looking up toward heaven? This Jesus, who has been taken up from you into heaven, will come in the same way as you saw him go into heaven."

The word of the Lord. **Thanks be to God.**

RESPONSORIAL PSALM *(Psalm 47)*

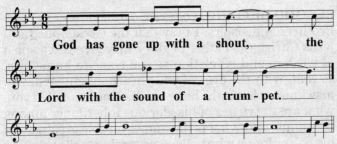

God has gone up with a shout, the Lord with the sound of a trum-pet.

℟. **God has gone up with a shout,
the Lord with the sound of a trumpet.**

or **Alleluia!**

Clap your hands, all · **you** peoples;
shout to God with loud songs · **of** joy.
For the Lord, the Most High, · **is** awesome,
a great king over · **all** the earth. ℟.

God has gone up · **with_a** shout,
the Lord with the sound of · **a** trumpet.
Sing praises to God, · **sing** praises;
sing praises to our · **King,** sing praises. ℟.

For God is the king of all · **the** earth;
sing praises · **with_a** Psalm.
God is king over · **the** nations;
God sits on his · **ho**-ly throne. ℟.

©2009 Gordon Johnston/Novalis

To hear the Sunday Psalms, visit www.livingwithchrist.ca.

An alternate reading follows.

SECOND READING *(Ephesians 1.17-23)*

Brothers and sisters: I pray that the God of our Lord Jesus Christ, the Father of glory, may give you a spirit of wisdom and revelation as you come to know him, so that, with the eyes of your heart enlightened, you may know what is the hope to which he has called you, what are the riches of his glorious inheritance among the saints, and what is the immeasurable greatness of his power for us who believe, according to the working of his great power.

God put this power to work in Christ when he raised him from the dead and seated him at his right hand in the heavenly places, far above all rule and authority and power and dominion, and above every name that is named, not only in this age but also in the age to come.

And he has put all things under his feet and has made him the head over all things for the Church, which is his body, the fullness of him who fills all in all.

The word of the Lord. **Thanks be to God.**

or

SECOND READING *(Ephesians 4.1-13)*

For the shorter version, omit the indented part.

Brothers and sisters: I, the prisoner in the Lord, beg you to lead a life worthy of the calling to which you have been called, with all humility and gentleness, with patience, bearing with one another in love, making every effort to maintain the unity of the Spirit in the bond of peace. There is one body and one Spirit, just as you were called to the one hope of your calling, one Lord, one faith, one baptism, one God and Father of all, who is above all and through all and in all. But each of us was given grace according to the measure of Christ's gift.

> Therefore it is said, "When he ascended on high he made captivity itself a captive; he gave gifts to his people." When it says, "He ascended," what does it mean but that he had also descended into the lower parts of the earth? He who descended is the same one who ascended far above all the heavens, so that he might fill all things.

The gifts he gave were that some would be Apostles, some Prophets, some evangelists, some pastors and teachers, to equip the saints for the work of ministry, for building up the body of Christ, until all of us come to the unity of the faith and of the knowledge of the Son of God, to maturity, to the measure of the full stature of Christ.

The word of the Lord. **Thanks be to God.**

GOSPEL ACCLAMATION (Matthew 28.19, 20)
Alleluia. Alleluia. Go make disciples of all nations. I am with you always, to the end of the age. **Alleluia.**

GOSPEL (Mark 16.15-20)
The Lord be with you. **And with your spirit.** A reading from the holy Gospel according to Mark. **Glory to you, O Lord.**

Jesus appeared to the eleven, and he said to them, "Go into all the world and proclaim the good news to the whole creation. The one who believes and is baptized will be saved; but the one who does not believe will be condemned. And these signs will accompany those who believe: by using my name they will cast out demons; they will speak in new tongues; they will pick up snakes in their hands, and if they drink any deadly thing, it will not hurt them; they will lay their hands on the sick, and they will recover."

So then the Lord Jesus, after he had spoken to them, was taken up into heaven and sat down at the right hand of God. And they went out and proclaimed the good news everywhere, while the Lord worked with them and confirmed the message by the signs that accompanied it.

The Gospel of the Lord. **Praise to you, Lord Jesus Christ.**

PROFESSION OF FAITH *(p. 14)*

PRAYER OF THE FAITHFUL
The following intentions are suggestions only.
There are more suggestions at www.livingwithchrist.ca.

R. **Lord, hear our prayer.**

For the Church, sent to proclaim the Good News to all, we pray to the Lord: R.

On this World Communications Day, for people in the different forms of media working to build a just society, we pray to the Lord: R.

For the sick, the dying and all who suffer, we pray to the Lord: R.

For mothers everywhere, nurturing the next generation, and for those who share in childrearing, we pray to the Lord: R.

For the members of this community, formed by our encounters with the risen Lord and sent forth to serve, we pray to the Lord: R.

PREPARATION OF THE GIFTS *(p. 17)*

PRAYER OVER THE OFFERINGS

We offer sacrifice now in supplication, O Lord, to honour the wondrous Ascension of your Son: grant, we pray, that through this most holy exchange we, too, may rise up to the heavenly realms. Through Christ our Lord. **Amen.**

PREFACE *(Ascension I-II, p. 28)*

COMMUNION ANTIPHON *(Matthew 28.20)*

Behold, I am with you always, even to the end of the age, alleluia.

PRAYER AFTER COMMUNION

Almighty ever-living God, who allow those on earth to celebrate divine mysteries, grant, we pray, that Christian hope may draw us onward to where our nature is united with you. Through Christ our Lord. **Amen.**

SOLEMN BLESSING — ASCENSION *(Optional)*

Bow down for the blessing.

May almighty God bless you, for on this very day his Only Begotten Son pierced the heights of heaven and unlocked for you the way to ascend to where he is. **Amen.**

May he grant that, as Christ after his Resurrection was seen plainly by his disciples, so when he comes as Judge he may show himself merciful to you for all eternity. **Amen.**

And may you, who believe he is seated with the Father in his majesty, know with joy the fulfillment of his promise to stay with you until the end of time. **Amen.**

And may the blessing of almighty God, the Father, and the Son, and the Holy Spirit, come down on you and remain with you for ever. **Amen.**

DISMISSAL *(p. 72)*

Pentecost Sunday

In today's first reading, we read a description of love in the midst of chaos. It's Pentecost and it's terrifying. Fire. Howling winds. The followers who had assembled in Jerusalem were gathered in this place. They must have been talking loudly among themselves in fear and confusion, each in their own language. Imagine the cacophony!

In this mayhem, what did God do? He used the spectacle to get their attention and then spoke to each in their own language. One voice, many languages. For what purpose? To share the good news, person to person. God was saying, here in the midst of bedlam, "I am calling you. I love YOU."

Fast forward to Sunday Mass in 2024, which is reverent worship in a peaceful place. Let this time and place get your attention. I know I have to check myself so as not to forget what is really taking place. Unlike Mass, life is noisy and our culture is chaotic. Maybe your life is both. With the psalmist, consider the majesty of God. His works in nature are astounding. When God sends forth his spirit, he renews the face of the earth. The psalmist end with this supplication: May the Lord rejoice in his works! We are the work of his hands and God wants us to know his love is personal. He is talking to *us*.

Johanne Brownrigg
Orleans, ON

ENTRANCE ANTIPHON *(Wisdom 1.7)*

The Spirit of the Lord has filled the whole world and that which contains all things understands what is said, alleluia.

or (Romans 5.5; cf. 8.11)

The love of God has been poured into our hearts through the Spirit of God dwelling within us, alleluia.

INTRODUCTORY RITES *(p. 8)*

COLLECT

O God, who by the mystery of today's great feast sanctify your whole Church in every people and nation, pour out, we pray, the gifts of the Holy Spirit across the face of the earth and, with the divine grace that was at work when the Gospel was first proclaimed, fill now once more the hearts of believers. Through our Lord Jesus Christ, your Son, who lives and reigns with you in the unity of the Holy Spirit, God, for ever and ever. **Amen.**

FIRST READING *(Acts 2.1-11)*

When the day of Pentecost had come, they were all together in one place. And suddenly from heaven there came a sound like the rush of a violent wind, and it filled the entire house where they were sitting. Divided tongues, as of fire, appeared among them, and a tongue rested on each of them. All of them were filled with the Holy Spirit and began to speak in other languages, as the Spirit gave them ability.

Now there were devout Jews from every nation under heaven living in Jerusalem. And at this sound the crowd gathered and was bewildered, because each one heard them speaking in their own language. Amazed and astonished, they asked, "Are not all these who are speaking Galileans? And how is it that we hear, each of us, in our own language? Parthians, Medes, Elamites, and residents of Mesopotamia, Judea and Cappadocia, Pontus and Asia, Phrygia and Pamphylia, Egypt and the parts of Libya belonging to Cyrene, and visitors from Rome, both Jews and converts, Cretans and Arabs — in our own languages we hear them speaking about God's deeds of power."

The word of the Lord. **Thanks be to God.**

RESPONSORIAL PSALM *(Psalm 104)*

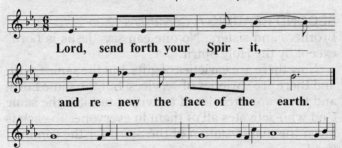

Lord, send forth your Spirit, and renew the face of the earth.

R. **Lord, send forth your Spirit,
and renew the face of the earth.**
or **Alleluia!**

Bless the Lord, O · **my** soul.
O Lord my God, you are very · **great.**
O Lord, how manifold · **are** your works!
The earth is full of · **your** creatures. R.

When you take away · **their** breath,
they die and return to their · **dust.**
When you send forth your spirit,
    they · **are** cre-ated;
and you renew the face of · **the** earth. R.

May the glory of the Lord endure · **for**-ever;
may the Lord rejoice in his · **works.**
May my meditation be · **pleasing** to him,
for I rejoice in · **the** Lord. R.

©2009 Gordon Johnston/Novalis

To hear the Sunday Psalms, visit www.livingwithchrist.ca.

An alternate reading follows.

SECOND READING *(1 Corinthians 12.3b-7, 12-13)*
Brothers and sisters: No one can say "Jesus is Lord"
except by the Holy Spirit.

Now there are varieties of gifts, but the same Spirit;
and there are varieties of services, but the same Lord;
and there are varieties of activities, but it is the same
God who activates all of them in everyone. To each is
given the manifestation of the Spirit for the common
good.

For just as the body is one and has many members,
and all the members of the body, though many, are one
body, so it is with Christ. For in the one Spirit we were
all baptized into one body — Jews or Greeks, slaves
or free — and we were all made to drink of one Spirit.

The word of the Lord. **Thanks be to God.**

or

SECOND READING *(Galatians 5.16-25)*

Brothers and sisters: Live by the Spirit, I say, and do not gratify the desires of the flesh. For what the flesh desires is opposed to the Spirit, and what the Spirit desires is opposed to the flesh; for these are opposed to each other, to prevent you from doing what you want.

But if you are led by the Spirit, you are not subject to the law. Now the works of the flesh are obvious: fornication, impurity, licentiousness, idolatry, sorcery, enmities, strife, jealousy, anger, quarrels, dissensions, factions, envy, drunkenness, carousing, and things like these. I am warning you, as I warned you before: those who do such things will not inherit the kingdom of God.

By contrast, the fruit of the Spirit is love, joy, peace, patience, kindness, generosity, faithfulness, gentleness, and self-control. There is no law against such things. And those who belong to Christ Jesus have crucified the flesh with its passions and desires. If we live by the Spirit, let us also be guided by the Spirit.

The word of the Lord. **Thanks be to God.**

SEQUENCE

1. Ho - ly Spir - it, Lord di - vine,
2. Come, O Fa - ther of the poor,

Come from heights of heav'n and shine,
Come, whose treas - ured gifts en - sure,

Come with bless - ed ra - diance bright!
Come, our heart's un - fail - ing light!

3. Of consolers, wisest, best,
   And our soul's most welcome guest,
   Sweet refreshment, sweet repose.

4. In our labour, rest most sweet,
   Pleasant coolness in the heat,
   Consolation in our woes.

5. Light most blessed, shine with grace
   In our heart's most secret place,
   Fill your faithful through and through.

6. Left without your presence here,
   Life itself would disappear,
   Nothing thrives apart from you!

7. Cleanse our soiled hearts of sin,
   Arid souls refresh within,
   Wounded lives to health restore.

8. Bend the stubborn heart and will,
   Melt the frozen, warm the chill,
   Guide the wayward home once more!

9. On the faithful who are true
   and profess their faith in you,
   In your sev'nfold gift descend!

10. Give us virtue's sure reward,
    Give us your salvation, Lord,
    Give us joys that never end!

Text: *Veni Sancte Spiritus;* tr. E. Caswell; adapt. © *Peter J. Scagnelli.*
Tune: ©*1995 Albert Dunn*

GOSPEL ACCLAMATION
Alleluia. Alleluia. Come, Holy Spirit, fill the hearts of
your faithful and kindle in them the fire of your love.
Alleluia.

An alternate Gospel follows.

GOSPEL *(John 20.19-23)*
The Lord be with you. **And with your spirit.**
A reading from the holy Gospel according to John.
Glory to you, O Lord.

It was evening on the day Jesus rose from the dead,
the first day of the week, and the doors of the house
where the disciples had met were locked for fear of
the Jews. Jesus came and stood among them and said,
"Peace be with you." After he said this, he showed
them his hands and his side. Then the disciples
rejoiced when they saw the Lord.

Jesus said to them again, "Peace be with you. As the
Father has sent me, so I send you."

When he had said this, he breathed on them and said to them, "Receive the Holy Spirit. If you forgive the sins of any, they are forgiven them; if you retain the sins of any, they are retained."

The Gospel of the Lord. **Praise to you, Lord Jesus Christ.**

or

GOSPEL *(John 15.26-27; 16.12-15)*
The Lord be with you. **And with your spirit.**
A reading from the holy Gospel according to John.
Glory to you, O Lord.

Jesus said to the disciples: "When the Advocate comes, whom I will send to you from the Father, the Spirit of truth who comes from the Father, he will testify on my behalf. You also are to testify because you have been with me from the beginning.

"I still have many things to say to you, but you cannot bear them now. When the Spirit of truth comes, he will guide you into all the truth; for he will not speak on his own, but will speak whatever he hears, and he will declare to you the things that are to come. He will glorify me, because he will take what is mine and declare it to you.

"All that the Father has is mine. For this reason I said that he will take what is mine and declare it to you."

The Gospel of the Lord. **Praise to you, Lord Jesus Christ.**

PROFESSION OF FAITH *(p. 14)*

PRAYER OF THE FAITHFUL

The following intentions are suggestions only.
There are more suggestions at www.livingwithchrist.ca.

R̥. **Send forth your Spirit, O Lord.**

For wisdom and courage among leaders in the Church, addressing the needs of the suffering and forgotten, we pray to the Lord: R̥.

For youth, eager to be of service to their neighbour in need, we pray to the Lord: R̥.

For the newest members of the Church, inspiring joy and faithful witness to the mission of Jesus in the world, we pray to the Lord: R̥.

For ourselves, guided by the Holy Spirit to renew the face of the earth, we pray to the Lord: R̥.

PREPARATION OF THE GIFTS (p. 17)

PRAYER OVER THE OFFERINGS
Grant, we pray, O Lord, that, as promised by your Son, the Holy Spirit may reveal to us more abundantly the hidden mystery of this sacrifice and graciously lead us into all truth. Through Christ our Lord. **Amen.**

PREFACE (Pentecost, p. 29)

COMMUNION ANTIPHON (Acts 2.4, 11)
They were all filled with the Holy Spirit and spoke of the marvels of God, alleluia.

PRAYER AFTER COMMUNION
O God, who bestow heavenly gifts upon your Church, safeguard, we pray, the grace you have given, that the gift of the Holy Spirit poured out upon her may retain all its force and that this spiritual food may gain her

abundance of eternal redemption. Through Christ our Lord. **Amen.**

SOLEMN BLESSING — THE HOLY SPIRIT
(Optional)
Bow down for the blessing.

May God, the Father of lights, who was pleased to enlighten the disciples' minds by the outpouring of the Spirit, the Paraclete, grant you gladness by his blessing and make you always abound with the gifts of the same Spirit. **Amen.**

May the wondrous flame that appeared above the disciples powerfully cleanse your hearts from every evil and pervade them with its purifying light. **Amen.**

And may God, who has been pleased to unite many tongues in the profession of one faith, give you perseverance in that same faith and, by believing, may you journey from hope to clear vision. **Amen.**

And may the blessing of almighty God, the Father, and the Son, and the Holy Spirit, come down on you and remain with you for ever. **Amen.**

DISMISSAL
1 Go forth, the Mass is ended, alleluia, alleluia!
2 Go in peace, alleluia, alleluia!

Thanks be to God, al-le-lu-ia, al-le - lu - ia!

R. **Thanks be to God, alleluia, alleluia!**

Most Holy Trinity

Today we celebrate Trinity Sunday. In the readings, we catch glimpses of some attributes of the Trinity. These glimpses can aid in our understanding of one of the mysteries of our faith and can inform our daily living.

While the readings have a common theme – God's eternal and steadfast love – the focus of the Gospel is discipleship. Here Jesus calls us to take up our identity as children of God and to share in the life of the Trinity. We may feel unworthy and hesitate to accept this divine invitation. However, we have nothing to fear. God is love and our only task is to love God in return.

This is easier said than done because love demands things of us. Love requires a high level of self-giving and engagement with others. We know this from our own experiences and from the example of Jesus. But, with the help of the Spirit, we are able to imitate, though imperfectly, Trinitarian love in our relationships with others and with creation.

I like to think of the Trinity as a perfect relationship. One that is informed by mutual respect and consideration. One where love flows freely and where each person delights in the others. We are so very blessed that God calls us to share in this life of grace.

Louise McEwan
Silverton, BC

ENTRANCE ANTIPHON
Blest be God the Father, and the Only Begotten Son of God, and also the Holy Spirit, for he has shown us his merciful love.

INTRODUCTORY RITES (p. 8)

COLLECT
God our Father, who by sending into the world the Word of truth and the Spirit of sanctification made known to the human race your wondrous mystery, grant us, we pray, that in professing the true faith, we may acknowledge the Trinity of eternal glory and adore your Unity, powerful in majesty. Through our Lord Jesus Christ, your Son, who lives and reigns with you in the unity of the Holy Spirit, God, for ever and ever. **Amen.**

FIRST READING (Deuteronomy 4.32-34, 39-40)
Moses spoke to the people saying, "Ask now about former ages, long before your own, ever since the day that God created man on the earth; ask from one end of heaven to the other: 'Has anything so great as this ever happened or has its like ever been heard of?'

"Has any people ever heard the voice of a god speaking out of a fire, as you have heard, and lived? Or has any god ever attempted to go and take a nation for himself from the midst of another nation, by trials, by signs and wonders, by war, by a mighty hand and an outstretched arm, and by terrifying displays of power, as the Lord your God did for you in Egypt before your very eyes?

"So acknowledge today and take to heart that the Lord is God in heaven above and on the earth beneath;

there is no other. Keep his statutes and his command-ments, which I am commanding you today for your own well-being and that of your descendants after you, so that you may long remain in the land that the Lord your God is giving you for all time."

The word of the Lord. **Thanks be to God.**

RESPONSORIAL PSALM *(Psalm 33)*

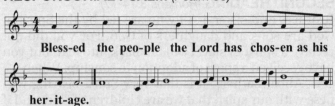

Bless-ed the peo-ple the Lord has chos-en as his her-it-age.

R̲. **Blessed the people the Lord has chosen
as his heritage.**

The word of the · **Lord** is upright,
and all his work is · **done** in faithfulness.
He loves · **righteousness** and justice;
the earth is full of the steadfast · **love_of**
    the Lord. R̲.

By the word of the Lord the · **heavens** were made,
and all their host by the breath · **of** his mouth.
For he spoke, and it · **came** to be;
he commanded, and · **it** stood firm. R̲.

Truly the eye of the Lord is on · **those**
    who fear_him,
on those who hope in his · **stead**-fast love,
to deliver their · **souls** from death,
and to keep them a·-**live** in famine. R̲.

Our soul waits · **for** the Lord;
he is our · **help** and shield.
Let your steadfast love, O Lord, · **be** up-on_us,
even as we · **hope** in you. R̶.

To hear the Sunday Psalms, visit www.livingwithchrist.ca.

SECOND READING *(Romans 8.14-17)*

Brothers and sisters: All who are led by the Spirit of God are sons and daughters of God. For you did not receive a spirit of slavery to fall back into fear, but you have received a spirit of adoption to sonship. When we cry, "Abba! Father!" it is that very Spirit bearing witness with our spirit that we are children of God, and if children, then heirs, heirs of God and joint heirs with Christ — if in fact, we suffer with him so that we may also be glorified with him.

The word of the Lord. **Thanks be to God.**

GOSPEL ACCLAMATION *(See Revelation 1.8)*

Alleluia. Alleluia. Glory to the Father, the Son, and the Holy Spirit: to God who is, who was, and who is to come. **Alleluia.**

GOSPEL *(Matthew 28.16-20)*

The Lord be with you. **And with your spirit.** A reading from the holy Gospel according to Matthew. **Glory to you, O Lord.**

The eleven disciples went to Galilee, to the mountain to which Jesus had directed them. When they saw him, they worshipped him; but some doubted.

And Jesus came and said to them, "All authority in heaven and on earth has been given to me. Go therefore and make disciples of all nations, baptizing them in the name of the Father and of the Son and of the Holy Spirit, and teaching them to obey everything that I have commanded you.

"And remember, I am with you always, to the end of the age."

The Gospel of the Lord. **Praise to you, Lord Jesus Christ.**

PROFESSION OF FAITH *(p. 14)*

PRAYER OF THE FAITHFUL

The following intentions are suggestions only.
There are more suggestions at www.livingwithchrist.ca.

℟. **Lord, hear our prayer.**

For the People of God, striving to embody the love of the Trinity, we pray to the Lord: ℟.

For leaders of nations, working for peace in war-torn regions of the world, we pray to the Lord: ℟.

For families responding to the call to be a community of God's love, we pray to the Lord: ℟.

For our parish community, especially in our efforts to reflect God's love, we pray to the Lord: ℟.

PREPARATION OF THE GIFTS *(p. 17)*

PRAYER OVER THE OFFERINGS
Sanctify by the invocation of your name, we pray, O Lord our God, this oblation of our service, and by it make of us an eternal offering to you. Through Christ our Lord. **Amen.**

PREFACE *(Trinity, p. 29)*

COMMUNION ANTIPHON *(Galatians 4.6)*
Since you are children of God, God has sent into your hearts the Spirit of his Son, the Spirit who cries out: Abba, Father.

PRAYER AFTER COMMUNION
May receiving this Sacrament, O Lord our God, bring us health of body and soul, as we confess your eternal holy Trinity and undivided Unity. Through Christ our Lord. **Amen.**

BLESSING AND DISMISSAL *(p. 72)*

June Saints' Days

The following saints are traditionally remembered in June in Canada.

Saint Justin . . . . Jun 1

Saints Marcellinus and Peter . . . . Jun 2

Saint Charles Lwanga and Companions . . . . Jun 3

Saint Boniface . . . . Jun 5

Saint Norbert . . . . Jun 6

Saint Ephrem . . . . Jun 9

Saint Barnabas . . . . Jun 11

Saint Anthony of Padua . . . . Jun 13

Saint Romuald . . . . Jun 19

Saint Aloysius Gonzaga . . . . Jun 21

Saint Paulinus of Nola . . . . Jun 22
Saints John Fisher and Thomas More

The Nativity of Saint John the Baptist . . . . Jun 24

Blesseds Nykyta Budka . . . . Jun 27
   and Vasyl Velychkowsky
Saint Cyril of Alexandria

Saint Irenaeus . . . . Jun 28

Saints Peter and Paul . . . . Jun 29

The First Martyrs of the . . . . Jun 30
   Holy Roman Church

Body and Blood of Christ

From the first time Abraham heard the Word, the people sought to offer sacrifices. The ancient Israelites were not alone in this custom; most ancient Near Eastern religions had some variation of this tradition.

The problem with offering sacrifices to atone for impurities and imperfections, however, is that nothing stays purified permanently. And the God of Abraham and Sarah ultimately desires mercy not sacrifice, forgiveness rather than atonement.

And so this God shows up in body and blood, an infant growing into a man, to offer us a human and divine self for our redemption and example. As the second reading indicates, once Jesus' blood is offered, no other sacrifice could ever compare. One death so that all could have eternal life. And more, this living and dying and rising is an invitation for us to offer ourselves back.

The One who gave a name to Abraham, whispered to Moses from the burning bush, inspired Esther, breathed a baby into Mary has only ever wanted us – as we are – in love. This feast celebrates the way that God holds nothing back from us, gives us all of Jesus, so that we might respond with nothing less than all of ourselves. May it be so.

Leah Perrault
Swift Current, SK

ENTRANCE ANTIPHON (Cf. Psalm 80.17)
He fed them with the finest wheat and satisfied them with honey from the rock.

INTRODUCTORY RITES (p. 8)

COLLECT
O God, who in this wonderful Sacrament have left us a memorial of your Passion, grant us, we pray, so to revere the sacred mysteries of your Body and Blood that we may always experience in ourselves the fruits of your redemption. Who live and reign with God the Father in the unity of the Holy Spirit, God, for ever and ever. **Amen.**

FIRST READING (Exodus 24.3-8)
Moses came and told the people all the words of the Lord and all the ordinances; and all the people answered with one voice, and said, "All the words that the Lord has spoken we will do." And Moses wrote down all the words of the Lord. He rose early in the morning, and built an altar at the foot of the mountain, and set up twelve pillars, corresponding to the twelve tribes of Israel. He sent young men of the children of Israel, who offered burnt offerings and sacrificed oxen as offerings of well-being to the Lord. Moses took half of the blood and put it in basins, and half of the blood he dashed against the altar. Then he took the book of the covenant, and read it in the hearing of the people; and they said, "All that the Lord has spoken we will do, and we will be obedient." Moses took the blood and dashed it on the people, and said, "See the blood of the covenant that the Lord has made with you in accordance with all these words."

   The word of the Lord. **Thanks be to God.**

RESPONSORIAL PSALM *(Psalm 116)*

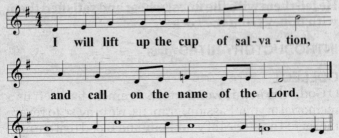

I will lift up the cup of sal - va - tion,

and call on the name of the Lord.

℞. **I will lift up the cup of salvation,**
   and call on the name of the Lord.
or **Alleluia!**

What shall I return to the · **Lord**
for all his bounty to · **me?**
I will lift up the cup of sal--**vation**
and call on the name · **of_the** Lord. ℞.

Precious in the sight of the · **Lord**
is the death of his · **faithful_ones.**
O Lord, I am your servant, the son
   of your · **serving_girl.**
You have loosed · **my** bonds. ℞.

I will offer to you a thanksgiving · **sacrifice**
and call on the name of the · **Lord.**
I will pay my vows to the · **Lord**
in the presence of all · **his** people. ℞.

To hear the Sunday Psalms, visit www.livingwithchrist.ca.

SECOND READING *(Hebrews 9.11-15)*

Brothers and sisters: When Christ came as a high priest of the good things that have come, then through the greater and perfect tent — not made with hands, that is, not of this creation — he entered once for all into the Holy Place, not with the blood of goats and calves, but with his own blood, thus obtaining eternal redemption.

For if the blood of goats and bulls, with the sprinkling of the ashes of a heifer, sanctifies those who have been defiled so that their flesh is purified, how much more will the blood of Christ, who through the eternal Spirit offered himself without blemish to God, purify our conscience from dead works to worship the living God!

For this reason Christ is the mediator of a new covenant, so that those who are called may receive the promised eternal inheritance, because a death has occurred that redeems them from the transgressions under the first covenant.

The word of the Lord. **Thanks be to God.**

SEQUENCE *(Optional)*

This sequence is to be sung. The shorter version begins at the asterisks (p. 413). An earlier version of this Sequence is set to music in CBW III, 693.

1. Laud, O Sion, your salvation,
   laud with hymns of exultation
   Christ, your King and Shepherd true:
   Bring him all the praise you know,
   He is more than you bestow;
   never can you reach his due.

2. Wondrous theme for glad thanksgiving
   is the living and life-giving
   Bread today before you set,
   from his hands of old partaken,
   As we know, by faith unshaken,
   where the Twelve at supper met.

3. Full and clear ring out your chanting,
   let not joy nor grace be wanting.
   From your heart let praises burst.
   For this day the Feast is holden,
   When the institution olden
   of that Supper was rehearsed.

4. Here the new law's new oblation,
   by the new King's revelation,
   Ends the forms of ancient rite.
   Now the new the old effaces,
   Substance now the shadow chases,
   light of day dispels the night.

5. What he did at supper seated,
   Christ ordained to be repeated,
   His remembrance not to cease.
   And his rule for guidance taking,
   Bread and wine we hallow, making,
   thus, our sacrifice of peace.

6. This the truth each Christian learns:
   bread into his own flesh Christ turns,
   To his precious Blood the wine.
   Sight must fail, no thought conceives,
   But a steadfast faith believes,
   resting on a power divine.

7. Here beneath these signs are hidden
   priceless things to sense forbidden.
   Signs alone, not things, we see:
   Blood and flesh as wine, bread broken;
   Yet beneath each wondrous token,
   Christ entire we know to be.

8. All who of this great food partake,
   they sever not the Lord, nor break:
   Christ is whole to all that taste.
   Be one or be a thousand fed
   They eat alike that living Bread,
   eat of him who cannot waste.

9. Good and guilty likewise sharing,
   though their different ends preparing:
   timeless death, or blessed life.
   Life to these, to those damnation,
   Even like participation
   is with unlike outcomes rife.

10. When the sacrament is broken,
    doubt not, but believe as spoken,
    That each severed outward token
    does the very whole contain.
    None that precious gift divides,
    breaking but the sign betides.
    Jesus still the same abides,
    still unbroken he remains.

* * *

11. Hail, the food of Angels given
    to the pilgrim who has striven,
    to the child as bread from heaven,

food alone for spirit meant:
Now the former types fulfilling —
Isaac bound, a victim willing,
Paschal Lamb, its life-blood spilling,
manna to the ancients sent.

12. Bread yourself, good Shepherd, tend us;
Jesus, with your love befriend us.
You refresh us and defend us;
to your lasting goodness send us
That the land of life we see.
Lord, who all things both rule and know,
who on this earth such food bestow,
Grant that with your saints we follow
to that banquet ever hallow,
With them heirs and guests to be.

Text: *translation ©2009 Concacan Inc.*

GOSPEL ACCLAMATION (John 6.51-52)
Alleluia. Alleluia. I am the living bread that came down from heaven, says the Lord; whoever eats of this bread will live forever. **Alleluia.**

GOSPEL (Mark 14.12-16, 22-26)
The Lord be with you. **And with your spirit.**
A reading from the holy Gospel according to Mark.
Glory to you, O Lord.

On the first day of Unleavened Bread, when the Passover lamb is sacrificed, the disciples said to Jesus, "Where do you want us to go and make the preparations for you to eat the Passover?"

So he sent two of his disciples, saying to them, "Go into the city, and a man carrying a jar of water will meet you; follow him, and wherever he enters, say to the owner of the house, 'The Teacher asks, "Where is my guest room where I may eat the Passover with my disciples?"' He will show you a large room upstairs, furnished and ready. Make preparations for us there."

So the disciples set out and went to the city, and found everything as he had told them; and they prepared the Passover meal.

While they were eating, he took a loaf of bread, and after blessing it he broke it, gave it to them, and said, "Take; this is my Body." Then he took a cup, and after giving thanks he gave it to them, and all of them drank from it. He said to them, "This is my Blood of the covenant, which is poured out for many. Truly I tell you, I will never again drink of the fruit of the vine until that day when I drink it new in the kingdom of God."

When they had sung the hymn, they went out to the Mount of Olives.

The Gospel of the Lord. **Praise to you, Lord Jesus Christ.**

PROFESSION OF FAITH *(p. 14)*

PRAYER OF THE FAITHFUL

The following intentions are suggestions only.
There are more suggestions at www.livingwithchrist.ca.

R. **Lord, hear our prayer.**

For the Church, striving to be bread for the world, we pray to the Lord: R.

For people who hunger and thirst for justice, we pray to the Lord: R.

For the sick and the dying, and for those who are lonely, we pray to the Lord: R.

For our parish community, meditating on the Word of Life and walking the path of action, we pray to the Lord: R.

PREPARATION OF THE GIFTS *(p. 17)*

PRAYER OVER THE OFFERINGS
Grant your Church, O Lord, we pray, the gifts of unity and peace, whose signs are to be seen in mystery in the offerings we here present. Through Christ our Lord. **Amen.**

PREFACE *(Holy Eucharist II-I, p. 30)*

COMMUNION ANTIPHON *(John 6.57)*
Whoever eats my flesh and drinks my blood remains in me and I in him, says the Lord.

PRAYER AFTER COMMUNION
Grant, O Lord, we pray, that we may delight for all eternity in that share in your divine life, which is foreshadowed in the present age by our reception of your precious Body and Blood. Who live and reign for ever and ever. **Amen.**

BLESSING AND DISMISSAL *(p. 72)*

10th Sunday in Ordinary Time

In countless tiny ways we are tempted to control others' perceptions of us, the way that we are defined or understood by them. But as painful as they may be, experiences of misunderstanding are an opportunity to develop humility. And they happen to everyone. Even Jesus, God made flesh is accused of being an agent of the devil in today's Gospel. What is his response?

Jesus doesn't defend his own honour when insulted (though he, more than anyone, would be entitled to do so). He doesn't respond with anxiety, or self-justification, or a frantic need to be understood. He doesn't respond out of his human need for approval. He already knows the Father is well pleased. That is enough.

Rather, Jesus responds in self-forgetfulness, out of concern for the ones before him. He responds will gentle, true and unflinching teaching. He points out the dangers in the spirit of division to which they have succumbed and calls them to repentance, for their own sakes.

Our instinct may be to flee from insults and humiliation, but these can be gifts, too, provided we submit to the working of grace. This "slight, momentary affliction" can produce in us "an eternal weight of glory beyond all measure." It is by accepting God's will, especially in difficult things, that we are made like Christ.

Gabrielle Johnson
Edmonton, AB

ENTRANCE ANTIPHON *(Cf. Psalm 26.1-2)*

The Lord is my light and my salvation; whom shall I fear? The Lord is the stronghold of my life; whom should I dread? When those who do evil draw near, they stumble and fall.

INTRODUCTORY RITES *(p. 8)*

COLLECT

O God, from whom all good things come, grant that we, who call on you in our need, may at your prompting discern what is right, and by your guidance do it. Through our Lord Jesus Christ, your Son, who lives and reigns with you in the unity of the Holy Spirit, God, for ever and ever. **Amen.**

FIRST READING *(Genesis 3.8-15)*

After the woman and the man had eaten from the tree, they heard the sound of the Lord God walking in the garden at the time of the evening breeze, and the man and his wife hid themselves from the presence of the Lord God among the trees of the garden. But the Lord God called to the man, and said to him, "Where are you?" He said, "I heard the sound of you in the garden, and I was afraid, because I was naked; and I hid myself." God said, "Who told you that you were naked? Have you eaten from the tree of which I commanded you not to eat?"

The man said, "The woman whom you gave to be with me, she gave me fruit from the tree, and I ate."

Then the Lord God said to the woman, "What is this that you have done?" The woman said, "The serpent tricked me, and I ate."

The Lord God said to the serpent, "Because you have done this, cursed are you among all animals and among all wild creatures; upon your belly you shall go, and dust you shall eat all the days of your life. I will put enmity between you and the woman, and between your offspring and hers; he will strike your head, and you will strike his heel."

The word of the Lord. **Thanks be to God.**

RESPONSORIAL PSALM (Psalm 130)

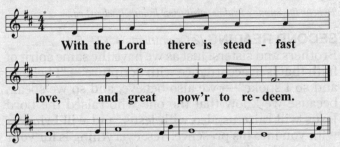

With the Lord there is stead - fast love, and great pow'r to re - deem.

R. **With the Lord there is steadfast love,
and great power to redeem.**

Out of the depths I cry to you, O · **Lord.**
Lord, hear · **my** voice!
Let your ears be at-·**tentive**
to the voice of my sup-·**pli**-cations! R.

If you, O Lord, should mark in-·**iquities,**
Lord, who · **could** stand?
But there is forgiveness with · **you,**
so that you may be · **re**-vered. R.

I wait for the · **Lord,**
my soul waits, and in his word · **I** hope;
my soul waits for the · **Lord**
more than watchmen for · **the** morning. R.

For with the Lord there is steadfast · **love,**
and with him is great power to · **re**-deem.
It is he who will redeem · **Israel**
from all its · **in**-iquities. R.

To hear the Sunday Psalms, visit www.livingwithchrist.ca.

SECOND READING *(2 Corinthians 4.13 – 5.1)*

Brothers and sisters: Just as we have the same spirit of faith that is in accordance with Scripture — "I believe, and so I spoke" — we also believe, and so we speak, because we know that the one who raised the Lord Jesus will raise us also with Jesus, and will bring us with you into his presence. Yes, everything is for your sake, so that grace, as it extends to more and more people, may increase thanksgiving, to the glory of God.

So we do not lose heart. Even though our outer self is wasting away, our inner self is being renewed day by day. For this slight momentary affliction is preparing us for an eternal weight of glory beyond all measure, because we look not at what can be seen but at what cannot be seen; for what can be seen is temporary, but what cannot be seen is eternal.

For we know that if the earthly tent we live in is destroyed, we have a building from God, a house not made with hands, eternal in the heavens.

The word of the Lord. **Thanks be to God.**

GOSPEL ACCLAMATION *(John 12.31-32)*
Alleluia. Alleluia. Now the ruler of this world will be driven out, and when I am lifted up from the earth, I will draw all people to myself. **Alleluia.**

GOSPEL *(Mark 3.20-35)*
The Lord be with you. **And with your spirit.** A reading from the holy Gospel according to Mark. **Glory to you, O Lord.**

Jesus went home and the crowd came together again, so that they could not even eat. When his family heard it, they went out to restrain him, for people were saying, "He has gone out of his mind."

And the scribes who came down from Jerusalem said, "He has Beelzebul, and by the ruler of the demons he casts out demons."

And Jesus called them to him, and spoke to them in parables, "How can Satan cast out Satan? If a kingdom is divided against itself, that kingdom cannot stand. And if a house is divided against itself, that house will not be able to stand. And if Satan has risen up against himself and is divided, he cannot stand, but his end has come. But no one can enter a strong man's house and plunder his property without first tying up the strong man; then indeed the house can be plundered.

"Truly I tell you, people will be forgiven for their sins and whatever blasphemies they utter; but whoever blasphemes against the Holy Spirit can never have forgiveness, but is guilty of an eternal sin" — for they had said, "He has an unclean spirit."

Then his mother and his brothers came; and standing outside, they sent to him and called him. A crowd was sitting around him; and they said to him, "Your mother and your brothers and sisters are outside, asking for you."

And Jesus replied, "Who are my mother and my brothers?" And looking at those who sat around him, he said, "Here are my mother and my brothers! Whoever does the will of God is my brother and sister and mother."

The Gospel of the Lord. **Praise to you, Lord Jesus Christ.**

PROFESSION OF FAITH (p. 14)

PRAYER OF THE FAITHFUL

The following intentions are suggestions only.
There are more suggestions at www.livingwithchrist.ca.

R. **Lord, hear our prayer.**

For the Church, a sign of God's compassion for the world, we pray to the Lord: R.

For nations and peoples seeking justice and peace, we pray to the Lord: R.

For love and forgiveness in our families, we pray to the Lord: R.

For our faith community as we strive to live with one heart, one mind and one spirit, we pray to the Lord: R.

PREPARATION OF THE GIFTS (p. 17)

PRAYER OVER THE OFFERINGS

Look kindly upon our service, O Lord, we pray, that what we offer may be an acceptable oblation to you and lead us to grow in charity. Through Christ our Lord. **Amen.**

PREFACE *(Sundays in Ordinary Time, p. 31)*

COMMUNION ANTIPHON *(Psalm 17.3)*

The Lord is my rock, my fortress, and my deliverer; my God is my saving strength.

or (1 John 4.16)

God is love, and whoever abides in love abides in God, and God in him.

PRAYER AFTER COMMUNION

May your healing work, O Lord, free us, we pray, from doing evil and lead us to what is right. Through Christ our Lord. **Amen.**

BLESSING AND DISMISSAL *(p. 72)*

11th Sunday in Ordinary Time

When I was a child, hearing the words "Once upon a time..." invited me into a land of wonder and possibility. The words called me to listen, to be ready to receive. Jesus – the gifted story-teller – uses the words "The kingdom of God is like..." to accomplish the same purpose. A wise and keen observer of the world around him, Jesus uses ordinary things – seeds and growing seeds, harvesting and nesting birds, to draw us into the wonder and awe of what the kingdom of God is like. And then he goes further, inviting you and me to build that kingdom.

So, what *is* the kingdom of God like? It is a place where we all have a part to play in the great work of God. It's a place where each worker knows that we are cooperating in a great and awesome dream – God's dream. God dreams of growth and possibility, of feeding the hungry, and of providing shelter for creatures big and small. Nothing in this parable is scanty or scarce! God's dream is of bountiful harvest, of small seeds becoming something massive, of huge numbers of creatures finding shelter.

Through this parable, God calls you and me to share God's mindset of abundance and possibility, and to act on it by co-creating a kingdom where no one goes hungry and where all are welcome.

Anne Walsh
St. John's, NL

ENTRANCE ANTIPHON *(Cf. Psalm 26.7, 9)*
O Lord, hear my voice, for I have called to you; be my help. Do not abandon or forsake me, O God, my Saviour!

INTRODUCTORY RITES *(p. 8)*

COLLECT
O God, strength of those who hope in you, graciously hear our pleas, and, since without you mortal frailty can do nothing, grant us always the help of your grace, that in following your commands we may please you by our resolve and our deeds. Through our Lord Jesus Christ, your Son, who lives and reigns with you in the unity of the Holy Spirit, God, for ever and ever. **Amen.**

FIRST READING *(Ezekiel 17.22-24)*
Thus says the Lord God:
"I myself will take a sprig from the lofty top of a cedar; I will set it out. I will break off a tender one from the topmost of its young twigs; I myself will plant it on a high and lofty mountain.

"On the mountain height of Israel I will plant it, in order that it may produce boughs and bear fruit, and become a noble cedar. Under it every kind of bird will live; in the shade of its branches will nest winged creatures of every kind.

"All the trees of the field shall know that I am the Lord. I bring low the high tree, I make high the low tree; I dry up the green tree and make the dry tree flourish. I the Lord have spoken; I will accomplish it."

The word of the Lord. **Thanks be to God.**

RESPONSORIAL PSALM *(Psalm 92)*

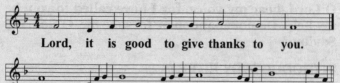

Lord, it is good to give thanks to you.

R. **Lord, it is good to give thanks to you.**

It is good to give thanks · **to** the Lord,
to sing praises to your name, · **O** Most High;
to declare your steadfast love · **in** the morning,
and your · **faithfulness** by night. R.

The righteous flourish · **like** the palm_tree,
and grow like a · **cedar** in Lebanon.
They are planted in the house · **of** the Lord;
they flourish in the · **courts_of** our God. R.

In old age they · **still_pro**-duce fruit;
they are always green and · **full** of sap,
showing that the · **Lord** is upright;
he is my rock, and there is no un·-**righteousness**
    in him. R.

©2009 Gordon Johnston/Novalis

To hear the Sunday Psalms, visit www.livingwithchrist.ca.

SECOND READING *(2 Corinthians 5.6-10)*
Brothers and sisters, we are always confident, even
though we know that while we are at home in the body
we are away from the Lord — for we walk by faith, not by
sight. Yes, we do have confidence, and we would rather
be away from the body and at home with the Lord.

So whether we are at home or away, we make it our aim to please him. For all of us must appear before the judgment seat of Christ, so that each may receive recompense for what he or she has done in the body, whether good or evil.

The word of the Lord. **Thanks be to God.**

GOSPEL ACCLAMATION
Alleluia. Alleluia. The seed is the word of God, Christ is the sower; all who come to him will live for ever. **Alleluia.**

GOSPEL (Mark 4.26-34)
The Lord be with you. **And with your spirit.** A reading from the holy Gospel according to Mark. **Glory to you, O Lord.**

Such a large crowd gathered around Jesus that he got into a boat and began to teach them using many parables.

Jesus said: "The kingdom of God is as if a man would scatter seed on the ground, and would sleep and rise night and day, and the seed would sprout and grow, without his knowing how. The earth produces of itself, first the stalk, then the head, then the full grain in the head. But when the grain is ripe, at once he goes in with the sickle, because the harvest has come."

Jesus also said, "With what can we compare the kingdom of God, or what parable will we use for it? It is like a mustard seed, which, when sown upon the ground, is the smallest of all the seeds on earth; yet when it is sown it grows up and becomes the greatest of all shrubs, and puts forth large branches, so that the birds of the air can make nests in its shade."

With many such parables Jesus spoke the word to them, as they were able to hear it; he did not speak to them except in parables, but he explained everything in private to his disciples.

The Gospel of the Lord. **Praise to you, Lord Jesus Christ.**

PROFESSION OF FAITH (p. 14)

PRAYER OF THE FAITHFUL

The following intentions are suggestions only.
There are more suggestions at www.livingwithchrist.ca.

R. **Lord, hear our prayer.**

For the Church, on the road to unity, we pray to the Lord: R.

For all world leaders in their commitment to peace and justice, we pray to the Lord: R.

For all who are disabled by fear, we pray to the Lord: R.

For fathers everywhere, called to model love and acceptance, we pray to the Lord: R.

For this community, celebrating the love, joy and peace of Christ, we pray to the Lord: R.

PREPARATION OF THE GIFTS (p. 17)

PRAYER OVER THE OFFERINGS

O God, who in the offerings presented here provide for the twofold needs of human nature, nourishing us with food and renewing us with your Sacrament, grant, we pray, that the sustenance they provide may not fail us in body or in spirit. Through Christ our Lord. **Amen.**

PREFACE *(Sundays in Ordinary Time, p. 31)*

COMMUNION ANTIPHON *(Psalm 26.4)*

There is one thing I ask of the Lord, only this do I seek: to live in the house of the Lord all the days of my life.

or (John 17.11)

Holy Father, keep in your name those you have given me, that they may be one as we are one, says the Lord.

PRAYER AFTER COMMUNION

As this reception of your Holy Communion, O Lord, foreshadows the union of the faithful in you, so may it bring about unity in your Church. Through Christ our Lord. **Amen.**

BLESSING AND DISMISSAL *(p. 72)*

JUN 23

12th Sunday in Ordinary Time

How appropriate is the Gospel reading of today. With the multitude of storms, winds, droughts, floods, fires in the last few years, we can easily cry out with the disciples: "We are perishing."

Yet we know the greatest mistake is to let fear take over our lives, even though we, like the disciples, live with many worries and unanswered questions. We know we must live by faith, which is the ability to trust even when despair knocks at our door; to do justice, even at great cost; to profess a firm love in a God we sometimes cannot find, knowing at the same time that God is always with us and never abandons us.

When the disciples experienced the calm after the sea and the wind obeyed Jesus' words, they were filled with awe even though they who had spent so long with Jesus still wondered: "Who can this be?" Sometimes we too continue to ponder this question in our own lives and seek for answers as we struggle to live our faith.

Our own experience of awe can be a source of encouragement for us to continue to work for justice, to know the joy and wisdom of helping each other through stormy times, knowing peace is not far behind.

Joan Doyle
Charlottetown, PE

ENTRANCE ANTIPHON (*Cf. Psalm 27.8-9*)
The Lord is the strength of his people, a saving refuge for the one he has anointed. Save your people, Lord, and bless your heritage, and govern them for ever.

INTRODUCTORY RITES (*p. 8*)

COLLECT
Grant, O Lord, that we may always revere and love your holy name, for you never deprive of your guidance those you set firm on the foundation of your love. Through our Lord Jesus Christ, your Son, who lives and reigns with you in the unity of the Holy Spirit, God, for ever and ever. **Amen.**

FIRST READING (*Job 38.1-4, 8-11*)
The Lord answered Job out of the whirlwind: "Who is this that darkens counsel by words without knowledge? I will question you, and you shall declare to me. Where were you when I laid the foundation of the earth? Tell me if you have understanding.

"Who shut in the sea with doors when it burst out from the womb? — when I made the clouds its garment, and prescribed bounds for it, and set bars and doors, and said, 'Thus far shall you come, and no farther, and here shall your proud waves be stopped'?"

The word of the Lord. **Thanks be to God.**

RESPONSORIAL PSALM *(Psalm 107)*

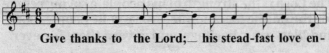

Give thanks to the Lord;— his stead-fast love en-

dures for-ev-er.

R̷. **Give thanks to the Lord;**
   his steadfast love endures forever.
or **Alleluia!**

Some went down to the sea in · **ships,**
doing business on the mighty · **waters;**
they saw the deeds of the · **Lord,**
his wondrous works in the · **deep.** R̷.

For he commanded and raised the stormy · **wind,**
which lifted up the waves of the · **sea.**
They mounted up to heaven and they went down
    to the · **depths;**
their courage melted away in their cal--**amity.** R̷.

Then they cried to the Lord in their · **trouble,**
and he brought them out from their dis--**tress;**
he made the storm be · **still,**
and the waves of the sea were · **hushed.** R̷.

Then they were glad when it grew · **calm,**
and he brought them to their desired · **haven.**
Let them thank the Lord for his steadfast · **love,**
for his wonderful works to the children
    of · **Adam.** R̷.

SECOND READING *(2 Corinthians 5.14-17)*
Brothers and sisters: The love of Christ urges us on, because we are convinced that one has died for all; therefore all have died. And he died for all, so that those who live might live no longer for themselves, but for him who died and was raised for them.

From now on, therefore, we regard no one from a human point of view. Even though we once knew Christ from a human point of view, we know him no longer in that way. So if anyone is in Christ, there is a new creation: everything old has passed away; see, everything has become new!

The word of the Lord. **Thanks be to God.**

GOSPEL ACCLAMATION *(Luke 7.16)*
Alleluia. Alleluia. A great Prophet has risen among us; God has looked favourably on his people. **Alleluia.**

GOSPEL *(Mark 4.35-41)*
The Lord be with you. **And with your spirit.** A reading from the holy Gospel according to Mark. **Glory to you, O Lord.**

When evening had come, Jesus said to his disciples, "Let us go across to the other side." And leaving the crowd behind, they took Jesus with them in the boat, just as he was. Other boats were with him.

A great windstorm arose, and the waves beat into the boat, so that the boat was already being swamped. But Jesus was in the stern, asleep on the cushion; and they woke him up and said to him, "Teacher, do you not care that we are perishing?" He woke up and rebuked the wind, and said to the sea, "Peace! Be still!" Then the wind ceased, and there was a dead calm.

Jesus said to them, "Why are you afraid? Have you still no faith?" And they were filled with great awe and said to one another, "Who then is this, that even the wind and the sea obey him?"

The Gospel of the Lord. **Praise to you, Lord Jesus Christ.**

PROFESSION OF FAITH *(p. 14)*

PRAYER OF THE FAITHFUL

The following intentions are suggestions only.
There are more suggestions at www.livingwithchrist.ca.

R. **Lord, hear our prayer.**

For the Church, calling for lasting peace among nations, we pray to the Lord: R.

For nations striving for the greater good of all people, we pray to the Lord: R.

For leaders of youth who model in faith the life of Christ, we pray to the Lord: R.

For this community, called to live our faith with humility, gentleness and love, we pray to the Lord: R.

PREPARATION OF THE GIFTS *(p. 17)*

PRAYER OVER THE OFFERINGS

Receive, O Lord, the sacrifice of conciliation and praise and grant that, cleansed by its action, we may make offering of a heart pleasing to you. Through Christ our Lord. **Amen.**

PREFACE *(Sundays in Ordinary Time, p. 31)*

COMMUNION ANTIPHON *(Psalm 144.15)*
The eyes of all look to you, Lord, and you give them their food in due season.

or (John 10.11, 15)
I am the Good Shepherd, and I lay down my life for my sheep, says the Lord.

PRAYER AFTER COMMUNION
Renewed and nourished by the Sacred Body and Precious Blood of your Son, we ask of your mercy, O Lord, that what we celebrate with constant devotion may be our sure pledge of redemption. Through Christ our Lord. **Amen.**

BLESSING AND DISMISSAL *(p. 72)*

JUN 30

13th Sunday in Ordinary Time

The faith of Jairus is inspiring. He believed Jesus could heal his daughter and sought him out for her physical healing.

To receive physical healing is a great gift. How much more does the Lord desire our spiritual healing so that we can receive God's salvation which has been won for us by our Lord Jesus Christ. Our free-will acceptance of God's love snatches us out of a destructive domain and takes us into the land of the living, where we will have a life-long journey towards holiness.

In tandem with spiritual healing is another kind of healing: inner healing, which can be found when we seek God in prayer. If we are candid with our Lord about what is going on in our hearts and ask him to ease our fears, hurts, burdens, poverty, and inadequacy, he will heal us and bless others through us. As we let God purify and sanctify us, our spirit will in time become pure and we will want to love only him, the Creator. Then we can be effective instruments of God's healing, peace and power.

Let us pray that God in his divine love will increase our faith in him, and give us the grace to persevere in loving him and serving others for his sake.

Sr. Michael Penelope Nguyen, SC
Ottawa, ON

ENTRANCE ANTIPHON *(Psalm 46.2)*
All peoples, clap your hands. Cry to God with shouts of joy!

INTRODUCTORY RITES *(p. 8)*

COLLECT
O God, who through the grace of adoption chose us to be children of light, grant, we pray, that we may not be wrapped in the darkness of error but always be seen to stand in the bright light of truth. Through our Lord Jesus Christ, your Son, who lives and reigns with you in the unity of the Holy Spirit, God, for ever and ever. **Amen.**

FIRST READING *(Wisdom 1.13-15; 2.23-24)*
God did not make death, and he does not delight in the death of the living. For he created all things so that they might exist; the generative forces of the world are wholesome, and there is no destructive poison in them, and the dominion of Hades is not on earth. For righteousness is immortal.

For God created man for incorruption, and made him in the image of his own eternity, but through the devil's envy death entered the world, and those who belong to his company experience it.

The word of the Lord. **Thanks be to God.**

RESPONSORIAL PSALM *(Psalm 30)*

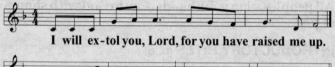

I will ex-tol you, Lord, for you have raised me up.

R. **I will extol you, Lord, for you have raised me up.**

I will extol you, O Lord,
    for you have drawn me · **up,**
and did not let my foes rejoice · **over_me.**
O Lord, you brought up my soul from · **Sheol,**
restored me to life from among those
    gone down · **to_the** Pit. R.

Sing praises to the Lord, O you his · **faithful_ones,**
and give thanks to his holy · **name.**
For his anger is but for a moment;
    his favour is for a · **lifetime.**
Weeping may linger for the night,
    but joy comes · **with_the** morning. R.

Hear, O Lord, and be gracious to · **me!**
O Lord, be my · **helper!**
You have turned my mourning into · **dancing.**
O Lord my God, I will give thanks to you
    · **for**-ever. R.

©2009 Gordon Johnston/Novalis

To hear the Sunday Psalms, visit www.livingwithchrist.ca.

SECOND READING *(2 Corinthians 8.7, 9, 13-15)*
Brothers and sisters: Now as you excel in everything — in faith, in speech, in knowledge, in utmost eagerness, and in our love for you — so we want you to excel also in this generous undertaking.

For you know the generous act of our Lord Jesus Christ, that though he was rich, yet for your sakes he became poor so that by his poverty you might become rich.

I do not mean that there should be relief for others and pressure on you, but it is a question of a fair balance between your present abundance and their need, so that their abundance may be for your need, in order that there may be a fair balance.

As it is written, "The one who had much did not have too much, and the one who had little did not have too little."

The word of the Lord. **Thanks be to God.**

GOSPEL ACCLAMATION *(2 Timothy 1.10)*
Alleluia. Alleluia. Our Saviour Jesus Christ has abolished death and has brought us life through the Gospel. **Alleluia.**

GOSPEL *(Mark 5.21-43)*
For the shorter version, omit the indented part.
The Lord be with you. **And with your spirit.**
A reading from the holy Gospel according to Mark. **Glory to you, O Lord.**

When Jesus had crossed in the boat to the other side, a great crowd gathered around him; and he was by the sea. Then one of the synagogue leaders named

Jairus came and, when he saw Jesus, fell at his feet and begged him repeatedly, "My little daughter is at the point of death. Come and lay your hands on her, so that she may be made well, and live." So Jesus went with him. And a large crowd followed him.

and pressed in on him. Now there was a woman who had been suffering from hemorrhages for twelve years. She had endured much under many physicians, and had spent all that she had; and she was no better, but rather grew worse. She had heard about Jesus, and came up behind him in the crowd and touched his cloak, for she said, "If I but touch his clothes, I will be made well." Immediately her hemorrhage stopped; and she felt in her body that she was healed of her disease. Immediately aware that power had gone forth from him, Jesus turned about in the crowd and said, "Who touched my clothes?" And his disciples said to him, "You see the crowd pressing in on you; how can you say, 'Who touched me'?" He looked all around to see who had done it. But the woman, knowing what had happened to her, came in fear and trembling, fell down before him, and told him the whole truth. Jesus said to her, "Daughter, your faith has made you well; go in peace, and be healed of your disease." While Jesus was still speaking,

Some people came from the leader's house to say, "Your daughter is dead. Why trouble the teacher any further?" But overhearing what they said, Jesus said to the leader of the synagogue, "Do not fear, only believe."

Jesus allowed no one to follow him. When they came to the house of the leader of the synagogue, he saw a commotion, people weeping and wailing loudly. When he had entered, he said to them, "Why do you make a commotion and weep? The child is not dead but sleeping." And they laughed at him.

Then Jesus put them all outside, and took the child's father and mother and those who were with him, and went in where the child was. He took her by the hand and said to her, "Talitha cum," which means, "Little girl, get up!" And immediately the girl got up and began to walk about for she was twelve years of age.

At this they were overcome with amazement. He strictly ordered them that no one should know this, and told them to give her something to eat.

The Gospel of the Lord. **Praise to you, Lord Jesus Christ.**

PROFESSION OF FAITH (p. 14)

PRAYER OF THE FAITHFUL

The following intentions are suggestions only.
There are more suggestions at www.livingwithchrist.ca.

R. **Lord, hear our prayer.**

For the Church, embraced by Jesus' unconditional love and acceptance, we pray to the Lord: R.

For public authorities bound to protect and meet the needs of all, we pray to the Lord: R.

For all who seek equality and justice, we pray to the Lord: R.

For our community, reaching out to others with the healing touch of God, we pray to the Lord: R.

PREPARATION OF THE GIFTS *(p. 17)*

PRAYER OVER THE OFFERINGS
O God, who graciously accomplish the effects of your
mysteries, grant, we pray, that the deeds by which we
serve you may be worthy of these sacred gifts. Through
Christ our Lord. **Amen.**

PREFACE *(Sundays in Ordinary Time, p. 31)*

COMMUNION ANTIPHON *(Cf. Psalm 102.1)*
**Bless the Lord, O my soul, and all within me, his
holy name.**

or (John 17.20-21)

**O Father, I pray for them, that they may be one in
us, that the world may believe that you have sent me,
says the Lord.**

PRAYER AFTER COMMUNION
May this divine sacrifice we have offered and received
fill us with life, O Lord, we pray, so that, bound to you
in lasting charity, we may bear fruit that lasts for ever.
Through Christ our Lord. **Amen.**

BLESSING AND DISMISSAL *(p. 72)*

July Saints' Days

The following saints are traditionally remembered in July in Canada.

Saint Thomas . . . . Jul 3

Saint Elizabeth of Portugal . . . . Jul 4

Saint Anthony Zaccaria . . . . Jul 5

Saint Maria Goretti . . . . Jul 6

Saint Augustine Zhao Rong . . . . Jul 9
  and Companions

Saint Benedict. . . . . Jul 11

Saint Henry. . . . . Jul 13

Saint Camillus de Lellis . . . . Jul 14

Saint Bonaventure. . . . . Jul 15

Our Lady of Mount Carmel . . . . Jul 16

Saint Apollinaris . . . . Jul 20

Saint Lawrence of Brindisi. . . . . Jul 21

Saint Mary Magdalene . . . . Jul 22

Saint Bridget. . . . . Jul 23

Saint Sharbel Makhlūf . . . . Jul 24

Saint James . . . . Jul 25

Saint Anne and Saint Joachim. . . . . Jul 26

Saints Martha, Mary and Lazarus . . . . Jul 29

Saint Peter Chrysologus. . . . . Jul 30

Saint Ignatius of Loyola . . . . Jul 31

14th Sunday in Ordinary Time

We believe all of creation is holy and has a sacramental capacity to "speak" of God. It follows that prophets, vehicles of God's self-revelation past and present, would be respectfully received and embraced as mediators between humanity and divinity.

Today's readings remind us, though, that prophets are not always welcomed. Mark's story of Jesus teaching in his hometown synagogue presents a curious situation. Though his listeners are initially astounded by his wisdom and deeds, doubt soon creeps into their hearts. Suspicion leads to rejection and to a dismissive unbelief that amazes even Jesus.

He is not heard. A poor itinerant preacher, a teacher without formal training or credentials, a carpenter, a local, one of the crowd, familiar and ordinary – he is judged to be unqualified to offer spiritual insight.

Mark's Gospel invites us to reflect on the voices we hear and those we exclude. As part of an institutional Church that has been shaped by centuries of patriarchy, clericalism, and colonialism, can we hear God's call to justice, reconciliation and transformation in the voices of the ordinary, the powerless, the rejected – the poor, women, Indigenous peoples – those among us who once were found unworthy? May we be prophets in our own hometowns.

Ella Allen
Fredericton, NB

ENTRANCE ANTIPHON *(Cf. Psalm 47.10-11)*
Your merciful love, O God, we have received in the midst of your temple. Your praise, O God, like your name, reaches the ends of the earth; your right hand is filled with saving justice.

INTRODUCTORY RITES *(p. 8)*

COLLECT
O God, who in the abasement of your Son have raised up a fallen world, fill your faithful with holy joy, for on those you have rescued from slavery to sin you bestow eternal gladness. Through our Lord Jesus Christ, your Son, who lives and reigns with you in the unity of the Holy Spirit, God, for ever and ever. **Amen.**

FIRST READING *(Ezekiel 2.3-5)*
A spirit entered into me and set me on my feet; and I heard one speaking to me: "Son of man, I am sending you to the children of Israel, to a nation of rebels who have rebelled against me; they and their ancestors have transgressed against me to this very day. The descendants are impudent and stubborn. I am sending you to them, and you shall say to them, 'Thus says the Lord God.' Whether they hear or refuse to hear (for they are a rebellious house), they shall know that there has been a Prophet among them."

The word of the Lord. **Thanks be to God.**

RESPONSORIAL PSALM *(Psalm 123)*

Our eyes look to the Lord, un-til he has mer-cy up-

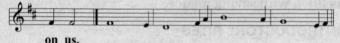

on us.

℟. **Our eyes look to the Lord,
until he has mercy upon us.**

To you I lift up my · **eyes —**
O you who are enthroned in · **the** heavens —
as the eyes of · **servants**
look to the hand of · **their** master. ℟.

As the eyes of a · **maid**
to the hand of · **her** mistress,
so our eyes look to the Lord our · **God,**
until he has mercy · **up**-on_us. ℟.

Have mercy upon us, O Lord, have · **mercy,**
for we have had more than enough of · **con**-tempt.
Our soul has had more than its fill of the · **scorn**
of those who are at ease, of the contempt
of · **the** proud. ℟.

To hear the Sunday Psalms, visit www.livingwithchrist.ca.

SECOND READING (*2 Corinthians 12.7-10*)
Brothers and sisters: Considering the exceptional character of the revelations, to keep me from being too elated, a thorn was given me in the flesh, a messenger of Satan to torment me, to keep me from being too elated.

Three times I appealed to the Lord about this, that it would leave me, but he said to me, "My grace is sufficient for you, for power is made perfect in weakness."

So, I will boast all the more gladly of my weaknesses, so that the power of Christ may dwell in me. Therefore I am content with weaknesses, insults, hardships, persecutions, and calamities for the sake of Christ; for whenever I am weak, then I am strong.

The word of the Lord. **Thanks be to God.**

GOSPEL ACCLAMATION (*Luke 4.18*)
Alleluia. Alleluia. The Spirit of the Lord is upon me; he has sent me to bring good news to the poor. **Alleluia.**

GOSPEL (*Mark 6.1-6*)
The Lord be with you. **And with your spirit.** A reading from the holy Gospel according to Mark. **Glory to you, O Lord.**

Jesus came to his hometown, and his disciples followed him. On the Sabbath he began to teach in the synagogue, and many who heard him were astounded. They said, "Where did this man get all this? What is this wisdom that has been given to him? What deeds of power are being done by his hands! Is not this the carpenter, the son of Mary and brother of James and Joses and Judas and Simon, and are not his sisters here with us?" And they took offence at him.

Then Jesus said to them, "A Prophet is not without honour, except in his hometown, and among his own kin, and in his own house."

And Jesus could do no deed of power there, except that he laid his hands on a few sick people and cured them. And Jesus was amazed at their unbelief.

Then he went about among the villages teaching.

The Gospel of the Lord. **Praise to you, Lord Jesus Christ.**

PROFESSION OF FAITH *(p. 14)*

PRAYER OF THE FAITHFUL

The following intentions are suggestions only.
There are more suggestions at www.livingwithchrist.ca.

R. **Lord, hear our prayer.**

For the Body of Christ, called to proclaim the dignity and worth of every human being, we pray to the Lord: R.

For all the world's citizens, entitled to benefit from a just distribution of the planet's resources, we pray to the Lord: R.

For all who face challenges in their work, we pray to the Lord: R.

For ourselves, trusting in the Lord to help us in our efforts to live the Gospel, we pray to the Lord: R.

PREPARATION OF THE GIFTS *(p. 17)*

PRAYER OVER THE OFFERINGS
May this oblation dedicated to your name purify us, O Lord, and day by day bring our conduct closer to the life of heaven. Through Christ our Lord. **Amen.**

PREFACE *(Sundays in Ordinary Time, p. 31)*

COMMUNION ANTIPHON *(Psalm 33.9)*
Taste and see that the Lord is good; blessed the man who seeks refuge in him.

or (Matthew 11.28)
Come to me, all who labour and are burdened, and I will refresh you, says the Lord.

PRAYER AFTER COMMUNION
Grant, we pray, O Lord, that, having been replenished by such great gifts, we may gain the prize of salvation and never cease to praise you. Through Christ our Lord. **Amen.**

BLESSING AND DISMISSAL *(p. 72)*

15th Sunday in Ordinary Time

The prophet Amos is met with violent resistance when he tries to do what God has sent him to do: preach God's word in the sanctuary of Bethel. It is the king's sanctuary, he is told, "a temple of the kingdom." The priests and royal court don't want to hear God's message unless it is a message that suits them, that ensures their wealth and power.

Contrast this with the humility of Amos. He won't even claim to be a prophet: he belongs to no prophetic guild, he is not the son of a prophet. He has no status, no power. But he hears God's word and obeys it.

This humility is what Jesus wants for his followers: "He ordered them to take nothing for their journey," the Gospel tells us. They are to go out to others in total humility and openness, to share God's love and mercy.

We have a long, sad history that shows the results of making Church and state temples of power, greed and selfishness: crusades, witch hunts, sex abuse scandals, residential schools, war, slavery, environmental degradation, trampling on the poor and needy. The Eucharist challenges us to change. Imagine what would happen if we followed Jesus' teaching, took on an attitude of humility and self-giving, and reached out to God and to others with open hands, open minds and open hearts.

Dinah Simmons
Halifax, NS

ENTRANCE ANTIPHON *(Cf. Psalm 16.15)*
As for me, in justice I shall behold your face; I shall be filled with the vision of your glory.

INTRODUCTORY RITES *(p. 8)*

COLLECT
O God, who show the light of your truth to those who go astray, so that they may return to the right path, give all who for the faith they profess are accounted Christians the grace to reject whatever is contrary to the name of Christ and to strive after all that does it honour. Through our Lord Jesus Christ, your Son, who lives and reigns with you in the unity of the Holy Spirit, God, for ever and ever. **Amen.**

FIRST READING *(Amos 7.12-15)*
Amaziah, the priest of Bethel, said to Amos, "O seer, go, flee away to the land of Judah, earn your bread there, and prophesy there; but never again prophesy at Bethel, for it is the king's sanctuary, and it is a temple of the kingdom."

Then Amos answered Amaziah, "I am no Prophet, nor a Prophet's son; but I am a herdsman, and a dresser of sycamore trees, and the Lord took me from following the flock, and the Lord said to me, 'Go, prophesy to my people Israel.'"

The word of the Lord. **Thanks be to God.**

RESPONSORIAL PSALM *(Psalm 85)*

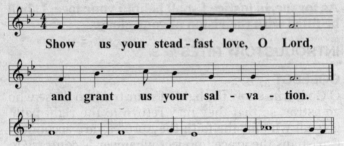

Show us your stead-fast love, O Lord,

and grant us your sal-va-tion.

R. **Show us your steadfast love, O Lord,
and grant us your salvation.**

Let me hear what God the Lord will · **speak,**
for he will speak peace to his · **people.**
Surely his salvation is at hand for those
    who · **fear_him,**
that his glory may dwell · **in_our** land. R.

Steadfast love and faithfulness will · **meet;**
righteousness and peace will · **kiss_each_other.**
Faithfulness will spring up from the · **ground,**
and righteousness will look down
    · **from_the** sky. R.

The Lord will give what is · **good,**
and our land will yield its · **increase.**
Righteousness will go be-·-**fore_him,**
and will make a path · **for_his** steps. R.

©2009 Gordon Johnston/Novalis

To hear the Sunday Psalms, visit www.livingwithchrist.ca.

SECOND READING *(Ephesians 1.3-14)*

The shorter version ends at the asterisks.

Blessed be the God and Father of our Lord Jesus Christ, who has blessed us in Christ with every spiritual blessing in the heavenly places, just as he chose us in Christ before the foundation of the world to be holy and blameless before him in love.

He destined us for adoption to sonship as his own through Jesus Christ, according to the good pleasure of his will, to the praise of his glorious grace that he freely bestowed on us in the Beloved.

In Christ we have redemption through his blood, the forgiveness of our trespasses, according to the riches of his grace that he lavished on us.

With all wisdom and insight God has made known to us the mystery of his will, according to his good pleasure that he set forth in Christ, as a plan for the fullness of time, to gather up all things in Christ, things in heaven and things on earth.

* * *

In Christ we have also obtained an inheritance, having been destined according to the purpose of him who accomplishes all things according to his counsel and will, so that we, who were the first to set our hope on Christ, might live for the praise of his glory.

In him you also, when you had heard the word of truth, the Gospel of your salvation, and had believed in him, were marked with the seal of the promised Holy Spirit.

This is the pledge of our inheritance toward redemption as God's own people, to the praise of his glory.

The word of the Lord. **Thanks be to God.**

GOSPEL ACCLAMATION (See Ephesians 1.17-18)
Alleluia. Alleluia. May the Father of our Lord Jesus Christ enlighten the eyes of our heart that we may know the hope to which we are called. **Alleluia.**

GOSPEL (Mark 6.7-13)
The Lord be with you. **And with your spirit.** A reading from the holy Gospel according to Mark. **Glory to you, O Lord.**

Jesus called the twelve and began to send them out two by two, and gave them authority over the unclean spirits. He ordered them to take nothing for their journey except a staff; no bread, no bag, no money in their belts; but to wear sandals and not to put on two tunics.

Jesus said to them, "Wherever you enter a house, stay there until you leave the place. If any place will not welcome you and they refuse to hear you, as you leave, shake off the dust that is on your feet as a testimony against them."

So the twelve went out and proclaimed that all should repent. They cast out many demons, and anointed with oil many who were sick and cured them.

The Gospel of the Lord. **Praise to you, Lord Jesus Christ.**

PROFESSION OF FAITH (p. 14)

PRAYER OF THE FAITHFUL
The following intentions are suggestions only.
There are more suggestions at www.livingwithchrist.ca.

℟. **Lord, hear our prayer.**

For the Church, attentive to the needs of the marginalized persons in our midst, we pray to the Lord: ℟.

For leaders, heeding the cry of those who feel excluded from society, we pray to the Lord: R.

For the isolated of the world, especially those in institutions, hospitals or prisons, we pray to the Lord: R.

For this community, reaching out to those in need, we pray to the Lord: R.

PREPARATION OF THE GIFTS *(p. 17)*

PRAYER OVER THE OFFERINGS
Look upon the offerings of the Church, O Lord, as she makes her prayer to you, and grant that, when consumed by those who believe, they may bring ever greater holiness. Through Christ our Lord. **Amen.**

PREFACE *(Sundays in Ordinary Time, p. 31)*

COMMUNION ANTIPHON *(Cf. Psalm 83.4-5)*
The sparrow finds a home, and the swallow a nest for her young: by your altars, O Lord of hosts, my King and my God. Blessed are they who dwell in your house, for ever singing your praise.

or (John 6.57)
Whoever eats my flesh and drinks my blood remains in me and I in him, says the Lord.

PRAYER AFTER COMMUNION
Having consumed these gifts, we pray, O Lord, that, by our participation in this mystery, its saving effects upon us may grow. Through Christ our Lord. **Amen.**

BLESSING AND DISMISSAL *(p. 72)*

16th Sunday in Ordinary Time

Today's readings invite us to reflect on the meaning of Jesus as our shepherd. The image of sheep and shepherd is not one to which we can readily relate. But most of us can relate to the apostles who don't even have time to eat! Don't we all, at times, long for someone to encourage us to come away and rest for a while? It is understandable why Psalm 23, today's psalm, is so well loved.

Today's Gospel calls us to focus our attention on the heart of Jesus. Faced with a vast crowd, we likely would not respond as Jesus did. Many of us would have turned the boat around to avoid all that human neediness. But, in truth, we too are often like that crowd, waiting for a leader whose vision and teaching about life we can trust. We all search for real answers to the challenges in our lives and have been disappointed by human leaders from all walks of life.

In the end, it is only when we take the risk to surrender to the compassion and love of Jesus as our shepherd that we will find rest, joy and peace for our hearts. This will give us the motivation to respond more generously, as did Jesus, to the needs of others around us.

Joe Egan
Toronto, ON

ENTRANCE ANTIPHON *(Psalm 53.6, 8)*

See, I have God for my help. The Lord sustains my soul. I will sacrifice to you with willing heart, and praise your name, O Lord, for it is good.

INTRODUCTORY RITES *(p. 8)*

COLLECT

Show favour, O Lord, to your servants and mercifully increase the gifts of your grace, that, made fervent in hope, faith and charity, they may be ever watchful in keeping your commands. Through our Lord Jesus Christ, your Son, who lives and reigns with you in the unity of the Holy Spirit, God, for ever and ever. **Amen.**

FIRST READING *(Jeremiah 23.1-6)*

"Woe to the shepherds who destroy and scatter the sheep of my pasture!" says the Lord. Therefore, thus says the Lord, the God of Israel, concerning the shepherds who shepherd my people: It is you who have scattered my flock, and have driven them away, and you have not attended to them. "So I will attend to you for your evil doings," says the Lord. "Then I myself will gather the remnant of my flock out of all the lands where I have driven them, and I will bring them back to their fold, and they shall be fruitful and multiply. I will raise up shepherds over them who will shepherd them, and they shall not fear any longer, or be dismayed, nor shall any be missing," says the Lord.

"The days are surely coming," says the Lord, "when I will raise up for David a righteous Branch, and he shall reign as king and deal wisely, and shall execute justice and righteousness in the land. In his days Judah will be saved and Israel will live in safety. And this is the name by which he will be called: 'The Lord is our righteousness.'"

The word of the Lord. **Thanks be to God.**

RESPONSORIAL PSALM *(Psalm 23)*

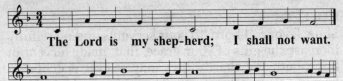

The Lord is my shep-herd; I shall not want.

R̷. **The Lord is my shepherd; I shall not want.**

The Lord is my shepherd, I shall · **not** want.
He makes me lie down in · **green** pastures;
he leads me be··**side** still waters;
he re··**stores** my soul. R̷.

He leads me in right paths for his · **name's** sake.
Even though I walk through the darkest valley,
  I fear · **no** evil;
for · **you** are with_me;
your rod and your · **staff** — they comfort_me. R̷.

You prepare a table · **be**-fore_me
in the presence · **of_my** enemies;
you anoint my · **head** with oil;
my · **cup** over-flows. R̷.

Surely goodness and mercy · **shall** follow_me
all the days of · **my** life,
and I shall dwell in the · **house_of** the Lord
my · **whole** life long. R̷.

©2009 Gordon Johnston/Novalis

SECOND READING *(Ephesians 2.13-18)*

Brothers and sisters: Now in Christ Jesus you who once were far off have been brought near by the blood of Christ. For he is our peace; in his flesh he has made both Jews and Gentiles into one and has broken down the dividing wall, that is, the hostility between us.

He has abolished the law with its commandments and ordinances, that he might create in himself one New Man in place of the two, thus making peace, and might reconcile both groups to God in one body through the Cross, thus putting to death that hostility through it.

So Christ Jesus came and proclaimed peace to you who were far off and peace to those who were near; for through him both of us have access in one Spirit to the Father.

The word of the Lord. **Thanks be to God.**

GOSPEL ACCLAMATION *(John 10.27)*

Alleluia. Alleluia. My sheep hear my voice, says the Lord; I know them, and they follow me. **Alleluia.**

GOSPEL *(Mark 6.30-34)*

The Lord be with you. **And with your spirit.** A reading from the holy Gospel according to Mark. **Glory to you, O Lord.**

The Apostles returned from their mission. They gathered around Jesus, and told him all that they had done and taught.

He said to them, "Come away to a deserted place all by yourselves and rest a while." For many were coming and going, and they had no leisure even to eat. And they went away in the boat to a deserted place by themselves.

Now many saw them going and recognized them, and they hurried there on foot from all the towns and arrived ahead of them. As Jesus went ashore, he saw a great crowd; and he had compassion for them, because they were like sheep without a shepherd; and he began to teach them many things.

The Gospel of the Lord. **Praise to you, Lord Jesus Christ.**

PROFESSION OF FAITH *(p. 14)*

PRAYER OF THE FAITHFUL

The following intentions are suggestions only.
There are more suggestions at www.livingwithchrist.ca.

R. **Lord, hear our prayer.**

For the Church, a sign of Christ's compassion for the world, we pray to the Lord: R.

For public leaders working for justice and peace, we pray to the Lord: R.

For those who are sick, suffering or lonely, we pray to the Lord: R.

For the compassionate witness of this faith community, we pray to the Lord: R.

PREPARATION OF THE GIFTS *(p. 17)*

PRAYER OVER THE OFFERINGS

O God, who in the one perfect sacrifice brought to completion varied offerings of the law, accept, we pray, this sacrifice from your faithful servants and make it holy, as you blessed the gifts of Abel, so that what each has offered to the honour of your majesty may benefit the salvation of all. Through Christ our Lord. **Amen.**

PREFACE *(Sundays in Ordinary Time, p. 31)*

COMMUNION ANTIPHON *(Psalm 110.4-5)*
The Lord, the gracious, the merciful, has made a memorial of his wonders; he gives food to those who fear him.

or (Revelation 3.20)

Behold, I stand at the door and knock, says the Lord. If anyone hears my voice and opens the door to me, I will enter his house and dine with him, and he with me.

PRAYER AFTER COMMUNION

Graciously be present to your people, we pray, O Lord, and lead those you have imbued with heavenly mysteries to pass from former ways to newness of life. Through Christ our Lord. **Amen.**

BLESSING AND DISMISSAL *(p. 72)*

17th Sunday in Ordinary Time
World Day for Grandparents and the Elderly

Our Gospel this weekend is one of the best known of all the miracles that Jesus performed when he walked this earth. He multiplied five barley loaves and two fish into enough food for more than five thousand people. This miracle is the only one reported by all four of the Gospel writers.

What was the significance of Jesus feeding all these people? What does he want to teach us by his actions? In the Hebrew Scriptures we learn that the Israelites wandered the desert for forty years. They had no food. God turned to Moses to provide manna for the people. Despite his reluctance, Moses obeyed. Lo and behold, the people have more than enough manna to sustain themselves. Similarly, the followers in today's Gospel are getting hungry and there's no food readily available. Jesus, with the aid of his disciples, provides more than enough food for everyone. Jesus is showing his compassion for us when we turn to him. The feeding of the hungry was both an act of compassion and a demonstration of the presence of the kingdom of God.

Note in this Gospel the importance of sharing. Jesus provided food for the people after the boy with loaves and fish offered them. Do I see the food I eat as a gift from God to be shared? In what ways am I feeding other people?

Gerry Sobie
Castlegar, BC

ENTRANCE ANTIPHON *(Cf. Psalm 67.6-7, 36)*

God is in his holy place, God who unites those who dwell in his house; he himself gives might and strength to his people.

INTRODUCTORY RITES *(p. 8)*

COLLECT

O God, protector of those who hope in you, without whom nothing has firm foundation, nothing is holy, bestow in abundance your mercy upon us and grant that, with you as our ruler and guide, we may use the good things that pass in such a way as to hold fast even now to those that ever endure. Through our Lord Jesus Christ, your Son, who lives and reigns with you in the unity of the Holy Spirit, God, for ever and ever. **Amen.**

FIRST READING *(2 Kings 4.42-44)*

A man came bringing food from the first fruits to Elisha, the man of God: twenty loaves of barley and fresh ears of grain in his sack. Elisha said, "Give it to the people and let them eat."

But his servant said, "How can I set this before a hundred people?" So Elisha repeated, "Give it to the people and let them eat, for thus says the Lord, 'They shall eat and have some left.'"

The servant set it before them, they ate, and had some left, according to the word of the Lord.

The word of the Lord. **Thanks be to God.**

RESPONSORIAL PSALM *(Psalm 145)*

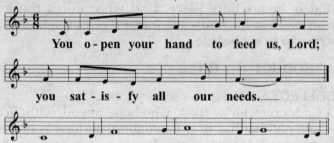

You o-pen your hand to feed us, Lord; you sat-is-fy all our needs.

℟. **You open your hand to feed us, Lord;
you satisfy all our needs.**

All your works shall give thanks to you, O · **Lord,**
and all your faithful shall · **bless_you.**
They shall speak of the glory of your · **kingdom,**
and tell of · **your** power. ℟.

The eyes of all look to · **you,**
and you give them their food in due · **season.**
You open your · **hand,**
satisfying the desire of every · **living** thing. ℟.

The Lord is just in all his · **ways,**
and kind in all his · **doings.**
The Lord is near to all who · **call_on_him,**
to all who call on him · **in** truth. ℟.

To hear the Sunday Psalms, visit www.livingwithchrist.ca.

SECOND READING *(Ephesians 4.1-6)*

Brothers and sisters: I, the prisoner in the Lord, beg you to lead a life worthy of the calling to which you have been called, with all humility and gentleness, with patience, bearing with one another in love, making every effort to maintain the unity of the Spirit in the bond of peace.

There is one body and one Spirit, just as you were called to the one hope of your calling, one Lord, one faith, one baptism, one God and Father of all, who is above all and through all and in all.

The word of the Lord. **Thanks be to God.**

GOSPEL ACCLAMATION *(Luke 7.16)*

Alleluia. Alleluia. A great Prophet has risen among us; God has looked favourably on his people. **Alleluia.**

GOSPEL *(John 6.1-15)*

The Lord be with you. **And with your spirit.** A reading from the holy Gospel according to John. **Glory to you, O Lord.**

Jesus went to the other side of the Sea of Galilee, also called the Sea of Tiberias. A large crowd kept following him, because they saw the signs that he was doing for the sick. Jesus went up the mountain and sat down there with his disciples. Now the Passover, the festival of the Jews, was near.

When he looked up and saw a large crowd coming toward him, Jesus said to Philip, "Where are we to buy bread for these people to eat?" He said this to test him, for he himself knew what he was going to do. Philip answered him, "Six months' wages would not buy enough bread for each of them to get a little."

One of his disciples, Andrew, Simon Peter's brother, said to Jesus, "There is a boy here who has five barley loaves and two fish. But what are they among so many people?" Jesus said, "Make the people sit down." Now there was a great deal of grass in the place; so they sat down, about five thousand in all.

Then Jesus took the loaves, and when he had given thanks, he distributed them to those who were seated; so also the fish, as much as they wanted. When they were satisfied, he told his disciples, "Gather up the fragments left over, so that nothing may be lost." So they gathered them up, and from the fragments of the five barley loaves, left by those who had eaten, they filled twelve baskets.

When the people saw the sign that he had done, they began to say, "This is indeed the Prophet who is to come into the world." When Jesus realized that they were about to come and take him by force to make him king, he withdrew again to the mountain by himself.

The Gospel of the Lord. **Praise to you, Lord Jesus Christ.**

PROFESSION OF FAITH (p. 14)

PRAYER OF THE FAITHFUL

The following intentions are suggestions only.
There are more suggestions at www.livingwithchrist.ca.

R. **Lord, hear our prayer.**

For the Church, embodying Christ's ministry of sharing and service, we pray to the Lord: R.

For young people discerning their vocation, we pray to the Lord: R.

For all those who hunger for food — food for the body, for the mind and for the soul, we pray to the Lord: R.

For this community, called to share our bread with others, we pray to the Lord: R.

PREPARATION OF THE GIFTS *(p. 17)*

PRAYER OVER THE OFFERINGS
Accept, O Lord, we pray, the offerings which we bring from the abundance of your gifts, that through the powerful working of your grace these most sacred mysteries may sanctify our present way of life and lead us to eternal gladness. Through Christ our Lord. **Amen.**

PREFACE *(Sundays in Ordinary Time, p. 31)*

COMMUNION ANTIPHON *(Psalm 102.2)*
Bless the Lord, O my soul, and never forget all his benefits.

or (Matthew 5.7-8)
Blessed are the merciful, for they shall receive mercy. Blessed are the clean of heart, for they shall see God.

PRAYER AFTER COMMUNION
We have consumed, O Lord, this divine Sacrament, the perpetual memorial of the Passion of your Son; grant, we pray, that this gift, which he himself gave us with love beyond all telling, may profit us for salvation. Through Christ our Lord. **Amen.**

BLESSING AND DISMISSAL *(p. 72)*

August Saints' Days

The following saints are traditionally remembered in August in Canada.

Saint Alphonsus Liguori . . . . Aug 1

Saint Eusebius of Vercelli . . . . Aug 2
Saint Peter Julian Eymard

Saint John Mary Vianney . . . . Aug 4

Blessed Frédéric Janssoone . . . . Aug 5

Saint Sixtus II and Companions . . . . Aug 7
Saint Cajetan

Saint Dominic . . . . Aug 8

Saint Teresa Benedicta of the Cross . . . . Aug 9

Saint Lawrence . . . . Aug 10

Saint Clare . . . . Aug 11

Saint Jane Frances de Chantal . . . . Aug 12

Saints Pontian and Hippolytus . . . . Aug 13

Saint Maximilian Kolbe . . . . Aug 14

Saint Stephen of Hungary . . . . Aug 16

Saint John Eudes . . . . Aug 19

Saint Bernard . . . . Aug 20

Saint Pius X . . . . Aug 21

Saint Rose of Lima . . . . Aug 23

Saint Bartholomew . . . . Aug 24

Saint Louis . . . . Aug 25
Saint Joseph Calasanz

Saint Monica . . . . Aug 27

Saint Augustine . . . . Aug 28

18th Sunday in Ordinary Time

Often when I am in the kitchen, someone stops by to ask what I am making. They come inquiring because there is something that piques curiosity or memory or, possibly, hope. This question is often followed by one about when it will be served – and then either joy or disappointment, depending on whether they will be present.

We want to be fed, to be nourished, by something enticing. And we seek it out by noticing what others are filling up on and then asking its source. Once we know, we sample for ourselves and come to an intimate awareness of why it called to us. And how frequently we then want more! Next, pieces are broken off and offered to those around us – Oh, try this! The whole process is life-giving, sustaining nourishment for body and spirit alike.

That Jesus would speak of bread when describing himself is not a surprise. Everything about his ministry was about people experiencing the nourishment of love and the transformation that can happen when we take that love into our being and then extend that love to others. To systems of authority, that love and its fruit can be a threat. To a people who hunger for it, that love is an endless banquet with enough seating for all. Let the people come.

Sr. Kimberly M. King, RSCJ
Halifax, NS

ENTRANCE ANTIPHON *(Psalm 69.2, 6)*
O God, come to my assistance; O Lord, make haste to help me! You are my rescuer, my help; O Lord, do not delay.

INTRODUCTORY RITES *(p. 8)*

COLLECT
Draw near to your servants, O Lord, and answer their prayers with unceasing kindness, that, for those who glory in you as their Creator and guide, you may restore what you have created and keep safe what you have restored. Through our Lord Jesus Christ, your Son, who lives and reigns with you in the unity of the Holy Spirit, God, for ever and ever. **Amen.**

FIRST READING *(Exodus 16.2-4, 12-15, 31a)*
The whole congregation of the children of Israel complained against Moses and Aaron in the wilderness. The children of Israel said to them, "If only we had died by the hand of the Lord in the land of Egypt, when we sat by the fleshpots and ate our fill of bread; for you have brought us out into this wilderness to kill this whole assembly with hunger."

Then the Lord said to Moses, "I am going to rain bread from heaven for you, and each day the people shall go out and gather enough for that day. In that way I will test them, whether they will follow my instruction or not.

"I have heard the complaining of the children of Israel; say to them, 'At twilight you shall eat meat, and in the morning you shall have your fill of bread; then you shall know that I am the Lord your God.'"

In the evening quails came up and covered the camp; and in the morning there was a layer of dew around the camp. When the layer of dew lifted, there on the surface of the wilderness was a fine flaky substance, as fine as frost on the ground.

When the children of Israel saw it, they said to one another, "What is it?" For they did not know what it was. Moses said to them, "It is the bread that the Lord has given you to eat."

The house of Israel called it manna.

The word of the Lord. **Thanks be to God.**

RESPONSORIAL PSALM *(Psalm 78)*

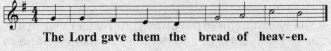

The Lord gave them the bread of heav-en.

R. **The Lord gave them the bread of heaven.**

Things that we have heard and known,
    that our ancestors have · **told_us,**
we will not · **hide;**
we will tell to the coming generation the glorious
    deeds of the Lord, and · **his** might,
and the wonders that he has · **done.** R.

He commanded the skies a-·**bove,**
and opened the doors of · **heaven;**
he rained down on them manna · **to** eat,
and gave them the bread of · **heaven.** R.

Man ate of the bread of · **Angels;**
he sent them food in a·-**bundance.**
And he brought them to his · **holy** hill,
to the mountain that his right hand had · **won.** R.

©2009 *Gordon Johnston/Novalis*

To hear the Sunday Psalms, visit www.livingwithchrist.ca.

SECOND READING *(Ephesians 4.17, 20-24)*

Brothers and sisters: Now this I affirm and insist on in the Lord: you must no longer live as the Gentiles live, in the futility of their minds.

That is not the way you learned Christ! For surely you have heard about him and were taught in him, as truth is in Jesus.

You were taught to put away your former way of life, your old self, corrupt and deluded by its lusts, and to be renewed in the spirit of your minds, and to clothe yourselves with the New Man, created according to the likeness of God in true righteousness and holiness.

The word of the Lord. **Thanks be to God.**

GOSPEL ACCLAMATION *(Matthew 4.4)*

Alleluia. Alleluia. Man does not live by bread alone, but by every word that comes from the mouth of God. **Alleluia.**

GOSPEL *(John 6.24-35)*

The Lord be with you. **And with your spirit.** A reading from the holy Gospel according to John. **Glory to you, O Lord.**

When the crowd saw that neither Jesus nor his disciples were at the place where Jesus had given the bread, they themselves got into the boats and went to Capernaum looking for Jesus.

When they found him on the other side of the sea, they said to him, "Rabbi, when did you come here?" Jesus answered them, "Very truly, I tell you, you are looking for me, not because you saw signs, but because you ate your fill of the loaves. Do not work for the food that perishes, but for the food that endures for eternal life, which the Son of Man will give you. For it is on him that God the Father has set his seal."

Then they said to Jesus, "What must we do to perform the works of God?" Jesus answered them, "This is the work of God, that you believe in him whom he has sent." So they said to him, "What sign are you going to give us then, so that we may see it and believe you? What work are you performing? Our ancestors ate the manna in the wilderness; as it is written, 'He gave them bread from heaven to eat.'"

Then Jesus said to them, "Very truly, I tell you, it was not Moses who gave you the bread from heaven, but it is my Father who gives you the true bread from heaven. For the bread of God is that which comes down from heaven and gives life to the world."

They said to him, "Sir, give us this bread always." Jesus said to them, "I am the bread of life. Whoever comes to me will never be hungry, and whoever believes in me will never be thirsty."

The Gospel of the Lord. **Praise to you, Lord Jesus Christ.**

PROFESSION OF FAITH (p. 14)

PRAYER OF THE FAITHFUL

The following intentions are suggestions only.
There are more suggestions at www.livingwithchrist.ca.

R. **Lord, hear our prayer.**

For the Church, joyful witness to the Resurrection of Christ, we pray to the Lord: R.

For civic leaders, working for the true good of all their people, we pray to the Lord: R.

For all who hunger and thirst for acceptance, we pray to the Lord: R.

For Christian communities everywhere, embodying the triumph of life over death, we pray to the Lord: R.

PREPARATION OF THE GIFTS *(p. 17)*

PRAYER OVER THE OFFERINGS

Graciously sanctify these gifts, O Lord, we pray, and, accepting the oblation of this spiritual sacrifice, make of us an eternal offering to you. Through Christ our Lord. **Amen.**

PREFACE *(Sundays in Ordinary Time, p. 31)*

COMMUNION ANTIPHON *(Wisdom 16.20)*

You have given us, O Lord, bread from heaven, endowed with all delights and sweetness in every taste.

or (John 6.35)

I am the bread of life, says the Lord; whoever comes to me will not hunger and whoever believes in me will not thirst.

PRAYER AFTER COMMUNION

Accompany with constant protection, O Lord, those you renew with these heavenly gifts and, in your never-failing care for them, make them worthy of eternal redemption. Through Christ our Lord. **Amen.**

BLESSING AND DISMISSAL *(p. 72)*

19th Sunday in Ordinary Time

When future historians look back on the early 21st century, they may identify "journey" as a defining characteristic of our time. In recent decades, hordes of people have surged across countries and continents, fleeing from climate disasters, war, oppression or starvation. In their desperate search for a better life, they often face unimaginable and life-threatening dangers.

Though perhaps in less dramatic circumstances, we are all undertaking a journey. The arc of every life involves change, leave-taking, risks, challenges. Each of us is inevitably confronted with times of struggle and pain, perhaps even to the point where we feel like giving up.

In today's Gospel, Jesus offers himself as the food for our journey, the bread of life. How do we experience this life-giving sustenance? In the Eucharist, to be sure, but also in so many other ways. It may be a phone call from a friend when we are feeling utterly alone, or a casserole delivered to a family dealing with illness or grief, or simply a word of encouragement when it is most needed.

As disciples of Jesus, we are called in turn to be bread for others. By giving of ourselves – gifts of time, resources, emotional or physical support – we too become bread, broken and shared for our suffering world.

Krystyna Higgins
Guelph, ON

ENTRANCE ANTIPHON *(Cf. Psalm 73.20, 19, 22, 23)*
Look to your covenant, O Lord, and forget not the life of your poor ones for ever. Arise, O God, and defend your cause, and forget not the cries of those who seek you.

INTRODUCTORY RITES *(p. 8)*

COLLECT
Almighty ever-living God, whom, taught by the Holy Spirit, we dare to call our Father, bring, we pray, to perfection in our hearts the spirit of adoption as your sons and daughters, that we may merit to enter into the inheritance which you have promised. Through our Lord Jesus Christ, your Son, who lives and reigns with you in the unity of the Holy Spirit, God, for ever and ever. **Amen.**

FIRST READING *(1 Kings 19.4-8)*
Elijah went a day's journey into the wilderness, and came and sat down under a solitary broom tree. He asked that he might die: "It is enough; now, O Lord, take away my life, for I am no better than my ancestors."

Then Elijah lay down under the broom tree and fell asleep. Suddenly an Angel touched him and said to him, "Get up and eat." He looked, and there at his head was a cake baked on hot stones, and a jar of water. He ate and drank, and lay down again.

The Angel of the Lord came a second time, touched him, and said, "Get up and eat, otherwise the journey will be too much for you." Elijah got up, and ate and drank; then he went in the strength of that food forty days and forty nights to Horeb the mountain of God.

The word of the Lord. **Thanks be to God.**

RESPONSORIAL PSALM *(Psalm 34)*

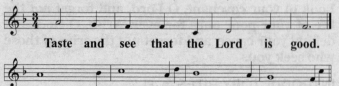

Taste and see that the Lord is good.

R. **Taste and see that the Lord is good.**

I will bless the Lord at all · **times;**
his praise shall continually be in · **my** mouth.
My soul makes its boast in the · **Lord;**
let the humble hear and · **be** glad. R.

O magnify the Lord with · **me,**
and let us exalt his name · **to-**gether.
I sought the Lord, and he · **answered_me,**
and delivered me from all · **my** fears. R.

Look to him, and be · **radiant;**
so your faces shall never · **be_a-**shamed.
The poor one called, and the Lord · **heard,**
and saved that person from ev--**ery** trouble. R.

The Angel of the Lord en--**camps**
around those who fear him, and · **de-**livers_them.
O taste and see that the Lord is · **good;**
blessed is the one who takes refuge · **in** him. R.

©2009 Gordon Johnston/Novalis

To hear the Sunday Psalms, visit www.livingwithchrist.ca.

SECOND READING *(Ephesians 4.30 – 5.2)*

Brothers and sisters: Do not grieve the Holy Spirit of God, with which you were marked with a seal for the day of redemption. Put away from you all bitterness and wrath and anger and wrangling and slander, together with all malice, and be kind to one another, tender-hearted, forgiving one another, as God in Christ has forgiven you.

Therefore be imitators of God, as beloved children, and live in love, as Christ loved us and gave himself up for us, a fragrant offering and sacrifice to God.

The word of the Lord. **Thanks be to God.**

GOSPEL ACCLAMATION *(John 6.51)*

Alleluia. Alleluia. I am the living bread that came down from heaven, says the Lord; whoever eats of this bread will live for ever. **Alleluia.**

GOSPEL *(John 6.41-51)*

The Lord be with you. **And with your spirit.**
A reading from the holy Gospel according to John. **Glory to you, O Lord.**

The people began to complain about Jesus because he said, "I am the bread that came down from heaven." They were saying, "Is not this Jesus, the son of Joseph, whose father and mother we know? How can he now say, 'I have come down from heaven'?"

Jesus answered them, "Do not complain among yourselves. No one can come to me unless the Father who sent me draw them; and I will raise that person up on the last day. It is written in the Prophets, 'And they shall all be taught by God.' Everyone who has heard and learned from the Father comes to me. Not that anyone has seen the Father except the one who is from God; he has seen the Father. Very truly, I tell you, whoever believes has eternal life.

"I am the bread of life. Your ancestors ate the manna in the wilderness, and they died. This is the bread that comes down from heaven, so that one may eat of it and not die. I am the living bread that came down from heaven. Whoever eats of this bread will live forever; and the bread that I will give for the life of the world is my flesh."

The Gospel of the Lord. **Praise to you, Lord Jesus Christ.**

PROFESSION OF FAITH *(p. 14)*

PRAYER OF THE FAITHFUL

The following intentions are suggestions only.
There are more suggestions at www.livingwithchrist.ca.

R. **Lord, hear our prayer.**

For the Church, called to celebrate healing and sustenance through the Eucharist, we pray to the Lord: R.

For leaders working to establish unity and peace among nations and peoples, we pray to the Lord: R.

For people suffering from mental and emotional distress, we pray to the Lord: R.

For our worshipping community gathered here today, we pray to the Lord: R.

PREPARATION OF THE GIFTS *(p. 17)*

PRAYER OVER THE OFFERINGS

Be pleased, O Lord, to accept the offerings of your Church, for in your mercy you have given them to be offered and by your power you transform them into the mystery of our salvation. Through Christ our Lord. **Amen.**

PREFACE *(Sundays in Ordinary Time, p. 31)*

COMMUNION ANTIPHON *(Psalm 147.12, 14)*

O Jerusalem, glorify the Lord, who gives you your fill of finest wheat.

or (Cf. John 6.51)

The bread that I will give, says the Lord, is my flesh for the life of the world.

PRAYER AFTER COMMUNION

May the communion in your Sacrament that we have consumed, save us, O Lord, and confirm us in the light of your truth. Through Christ our Lord. **Amen.**

BLESSING AND DISMISSAL *(p. 72)*

20th Sunday in Ordinary Time

When Jesus announced that we are to eat his body and drink his blood to attain salvation, he appalled his hearers. Jewish people were, and are, forbidden to consume blood. And his disciples found it a difficult teaching to accept. We have since come to understand that Christ was offering his entire self to us by being fully present in the Eucharist.

This is a matter of faith, not logical or scientific fact, that can only be grasped through the wisdom of faith. Wisdom invites us to a mature faith that is not dependent on earthly knowledge, but a deep understanding that we encounter Christ each time at Mass. When we receive Jesus, we become tabernacles bringing Jesus to the world. Through our encounter with the mystery of Christ's eucharistic presence, we become that very presence for all we encounter.

We do this by witnessing to our awe and wonder before God, speaking and doing no evil, dedicating ourselves to good works, and pursuing peace in our lives. We live as wise people who offer thanksgiving for all we have been given. We are particularly thankful that Jesus offered his entire self to us in his body and blood. Likewise, we Christ-bearers offer our whole selves to others, and to God's wise plan for justice and peace in our world. Therein lies our salvation.

Michael Way Skinner
Newmarket, ON

ENTRANCE ANTIPHON *(Psalm 83.10-11)*

Turn your eyes, O God, our shield; and look on the face of your anointed one; one day within your courts is better than a thousand elsewhere.

INTRODUCTORY RITES *(p. 8)*

COLLECT

O God, who have prepared for those who love you good things which no eye can see, fill our hearts, we pray, with the warmth of your love, so that, loving you in all things and above all things, we may attain your promises, which surpass every human desire. Through our Lord Jesus Christ, your Son, who lives and reigns with you in the unity of the Holy Spirit, God, for ever and ever. **Amen.**

FIRST READING *(Proverbs 9.1-6)*

Wisdom has built her house,
she has hewn her seven pillars.
She has slaughtered her animals,
she has mixed her wine,
she has also set her table.
She has sent out her servant girls,
she calls from the highest places in the town,
"You that are simple, turn in here!"

To those without sense she says,
"Come, eat of my bread
and drink of the wine I have mixed.
Lay aside immaturity, and live,
and walk in the way of insight."

The word of the Lord. **Thanks be to God.**

RESPONSORIAL PSALM *(Psalm 34)*

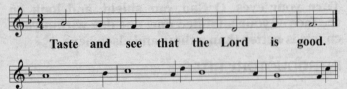

Taste and see that the Lord is good.

R̷. **Taste and see that the Lord is good.**

I will bless the Lord at all · **times;**
his praise shall continually be in · **my** mouth.
My soul makes its boast in the · **Lord;**
let the humble hear and · **be** glad. R̷.

O fear the Lord, you his · **holy_ones,**
for those who fear him have · **no** want.
The young lions suffer want and · **hunger,**
but those who seek the Lord
  lack no · **good** thing. R̷.

Come, O children, · **listen_to_me;**
I will teach you the fear of · **the** Lord.
Which of you desires · **life,**
and covets many days to en-·**joy** good? R̷.

Keep your tongue from · **evil,**
and your lips from speaking · **de**-ceit.
Depart from evil, and do · **good;**
seek peace, and · **pur**-sue_it. R̷.

©2009 Gordon Johnston/Novalis

To hear the Sunday Psalms, visit www.livingwithchrist.ca.

SECOND READING *(Ephesians 5.15-20)*

Brothers and sisters, be careful how you live, not as unwise people but as wise, making the most of the time, because the days are evil. So do not be foolish, but understand what the will of the Lord is.

Do not get drunk with wine, for that is debauchery; but be filled with the Spirit, as you sing Psalms and hymns and spiritual songs among yourselves, singing and making music to the Lord in your hearts, giving thanks to God the Father at all times and for everything in the name of our Lord Jesus Christ.

The word of the Lord. **Thanks be to God.**

GOSPEL ACCLAMATION *(John 6.56)*

Alleluia. Alleluia. Whoever eats my flesh and drinks my blood abides in me, and I in them, says the Lord. **Alleluia.**

GOSPEL *(John 6.51-58)*

The Lord be with you. **And with your spirit.** A reading from the holy Gospel according to John. **Glory to you, O Lord.**

Jesus said to the people: "I am the living bread that came down from heaven. Whoever eats of this bread will live forever; and the bread that I will give for the life of the world is my flesh."

The people then disputed among themselves, saying, "How can this man give us his flesh to eat?"

So Jesus said to them, "Very truly, I tell you, unless you eat the flesh of the Son of Man and drink his blood, you have no life in you. Whoever eats my flesh and drinks my blood has eternal life, and I will raise them up on the last day; for my flesh is true food and my blood is true drink. Whoever eats my flesh and drinks my blood abides in me, and I in them.

"Just as the living Father sent me, and I live because of the Father, so whoever eats me will live because of me. This is the bread that came down from heaven, not like that which your ancestors ate, and they died. But the one who eats this bread will live forever."

The Gospel of the Lord. **Praise to you, Lord Jesus Christ.**

PROFESSION OF FAITH (p. 14)

PRAYER OF THE FAITHFUL

The following intentions are suggestions only.
There are more suggestions at www.livingwithchrist.ca.

R. **Lord, hear our prayer.**

For the Church, whose very life proclaims the joy of the kingdom, we pray to the Lord: R.

For leaders of nations, seeking justice for their people, we pray to the Lord: R.

For the poor who lack the basic necessities of life, we pray to the Lord: R.

For our community, striving to be a model of fullness of life in Christ, we pray to the Lord: R.

PREPARATION OF THE GIFTS (p. 17)

PRAYER OVER THE OFFERINGS

Receive our oblation, O Lord, by which is brought about a glorious exchange, that, by offering what you have given, we may merit to receive your very self. Through Christ our Lord. **Amen.**

PREFACE *(Sundays in Ordinary Time, p. 31)*

COMMUNION ANTIPHON *(Psalm 129.7)*

With the Lord there is mercy; in him is plentiful redemption.

or (John 6.51-52)

I am the living bread that came down from heaven, says the Lord. Whoever eats of this bread will live for ever.

PRAYER AFTER COMMUNION

Made partakers of Christ through these Sacraments, we humbly implore your mercy, Lord, that, conformed to his image on earth, we may merit also to be his co-heirs in heaven. Who lives and reigns for ever and ever. **Amen.**

BLESSING AND DISMISSAL *(p. 72)*

**AUG
25**

21st Sunday in Ordinary Time

In today's Gospel, Jesus invites us to eat his flesh and drink his blood, to be one with him. We are challenged, as the disciples were, to understand this mystery and what it means to be a eucharistic people.

For the two of us, this invitation to imitate Christ finds its expression in part through our marriage. Amidst the competing priorities of family, work and community life, it is not always easy to see which choices draw us closer to Christ. But as Saint Paul encourages the Ephesians, when we choose to imitate Christ by loving each other with abandon, we come to know the Holy One of God more fully. Our deepening relationship with God helps us to create space for him even amidst the busyness of daily life. And this deepening union in turn deepens our marital union, helping us to choose forgiveness over anger, intimate encounter over distraction.

Through the grace of the Eucharist we are nourished and sustained in our calling to imitate Christ through acts of loving service in our world. Christ wishes to reveal himself to us as the only clear choice, as he did for Simon Peter. This deep knowing does not mean we will not stumble like Peter did. It does mean that Jesus, who is ever loving and forgiving, unceasingly invites us to a fullness of life.

*Michael & Vanessa Nicholas-Schmidt
Toronto, ON*

ENTRANCE ANTIPHON (Cf. Psalm 85.1-3)

Turn your ear, O Lord, and answer me; save the servant who trusts in you, my God. Have mercy on me, O Lord, for I cry to you all the day long.

INTRODUCTORY RITES (p. 8)

COLLECT

O God, who cause the minds of the faithful to unite in a single purpose, grant your people to love what you command and to desire what you promise, that, amid the uncertainties of this world, our hearts may be fixed on that place where true gladness is found. Through our Lord Jesus Christ, your Son, who lives and reigns with you in the unity of the Holy Spirit, God, for ever and ever. **Amen.**

FIRST READING (Joshua 24.1-2a, 15-17, 18b)

Joshua gathered all the tribes of Israel to Shechem, and summoned the elders, the heads, the judges, and the officers of Israel; and they presented themselves before God.

And Joshua said to all the people, "If you are unwilling to serve the Lord, choose this day whom you will serve, whether the gods your ancestors served in the region beyond the River or the gods of the Amorites in whose land you are living. As for me and my household, we will serve the Lord."

Then the people answered, "Far be it from us that we should forsake the Lord to serve other gods; for it is the Lord our God who brought us and our ancestors up from the land of Egypt, out of the house of slavery, and who did those great signs in our sight. He protected us along all the way that we went, and among all the peoples through whom we passed. Therefore we also will serve the Lord, for he is our God."

The word of the Lord. **Thanks be to God.**

RESPONSORIAL PSALM *(Psalm 34)*

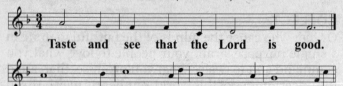

Taste and see that the Lord is good.

R̷ **Taste and see that the Lord is good.**

I will bless the Lord at all · **times;**
his praise shall continually be in · **my** mouth.
My soul makes its boast in the · **Lord;**
let the humble hear and · **be** glad. R̷

The eyes of the Lord are on the · **righteous,**
and his ears are open · **to_their** cry.
The face of the Lord is against · **evildoers,**
to cut off the remembrance of them
  · **from_the** earth. R̷

When the righteous cry for help, the Lord · **hears,**
and rescues them from all · **their** troubles.
The Lord is near to the broken--**hearted,**
and saves the crushed · **in** spirit. R̷

Many are the afflictions of the · **righteous_one,**
but the Lord rescues him from · **them** all.
He keeps all his · **bones;**
not one of them will · **be** broken. R̷

Evil brings death to the · **wicked,**
and those who hate the righteous will be
· **con**-demned.
The Lord redeems the life of his · **servants;**
none of those who take refuge in him will be
· **con**-demned. R.

©2009 Gordon Johnston/Novalis

To hear the Sunday Psalms, visit www.livingwithchrist.ca.

SECOND READING *(Ephesians 4.32 – 5.1-2, 21-32)*

Brothers and sisters: Be kind to one another, tender-hearted, forgiving one another, as God in Christ has forgiven you. Therefore be imitators of God, as beloved children, and live in love, as Christ loved us and gave himself up for us, a fragrant offering and sacrifice to God. Be subject to one another out of reverence for Christ.

Wives, be subject to your husbands as you are to the Lord. For the husband is the head of the wife just as Christ is the head of the Church, the body of which he is the Saviour. Just as the Church is subject to Christ, so also wives ought to be, in everything, to their husbands.

Husbands, love your wives, just as Christ loved the Church and gave himself up for her, in order to make her holy by cleansing her with the washing of water by the word, so as to present the Church to himself in splendour, without a spot or wrinkle or anything of the kind — yes, so that she may be holy and without blemish. In the same way, husbands should love their wives as they do their own bodies. He who loves his wife loves himself. For no one ever hates his own body, but he nourishes and tenderly cares for it, just as

Christ does for the Church, because we are members of his body.

For this reason a man will leave his father and mother and be joined to his wife, and the two will become one flesh. This is a great mystery, and I am applying it to Christ and the Church.

The word of the Lord. **Thanks be to God.**

GOSPEL ACCLAMATION (John 6.63, 68)
Alleluia. Alleluia. Your words, Lord, are spirit and life; you have the words of eternal life. **Alleluia.**

GOSPEL (John 6.53, 60-69)
The Lord be with you. **And with your spirit.** A reading from the holy Gospel according to John. **Glory to you, O Lord.**

Jesus said to the people: "Very truly, I tell you, unless you eat the flesh of the Son of Man and drink his blood, you have no life in you."

When many of his disciples heard this, they said: "This teaching is difficult; who can accept it?"

But Jesus, being aware that his disciples were complaining about it, said to them, "Does this offend you? Then what if you were to see the Son of Man ascending to where he was before? It is the spirit that gives life; the flesh is useless. The words that I have spoken to you are spirit and life. But among you there are some who do not believe." For Jesus knew from the first who were the ones that did not believe, and who was the one that would betray him.

And he said, "For this reason I have told you that no one can come to me unless it is granted them by my Father."

Because of this many of his disciples turned back, and no longer went about with him. So Jesus asked the twelve, "Do you also wish to go away?"

Simon Peter answered him, "Lord, to whom can we go? You have the words of eternal life. We have come to believe and know that you are the Holy One of God."

The Gospel of the Lord. **Praise to you, Lord Jesus Christ.**

PROFESSION OF FAITH (p. 14)

PRAYER OF THE FAITHFUL

The following intentions are suggestions only.
There are more suggestions at www.livingwithchrist.ca.

R. **Lord, hear our prayer.**

For the Church, witness to God's mercy and love, we pray to the Lord: R.

For leaders of nations working for the peace and well-being of all citizens, we pray to the Lord: R.

For the sick and suffering, and for those who care for them, we pray to the Lord: R.

For all of us gathered here in faith, hope and love, we pray to the Lord: R.

PREPARATION OF THE GIFTS (p. 17)

PRAYER OVER THE OFFERINGS

O Lord, who gained for yourself a people by adoption through the one sacrifice offered once for all, bestow graciously on us, we pray, the gifts of unity and peace in your Church. Through Christ our Lord. **Amen.**

PREFACE *(Sundays in Ordinary Time, p. 31)*

COMMUNION ANTIPHON *(Cf. Psalm 103.13-15)*
The earth is replete with the fruits of your work, O Lord; you bring forth bread from the earth and wine to cheer the heart.

or (Cf. John 6.54)
Whoever eats my flesh and drinks my blood has eternal life, says the Lord, and I will raise him up on the last day.

PRAYER AFTER COMMUNION
Complete within us, O Lord, we pray, the healing work of your mercy and graciously perfect and sustain us, so that in all things we may please you. Through Christ our Lord. **Amen.**

BLESSING AND DISMISSAL *(p. 72)*

September Saints' Days

The following saints are traditionally remembered in September in Canada.

Blessed André Grasset . . . . Sep 2

Saint Gregory the Great . . . . Sep 3

Blessed Dina Bélanger . . . . Sep 4

Saint Peter Claver . . . . Sep 9

Saint John Chrysostom. . . . . Sep 13

Our Lady of Sorrows. . . . . Sep 15

Saints Cornelius and Cyprian . . . . Sep 16

Saint Robert Bellarmine. . . . . , . Sep 17
Saint Hildegard of Bingen

Saint Januarius. . . . . Sep 19

Saints Andrew Kim Tae-gŏn, ... Sep 20
  Paul Chŏng Ha-sang and Companions

Saint Matthew . . . . Sep 21

Saint Pius of Pietrelcina . . . . Sep 23

Blessed Émilie Tavernier-Gamelin. . . . . Sep 24

Saints Cosmas and Damian . . . . Sep 25

Saints John de Brébeuf, Isaac Jogues . . . . Sep 26
  and Companions
Secondary Patrons of Canada

Saint Vincent de Paul . . . . Sep 27

Saint Wenceslaus. . . . . Sep 28
Saint Lawrence Ruiz and Companions

Saints Michael, Gabriel and Raphael. . . . . Sep 29

Saint Jerome . . . . Sep 30

22nd Sunday in Ordinary Time
World Day of Prayer for the Care of Creation

In today's Gospel, Jesus is encouraging us to listen and understand that the deepest desires of our hearts are reflected in our everyday actions, words and decisions. He is stirring our hearts and inviting us to reflect on the source of our spiritual well-being. Are we motivated by the world around us or choosing to learn from Jesus how to love with a faithful heart full of care, compassion and mercy?

Jesus understands we struggle in our human weakness. We live in a secular world that measures our worth by what we accomplish and possess. This focus, even when it is not what we want, leads us away from God who deeply loves us, to the point of giving us his very self.

God wants to draw us closer into a loving relationship with him. Only in this way can we discover the joy of our truest selves, transforming our hearts to love, seek peace, and walk in companionship with the poor and marginalized.

When we can enter prayerfully and sacramentally into the depths of our heart, we will find Christ's grace-filled love waiting there for us. In this sacred place, we are invited to renew our spirits and cleanse our hearts. Here, we touch and receive the beauty of God's love for us and for our world that he loves so much.

Julie Cachia
Toronto, ON

ENTRANCE ANTIPHON *(Cf. Psalm 85.3, 5)*
Have mercy on me, O Lord, for I cry to you all the day long. O Lord, you are good and forgiving, full of mercy to all who call to you.

INTRODUCTORY RITES *(p. 8)*

COLLECT
God of might, giver of every good gift, put into our hearts the love of your name, so that, by deepening our sense of reverence, you may nurture in us what is good and, by your watchful care, keep safe what you have nurtured. Through our Lord Jesus Christ, your Son, who lives and reigns with you in the unity of the Holy Spirit, God, for ever and ever. **Amen.**

FIRST READING *(Deuteronomy 4.1-2, 6-8)*
"Now, Israel, give heed to the statutes and ordinances that I am teaching you to observe, so that you may live to enter and occupy the land that the Lord, the God of your fathers, is giving you. You must neither add anything to what I command you nor take away anything from it, but keep the commandments of the Lord your God with which I am charging you.

"You must observe them diligently, for this will show your wisdom and discernment to the peoples, who, when they hear all these statutes, will say, 'Surely this great nation is a wise and discerning people!' For what other great nation has a god so near to it as the Lord our God is whenever we call to him? And what other great nation has statutes and ordinances as just as this entire law that I am setting before you today?"

The word of the Lord. **Thanks be to God.**

RESPONSORIAL PSALM *(Psalm 15)*

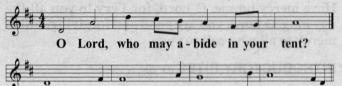

O Lord, who may a-bide in your tent?

R. **O Lord, who may abide in your tent?**

Whoever walks · **blamelessly,**
and does what is · **right,**
and speaks the truth from their · **heart;**
whoever does not slander · **with their** tongue. R.

Whoever does no evil to a · **friend,**
nor takes up a reproach against a · **neighbour;**
in whose eyes the wicked one is de··**spised,**
but who honours those who fear · **the** Lord. R.

Whoever stands by their oath even to their · **hurt;**
who does not lend money at · **interest,**
and does not take a bribe against the · **innocent.**
One who does these things shall never
· **be** moved. R.

©2009 Gordon Johnston/Novalis

To hear the Sunday Psalms, visit www.livingwithchrist.ca.

SECOND READING *(James 1.17-18, 21-22, 27)*
Every generous act of giving, with every perfect gift,
is from above, coming down from the Father of lights,
with whom there is no variation or shadow due to
change. In fulfillment of his own purpose he gave us

birth by the word of truth, so that we would become a kind of first fruits of his creatures.

Welcome with meekness the implanted word that has the power to save your souls. But be doers of the word, and not merely hearers who deceive themselves.

Religion that is pure and undefiled before God, the Father, is this: to care for orphans and widows in their distress, and to keep oneself unstained by the world.

The word of the Lord. **Thanks be to God.**

GOSPEL ACCLAMATION *(James 1.18)*
Alleluia. Alleluia. The Father gave us birth by the word of truth, that we would become first fruits of his creation. **Alleluia.**

GOSPEL *(Mark 7.1-8, 14-15, 21-23)*
The Lord be with you. **And with your spirit.** A reading from the holy Gospel according to Mark. **Glory to you, O Lord.**

When the Pharisees and some of the scribes who had come from Jerusalem gathered around Jesus, they noticed that some of his disciples were eating with defiled hands, that is, without washing them. For the Pharisees, and all the Jews, do not eat unless they thoroughly wash their hands, thus observing the tradition of the elders; and they do not eat anything from the market unless they wash it; and there are also many other traditions that they observe, the washing of cups, pots, and bronze kettles. So the Pharisees and the scribes asked him, "Why do your disciples not live according to the tradition of the elders, but eat with defiled hands?"

Jesus said to them, "Isaiah prophesied rightly about you hypocrites, as it is written, 'This people honours me with their lips, but their hearts are far from me; in vain do they worship me, teaching human precepts as doctrines.' You abandon the commandment of God and hold to human tradition."

Then Jesus called the crowd again and said to them, "Listen to me, all of you, and understand: there is nothing outside a person that by going in can defile them, but the things that come out of a person are what defile them.

"For it is from within, from the human heart, that evil intentions come: fornication, theft, murder, adultery, avarice, wickedness, deceit, licentiousness, envy, slander, pride, folly. All these evil things come from within, and they defile a person."

The Gospel of the Lord. **Praise to you, Lord Jesus Christ.**

PROFESSION OF FAITH (p. 14)

PRAYER OF THE FAITHFUL

The following intentions are suggestions only.
There are more suggestions at www.livingwithchrist.ca.

R. **Lord, hear our prayer.**

For the Church, witness to the kingdom of God throughout the world, we pray to the Lord: R.

For civic leaders, working for the good of all people, we pray to the Lord: R.

For people living in poverty, pain and injustice, we pray to the Lord: R.

For our community, diligently striving to live the commandment of love, we pray to the Lord: R̥

PREPARATION OF THE GIFTS *(p. 17)*

PRAYER OVER THE OFFERINGS
May this sacred offering, O Lord, confer on us always the blessing of salvation, that what it celebrates in mystery it may accomplish in power. Through Christ our Lord. **Amen.**

PREFACE *(Sundays in Ordinary Time, p. 31)*

COMMUNION ANTIPHON *(Psalm 30.20)*
How great is the goodness, Lord, that you keep for those who fear you.

or (Matthew 5.9-10)

Blessed are the peacemakers, for they shall be called children of God. Blessed are they who are persecuted for the sake of righteousness, for theirs is the Kingdom of Heaven.

PRAYER AFTER COMMUNION
Renewed by this bread from the heavenly table, we beseech you, Lord, that, being the food of charity, it may confirm our hearts and stir us to serve you in our neighbour. Through Christ our Lord. **Amen.**

BLESSING AND DISMISSAL *(p. 72)*

23rd Sunday in Ordinary Time

Oh, the power of a simple word! "Ephphatha!" Jesus says in today's Gospel, and with that one word, the deaf man's life changes forever. No longer would he be set apart, isolated from everyone around him. No more would he have to endure the looks that said his disability was somehow his own fault. "Be opened," Jesus commands, and his life begins anew.

And what about his friends, those who had brought him to Jesus? They would have been familiar with the words of the prophets, like Isaiah in the first reading, who spoke of the coming of God as a time when the ears of the deaf would be unstopped and the speechless would sing for joy. Imagine their amazement, then, when it happened to one of their own, in their very midst. To them, too, Jesus speaks: Ephphatha! Be open, always, to the signs that God is right here among you.

We hear the same word spoken in today's celebration: Ephphatha! Perhaps we need to open ourselves to the surprising ways God enters our lives anew, disguised in the ordinary events of each day. Or we need to be open to new ways in which we are being called to bring God's love into a world wounded by division and despair. With gratitude and humility, we pray for hearts open to hear God's call.

Teresa Whalen Lux
Regina, SK

ENTRANCE ANTIPHON *(Psalm 118.137, 124)*
**You are just, O Lord, and your judgment is right;
treat your servant in accord with your merciful love.**

INTRODUCTORY RITES *(p. 8)*

COLLECT
O God, by whom we are redeemed and receive adoption, look graciously upon your beloved sons and daughters, that those who believe in Christ may receive true freedom and an everlasting inheritance. Through our Lord Jesus Christ, your Son, who lives and reigns with you in the unity of the Holy Spirit, God, for ever and ever. **Amen.**

FIRST READING *(Isaiah 35.4-7)*
Say to those who are of a fearful heart,
"Be strong, do not fear!
Here is your God.
He will come with vengeance,
with terrible recompense.
He will come and save you."

Then the eyes of the blind shall be opened,
and the ears of the deaf unstopped;
then the lame shall leap like a deer,
and the tongue of the mute sing for joy.

For waters shall break forth in the wilderness,
and streams in the desert;
the burning sand shall become a pool,
and the thirsty ground springs of water.

The word of the Lord. **Thanks be to God.**

RESPONSORIAL PSALM *(Psalm 146)*

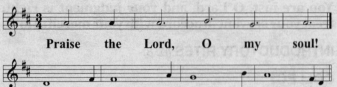

Praise   the   Lord,   O   my   soul!

R. **Praise the Lord, O my soul!**
or **Alleluia!**

It is the Lord who keeps faith for··**ever,**
who executes justice for the op··**pressed;**
who gives food to the · **hungry.**
The Lord sets the · **prisoners** free. R.

The Lord opens the eyes of the · **blind**
and lifts up those who are bowed · **down;**
the Lord loves the · **righteous**
and watches over · **the** strangers. R.

The Lord upholds the orphan and the · **widow,**
but the way of the wicked he brings to · **ruin.**
The Lord will reign for··**ever,**
your God, O Zion, for all · **gener**-ations. R.

©2009 Gordon Johnston/Novalis

To hear the Sunday Psalms, visit www.livingwithchrist.ca.

SECOND READING *(James 2.1-5)*

My brothers and sisters, do you with your acts of favour-
itism really believe in our glorious Lord Jesus Christ? For
if a man with gold rings and in fine clothes comes into
your assembly, and if a poor person in dirty clothes
also comes in, and if you take notice of the one wearing

the fine clothes and say, "Have a seat here, please," while to the one who is poor you say, "Stand there," or, "Sit at my feet," have you not made distinctions among yourselves, and become judges with evil thoughts?

Listen, my beloved brothers and sisters. Has not God chosen the poor in the world to be rich in faith and to be heirs of the kingdom that he has promised to those who love him?

The word of the Lord. **Thanks be to God.**

GOSPEL ACCLAMATION *(Matthew 4.23)*
Alleluia. Alleluia. Jesus proclaimed the good news of the kingdom and cured every sickness among the people. **Alleluia.**

GOSPEL *(Mark 7.31-37)*
The Lord be with you. **And with your spirit.** A reading from the holy Gospel according to Mark. **Glory to you, O Lord.**

Returning from the region of Tyre, Jesus went by way of Sidon towards the Sea of Galilee, in the region of the Decapolis.

They brought to him a man who was deaf and who had an impediment in his speech; and they begged him to lay his hand on him. Jesus took him aside in private, away from the crowd, and put his fingers into his ears, and he spat and touched his tongue. Then looking up to heaven, he sighed and said to him, "Ephphatha," that is, "Be opened." And immediately the man's ears were opened, his tongue was released, and he spoke plainly.

Then Jesus ordered them to tell no one; but the more he ordered them, the more zealously they proclaimed it. They were astounded beyond measure, saying, "He has done everything well; he even makes the deaf to hear and the mute to speak."

The Gospel of the Lord. **Praise to you, Lord Jesus Christ.**

PROFESSION OF FAITH (p. 14)

PRAYER OF THE FAITHFUL

The following intentions are suggestions only.
There are more suggestions at www.livingwithchrist.ca.

R. **Lord, hear our prayer.**

For the Church, welcoming all God's children, we pray to the Lord: R.

For world leaders, bringing strength and wisdom to their care for the poor, we pray to the Lord: R.

For all who hunger and thirst for acceptance, we pray to the Lord: R.

For God's people gathered here, we pray to the Lord: R.

PREPARATION OF THE GIFTS (p. 17)

PRAYER OVER THE OFFERINGS

O God, who give us the gift of true prayer and of peace, graciously grant that, through this offering, we may do fitting homage to your divine majesty and, by partaking of the sacred mystery, we may be faithfully united in mind and heart. Through Christ our Lord. **Amen.**

PREFACE (Sundays in Ordinary Time, p. 31)

COMMUNION ANTIPHON *(Cf. Psalm 41.2-3)*
Like the deer that yearns for running streams, so my soul is yearning for you, my God; my soul is thirsting for God, the living God.

or (John 8.12)
I am the light of the world, says the Lord; whoever follows me will not walk in darkness, but will have the light of life.

PRAYER AFTER COMMUNION
Grant that your faithful, O Lord, whom you nourish and endow with life through the food of your Word and heavenly Sacrament, may so benefit from your beloved Son's great gifts that we may merit an eternal share in his life. Who lives and reigns for ever and ever. **Amen.**

BLESSING AND DISMISSAL *(p. 72)*

24th Sunday in Ordinary Time

Today's Gospel has Jesus expressing some pretty strong words for Peter. When Peter challenges what Jesus is telling the disciples about his death and resurrection, Jesus tells him that he thinks like a human and not like God. "Get behind me, Satan" is so strong it's easy to see that it's not a good thing. One has to wonder – how can we humans ever think like God does?

One clue is to consider losing vs. saving our lives. If we can lose our human way of seeing the world – give up our worldly expectations – maybe we can train ourselves to think differently and be open to what God wants. If we can think more like God, maybe we can embrace the crosses we need to bear more readily, or respond more quickly to the needs of others.

We may already be struggling with our daily prayer routine. We may not have time to join a Bible study, or catch an inspirational video or podcast. Any of these might help save ourselves from our limited and often selfish human ways of thinking. While there are many options for learning more about the mind of Jesus in our connected world, our time is still limited. What part of our lives could we lose in order to save the parts that need to be more Christ-like?

Jeanne Lambert
Oxford Station, ON

ENTRANCE ANTIPHON (Cf. Sirach 36.18)
Give peace, O Lord, to those who wait for you, that your prophets be found true. Hear the prayers of your servant, and of your people Israel.

INTRODUCTORY RITES (p. 8)

COLLECT
Look upon us, O God, Creator and ruler of all things, and, that we may feel the working of your mercy, grant that we may serve you with all our heart. Through our Lord Jesus Christ, your Son, who lives and reigns with you in the unity of the Holy Spirit, God, for ever and ever. **Amen.**

FIRST READING (Isaiah 50.5-9)
The Lord God has opened my ear,
and I was not rebellious, I did not turn backward.
I gave my back to those who struck me,
and my cheeks to those who pulled out the beard;
I did not hide my face from insult and spitting.

The Lord God helps me;
therefore I have not been disgraced;
therefore I have set my face like flint,
and I know that I shall not be put to shame;
he who vindicates me is near.

Who will contend with me? Let us stand up together.
Who are my adversaries? Let them confront me.
It is the Lord God who helps me;
who will declare me guilty?

The word of the Lord. **Thanks be to God.**

RESPONSORIAL PSALM *(Psalm 116)*

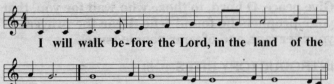

I will walk be-fore the Lord, in the land of the liv-ing.

℟. **I will walk before the Lord,**
   in the land of the living.
or **Alleluia!**

I love the Lord, because he has · **heard**
my voice and my · suppli-cations.
Because he inclined his ear to · **me,**
therefore I will call on him as long as · **I live.** ℟.

The snares of death encompassed me;
   the pangs of Sheol laid · **hold_on_me;**
I suffered distress · **and** anguish.
Then I called on the name of the · **Lord:**
"O Lord, I pray, save · **my life!"** ℟.

Gracious is the Lord, and · **righteous;**
our God · **is** merciful.
The Lord protects the · **simple;**
when I was brought low, · **he** saved_me. ℟.

For you have delivered my soul from · **death,**
my eyes from tears, my feet · **from** stumbling.
I will walk before the · **Lord**
in the land of · **the** living. ℟.

©2009 *Gordon Johnston/Novalis*

SECOND READING *(James 2.14-18)*

What good is it, my brothers and sisters, if you say you have faith but do not have works? Can faith save you?

If a brother or a sister is without clothing and lacks daily food, and one of you says to them, "Go in peace; keep warm and eat your fill," and yet you do not supply their bodily needs, what is the good of that? So faith by itself, if it has no works, is dead.

But someone will say, "You have faith and I have works." Show me your faith apart from your works, and I by my works will show you my faith.

The word of the Lord. **Thanks be to God.**

GOSPEL ACCLAMATION *(Galatians 6.14)*

Alleluia. Alleluia. May I never boast of anything except the Cross of the Lord, by which the world has been crucified to me, and I to the world. **Alleluia.**

GOSPEL *(Mark 8.27-35)*

The Lord be with you. **And with your spirit.** A reading from the holy Gospel according to Mark. **Glory to you, O Lord.**

Jesus went on with his disciples to the villages of Caesarea Philippi; and on the way he asked his disciples, "Who do people say that I am?" And they answered him, "John the Baptist; and others, Elijah; and still others, one of the Prophets."

Jesus asked them, "But who do you say that I am?" Peter answered him, "You are the Christ." And he sternly ordered them not to tell anyone about him.

Then he began to teach them that the Son of Man must undergo great suffering, and be rejected by the elders, the chief priests, and the scribes, and be killed, and after three days rise again. He said all this quite openly.

And Peter took Jesus aside and began to rebuke him. But turning and looking at his disciples, he rebuked Peter and said, "Get behind me, Satan! For you are thinking not as God does, but as humans do."

Jesus called the crowd with his disciples, and said to them, "Whoever wants to become my follower, let him deny himself and take up his cross and follow me. For whoever wants to save their life will lose it, and whoever loses their life for my sake, and for the sake of the Gospel, will save it."

The Gospel of the Lord. **Praise to you, Lord Jesus Christ.**

PROFESSION OF FAITH (p. 14)

PRAYER OF THE FAITHFUL

The following intentions are suggestions only.
There are more suggestions at www.livingwithchrist.ca.

R. **Lord, hear our prayer.**

For the Church, walking in the presence of the Lord, we pray to the Lord: R.

For world leaders who work for justice, peace and the integrity of creation, we pray to the Lord: R.

For those suffering from illness, violence, poverty or hunger, we pray to the Lord: R.

For the members of this community, called to listen for the stirrings of God's spirit, we pray to the Lord: R.

PREPARATION OF THE GIFTS *(p. 17)*

PRAYER OVER THE OFFERINGS
Look with favour on our supplications, O Lord, and in your kindness accept these, your servants' offerings, that what each has offered to the honour of your name may serve the salvation of all. Through Christ our Lord. **Amen.**

PREFACE *(Sundays in Ordinary Time, p. 31)*

COMMUNION ANTIPHON *(Cf. Psalm 35.8)*
How precious is your mercy, O God! The children of men seek shelter in the shadow of your wings.

or (Cf. 1 Corinthians 10.16)
The chalice of blessing that we bless is a communion in the Blood of Christ; and the bread that we break is a sharing in the Body of the Lord.

PRAYER AFTER COMMUNION
May the working of this heavenly gift, O Lord, we pray, take possession of our minds and bodies, so that its effects, and not our own desires, may always prevail in us. Through Christ our Lord. **Amen.**

BLESSING AND DISMISSAL *(p. 72)*

25th Sunday in Ordinary Time

As someone who wears glasses, I know that it doesn't take much for them to become ineffective. They might just have been cleaned, but eat a salad and they are suddenly spotted with dressing; or go outside in cold weather and they are fogged up. Likewise, our ego can prevent us from seeing clearly and living out our faith.

When Jesus tells the disciples about his impending death and resurrection, it doesn't sink in. Perhaps this is because his death is too awful to contemplate or because resurrection is a difficult concept. However, the timing of their argument about who is the greatest suggests that they are too busy thinking about themselves, to think about him. Jesus is someone they dearly love, yet they are unable to respond to his news with compassion. Jesus has taught them not to be afraid, yet they cannot summon the courage to ask him to explain. They are hamstrung by their ego. As Jesus shows by likening welcoming a child to welcoming God, his definition of greatness is our ability to love.

Perhaps today is an opportunity for us to ask Jesus to subdue our egos so that we can see him as he is and ourselves as he is asking us to be.

Kate Larson
Nepean, ON

ENTRANCE ANTIPHON
I am the salvation of the people, says the Lord. Should they cry to me in any distress, I will hear them, and I will be their Lord for ever.

INTRODUCTORY RITES (p. 8)

COLLECT
O God, who founded all the commands of your sacred Law upon love of you and of our neighbour, grant that, by keeping your precepts, we may merit to attain eternal life. Through our Lord Jesus Christ, your Son, who lives and reigns with you in the unity of the Holy Spirit, God, for ever and ever. **Amen.**

FIRST READING (Wisdom 2.12, 17-20)
The godless say, "Let us lie in wait for the righteous one, who makes life inconvenient to us and opposes our actions; who reproaches us for sins against the law, and accuses us of sins against our training.

"Let us see if his words are true, and let us test what will happen at the end of his life; for if the righteous one is God's son, God will help him, and will deliver him from the hand of his adversaries.

"Let us test him with insult and torture, so that we may find out how gentle he is, and make trial of his forbearance. Let us condemn him to a shameful death, for, according to what he says, he will be protected."

The word of the Lord. **Thanks be to God.**

RESPONSORIAL PSALM *(Psalm 54)*

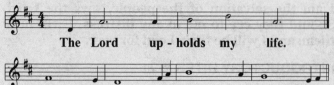

The Lord up - holds my life.

R. **The Lord upholds my life.**

Save me, O God, by your · **name,**
and vindicate me by · **your** might.
Hear my prayer, O · **God;**
give ear to the words of · **my** mouth. R.

1 - For the insolent have risen a-·**gainst_me,**
2 - the ruthless seek · **my** life;
4 - they do not set God · **be**-fore_them. R.

But surely, God is my · **helper;**
the Lord is the upholder of · **my** life.
With a freewill offering I will · **sacrifice_to_you;**
I will give thanks to your name, for · **it_is** good. R.

©2009 Gordon Johnston/Novalis

To hear the Sunday Psalms, visit www.livingwithchrist.ca.

SECOND READING *(James 3.16 – 4.3)*

Beloved: Where there is envy and selfish ambition, there will also be disorder and wickedness of every kind. But the wisdom from above is first pure, then peaceable, gentle, willing to yield, full of mercy and good fruits, without a trace of partiality or hypocrisy. And a harvest of righteousness is sown in peace for those who make peace.

Those conflicts and disputes among you, where do they come from? Do they not come from your cravings that are at war within you? You want something and do not have it; so you commit murder. And you covet something and cannot obtain it; so you engage in disputes and conflicts.

You do not have, because you do not ask. You ask and do not receive, because you ask wrongly, in order to spend what you get on your pleasures.

The word of the Lord. **Thanks be to God.**

GOSPEL ACCLAMATION *(2 Thessalonians 2.14)*
Alleluia. Alleluia. God has called us through the good news, to obtain the glory of our Lord Jesus Christ. **Alleluia.**

GOSPEL *(Mark 9.30-37)*
The Lord be with you. **And with your spirit.**
A reading from the holy Gospel according to Mark. **Glory to you, O Lord.**

After leaving the mountain Jesus and his disciples went on from there and passed through Galilee. He did not want anyone to know it; for he was teaching his disciples, saying to them, "The Son of Man is to be betrayed into the hands of men, and they will kill him, and three days after being killed, he will rise again." But they did not understand what he was saying and were afraid to ask him.

Then they came to Capernaum; and when he was in the house Jesus asked them, "What were you arguing about on the way?" But they were silent, for on the way they had argued with one another who was the greatest.

Jesus sat down, called the twelve, and said to them, "Whoever wants to be first must be last of all and servant of all."

Then he took a little child and put it among them; and taking it in his arms, he said to them, "Whoever welcomes one such child in my name welcomes me, and whoever welcomes me welcomes not me but the one who sent me."

The Gospel of the Lord. **Praise to you, Lord Jesus Christ.**

PROFESSION OF FAITH *(p. 14)*

PRAYER OF THE FAITHFUL

The following intentions are suggestions only.
There are more suggestions at www.livingwithchrist.ca.

R. **Lord, hear our prayer.**

For the Church, called to be a humble servant of all, we pray to the Lord: R.

For discerning service by all those who hold public office, we pray to the Lord: R.

For children everywhere, blessed and loved by God, we pray to the Lord: R.

For this community, called to welcome children in the name of Jesus, we pray to the Lord: R.

PREPARATION OF THE GIFTS *(p. 17)*

PRAYER OVER THE OFFERINGS
Receive with favour, O Lord, we pray, the offerings of your people, that what they profess with devotion and faith may be theirs through these heavenly mysteries. Through Christ our Lord. **Amen.**

PREFACE *(Sundays in Ordinary Time, p. 31)*

COMMUNION ANTIPHON *(Psalm 118.4-5)*
You have laid down your precepts to be carefully kept; may my ways be firm in keeping your statutes.

or (John 10.14)
I am the Good Shepherd, says the Lord; I know my sheep, and mine know me.

PRAYER AFTER COMMUNION
Graciously raise up, O Lord, those you renew with this Sacrament, that we may come to possess your redemption both in mystery and in the manner of our life. Through Christ our Lord. **Amen.**

BLESSING AND DISMISSAL *(p. 72)*

**SEP
29**

26th Sunday in Ordinary Time
World Day of Migrants and Refugees

In today's second reading, James writes with a disciplinary earnestness addressing "you rich people." He describes punishment awaiting those who exploit others. Tragically, today the world continues to be flooded by exploitation and oppression. It is fitting that this reading falls on the 110th World Day of Migrants and Refugees. Conflict, socio-economic crises and natural disasters continue to displace millions from their homes. This displacement puts them at risk of exploitation.

While we may not be contributing directly to the problem, are we working towards a solution? Media tend to paint a narrow picture of the ongoing worldwide refugee crisis, often only focusing on one or two countries. Working with the refugee community, I have learned that while there are many positive stories of brighter futures, there is also a darker side that can include human trafficking.

Being rich does not only refer to monetary wealth. You may be rich in resources, knowledge, or even social and political agency. On this World Day of Migrants and Refugees, reflect on how you can use your own riches to work towards the end of human exploitation. Following today's Gospel, "be not a stumbling block before one of these little ones" but rather "give [...] a cup of water to drink because you bear the name of Christ."

Julianna Deutscher, Kingston, ON

National Collection for the Needs of the Church in Canada

ENTRANCE ANTIPHON *(Daniel 3.31, 29, 30, 43, 42)*
All that you have done to us, O Lord, you have done with true judgment, for we have sinned against you and not obeyed your commandments. But give glory to your name and deal with us according to the bounty of your mercy.

INTRODUCTORY RITES *(p. 8)*

COLLECT
O God, who manifest your almighty power above all by pardoning and showing mercy, bestow, we pray, your grace abundantly upon us and make those hastening to attain your promises heirs to the treasures of heaven. Through our Lord Jesus Christ, your Son, who lives and reigns with you in the unity of the Holy Spirit, God, for ever and ever. **Amen.**

FIRST READING *(Numbers 11.25-29)*
The Lord came down in the cloud, took some of the spirit that was on Moses and put it on the seventy elders. When the spirit rested upon them, they prophesied. But they did not do so again.

Two men remained in the camp, one named Eldad, and the other named Medad, and the spirit rested on them; they were among those registered, but they had not gone out to the tent, and so they prophesied in the camp. A young man ran and told Moses, "Eldad and Medad are prophesying in the camp."

Joshua son of Nun, the assistant of Moses, one of his chosen men, said, "My lord Moses, stop them!" But Moses said to him, "Are you jealous for my sake?

Would that all the Lord's people were Prophets, and
that the Lord would put his spirit on them!"
  The word of the Lord. **Thanks be to God.**

RESPONSORIAL PSALM *(Psalm 19)*

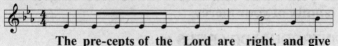

The pre-cepts of the Lord are right, and give

joy to the heart.

R. **The precepts of the Lord are right,
  and give joy to the heart.**

The law of the Lord is · **perfect,**
reviving the · **soul;**
the decrees of the Lord are · **sure,**
making wise · **the** simple. R.

The fear of the Lord is · **pure,**
enduring for-**ever;**
the ordinances of the Lord are · **true**
and righteous · **alto**-gether. R.

By them is your servant · **warned;**
in keeping them there is great re-**ward.**
But who can detect unmindful · **errors?**
Clear me from · **hidden** faults. R.

Keep back your servant also from the · **insolent;**
do not let them have dominion · **over_me.**
Then I shall be · **blameless,**
and innocent of · **great_trans**-gression. R.

©2009 Gordon Johnston/Novalis

SECOND READING *(James 5.1-6)*
Come now, you rich people, weep and wail for the miseries that are coming to you. Your riches have rotted, and your clothes are moth-eaten. Your gold and silver have rusted, and their rust will be evidence against you, and it will eat your flesh like fire.

You have laid up treasure for the last days. Listen! The wages of the labourers who mowed your fields, which you kept back by fraud, cry out, and the cries of the harvesters have reached the ears of the Lord of hosts.

You have lived on the earth in luxury and in pleasure; you have fattened your hearts in a day of slaughter. You have condemned and murdered the righteous one, who does not resist you.

The word of the Lord. **Thanks be to God.**

GOSPEL ACCLAMATION *(John 17.17)*
Alleluia. Alleluia. Your word, O Lord, is truth; sanctify us in the truth. **Alleluia.**

GOSPEL *(Mark 9.38-43, 45, 47-48)*
The Lord be with you. **And with your spirit.**
A reading from the holy Gospel according to Mark.
Glory to you, O Lord.

After Jesus had finished teaching the disciples, John said to him, "Teacher, we saw someone casting out demons in your name, and we tried to stop him, because he was not following us." But Jesus said, "Do not stop him; for no one who does a deed of power in my name will be able soon afterward to speak evil of me. Whoever is not against us is for us.

"For truly I tell you, whoever gives you a cup of water to drink because you bear the name of Christ will by no means lose the reward.

"If any of you put a stumbling block before one of these little ones who believe in me, it would be better for you if a great millstone were hung around your neck and you were thrown into the sea.

"If your hand causes you to stumble, cut it off; it is better for you to enter life maimed than to have two hands and to go to hell, to the unquenchable fire. And if your foot causes you to stumble, cut it off; it is better for you to enter life lame than to have two feet and to be thrown into hell. And if your eye causes you to stumble, tear it out; it is better for you to enter the kingdom of God with one eye than to have two eyes and to be thrown into hell, where their worm never dies, and the fire is never quenched."

The Gospel of the Lord. **Praise to you, Lord Jesus Christ.**

PROFESSION OF FAITH *(p. 14)*

PRAYER OF THE FAITHFUL

The following intentions are suggestions only.
There are more suggestions at www.livingwithchrist.ca.

R. **Lord, hear our prayer.**

For all religious leaders who seek to foster love and forgiveness in the world, we pray to the Lord: R.

For leaders of nations, working to bring peace and security to troubled areas of the world, we pray to the Lord: R.

For those who keep the flame of hope burning in the midst of injustice and need, we pray to the Lord: R.

For all refugees, searching for welcome, peace and security in a new homeland, we pray to the Lord: R.

For this assembly, always striving to live the Good News, we pray to the Lord: R.

PREPARATION OF THE GIFTS *(p. 17)*

PRAYER OVER THE OFFERINGS
Grant us, O merciful God, that this our offering may find acceptance with you and that through it the wellspring of all blessing may be laid open before us. Through Christ our Lord. **Amen.**

PREFACE *(Sundays in Ordinary Time, p. 31)*

COMMUNION ANTIPHON *(Cf. Psalm 118.49-50)*
Remember your word to your servant, O Lord, by which you have given me hope. This is my comfort when I am brought low.

or (1 John 3.16)
By this we came to know the love of God: that Christ laid down his life for us; so we ought to lay down our lives for one another.

PRAYER AFTER COMMUNION
May this heavenly mystery, O Lord, restore us in mind and body, that we may be co-heirs in glory with Christ, to whose suffering we are united whenever we proclaim his Death. Who lives and reigns for ever and ever. **Amen.**

BLESSING AND DISMISSAL *(p. 72)*

October Saints' Days

The following saints are traditionally remembered in October in Canada.

Saint Thérèse of the Child Jesus . . . . Oct 1

The Holy Guardian Angels . . . . Oct 2

Saint Francis of Assisi. . . . . Oct 4

Saint Faustina Kowalska . . . . Oct 5

Blessed Marie-Rose Durocher . . . . Oct 6
Saint Bruno

Our Lady of the Rosary . . . . Oct 7

Saint Denis and Companions . . . . Oct 9
Saint John Leonardi

Saint John XXIII. . . . . Oct 11

Saint Callistus I . . . . Oct 14

Saint Teresa of Jesus . . . . Oct 15

Saint Marguerite d'Youville. . . . . Oct 16

Saint Ignatius of Antioch . . . . Oct 17

Saint Luke . . . . Oct 18

Saint Paul of the Cross . . . . Oct 19

Saint Hedwig . . . . Oct 20
Saint Margaret Mary Alacoque

Saint John Paul II. . . . . Oct 22

Saint John of Capistrano. Oct 23

Saint Anthony Mary Claret . . . . Oct 24

Saints Simon and Jude . . . . Oct 28

27th Sunday in Ordinary Time

I'm holding my sleeping granddaughter while contemplating the lines from today's Gospel: "Whoever does not receive the kingdom of God as a little child will never enter it." She's lying peacefully in my arms, not knowing the words to any prayers yet; but, in a sense, she is a living prayer teaching essential wisdom. She hasn't learned to consciously listen for God's voice, yet she communicates God's grace. Just by being alive and resting in divine presence, she teaches me that there is prayer before words. It is this simplicity in prayer preceding language that helps me toward heaven. This divine simplicity is akin to the breath of life that God breathed into the man in today's first reading, making human community possible.

Jesus encourages this simplicity of heart as a prayer path. In abiding in God's grace, I glimpse the glory of heaven. In the busyness of my life, littered with worries and preoccupations, I can easily lose touch with the joy of simply resting in God's love.

How can we recover this divine, child-like simplicity in our own prayer lives? Perhaps it is through silent contemplation of the beauty that surrounds us. The visual language of our churches wraps us in grace, as do the natural wonders around us. Maybe we can abide in that wonder as a way of being with God in a child-like way.

Les Miller
Richmond Hill, ON

ENTRANCE ANTIPHON *(Cf. Esther 4.17)*
Within your will, O Lord, all things are established, and there is none that can resist your will. For you have made all things, the heaven and the earth, and all that is held within the circle of heaven; you are the Lord of all.

INTRODUCTORY RITES *(p. 8)*

COLLECT
Almighty ever-living God, who in the abundance of your kindness surpass the merits and the desires of those who entreat you, pour out your mercy upon us to pardon what conscience dreads and to give what prayer does not dare to ask. Through our Lord Jesus Christ, your Son, who lives and reigns with you in the unity of the Holy Spirit, God, for ever and ever. **Amen.**

FIRST READING *(Genesis 2.7ab, 15, 18-24)*
The Lord God formed man from the dust of the ground, and breathed into his nostrils the breath of life, and put him in the garden of Eden to till it and keep it.

Then the Lord God said, "It is not good that the man should be alone; I will make him a helper as his partner." So out of the ground the Lord God formed every animal of the field and every bird of the air, and brought them to the man to see what he would call them; and whatever the man called every living creature, that was its name. The man gave names to all cattle, and to the birds of the air, and to every animal of the field; but for the man there was not found a helper as his partner.

So the Lord God caused a deep sleep to fall upon the man, and he slept; then he took one of his ribs and closed up its place with flesh. And the rib that the Lord God had taken from the man he made into a woman and brought her to the man.

Then the man said, "This at last is bone of my bones and flesh of my flesh; this one shall be called Woman, for out of Man this one was taken."

Therefore a man leaves his father and his mother and clings to his wife, and they become one flesh.

The word of the Lord. **Thanks be to God.**

RESPONSORIAL PSALM *(Psalm 128)*

May the Lord bless us all the days of   our lives.

R. **May the Lord bless us all the days of our lives.**

Blessed is everyone who fears · **the** Lord,
who walks in · **his** ways.
You shall eat the fruit of the labour
   of · **your** hands;
you shall be happy, and it shall go well
   · **with** you. R.

Your wife will be like a fruit·-**ful** vine
within · **your** house;
your children will be · **like** olive_shoots
around · **your** table. R.

Thus shall the man be blessed
> who fears · **the** Lord.
The Lord bless you · **from** Zion.
May you see the prosperity of · **Je**-rusalem
all the days of · **your** life. R.

©2009 Gordon Johnston/Novalis

To hear the Sunday Psalms, visit www.livingwithchrist.ca.

SECOND READING *(Hebrews 2.9-11)*

We do indeed see Jesus, who for a little while was made lower than the Angels, now crowned with glory and honour because of the suffering of death, so that by the grace of God he might taste death for everyone.

It was fitting that God, for whom and through whom all things exist, in bringing many sons and daughters to glory should make the pioneer of their salvation perfect through sufferings. For the one who sanctifies and those who are sanctified are all from one. For this reason he is not ashamed to call them brothers and sisters.

The word of the Lord. **Thanks be to God.**

GOSPEL ACCLAMATION *(1 John 4.12)*

Alleluia. Alleluia. If we love one another, God will live in us in perfect love. **Alleluia.**

GOSPEL *(Mark 10.2-16)*

The shorter version ends at the asterisks.

The Lord be with you. **And with your spirit.**
A reading from the holy Gospel according to Mark.
Glory to you, O Lord.

Some Pharisees came, and to test Jesus they asked, "Is it lawful for a man to divorce his wife?" Jesus answered them, "What did Moses command you?" They said, "Moses allowed a man to write a certificate of dismissal and to divorce her."

But Jesus said to them, "Because of your hardness of heart he wrote this commandment for you. But from the beginning of creation, 'God made them male and female.' 'For this reason a man shall leave his father and mother and be joined to his wife, and the two shall become one flesh.' So they are no longer two, but one flesh. Therefore what God has joined together, let no one separate."

Then in the house the disciples asked him again about this matter. Jesus said to them, "Whoever divorces his wife and marries another commits adultery against her; and if she divorces her husband and marries another, she commits adultery."

* * *

People were bringing little children to him in order that Jesus might touch them; and the disciples spoke sternly to them. But when Jesus saw this, he was indignant and said to them, "Let the little children come to me; do not stop them: for it is to such as these that the kingdom of God belongs. Truly I tell you, whoever does not receive the kingdom of God as a little child will never enter it."

And Jesus took them up in his arms, laid his hands on them, and blessed them.

The Gospel of the Lord. **Praise to you, Lord Jesus Christ.**

PROFESSION OF FAITH *(p. 14)*

PRAYER OF THE FAITHFUL
The following intentions are suggestions only.
There are more suggestions at www.livingwithchrist.ca.

R. **Lord, hear our prayer.**

For the Church, instrument of God's healing, we pray to the Lord: R.

For corporate and political leaders who have the power to promote peace, we pray to the Lord: R.

For healing for all victims of abuse and violence, we pray to the Lord: R.

For the community of faith gathered here today, we pray to the Lord: R.

PREPARATION OF THE GIFTS *(p. 17)*

PRAYER OVER THE OFFERINGS
Accept, O Lord, we pray, the sacrifices instituted by your commands and, through the sacred mysteries, which we celebrate with dutiful service, graciously complete the sanctifying work by which you are pleased to redeem us. Through Christ our Lord. **Amen.**

PREFACE *(Sundays in Ordinary Time, p. 31)*

COMMUNION ANTIPHON *(Lamentations 3.25)*

The Lord is good to those who hope in him, to the soul that seeks him.

   or (Cf. 1 Corinthians 10.17)

Though many, we are one bread, one body, for we all partake of the one Bread and one Chalice.

PRAYER AFTER COMMUNION

Grant us, almighty God, that we may be refreshed and nourished by the Sacrament which we have received, so as to be transformed into what we consume. Through Christ our Lord. **Amen.**

BLESSING AND DISMISSAL *(p. 72)*

28th Sunday in Ordinary Time

I write to deadlines and to available space. I allot the time and space required for the project and move on. For many, especially those who procrastinate, this is difficult to do. Many people yearn to achieve things, but they don't *burn*.

In today's Gospel, the rich, young man yearns for salvation, but he isn't burning. He is willing to do the minimum to gain eternal life, but he is very hesitant to step outside his comfort zone and go the extra mile.

He is much like many of us. Do we burn with a passion for eternal life? Are we willing to do more than the minimum, which may be in our comfort zone, to gain eternal life? We may have good intentions, but are good intentions going to help us meet the deadline?

We fool ourselves if we think we can gain eternal life by our own merit. We need wisdom which comes from God. We need the Word of God to judge the "intentions of the heart." "For humans, [salvation] is impossible, but not for God."

Today, let us pray for the wisdom of God to fill our hearts so that we may give ourselves over to God. Then we can step out of our comfort zone and burn with a desire to serve God.

Anthony Chezzi
Sudbury, ON

ENTRANCE ANTIPHON *(Psalm 129.3-4)*
If you, O Lord, should mark iniquities, Lord, who could stand? But with you is found forgiveness, O God of Israel.

INTRODUCTORY RITES *(p. 8)*

COLLECT
May your grace, O Lord, we pray, at all times go before us and follow after and make us always determined to carry out good works. Through our Lord Jesus Christ, your Son, who lives and reigns with you in the unity of the Holy Spirit, God, for ever and ever. **Amen.**

FIRST READING *(Wisdom 7.7-11)*
I prayed, and understanding was given me;
I called on God, and the spirit of wisdom came to me.

I preferred her to sceptres and thrones,
and I accounted wealth as nothing in comparison
   with her.
Neither did I liken to her any priceless gem,
because all gold is but a little sand in her sight,
and silver will be accounted as clay before her.

I loved her more than health and beauty,
and I chose to have her rather than light,
because her radiance never ceases.
All good things came to me along with her,
and in her hands uncounted wealth.

The word of the Lord. **Thanks be to God.**

RESPONSORIAL PSALM *(Psalm 90)*

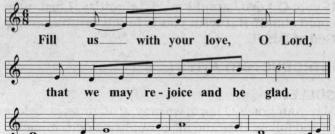

Fill us with your love, O Lord, that we may rejoice and be glad.

℟. **Fill us with your love, O Lord,**
that we may rejoice and be glad.

Teach us to count our · **days**
that we may gain a wise · **heart.**
Turn, O Lord! How · **long?**
Have compassion · **on_your** servants! ℟.

Satisfy us in the morning
    with your steadfast · **love,**
so that we may rejoice and be glad all our · **days.**
Make us glad as many days
    as you have af-·**flicted_us,**
and as many years as we have · **seen** evil. ℟.

Let your work be manifest to your · **servants,**
and your glorious power to their · **children.**
Let the favour of the Lord our God be up-·**on_us,**
and prosper for us the work of · **our** hands. ℟.

SECOND READING *(Hebrews 4.12-13)*
The word of God is living and active, sharper than
any two-edged sword, piercing until it divides soul

from spirit, joints from marrow; it is able to judge the thoughts and intentions of the heart.

And before God no creature is hidden, but all are naked and laid bare to the eyes of the one to whom we must render an account.

The word of the Lord. **Thanks be to God.**

GOSPEL ACCLAMATION *(Matthew 5.3)*
Alleluia. Alleluia. Blessed are the poor in spirit; for theirs is the kingdom of heaven! **Alleluia.**

GOSPEL *(Mark 10.17-30)*
The shorter version ends at the asterisks.
The Lord be with you. **And with your spirit.** A reading from the holy Gospel according to Mark. **Glory to you, O Lord.**

As Jesus was setting out on a journey, a man ran up and knelt before him, and asked him, "Good Teacher, what must I do to inherit eternal life?"

Jesus said to him, "Why do you call me good? No one is good but God alone. You know the commandments: 'You shall not murder; You shall not commit adultery; You shall not steal; You shall not bear false witness; You shall not defraud; Honour your father and mother.'"

He said to Jesus, "Teacher, I have kept all these since my youth." Jesus, looking at him, loved him and said, "You lack one thing; go, sell what you own, and give the money to the poor, and you will have treasure in heaven; then come, follow me."

When the man heard this, he was shocked and went away grieving, for he had many possessions.

Then Jesus looked around and said to his disciples, "How hard it will be for those who have wealth to enter the kingdom of God!" And the disciples were perplexed at these words. But Jesus said to them again, "Children, how hard it is to enter the kingdom of God! It is easier for a camel to go through the eye of a needle than for someone who is rich to enter the kingdom of God."

They were greatly astounded and said to one another, "Then who can be saved?" Jesus looked at them and said, "For humans it is impossible, but not for God; for God all things are possible."

* * *

Peter began to say to him, "Look, we have left everything and followed you." Jesus said, "Truly I tell you, there is no one who has left house or brothers or sisters or mother or father or children or fields, for my sake and for the sake of the good news, who will not receive a hundredfold now in this age — houses, brothers and sisters, mothers and children, and fields — but with persecutions — and in the age to come, eternal life."

The Gospel of the Lord. **Praise to you, Lord Jesus Christ.**

PROFESSION OF FAITH (p. 14)

PRAYER OF THE FAITHFUL

The following intentions are suggestions only.
There are more suggestions at www.livingwithchrist.ca.

R. **Lord, hear our prayer.**

For all God's people, open to responding to the call of Jesus, we pray to the Lord: R.

For all leaders, summoned by God to help bring about the reign of love, we pray to the Lord: R.

For persons who struggle with poverty, and for those who choose to live in voluntary simplicity, we pray to the Lord: R.

For God's People gathered here, called to recognize God among us, we pray to the Lord: R.

PREPARATION OF THE GIFTS *(p. 17)*

PRAYER OVER THE OFFERINGS
Accept, O Lord, the prayers of your faithful with the sacrificial offerings, that, through these acts of devotedness, we may pass over to the glory of heaven. Through Christ our Lord. **Amen.**

PREFACE *(Sundays in Ordinary Time, p. 31)*

COMMUNION ANTIPHON *(Cf. Psalm 33.11)*
The rich suffer want and go hungry, but those who seek the Lord lack no blessing.

or (1 John 3.2)
When the Lord appears, we shall be like him, for we shall see him as he is.

PRAYER AFTER COMMUNION
We entreat your majesty most humbly, O Lord, that, as you feed us with the nourishment which comes from the most holy Body and Blood of your Son, so you may make us sharers of his divine nature. Who lives and reigns for ever and ever. **Amen.**

BLESSING AND DISMISSAL *(p. 72)*

29th Sunday in Ordinary Time
World Mission Sunday

We know that James and John were fishermen. These brothers were probably working long hours, up before dawn and making sure they could reap the benefits of their catch. They left it all to become close followers of Jesus of Nazareth.

"Grant us to sit, one at your right hand and one at your left, in your glory." A pretty bold request. When Jesus asks if they are prepared to be baptized as he is and drink the cup that he is to drink, they are still enthused. "We are able." We know that the cup Jesus is to drink results in his torture and suffering. James and John were missing this. Their vision of glory was very unlike the labour-intensive life of fishermen.

As Christians, are we prepared to be the servant rather than the served? It is hard to rise to this calling. It requires that we become the last, not the first in line. We sometimes see ourselves as an exclusive bunch who are earning points for a prize. Jesus presents us with a different idea of success.

As we gather today to celebrate Jesus and receive him in the Eucharist, may we be mindful of the glory of being the servant, not the served. We join in prayer with grateful hearts for the gift of humility and the glory it brings.

Jan Bentham
Ottawa, ON

ENTRANCE ANTIPHON *(Cf. Psalm 16.6, 8)*

To you I call; for you will surely heed me, O God; turn your ear to me; hear my words. Guard me as the apple of your eye; in the shadow of your wings protect me.

INTRODUCTORY RITES *(p. 8)*

COLLECT

Almighty ever-living God, grant that we may always conform our will to yours and serve your majesty in sincerity of heart. Through our Lord Jesus Christ, your Son, who lives and reigns with you in the unity of the Holy Spirit, God, for ever and ever. **Amen.**

FIRST READING *(Isaiah 53.10-11)*

It was the will of the Lord to crush him with pain. When you make his life an offering for sin, he shall see his offspring, and shall prolong his days; through him the will of the Lord shall prosper. Out of his anguish he shall see light; he shall find satisfaction through his knowledge. The righteous one, my servant, shall make many righteous, and he shall bear their iniquities.

The word of the Lord. **Thanks be to God.**

RESPONSORIAL PSALM *(Psalm 33)*

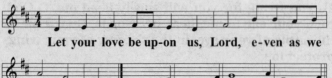

Let your love be up-on us, Lord, e-ven as we
hope in you.

R. **Let your love be upon on us, Lord,
even as we hope in you.**

The word of the Lord is · **upright,**
and all his work is done in · **faithfulness.**
He loves righteousness and · **justice;**
the earth is full of the steadfast love
of the · **Lord.** R.

Truly the eye of the Lord is on those
who · **fear_him,**
on those who hope in his steadfast · **love,**
to deliver their soul from · **death,**
and to keep them alive in · **famine.** R.

Our soul waits for the · **Lord;**
he is our help and · **shield.**
Let your steadfast love, O Lord, be up-·**on_us,**
even as we hope in · **you.** R.

©2009 Gordon Johnston/Novalis

To hear the Sunday Psalms, visit www.livingwithchrist.ca.

SECOND READING *(Hebrews 4.14-16)*

Brothers and sisters: Since we have a great high priest who has passed through the heavens, Jesus, the Son of God, let us hold fast to our confession. For we do not have a high priest who is unable to sympathize with our weaknesses, but we have one who in every respect has been tested as we are, yet without sin.

Let us therefore approach the throne of grace with boldness, so that we may receive mercy and find grace to help in time of need.

The word of the Lord. **Thanks be to God.**

GOSPEL ACCLAMATION *(Mark 10.45)*

Alleluia. Alleluia. The Son of Man came to serve and to give his life as a ransom for many. **Alleluia.**

GOSPEL *(Mark 10.35-45)*

The shorter version begins at the asterisks.

The Lord be with you. **And with your spirit.**
A reading from the holy Gospel according to Mark.
Glory to you, O Lord.

James and John, the sons of Zebedee, came forward to Jesus and said to him, "Teacher, we want you to do for us whatever we ask of you." And Jesus said to them, "What is it you want me to do for you?" And they said to him, "Grant us to sit, one at your right hand and one at your left, in your glory."

But Jesus said to them, "You do not know what you are asking. Are you able to drink the cup that I drink, or be baptized with the baptism that I am baptized with?" They replied, "We are able."

Then Jesus said to them, "The cup that I drink you will drink; and with the baptism with which I am baptized, you will be baptized; but to sit at my right hand or at my left is not mine to grant, but it is for those for whom it has been prepared."

When the ten heard this, they began to be angry with James and John.

* * *

So Jesus called them and said to them, "You know that among the Gentiles those whom they recognize as their rulers lord it over them, and their great ones are tyrants over them. But it is not so among you; whoever wishes to become great among you must be your servant, and whoever wishes to be first among you must be slave of all. For the Son of Man came not to be served but to serve, and to give his life as a ransom for many."

The Gospel of the Lord. **Praise to you, Lord Jesus Christ.**

PROFESSION OF FAITH (p. 14)

PRAYER OF THE FAITHFUL

The following intentions are suggestions only.
There are more suggestions at www.livingwithchrist.ca.

R. **Lord, hear our prayer.**

For the mission of the Church in the world, we pray to the Lord: R.

For leaders who work for justice and peace in the world, we pray to the Lord: R.

For all who suffer from poverty or isolation, we pray to the Lord: R.

For each of us called to witness to God's love and compassion, we pray to the Lord: R.

PREPARATION OF THE GIFTS *(p. 17)*

PRAYER OVER THE OFFERINGS
Grant us, Lord, we pray, a sincere respect for your gifts, that, through the purifying action of your grace, we may be cleansed by the very mysteries we serve. Through Christ our Lord. **Amen.**

PREFACE *(Sundays in Ordinary Time, p. 31)*

COMMUNION ANTIPHON *(Cf. Psalm 32.18-19)*
Behold, the eyes of the Lord are on those who fear him, who hope in his merciful love, to rescue their souls from death, to keep them alive in famine.

or (Mark 10.45)
The Son of Man has come to give his life as a ransom for many.

PRAYER AFTER COMMUNION
Grant, O Lord, we pray, that, benefiting from participation in heavenly things, we may be helped by what you give in this present age and prepared for the gifts that are eternal. Through Christ our Lord. **Amen.**

BLESSING AND DISMISSAL *(p. 72)*

30th Sunday in Ordinary Time

Nothing is more unsettling than the inability to understand the world around us. Physical blindness is a terrifying prospect for most of us, but even the moments of being metaphorically blind while chaos reigns in our life can be equally terrifying. When our lives seem to be spiralling downward and we feel that we're overwhelmed by danger and pain, these can be moments of complete distress.

In such a situation, when full of alarm and terror, and all our efforts produce no solutions, we can do one of two things. We can give into despair and surrender to the belief that things are hopeless. Alternatively, we can do what Bartimaeus does in today's Gospel: go deeper in prayer. Bartimaeus' pleas to Christ are prayers made by a desperate man.

When Bartimaeus begins shouting "Jesus, Son of David, have mercy on me!" he is met by scorn from the crowds. This serves as a stark reminder that prayer doesn't always yield an instant fix to our problems. However, Bartimaeus persists in prayer, and the outcome is ultimately one that sees a solution to his plight. Whether or not we get the answer we expect, we can take consolation in today's Gospel that for those who persist in prayer in dire circumstances, Christ will not leave us abandoned. Our faith will make us well.

Andrew Hume
Toronto, ON

ENTRANCE ANTIPHON *(Cf. Psalm 104.3-4)*
Let the hearts that seek the Lord rejoice; turn to the Lord and his strength; constantly seek his face.

INTRODUCTORY RITES *(p. 8)*

COLLECT
Almighty ever-living God, increase our faith, hope and charity, and make us love what you command, so that we may merit what you promise. Through our Lord Jesus Christ, your Son, who lives and reigns with you in the unity of the Holy Spirit, God, for ever and ever. **Amen.**

FIRST READING *(Jeremiah 31.7-9)*
Thus says the Lord: "Sing aloud with gladness for Jacob, and raise shouts for the chief of the nations; proclaim, give praise, and say, 'Save, O Lord, your people, the remnant of Israel.'

"See, I am going to bring them from the land of the north, and gather them from the farthest parts of the earth, among them those who are blind and those who are lame, those with child and those in labour, together; a great company, they shall return here.

"With weeping they shall come, and with consolations I will lead them back, I will let them walk by brooks of water, in a straight path in which they shall not stumble; for I have become a father to Israel, and Ephraim is my firstborn."

The word of the Lord. **Thanks be to God.**

RESPONSORIAL PSALM *(Psalm 126)*

The Lord has done great things for us; we are filled with

joy.

R. **The Lord has done great things for us;**
we are filled with joy.

When the Lord restored the fortunes of · **Zion,**
we were like those who · **dream.**
Then our mouth was filled with · **laughter,**
and our tongue with shouts · **of** joy. R.

Then it was said among the · **nations,**
"The Lord has done great things for · **them."**
The Lord has done great things for · **us,**
and we · **re**-joiced. R.

Restore our fortunes, O · **Lord,**
like the watercourses in the desert of the · **Negev.**
May those who sow in · **tears**
reap with shouts · **of** joy. R.

Those who go out · **weeping,**
bearing the seed for · **sowing,**
shall come home with shouts of · **joy,**
carrying · **their** sheaves. R.

©2009 Gordon Johnston/Novalis

To hear the Sunday Psalms, visit www.livingwithchrist.ca.

SECOND READING *(Hebrews 5.1-6)*

Every high priest chosen from among men is put in charge of things pertaining to God on their behalf, to offer gifts and sacrifices for sins. He is able to deal gently with the ignorant and wayward, since he himself is subject to weakness; and because of this he must offer sacrifice for his own sins as well as for those of the people. And one does not presume to take this honour, but takes it only when called by God, just as Aaron was.

So also Christ did not glorify himself in becoming a high priest, but was appointed by the one who said to him, "You are my Son, today I have begotten you"; as he says also in another place, "You are a priest forever, according to the order of Melchizedek."

The word of the Lord. **Thanks be to God.**

GOSPEL ACCLAMATION *(2 Timothy 1.10)*

Alleluia. Alleluia. Our Saviour Jesus Christ has abolished death and brought us life through the Gospel. **Alleluia.**

GOSPEL *(Mark 10.46-52)*

The Lord be with you. **And with your spirit.** A reading from the holy Gospel according to Mark. **Glory to you, O Lord.**

As Jesus and his disciples and a large crowd were leaving Jericho, Bartimaeus son of Timaeus, a blind beggar, was sitting by the roadside. When he heard that it was Jesus of Nazareth, he began to shout out and say, "Jesus, Son of David, have mercy on me!" Many sternly ordered him to be quiet, but he cried out even more loudly, "Son of David, have mercy on me!"

Jesus stood still and said, "Call him here." And they called the blind man, saying to him, "Take heart; get up, he is calling you." So throwing off his cloak, he sprang up and came to Jesus.

Then Jesus said to him, "What do you want me to do for you?" The blind man said to him, "My teacher, let me see again." Jesus said to him, "Go; your faith has made you well."

Immediately the man regained his sight and followed Jesus on the way.

The Gospel of the Lord. **Praise to you, Lord Jesus Christ.**

PROFESSION OF FAITH *(p. 14)*

PRAYER OF THE FAITHFUL

The following intentions are suggestions only.
There are more suggestions at www.livingwithchrist.ca.

R. **Lord, hear our prayer.**

For the Church, striving to grow in holiness, we pray to the Lord: R.

For world leaders, called to govern with wisdom, mercy and compassion, we pray to the Lord: R.

For all who hunger for the justice denied to them, we pray to the Lord: R.

For young people and their families in their desire to live and grow in discipleship with Jesus, we pray to the Lord: R.

PREPARATION OF THE GIFTS *(p. 17)*

PRAYER OVER THE OFFERINGS

Look, we pray, O Lord, on the offerings we make to your majesty, that whatever is done by us in your service may be directed above all to your glory. Through Christ our Lord. **Amen.**

PREFACE *(Sundays in Ordinary Time, p. 31)*

COMMUNION ANTIPHON *(Cf. Psalm 19.6)*

We will ring out our joy at your saving help and exult in the name of our God.

or (Ephesians 5.2)

Christ loved us and gave himself up for us, as a fragrant offering to God.

PRAYER AFTER COMMUNION

May your Sacraments, O Lord, we pray, perfect in us what lies within them, that what we now celebrate in signs we may one day possess in truth. Through Christ our Lord. **Amen.**

BLESSING AND DISMISSAL *(p. 72)*

November Saints' Days

The following saints are traditionally remembered in November in Canada.

All Saints . . . . Nov 1

All Souls' Day . . . . Nov 2

Saint Martin de Porres . . . . Nov 3

Saint Charles Borromeo . . . . Nov 4

Saint Leo the Great . . . . Nov 10

Saint Martin of Tours . . . . Nov 11

Saint Josaphat . . . . Nov 12

Saint Albert the Great . . . . Nov 15

Saint Margaret of Scotland . . . . Nov 16
Saint Gertrude

Saint Elizabeth of Hungary . . . . Nov 17

Saint Cecilia . . . . Nov 22

Saint Clement I . . . . Nov 23
Saint Columban

Saint Andrew Dũng-Lạc . . . . Nov 24
   and Companions

Saint Catherine of Alexandria . . . . Nov 25

Saint Andrew . . . . Nov 30

31st Sunday in Ordinary Time

The churches in British Columbia had been allowed to re-open, after the first COVID-induced shut-down. Attendance required pre-registration and the doors were closed to latecomers. It felt wonderful to be allowed back to our traditional form of worship. I was walking to Mass when I thought I heard my name being called. Then I heard my name being called again.

When I turned round, I saw Steve, the panhandler who used to keep an eye on my bicycle. He was running to catch up, so I stopped. He wanted to say hello, to know how I was. We chatted. He was doing okay. After we said our goodbyes I hurried to church, but the doors were locked. For a second, I was sad to have missed Mass. Then I realized: Our Lord was right here, on the street. He was the Love in this unexpected encounter.

In today's Gospel Jesus tells us that the most important way to love God is through our neighbour. The crowd around Jesus was discussing the importance of traditional sacrifices. The wise scribe did not join the argument. Instead, he stopped and listened to Jesus. When the scribe took Jesus' answer into his heart, he was given the grace to understand the New Covenant.

Jesus teaches us to look at tradition with discernment and to love God through each of our neighbours.

Liz Summers
Victoria, BC

ENTRANCE ANTIPHON *(Cf. Psalm 37.22-23)*
Forsake me not, O Lord, my God; be not far from me! Make haste and come to my help, O Lord, my strong salvation!

INTRODUCTORY RITES *(p. 8)*

COLLECT
Almighty and merciful God, by whose gift your faithful offer you right and praiseworthy service, grant, we pray, that we may hasten without stumbling to receive the things you have promised. Through our Lord Jesus Christ, your Son, who lives and reigns with you in the unity of the Holy Spirit, God, for ever and ever. **Amen.**

FIRST READING *(Deuteronomy 6.2-6)*
Moses spoke to the people: "May you and your children and your children's children fear the Lord your God all the days of your life, and keep all his decrees and his commandments that I am commanding you, so that your days may be long.

"Hear therefore, O Israel, and observe them diligently, so that it may go well with you, and so that you may multiply greatly in a land flowing with milk and honey, as the Lord, the God of your Fathers, has promised you.

"Hear, O Israel: The Lord is our God, the Lord alone. You shall love the Lord your God with all your heart, and with all your soul, and with all your might. Keep these words that I am commanding you today in your heart."

The word of the Lord. **Thanks be to God.**

RESPONSORIAL PSALM *(Psalm 18)*

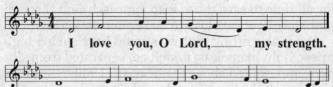

R. **I love you, O Lord, my strength.**

I love you, O Lord, my · **strength.**
The Lord is my rock, my fortress,
    and my de-·**liverer.**
My God, my rock in whom I take · **refuge,**
my shield, and the source of my salvation,
    · **my** stronghold. R.

I call upon the Lord, who is worthy
    to be · **praised,**
so I shall be saved from my · **enemies.**
From his temple he heard my · **voice,**
and my cry to him reached · **his** ears. R.

The Lord lives! Blessed be my · **rock,**
and exalted be the God of my sal-·**vation.**
Great triumphs he gives to his · **king,**
and shows steadfast love to · **his_a**-nointed. R.

©2009 Gordon Johnston/Novalis

To hear the Sunday Psalms, visit www.livingwithchrist.ca.

SECOND READING *(Hebrews 7.23-28)*
**The priests of the first covenant were many in number,
because they were prevented by death from continuing
in office; but Jesus holds his priesthood permanently,**

because he continues forever. Consequently he is able for all time to save those who approach God through him, since he always lives to make intercession for them.

For it was fitting that we should have such a high priest, holy, blameless, undefiled, separated from sinners, and exalted above the heavens. Unlike the other high priests, he has no need to offer sacrifices day after day, first for his own sins, and then for those of the people; this he did once for all when he offered himself.

For the law appoints as high priests those who are subject to weakness, but the word of the oath, which came later than the law, appoints a Son who has been made perfect forever.

The word of the Lord. **Thanks be to God.**

GOSPEL ACCLAMATION *(John 14.23)*
Alleluia. Alleluia. Whoever loves me will keep my word, and my Father will love him, and we will come to him. **Alleluia.**

GOSPEL *(Mark 12.28-34)*
The Lord be with you. **And with your spirit.** A reading from the holy Gospel according to Mark. **Glory to you, O Lord.**

One of the scribes came near and heard the religious authorities disputing with one another, and seeing that Jesus answered them well, he asked him, "Which commandment is the first of all?"

Jesus answered, "The first is, 'Hear, O Israel: the Lord our God, the Lord is one; you shall love the Lord your God with all your heart, and with all your soul, and with all your mind, and with all your strength.'

The second is this, 'You shall love your neighbour as yourself.' There is no other commandment greater than these."

Then the scribe said to him, "You are right, Teacher; you have truly said that 'he is one, and besides him there is no other'; and 'to love him with all the heart, and with all the understanding, and with all the strength,' and 'to love one's neighbour as oneself,' — this is much more important than all whole burnt offerings and sacrifices."

When Jesus saw that the scribe answered wisely, he said to him, "You are not far from the kingdom of God."

After that no one dared to ask Jesus any question.

The Gospel of the Lord. **Praise to you, Lord Jesus Christ.**

PROFESSION OF FAITH (p. 14)

PRAYER OF THE FAITHFUL

The following intentions are suggestions only.
There are more suggestions at www.livingwithchrist.ca.

R. **Lord, hear our prayer.**

For the Church and its mission of justice and peace, we pray to the Lord: R.

For a fair distribution of resources, talent, time and possessions in our society, we pray to the Lord: R.

For those excluded from sharing in the fullness of creation, we pray to the Lord: R.

For a strong witness to the greatest commandment in this faith community, we pray to the Lord: R.

PREPARATION OF THE GIFTS *(p. 17)*

PRAYER OVER THE OFFERINGS
May these sacrificial offerings, O Lord, become for you a pure oblation, and for us a holy outpouring of your mercy. Through Christ our Lord. **Amen.**

PREFACE *(Sundays in Ordinary Time, p. 31)*

COMMUNION ANTIPHON *(Cf. Psalm 15.11)*
You will show me the path of life, the fullness of joy in your presence, O Lord.

   or (John 6.58)
Just as the living Father sent me and I have life because of the Father, so whoever feeds on me shall have life because of me, says the Lord.

PRAYER AFTER COMMUNION
May the working of your power, O Lord, increase in us, we pray, so that, renewed by these heavenly Sacraments, we may be prepared by your gift for receiving what they promise. Through Christ our Lord. **Amen.**

BLESSING AND DISMISSAL *(p. 72)*

32nd Sunday in Ordinary Time

The clattering coins of the wealthy donations likely turned heads. But it's the poor widow's offering that gets Jesus really excited. *Clink. Clink.* Two copper coins. A penny's worth. Hardly noticeable, really. Except to Jesus. He's so moved by the widow's generosity, he calls the disciples over. A teachable moment for them. And for us.

Be it our treasure, talent or time, it's hard not to be tightfisted with our "last penny." *I would donate but... I would be more patient but... I would volunteer but...* It's so easy to rationalize it to ourselves.

Now, imagine if the boy in John 6.9 had done that with his loaves and fish. "Sorry, Jesus. I can't. I need it. I'm hungry. Besides, it wouldn't feed 5,000 people anyway." But because Jesus asks, the boy – hungry as he is – gives. Because God asks, the widow – poor as she is – gives. Their trust in God helps them see the opportunity of giving. It inspires true generosity. And God works through them.

God calls us to be cheerful givers. To give what we can with gratitude. To be generous, simply because God asks us through the needs of others. Generosity is not about turning heads, it's about touching hearts. What time, talent or treasure is God asking of you this week? It's a great opportunity. Are you all in?

Caroline Pignat
Kanata, ON

ENTRANCE ANTIPHON *(Cf. Psalm 87.3)*
Let my prayer come into your presence. Incline your ear to my cry for help, O Lord.

INTRODUCTORY RITES *(p. 8)*

COLLECT
Almighty and merciful God, graciously keep from us all adversity, so that, unhindered in mind and body alike, we may pursue in freedom of heart the things that are yours. Through our Lord Jesus Christ, your Son, who lives and reigns with you in the unity of the Holy Spirit, God, for ever and ever. **Amen.**

FIRST READING *(1 Kings 17.10-16)*
Elijah, the Prophet, set out and went to Zarephath. When he came to the gate of the town, a widow was there gathering sticks; he called to her and said, "Bring me a little water in a vessel, so that I may drink." As she was going to bring it, he called to her and said, "Bring me a morsel of bread in your hand."

But she said, "As the Lord your God lives, I have nothing baked, only a handful of meal in a jar, and a little oil in a jug; I am now gathering a couple of sticks, so that I may go home and prepare it for myself and my son, that we may eat it, and die."

Elijah said to her, "Do not be afraid; go and do as you have said; but first make me a little cake of it and bring it to me, and afterwards make something for yourself and your son. For thus says the Lord the God of Israel: 'The jar of meal will not be emptied and the jug of oil will not fail until the day that the Lord sends rain on the earth.'"

She went and did as Elijah said, so that she as well as he and her household ate for many days. The jar of meal was not emptied, neither did the jug of oil fail, according to the word of the Lord that he spoke by Elijah.

The word of the Lord. **Thanks be to God.**

RESPONSORIAL PSALM *(Psalm 146)*

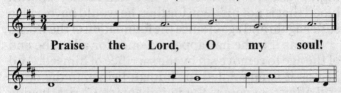

Praise the Lord, O my soul!

R. **Praise the Lord, O my soul!**
or **Alleluia!**

It is the Lord who keeps faith for·-**ever,**
who executes justice for the op·-**pressed;**
who gives food to the · **hungry.**
The Lord sets the · **prisoners** free. R.

The Lord opens the eyes of the · **blind**
and lifts up those who are bowed · **down;**
the Lord loves the · **righteous**
and watches over · **the** strangers. R.

The Lord upholds the orphan and the · **widow,**
but the way of the wicked he brings to · **ruin.**
The Lord will reign for·-**ever,**
your God, O Zion, for all · **gener**-ations. R.

©2009 Gordon Johnston/Novalis

To hear the Sunday Psalms, visit www.livingwithchrist.ca.

SECOND READING *(Hebrews 9.24-28)*

Christ did not enter a sanctuary made by human hands, a mere copy of the true one, but he entered into heaven itself, now to appear in the presence of God on our behalf.

Nor was it to offer himself again and again, as the high priest enters the Holy Place year after year with blood that is not his own; for then he would have had to suffer again and again since the foundation of the world.

But as it is, he has appeared once for all at the end of the age to remove sin by the sacrifice of himself. And just as it is appointed for human beings to die once, and after that comes the judgment, so Christ, having been offered once to bear the sins of many, will appear a second time, not to deal with sin, but to save those who are eagerly waiting for him.

The word of the Lord. **Thanks be to God.**

GOSPEL ACCLAMATION *(Matthew 5.3)*

Alleluia. Alleluia. Blessed are the poor in spirit; for theirs is the kingdom of heaven! **Alleluia.**

GOSPEL *(Mark 12.38-44)*

The shorter version begins at the asterisks.

The Lord be with you. **And with your spirit.** A reading from the holy Gospel according to Mark. **Glory to you, O Lord.**

Jesus was teaching in the temple, and a large crowd was listening to him. He said, "Beware of the scribes, who like to walk around in long robes, and to be greeted with respect in the marketplaces, and to have the best seats in the synagogues and places of honour at banquets! They devour widows' houses and for the sake of appearance say long prayers. They will receive the greater condemnation."

* * *

Jesus sat down opposite the treasury, and watched the crowd putting money into the treasury. Many rich people put in large sums. A poor widow came and put in two small copper coins, which are worth a penny. Then he called his disciples and said to them, "Truly I tell you, this poor widow has put in more than all those who are contributing to the treasury. For all of them have contributed out of their abundance; but she out of her poverty has put in everything she had, all she had to live on."

The Gospel of the Lord. **Praise to you, Lord Jesus Christ.**

PROFESSION OF FAITH (p. 14)

PRAYER OF THE FAITHFUL

The following intentions are suggestions only.
There are more suggestions at www.livingwithchrist.ca.

R. **Lord, hear our prayer.**

For leaders in the Church, as they strive to serve their communities in fidelity and trust, we pray to the Lord: R.

For all who suffer from war, famine and other threats to their security, we pray to the Lord: R.

For those who live without adequate shelter, food or employment, we pray to the Lord: R.

For ourselves, called to fulfill our vocation as people of faith and hope, we pray to the Lord: R.

PREPARATION OF THE GIFTS (p. 17)

PRAYER OVER THE OFFERINGS
Look with favour, we pray, O Lord, upon the sacrificial gifts offered here, that, celebrating in mystery the Passion of your Son, we may honour it with loving devotion. Through Christ our Lord. **Amen.**

PREFACE (Sundays in Ordinary Time, p. 31)

COMMUNION ANTIPHON (Cf. Psalm 22.1-2)
The Lord is my shepherd; there is nothing I shall want. Fresh and green are the pastures where he gives me repose, near restful waters he leads me.

or (Cf. Luke 24.35)
The disciples recognized the Lord Jesus in the breaking of bread.

PRAYER AFTER COMMUNION
Nourished by this sacred gift, O Lord, we give you thanks and beseech your mercy, that, by the pouring forth of your Spirit, the grace of integrity may endure in those your heavenly power has entered. Through Christ our Lord. **Amen.**

BLESSING AND DISMISSAL (p. 72)

33rd Sunday in Ordinary Time

World Day of the Poor

The news was curt. It was not, however, unexpected. After ten years with the company in a struggling industry, I lost my job.

What can get us through the darkness? I admit, I first grappled with despair and fears about the future. As I heal from being laid off, I am finding hope and peace, knowing suffering is temporary. Most of all, I know God's purpose for us is to be with him in heaven.

Today's readings highlight the need to be vigilant about what matters: setting our sights on God and following his path to eternity. Hopelessness is useless because God won't abandon us. He wants us to use our gifts, in our jobs and all aspects of our lives, as a way to help fulfill his will. And ultimately, the end times will come one day. Suffering will end for God's children.

On this World Day of the Poor, we remember those who suffer and struggle to make ends meet. Let us give thanks to God for giving us the hope of heaven. With God, darkness won't extinguish hope. We only have to follow the light of our faith. One day, that little light will lead us to a place where brightness in all its glory endures, and we will be united with God forever.

Christl Dabu
Hamilton, ON

ENTRANCE ANTIPHON *(Jeremiah 29.11, 12, 14)*

The Lord said: I think thoughts of peace and not of affliction. You will call upon me, and I will answer you, and I will lead back your captives from every place.

INTRODUCTORY RITES *(p. 8)*

COLLECT

Grant us, we pray, O Lord our God, the constant gladness of being devoted to you, for it is full and lasting happiness to serve with constancy the author of all that is good. Through our Lord Jesus Christ, your Son, who lives and reigns with you in the unity of the Holy Spirit, God, for ever and ever. **Amen.**

FIRST READING *(Daniel 12.1-3)*

At that time Michael, the great prince, the protector of your people, shall arise. There shall be a time of anguish, such as has never occurred since nations first came into existence. But at that time your people shall be delivered, everyone who is found written in the book. Many of those who sleep in the dust of the earth shall awake, some to everlasting life, and some to shame and everlasting contempt.

Those who are wise shall shine like the brightness of the sky, and those who lead many to righteousness, like the stars forever and ever.

The word of the Lord. **Thanks be to God.**

RESPONSORIAL PSALM *(Psalm 16)*

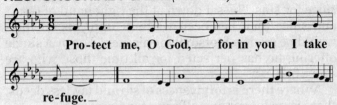

Pro-tect me, O God, ___ for in you I take re-fuge. ___

R. **Protect me, O God, for in you I take refuge.**

The Lord is my chosen portion · **and_my** cup;
you hold · **my** lot.
I keep the Lord always · **be**-fore_me;
because he is at my right hand,
  I shall · **not** be moved. R.

Therefore my heart is glad,
  and my soul · **re**-joices;
my body also rests · **se**-cure.
For you do not give me up · **to** Sheol,
or let your faithful one · **see** the Pit. R.

You show me the path · **of** life.
In your presence there is fullness · **of** joy;
in your right hand · **are** pleasures
for--**ev**-er-more. R.

©2009 Gordon Johnston/Novalis

To hear the Sunday Psalms, visit www.livingwithchrist.ca.

SECOND READING *(Hebrews 10.11-14, 18)*
Every priest stands day after day at his service, offering again and again the same sacrifices that can never take away sins.

But when Christ had offered for all time a single sacrifice for sins, "he sat down at the right hand of God," and since then has been waiting "until his enemies would be made a footstool for his feet." For by a single offering he has perfected for all time those who are sanctified.

Where there is forgiveness of sin and lawless deeds, there is no longer any offering for sin.

The word of the Lord. **Thanks be to God.**

GOSPEL ACCLAMATION *(Luke 21.36)*
Alleluia. Alleluia. Be alert at all times, praying that you may be able to stand before the Son of Man. **Alleluia.**

GOSPEL *(Mark 13.24-32)*
The Lord be with you. **And with your spirit.** A reading from the holy Gospel according to Mark. **Glory to you, O Lord.**

Jesus spoke to his disciples about the end which is to come:

"In those days, after the time of suffering, the sun will be darkened, and the moon will not give its light, and the stars will be falling from heaven, and the powers in the heavens will be shaken.

"Then they will see 'the Son of Man coming in clouds' with great power and glory. Then he will send out the Angels, and gather his elect from the four winds, from the ends of the earth to the ends of heaven.

"From the fig tree learn its lesson: as soon as its branch becomes tender and puts forth its leaves, you know that summer is near. So also, when you see these things taking place, you know that he is near, at the very gates.

"Truly I tell you, this generation will not pass away until all these things have taken place. Heaven and earth will pass away, but my words will not pass away.

"But about that day or hour no one knows, neither the Angels in heaven, nor the Son, but only the Father."

The Gospel of the Lord. **Praise to you, Lord Jesus Christ.**

PROFESSION OF FAITH (p. 14)

PRAYER OF THE FAITHFUL

The following intentions are suggestions only.
There are more suggestions at www.livingwithchrist.ca.

℟. **Lord, hear our prayer.**

For the Church, working to overcome divisions between persons, races and nations, we pray to the Lord: ℟.

For the world, longing for its promised salvation, we pray to the Lord: ℟.

For all who desire freedom from oppression in their lives, we pray to the Lord: ℟.

For all who experience the pain of poverty, and those who work to address poverty, we pray to the Lord: ℟.

For our parish community, striving each day to become a more authentic witness to the gospel, we pray to the Lord: ℟.

PREPARATION OF THE GIFTS (p. 17)

PRAYER OVER THE OFFERINGS

Grant, O Lord, we pray, that what we offer in the sight
of your majesty may obtain for us the grace of being
devoted to you and gain us the prize of everlasting happiness. Through Christ our Lord. **Amen.**

PREFACE *(Sundays in Ordinary Time, p. 31)*

COMMUNION ANTIPHON *(Psalm 72.28)*
**To be near God is my happiness, to place my hope
in God the Lord.**

or (Mark 11.23-24)
**Amen, I say to you: Whatever you ask in prayer,
believe that you will receive, and it shall be given to
you, says the Lord.**

PRAYER AFTER COMMUNION

We have partaken of the gifts of this sacred mystery,
humbly imploring, O Lord, that what your Son commanded us to do in memory of him may bring us
growth in charity. Through Christ our Lord. **Amen.**

BLESSING AND DISMISSAL *(p. 72)*

Our Lord Jesus Christ, King of the Universe

World Day of Youth

Today, as we mark the end of the liturgical year with a feast highlighting the kingship of Jesus, we can ask: what kind of king is Jesus?

In today's Gospel, Jesus is far removed from conventional kingship – in fact, he is a prisoner. And yet the interplay of words between Jesus and his interrogator is telling. Pilate's flippant reply ("I am not a Jew, am I?") is not the response of a self-assured leader. Pilate represents the power of the colonizer, and so he shows little respect for Jesus. Who is more king-like – the insecure Roman functionary, or the humble servant–leader? Who testifies to the truth? From our vantage point in history and in faith, we believe Jesus' testimony that his kingdom is not of this world and know him to be truth incarnate.

These days, we live in confusing times; many voices claim to speak the truth, but their words do not ring true. This can cause us to question our faith, to have doubts about what is true, what is truth. "Fake news" is a phrase that can quickly heighten our anxiety levels. As we gather in our eucharistic communities this weekend, let us support one another in our belief that Jesus is Christ the King, and give thanks to God for Jesus' true and humble leadership.

Sr. Pat Carter, CSJ
Sault Ste. Marie, ON

ENTRANCE ANTIPHON *(Revelation 5.12; 1.6)*
How worthy is the Lamb who was slain, to receive power and divinity, and wisdom and strength and honour. To him belong glory and power for ever and ever.

INTRODUCTORY RITES *(p. 8)*

COLLECT
Almighty ever-living God, whose will is to restore all things in your beloved Son, the King of the universe, grant, we pray, that the whole creation, set free from slavery, may render your majesty service and ceaselessly proclaim your praise. Through our Lord Jesus Christ, your Son, who lives and reigns with you in the unity of the Holy Spirit, God, for ever and ever. **Amen.**

FIRST READING *(Daniel 7.13-14)*
I had a dream and visions as I lay in bed. As I watched in the night visions, I saw one like a son of man coming with the clouds of heaven. And he came to the One who is Ancient of Days and was presented before him.

To him was given dominion and glory and kingship, that all peoples, nations and languages should serve him. His dominion is an everlasting dominion that shall not pass away, and his kingship is one that shall never be destroyed.

The word of the Lord. **Thanks be to God.**

RESPONSORIAL PSALM *(Psalm 93)*

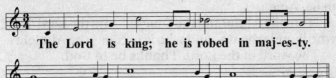

The Lord   is   king;   he is robed   in maj-es-ty.

R. **The Lord is king; he is robed in majesty.**

The Lord is king, he is robed · **in** majesty;
the Lord · **is** robed,
he is · **girded** with strength. R.

He has established the world;
  it shall never · **be** moved;
your throne is established · **from_of** old;
you are from · **ev**-er-lasting. R.

Your decrees are · **very** sure;
holiness befits · **your** house,
O Lord, for·-**ev**-er-more. R.

To hear the Sunday Psalms, visit www.livingwithchrist.ca.

SECOND READING *(Revelation 1.5-8)*
Jesus Christ is the faithful witness, the firstborn of the dead, and the ruler of the kings of the earth. To him who loves us and freed us from our sins by his blood, and made us to be a kingdom, priests serving his God and Father, to him be glory and dominion forever and ever. Amen.

Look! He is coming with the clouds; every eye will see him, even those who pierced him; and on his account all the tribes of the earth will lament. So it is to be. Amen.

"I am the Alpha and the Omega," says the Lord God, who is and who was and who is to come, the Almighty.

The word of the Lord. **Thanks be to God.**

GOSPEL ACCLAMATION *(Mark 11.9-10)*
Alleluia. Alleluia. Blessed is the coming kingdom of our father David; blessed is the one who comes in the name of the Lord! **Alleluia.**

GOSPEL *(John 18.33b-37)*
The Lord be with you. **And with your spirit.** A reading from the holy Gospel according to John. **Glory to you, O Lord.**

Pilate asked Jesus, "Are you the King of the Jews?"

Jesus answered, "Do you ask this on your own, or did others tell you about me?"

Pilate replied, "I am not a Jew, am I? Your own nation and the chief priests have handed you over to me. What have you done?"

Jesus answered, "My kingdom is not from this world. If my kingdom were from this world, my followers would be fighting to keep me from being handed over to the Jews. But as it is, my kingdom is not from here."

Pilate asked him, "So you are a king?"

Jesus answered, "You say that I am a king. For this I was born, and for this I came into the world, to testify to the truth. Everyone who belongs to the truth listens to my voice."

The Gospel of the Lord. **Praise to you, Lord Jesus Christ.**

PROFESSION OF FAITH *(p. 14)*

PRAYER OF THE FAITHFUL

The following intentions are suggestions only.
There are more suggestions at www.livingwithchrist.ca.

R. **Lord, hear our prayer.**

For the Church, called to work together to bring about God's kingdom of truth and love, we pray to the Lord: R.

For world leaders who follow Christ's example of humility and service, we pray to the Lord: R.

For those struggling with injustice, privation and a loss of hope, we pray to the Lord: R.

For this parish, working to build up the kingdom of God, we pray to the Lord: R.

PREPARATION OF THE GIFTS *(p. 17)*

PRAYER OVER THE OFFERINGS

As we offer you, O Lord, the sacrifice by which the human race is reconciled to you, we humbly pray that your Son himself may bestow on all nations the gifts of unity and peace. Through Christ our Lord. **Amen.**

PREFACE *(Christ the King, p. 31)*

COMMUNION ANTIPHON *(Psalm 28.10-11)*
The Lord sits as King for ever. The Lord will bless his people with peace.

PRAYER AFTER COMMUNION

Having received the food of immortality, we ask, O
Lord, that, glorying in obedience to the commands
of Christ, the King of the universe, we may live with
him eternally in his heavenly Kingdom. Who lives and
reigns for ever and ever. **Amen.**

BLESSING AND DISMISSAL (p. 72)

THE POPE'S PRAYER INTENTIONS FOR 2023-2024

DECEMBER 2023

For persons with disabilities

We pray that people living with disabilities may be at the centre of attention in society, and that institutions may offer inclusive programmes which value their active participation.

JANUARY 2024

For the gift of diversity in the Church

We pray that the Holy Spirit may help us to recognize the gift of different charisms within the Christian community and to discover the richness of different traditions and rituals in the Catholic Church.

FEBRUARY 2024

For the terminally ill

We pray that those with a terminal illness, and their families, receive the necessary physical and spiritual care and accompaniment.

MARCH 2024

For the new martyrs

We pray that those who risk their lives for the Gospel in various parts of the world inflame the Church with their courage and missionary enthusiasm.

APRIL 2024

For the role of women

We pray that the dignity and immense value of women be recognized in every culture, and for the end of discrimination that they experience in different parts of the world.

MAY 2024

For the formation of religious and seminarians

We pray that religious women and men, and seminarians, grow in their own vocations through their human, pastoral, spiritual and community formation, leading them to be credible witnesses to the Gospel.

JUNE 2024

For migrants fleeing their homes

We pray that migrants fleeing from war or hunger, forced to undertake journeys full of danger and violence, find welcome and new opportunities in the countries that receive them.

JULY 2024

For the pastoral care of the sick

We pray that the Sacrament of the Anointing of the Sick confer to those who receive it and their loved ones the power of the Lord and become ever more a visible sign of compassion and hope for all.

AUGUST 2024

For political leaders

We pray that political leaders be at the service of their own people, working for integral human development and for the common good, especially caring for the poor and those who have lost their jobs.

SEPTEMBER 2024

For the cry of the earth

We pray that each one of us will hear and take to heart the cry of the Earth and of victims of natural disasters and climactic change, and that all will undertake to personally care for the world in which we live.

OCTOBER 2024

For a shared mission

We pray that the Church continue to sustain in all ways a Synodal lifestyle, as a sign of co-responsibility, promoting the participation, the communion, and the mission shared among priests, religious and lay people.

NOVEMBER 2024

For anyone who has lost a child

We pray that all parents who mourn the loss of a son or daughter find support in their community and receive peace and consolation from the Holy Spirit.

ABOUT PRAYER

It's about humility, not merit.
It's about honesty, not best behaviour.
It's about the heart, not the head.
It's about faith, not certainty.
It's about simplicity, not complexity.
It's about friendship, not fear.
It's about intimacy, not distance.
It's about community, not just me.
It's about routine, not whenever.
It's about changing our mind, not God's.
It's about what we undergo, not what we do.
It's about being called into being.
It's about being loved.
And, being loved, loving others, loving the world...

Raymond Friel and David Wells, *At Your Side: Prayers for Messy, Delightful, Complicated, Outrageous, Everyday Life* (Toronto: Novalis, 2020), p. 112.

TRADITIONAL PRAYERS

HAIL MARY

Hail Mary, full of grace, the Lord is with thee. Blessed art thou among women and blessed is the fruit of thy womb, Jesus.

Holy Mary, Mother of God, pray for us sinners, now and at the hour of our death. Amen.

GLORY BE TO THE FATHER

Glory be to the Father, and to the Son, and to the Holy Spirit. As it was in the beginning, is now, and ever shall be, world without end. Amen.

COME, HOLY SPIRIT

Come, Holy Spirit, fill the hearts of your faithful and kindle in them the fire of your love. Send forth your Spirit, O Lord, and renew the face of the earth. Amen.

ACT OF FAITH

O my God, I firmly believe that you are one God in three divine Persons, Father, Son, and Holy Spirit. I believe that your divine Son became man, died for our sins, and that he will come to judge the living and the dead. I believe these and all the truths which the holy Catholic Church teaches, because you have revealed them, who can neither deceive nor be deceived. Amen.

ACT OF HOPE

O my God, relying on your almighty power and infinite mercy and promises, I hope to obtain pardon of my sins, the help of your grace, and life everlasting through the merits of Jesus Christ, my Lord and Redeemer. Amen.

ACT OF LOVE

O my God, I love you above all things, with my whole heart and soul, because you are all good and worthy of all love. I love my neighbour as myself for the love of you. I forgive all who have injured me, and ask pardon of all whom I have injured. Amen.

DIVINE PRAISES

Blessed be God.
Blessed be his holy name.

Blessed be Jesus Christ, true God and true man.
Blessed be the name of Jesus.
Blessed be his most sacred heart.
Blessed be his most precious blood.
Blessed be Jesus in the sacrament of the altar.

Blessed be the Holy Spirit, the Paraclete.

Blessed be the Mother of God, Mary most holy.
Blessed be her holy and immaculate conception.
Blessed be her glorious assumption.
Blessed be the name of Mary, virgin and mother.

Blessed be Saint Joseph, her most chaste spouse.
Blessed be God in his angels and in his saints.

PRAYER TO ST. MICHAEL THE ARCHANGEL

St. Michael the Archangel,
defend us in battle.
Be our safeguard against the wickedness
and snares of the Devil.
May God rebuke him,
we humbly pray,
and do thou,
O Prince of the heavenly hosts,
by the power of God,
cast into hell Satan,
and all evil spirits,
who prowl about the world
seeking the ruin of souls. Amen.

ANGELUS

The angel of the Lord declared unto Mary, and she conceived of the Holy Spirit. *Hail Mary...*

Behold, the handmaid of the Lord; be it done to me according to your word. *Hail Mary...*

And the word was made flesh, and dwelt among us. *Hail Mary...*

Pray for us, O holy Mother of God; that we may be made worthy of the promises of Christ.

Pour forth, we beseech you, O Lord, your grace into our hearts that we, to whom the incarnation of your Son was made known by the message of an angel, may by his passion and cross be brought to the glory of his resurrection. We ask this through the same Christ, our Lord. Amen.

HAIL, HOLY QUEEN

Hail, holy Queen, mother of mercy, our life, our sweetness and our hope. To you we cry, poor banished children of Eve. To you we send up our sighs, mourning and weeping in this valley of tears. Turn then, most gracious advocate, your eyes of mercy upon us, and after this, our exile, show unto us the blessed fruit of your womb, Jesus. O clement, O loving, O kind Virgin Mary.

MEMORARE

Remember, O most gracious Virgin Mary, that never was it known that anyone who fled to thy protection, implored thy help or sought thy intercession, was left unaided. Inspired with this confidence, I fly unto thee, O Virgin of virgins my Mother; to thee I come, before thee I stand, sinful and sorrowful; O Mother of the Word Incarnate, despise not my petitions, but in thy mercy hear and answer me. Amen.

MAGNIFICAT

My soul proclaims the greatness of the Lord, my spirit rejoices in God my Saviour; for he has looked with favour on his lowly servant.

From this day all generations will call me blessed: the Almighty has done great things for me, and holy is his Name.

He has mercy on those who fear him in every generation. He has shown the strength of his arm, he has scattered the proud in their conceit.

He has cast down the mighty from their thrones, and has lifted up the lowly. He has filled the hungry with good things, and the rich he has sent away empty.

He has come to the help of his servant Israel for he has remembered his promise of mercy, the promise he made to our fathers, to Abraham and his children forever.

ICEL

PRAYER TO SAINT JOSEPH

Hail, Guardian of the Redeemer,
Spouse of the Blessed Virgin Mary.
To you God entrusted his only Son;
in you Mary placed her trust;
with you Christ became man.

Blessed Joseph, to us too,
show yourself a father
and guide us in the path of life.
Obtain for us grace, mercy and courage,
and defend us from every evil. Amen.

Pope Francis, Patris Corde (With a Father's Heart)

THE ROSARY

In the Rosary we focus on 20 events or mysteries in the life and death of Jesus and meditate on how we share with Mary in the redemptive work of Christ. Reading a pertinent passage from the Bible helps to deepen meditation on a particular mystery. The scriptural references given here are not exhaustive. In many instances, other biblical texts are equally suitable for meditation.

~ Begin the Rosary at the crucifix by praying the Apostles' Creed (p. 16)
~ At each large bead, pray the Lord's Prayer (p. 70)
~ At each small bead, pray the Hail Mary (p. 581)
~ At the first three beads it is customary to pray a Hail Mary for each of the gifts of faith, hope, and love
~ For each mystery, pray the Lord's Prayer, Hail Mary ten times, Glory Be to the Father (p. 581), and end with the Fatima prayer:

O my Jesus, forgive us our sins, save us from the fires of hell; lead all souls to heaven, especially those most in need of your mercy.

The Five Joyful Mysteries:

The Annunciation (Luke 1.26-38)
The Visitation (Luke 1.39-56)
The Nativity (Luke 2.1-20)
The Presentation (Luke 2.22-38)
The Finding in the Temple (Luke 2.41-52)

The Five Mysteries of Light:

The Baptism in the Jordan (Matthew 3.13-17)
The Wedding at Cana (John 2.1-12)
The Proclamation of the Kingdom (Mark 1.15)
The Transfiguration (Luke 9.28-36)
The First Eucharist (Matthew 26.26-29)

The Five Sorrowful Mysteries:

The Agony in the Garden (Matthew 26.36-56)
The Scourging at the Pillar (Matthew 27.20-26)
The Crowning with Thorns (Matthew 27.27-30)
The Carrying of the Cross (Matthew 27.31-33)
The Crucifixion (Matthew 27.34-60)

The Five Glorious Mysteries:

The Resurrection (John 20.1-18)
The Ascension (Acts 1.9-11)
The Descent of the Holy Spirit (John 20.19-23)
The Assumption of Mary (John 11.26)
The Crowning of Mary (Philippians 2.1-11)

PHOTO: SHUTTERSTOCK

THE WAY OF THE CROSS

(Revised version: The Sacred Congregation for Divine Worship recommends that the traditional Stations be revised to emphasize that the sufferings and resurrection of Christ are one redemptive mystery.)

OPENING PRAYER

Lord Jesus, all of your life led up to the Way of the Cross. In this final journey you lay down your life for your friends.

Jesus, you consider us your friends. You walk side by side with us on the journey of life. You know its joys and hopes, its suffering and pain. Today we want to walk side by side with you on your way to the Cross. Your suffering, your death, your rising from the dead give meaning to our lives. The way of the Cross is the way of life.

Lord, as you took the bread, your body, take us, bless us, break us, give us to others, so that in you we may be instruments of salvation for the world. **Amen.**

1. THE LAST SUPPER

Jesus said to them, "I have wanted so much to eat this Passover meal with you before I suffer! For I tell you, I will never eat it until it is given its full meaning in the Kingdom of God."

Then Jesus took a cup, gave thanks to God, and said, "Take this and share it among yourselves. I tell you that from now on I will not drink this wine until the Kingdom of God comes."

Then he took a loaf of bread, gave thanks to God, broke it, and gave it to them, saying, "This is my body, which is given for you. Do this in memory of me." In the same way, he gave them the cup after supper, saying, "This cup is God's new covenant sealed with my blood, which is poured out for you." *(Luke 22.15-20)*

Jesus, you love us. Make us realize we are a covenant people, make our Eucharists moments when we feel your friendship, so that we may live this out for all humankind.

2. IN THE GARDEN OF GETHSEMANE

Then Jesus went with his disciples to a place called Gethsemane, and said to them, "Sit here while I go over there and pray." He took with him Peter and the two sons of Zebedee. Grief and anguish came over him, and he said to them, "The sorrow in my heart is so great that it almost crushes me. Stay here and keep watch with me." *(Matthew 26.36-38)*

Jesus, you love us. Comfort us in times of distress. Help us to see beyond ourselves; help us to overcome the feeling of senseless chaos; help us to see the joy and hope of those who truly suffer and who truly believe. Remind us of your covenant of friendship with us.

3. BEFORE THE SANHEDRIN

Jesus was taken to the High Priest's house, where the chief priests, the elders, and the teachers of the Law were gathering. Peter followed at a distance and went into the courtyard, where he sat down with the guards, keeping himself warm by the fire. The chief priests and the whole Council tried to find some evidence against Jesus in order to put him to death, but they could not find any. *(Mark 14.53-55)*

Jesus, you love us. Help us live out your covenant of friend-ship; give us strength to stand against authorities who exercise power for evil. Make us nonviolent, but strong in this struggle for humankind. Jesus, strengthen us.

4. BEFORE PONTIUS PILATE

Early in the morning Jesus was taken from Caiaphas' house to the governor's palace. The Jewish authorities did not go inside the palace, for they wanted to keep themselves ritually clean in order to be able to eat the Passover meal. So Pilate went outside to them and asked, "What do you accuse this man of?" Their answer was, "We would not have brought him to you if he had not committed a crime." *(John 18.28-30)*

Jesus, you love us. You stand with the victims in this world. Is that one meaning of the covenant for us: that we too should side with the oppressed against the oppressor? Lord, this is hard for us, teach us how to side with the oppressed, with the victims.

5. THE WHIPPING AND CROWNING WITH THORNS

Then Pilate took Jesus and had him whipped. The soldiers made a crown of thorny branches, put it on his head, then put a purple robe on him. They came to him and said, "Long live the King of the Jews!" and slapped him. *(John 19.1-3)*

Jesus, you love us. Turn our sympathies to the poor victims of desperate soldiers all over the world. Empower us to stop the sale of arms to ruthless armies. Show us the way to curb senseless attacks by states against their own people. Jesus, teach us how to resist evil.

6. THE CARRYING OF THE CROSS

So they took charge of Jesus. He went out, carrying his cross, and came to the 'Place of the Skull,' as it is called. (In Hebrew it is called 'Golgotha.') *(John 19.16-17)*

Jesus, you love us. Your love for us affirms the goodness of our humanity. We are the friends for whom you suffered. Teach us to respect others, not to dismiss or diminish them as less human.

7. SIMON OF CYRENE

On the way they met a man named Simon, who was coming into the city from the country. The soldiers forced him to carry Jesus' cross. *(Mark 15.21)*

Jesus, you love us. We don't like carrying crosses, but many times our cross is of our own making. It is a self-centred cross. Help us find the true cross in the lives of the poor. Help us to help carry their burden. Jesus, help us!

8. THE WOMEN OF JERUSALEM

A large crowd of people followed him; among them were some women who were weeping and wailing for him. Jesus turned to them and said, "Women of Jerusalem! Do not cry for me, but for yourselves and your children. For the days are coming when people will say, 'How lucky are the women who never had children, who never bore babies, who never nursed them!' " *(Luke 23.27-31)*

Jesus, you love us. Allow us to comfort the grieving women of our time. But even more, enable us to prevent their grief, which so often could be avoided. Help us to break down the human systems which starve and kill. Jesus, make us angry about this unnecessary grief and suffering. Teach us to weep, knowing all the time that tears are never enough.

9. THE STRIPPING AND CRUCIFIXION

They came to a place called Golgotha, which means 'Place of the Skull.' There they offered Jesus wine mixed with a bitter substance; but after tasting it, he would not drink it.

They crucified him and then divided his clothes among them by throwing dice. *(Matthew 27.33-35)*

Jesus, you love us. Stripped naked, nailed to the cross, you have given your all for us. Jesus, help us break the bonds of our selfishness and materialism. Show us how we can give our life for others, in your covenant.

10. THE SECOND THIEF

One of the criminals hanging there hurled insults at him: "Aren't you the Messiah? Save yourself and us!"

The other one, however, rebuked him, saying, "Don't you fear God? You received the same sentence he did. Ours, however, is only right because we are getting what we deserve; but he has done no wrong." And he said to Jesus, "Remember me, Jesus, when you come as King!"

Jesus said to him, "I promise you that today you will be in Paradise with me." *(Luke 23.39-43)*

Jesus, you love us. Impress on us that the lives we live, the work we do, have consequences for others. Awaken our awareness to real evil and real faith. Help us honour your covenant of friendship in our lives.

11. MARY AND JOHN

Standing close to Jesus' cross were his mother, his mother's sister, Mary the wife of Clopas, and Mary Magdalene. Jesus saw his mother and the disciple he loved standing there; so he said to his mother, "He is your son."

Then he said to the disciple, "She is your mother." From that time the disciple took her to live in his home. *(John 19.25-27)*

Jesus, you love us. You gave us your mother Mary as our own mother. Touch our hearts with her sorrow at your death. Lift our eyes so we may see in her the beauty of your covenant; the beauty of her gift of herself to you and to us.

12. DEATH ON THE CROSS

But when they came to Jesus, they saw that he was already dead, so they did not break his legs. One of the soldiers, however, plunged his spear into Jesus' side, and at once blood and water poured out. *(John 19.33-34)*

Jesus, you love us. Teach us your way. Give us the wisdom to recognize evil. Give us the courage to confront it, to struggle against it, so that we may truly be your friends.

13. THE NEW SEPULCHRE

When it was evening, a rich man from Arimathea arrived; his name was Joseph, and he also was a disciple of Jesus. He went to Pilate and asked for the body of Jesus. Pilate gave orders for the body to be given to Joseph. So Joseph took it, wrapped it in a new linen sheet, and placed it in his own tomb which he had just recently dug out of solid rock. Then he rolled a large stone across the entrance to the tomb and went away. *(Matthew 27.57-60)*

Jesus, you love us. Help us to distinguish justice and charity. Sometimes it is easier to do charity than to do justice. Let us know which should be our response and when, in our lives. Give us the grace to act charitably and justly.

14. THE RESURRECTION

Very early on Sunday morning the women went to the tomb, carrying the spices they had prepared. They found the stone rolled away from the entrance to the tomb, so they went in; but they did not find the body of the Lord Jesus. *(Luke 24.1-3)*

Jesus, you love us. You have returned from the dead to be with us. Be our promise, our hope that all evil will be overcome. Bless us with full life for all humankind, under your covenant.

FINAL PRAYER

We know that Christ has been raised from death and will never die again — death will no longer rule over him. And so, because he died, sin has no power over him; and now he lives his life in fellowship with God. In the same way, you are to think of yourselves as dead, so far as sin is concerned, but living in fellowship with God through Christ Jesus. *(Romans 6.9-11)*

Father, your only Son gave up his life for us, his friends. Help us understand the meaning of that friendship. Help us grow in that friendship.

We are a weak and distracted people. Often we neglect you, but you never abandon us. You love us. Make us a less self-ish and a more caring people. Help us to share the crosses of others, as Simon did. Show us how to live your covenant of friendship day by day with the victims and the poor of this world. Father, we depend on you.

We pray this through Jesus, the Christ, your Son who has risen from the dead. Amen.

PRAYING WITH THE EUCHARIST

ANIMA CHRISTI *(Soul of Christ)*
Soul of Christ, sanctify me.
Body of Christ, heal me.
Blood of Christ, drench me.
Water from the side of Christ, wash me.
Passion of Christ, strengthen me.
Good Jesus, hear me.
In your wounds shelter me.
From turning away keep me.
From the evil one protect me.
At the hour of death call me.
Into your presence lead me,
to praise you with all your saints
for ever and ever. Amen.

* * *

My Lord, I offer Thee myself in turn as a sacrifice of thanksgiving. Thou hast died for me, and I in turn make myself over to Thee. I am not my own. Thou hast bought me; I will by my own act and deed complete the purchase. My wish is to be separated from everything of this world; to cleanse myself simply from sin; to put away from me even what is innocent, if used for its own sake, and not for Thine. I put away reputation and honour, and influence, and power, for my praise and strength shall be in Thee. Enable me to carry on what I profess. Amen.

Saint John Henry Newman

I believe Thou art present in the Blessed Sacrament, O Jesus. I love Thee and desire Thee. Come into my heart. I embrace Thee, O never leave me. I beseech Thee, O Lord Jesus, may the burning and most sweet power of Thy love absorb my mind, that I may die through love of Thy love, Who wast graciously pleased to die through love of my love.

Saint Francis of Assisi

* * *

Lord Jesus, Who in the Eucharist make your dwelling among us and become our traveling companion, sustain our Christian communities so that they may be ever more open to listening and accepting your Word. May they draw from the Eucharist a renewed commitment to spreading in society, by the proclamation of your Gospel, the signs and deeds of an attentive and active charity.

Saint John Paul II

AN ACT OF SPIRITUAL COMMUNION

My Jesus, I believe that you are present in the most Blessed Sacrament. I love You above all things and I desire to receive You into my soul. Since I cannot now receive You sacramentally, come at least spiritually into my heart. I embrace You as if You have already come, and unite myself wholly to You. Never permit me to be separated from You. Amen.

Saint Alphonsus Liguori

PRAYER FOR REVERENCE FOR LIFE

Almighty God, giver of all that is good, we thank you for the precious gift of human life:

For life in the womb, coming from your creative power,
For the life of children, making us glad with their
    freshness and promise,
For the life of young people, hoping for a better world,
For the life of the people who are disabled, teaching
    us that every life has value,
For the life of the elderly, witnessing to the ageless values
    of patience and wisdom.

Like Blessed Mary, may we always say "yes" to your gift. May we defend it and promote it from conception to its natural end. And bring us at last, O Father, to the fullness of eternal life in Jesus Christ, our Lord. Amen.

© Archdiocese of Vancouver

PRAYER FOR VOCATIONS

O God, you have chosen the Apostles
to make disciples of all nations
and by Baptism and Confirmation
have called all of us to build up your Holy Church.
We earnestly implore you to choose from among us,
    your children,
many priests, deacons, brothers, and sisters
who will love you with their whole heart
and will gladly spend their entire lives
to make you known and loved by all. Amen.

© Archdiocese of Vancouver

A PRAYER FOR OUR EARTH

All-powerful God, you are present in the whole universe
and in the smallest of your creatures.
You embrace with your tenderness all that exists.
Pour out upon us the power of your love,
that we may protect life and beauty.
Fill us with peace, that we may live
as brothers and sisters, harming no one.
O God of the poor,
help us to rescue the abandoned and forgotten
   of this earth,
so precious in your eyes.
Bring healing to our lives,
that we may protect the world and not prey on it,
that we may sow beauty, not pollution and destruction.
Touch the hearts
of those who look only for gain
at the expense of the poor and the earth.
Teach us to discover the worth of each thing,
to be filled with awe and contemplation,
to recognize that we are profoundly united
with every creature
as we journey towards your infinite light.
We thank you for being with us each day.
Encourage us, we pray, in our struggle
for justice, love and peace.

Pope Francis, Laudato Si'

PRAYER FOR PEACE IN THE WORLD

Loving Father,
We bring to you the suffering of our world today.
Look kindly upon every person living in fear,
    suffering persecution, or facing death.
Help us to remember that you are the Father of all
    of your children on earth.
Fill each heart with an unwavering trust in
    your Fatherly love.
Forgive us when we have not cared for our earth,
    the home you have given.
Forgive us when we choose the path of selfishness
    rather than the path of Love.
Forgive us when we forget to live as brothers
    and sisters on this earth,
the way you have shown in fellowship with
    your disciples.
Look upon us with your compassion,
the way you looked upon the world from the cross.
Remember not the evil we have done,
but see the depth of our repentance.
Give peace to the world;
help us to live anew.
Send your Spirit to teach us
to build rather than to destroy,
to love rather than to hate,
to live rather than to die.
In Jesus' name,
we pray.
Amen.

Novalis staff

INSPIRATION FROM THE SAINTS

LIVING HOPE

Consult not your fears but your hopes and your dreams. Think not about your frustrations, but about your unfulfilled potential. Concern yourself not with what you tried and failed in, but with what it is still possible for you to do.

Saint John XXIII

SEEKING JESUS

It is Jesus that you seek when you dream of happiness; He is waiting for you when nothing else you find satisfies you; He is the beauty to which you are so attracted; it is He who provoked you with that thirst for fullness that will not let you settle for compromise; it is He who urges you to shed the masks of a false life; it is He who reads in your heart your most genuine choices, the choices that others try to stifle.

It is Jesus who stirs in you the desire to do something great with your lives, the will to follow an ideal, the refusal to allow yourselves to be ground down by mediocrity, the courage to commit yourselves humbly and patiently to improving yourselves and society, making the world more human.

Saint John Paul II, World Youth Day, August 19, 2000

GOD'S HANDIWORK

It is with the smallest brushes that the artist paints the most exquisitely beautiful pictures.

Saint André Bessette

PRAYER OF ST. THOMAS AQUINAS

Grant me, O Lord my God,
a mind to know you,
a heart to seek you,
wisdom to find you,
conduct pleasing to you,
faithful perseverance in waiting for you,
and a hope of finally embracing you.

Saint Thomas Aquinas

DOING GOD'S WILL

Lord Jesus, teach me to be generous;
teach me to serve you as you deserve;
to give and not count the cost,
to fight and not heed the wounds,
to toil and not seek for rest,
to labour and not to seek reward,
except that of knowing that I do your will.

Saint Ignatius of Loyola

* * *

Give me, Lord, a full faith, a firm hope and a fervent love, a love for you incomparably above the love of myself. These things, good Lord, that I pray for, give me your grace also to labour for.

Saint Thomas More

THE PEACE PRAYER OF ST. FRANCIS

Lord, make me an instrument of your peace.
Where there is hatred let me sow love;
where there is injury, pardon;
where there is doubt, faith;
where there is despair, hope;
where there is darkness, light;
and where there is sadness, joy.

Divine Master,
grant that I may not so much seek
to be consoled as to console,
to be understood as to understand,
to be loved as to love.

For it is in giving that we receive,
in pardoning that we are pardoned,
and in dying that we are brought to eternal life.

Unknown, ca. 1915

IN SERVICE TO GOD

Govern everything by your wisdom, O Lord,
so that my soul may always be serving you
in the way you will
and not as I choose.
Let me die to myself so that I may serve you;
let me live to you who are life itself.

Saint Teresa of Avila

LORD, BLESS ALL PEOPLE

Lord, bless all who are filled with sadness.
Bless the broken spirits of those who suffer,
the oppressive solitude of lonely people,
the person who knows no rest,
the suffering that we confide to no one.

Bless the procession
of night owls
that do not fear the spectre
of unknown roads.

Bless the suffering of those who are dying this day.
Dear God, give them a good death.

Bless hearts, Lord,
hearts that are bitter.
Above all,
comfort the sick,
teach forgetfulness
to those who have lost
the one they love most.
Leave no one on the whole Earth
in distress.

Bless those who are full of joy,
and protect them, Lord.
So far, you have never
delivered me from sadness.
It sometimes weighs heavily on me,
but you give me your strength
and so I can bear it. Amen.

Saint Teresa Benedicta of the Cross

HELP US TO LIVE

Crucified and risen Lord,
teach us to face
the struggles of daily life,
so that we may live more fully.

You humbly and patiently welcomed
the setbacks of human life,
even the suffering of your crucifixion.
Help us to live the sorrows and struggles
of each day
as opportunities to grow
and to become more like you.
Make us able to face them
patiently and bravely,
full of trust in your support.

Make us understand that
we will find fullness of life
only when we continually die to ourselves
and to our selfish desires.

For it is only in dying with you
that we can rise with you.
From now on,
nothing can make us suffer or cry
to the point of forgetting the joy of your resurrection!
You are the sun that bursts forth from the Father's love.

May the joy of Jesus give us strength,
and may it create between us a bond of peace,
unity and love. Amen.

Saint Teresa of Calcutta

PRAYERS FOR CEMETERY VISITS

PSALM 23 — THE DIVINE SHEPHERD

The Lord is my shepherd, I shall not want.
He makes me lie down in green pastures;
he leads me beside still waters;
he restores my soul.
He leads me in right paths
for his name's sake.

Even though I walk through the darkest valley,
I fear no evil;
for you are with me;
your rod and your staff —
they comfort me.

You prepare a table before me
in the presence of my enemies;
you anoint my head with oil;
my cup overflows.

Surely goodness and mercy shall follow me
all the days of my life,
and I shall dwell in the house of the Lord
my whole life long.

ETERNAL REST

Eternal rest grant unto them, O Lord,
and let perpetual light shine upon them.
May the souls of the faithful departed,
through the mercy of God,
rest in peace. Amen.

DE PROFUNDIS *(Psalm 130)*

Out of the depths I cry to You, O Lord;
Lord, hear my voice.
Let Your ears be attentive
to my voice in supplication.
If You, O Lord, mark iniquities,
Lord, who can stand?
But with You is forgiveness,
that You may be revered.

I trust in the Lord;
my soul trusts in His word.
My soul waits for the Lord
more than sentinels wait for the dawn.
More than sentinels wait for the dawn,
let Israel wait for the Lord,

For with the Lord is kindness
and with Him is plenteous redemption;
And He will redeem Israel
from all their iniquities.

* * *

Lord, support us all the day long,
until the shadows lengthen
    and the evening comes,
and the busy world is hushed
and the fever of life is over
and our work is done.
Then in thy mercy grant us
a safe lodging,
and a holy rest,
and peace at the last.

Saint John Henry Newman

A WONDERFUL BIRTH

Death
is the ultimate grace
and the culmination
of our Christian life.
It is not the end,
as too many think,
but the beginning of a wonderful birth.

It marks not the end of a creature,
but their true development,
their full realization in love.
It fulfills our belonging in God's life,
removing the barriers that, here on Earth,
prevent us from enjoying life in God completely.

Death allows us to attend freely
to Love Eternal,
to be aware
that Love gives itself to us
and to live in God forever...
When I think about my approaching death,
I say to myself,
"Good – soon I will see God!"

Ven. Marthe Robin

WHERE DO THE READINGS AT MASS COME FROM?

One of the key teachings of Vatican II on the nature of the liturgy was on the significance of Scripture: "*Sacred scripture is of the greatest importance in the celebration of the liturgy*... Thus to achieve the restoration, progress, and adaptation of the sacred liturgy, *it is essential to promote that warm and living love for scripture to which the venerable tradition of both eastern and western rites gives testimony.*" (*Constitution on the Sacred Liturgy*, 24 [emphasis added])

Thus, "The treasures of the bible are to be opened up more lavishly, *so that richer fare may be provided for the faithful at the table of God's word.* In this way a more representative portion of the holy scriptures will be read to the people in the course of a prescribed number of years." *(CSL,* 51 [emphasis added]) Working from a renewed understanding of the nature of Scripture as God's Word, the scholars who were made responsible for the reform of the lectionary were able to produce the "richer fare" to be "provided for the faithful at the table of God's Word."

During the seasons of Lent, Easter, Advent, and Christmas, the choice and order of readings are aimed at giving the people of God an ever-greater understanding of the fundamentals of their faith and of the history of salvation. The season of Ordinary Time expands and develops these elements and presents more of Christ's teaching for the faithful to reflect on in relation to themselves and their participation in Christ's mission.

Within this broad framework, two principles were used to select and order Scripture texts: a principle of *continuous reading* of a bible book, and a principle of *harmony*. Each of three years focuses on a continuous reading of a Synoptic Gospel (Matthew, Mark or Luke). (The Gospel of John, due to its spiritual and theological richness, is read every year during Lent, Easter, and Christmas, and to a lesser extent during the year of Mark.) In order to understand better how the other Scripture readings in the three-year Sunday cycle are arranged, let us take up each liturgical season one by one.

The season of *Lent* begins with five Sundays that focus on repentance and conversion, and on the preparation of catechumens for baptism at Easter. On the first two Sundays of Lent each year, we hear the temptation of Christ, followed by the Transfiguration. Then in Year A, the gospels focus on baptismal preparation and the basic gifts Christ brings: living water, light and resurrection from the dead. In Year B, the focus is on the person of Jesus and his role in salvation according to the Gospel of John. In Year C, the gospels remind us of God's tireless patience, love and forgiveness. The last two weeks of Lent, including Palm Sunday and Holy Week, focus on the Passion of Jesus and what led to it.

The first reading of each Sunday of Lent is chosen according to the principle of *harmony*, connecting a person, theme, symbol, or event from the Hebrew Scriptures to the gospel reading. The second reading from the New Testament letters also connects to the theme of that particular Sunday, making it more explicit or commenting on it in some way.

Throughout the season of *Easter*, the Church rejoices in Jesus' overcoming of sin and death sealed in the new life of the resurrection. Before the Ascension, the gospel readings celebrate various apparitions of the Risen Christ, before shifting to John's Gospel which provides deeper meditation on the meaning of the Risen Christ for us. After the Ascension, we wait patiently for the coming of the Holy Spirit. The first reading throughout is from the Acts of the Apostles from beginning to end. The second reading, usually from the letters of Paul, stresses our living out of the Paschal Mystery of Christ.

The season of *Advent* focuses our attention on the threefold coming of Christ: his incarnation and birth at Bethlehem, his spiritual coming to each believer here and now, and his coming again at the end of the world. On the first Sunday of Advent each year, the gospel is always taken from one of the end-time teachings of Jesus in the Synoptic Gospels. On the Second Sunday, we meet John the Baptist who prepared the way for Christ's first coming. On the Third Sunday, we meet John the Baptist again, but this time experiencing the joy we feel at the world's salvation here and now. The Fourth Sunday gospels relate events more immediately connected to the first coming of Jesus: the dreams of Joseph (Year A), the Annunciation (Year B), and the Visitation (Year C). The first readings are prophecies of the Lord's coming, with a heavy emphasis on the prophet Isaiah, while the second readings emphasize the various themes of Advent hope.

The *Christmas* season consists mainly of a series of feasts: Christmas Day, Holy Family, Mary the Mother of God, Epiphany and the Baptism of Jesus. The gospel readings are connected to the events being celebrated in the feast, and the first and second readings are chosen thematically according to the feast.

The gospels of *Ordinary Time* are a continuous reading of Christ's ministry and teaching. The first reading for each Sunday in Ordinary Time is chosen according to the principle of harmony, so that a person, event, symbol or theme of the Hebrew Scriptures is related to the teaching of Christ for that Sunday. The second reading is independent, based on a principle of continuous reading of the New Testament letters.

A word about weekdays. Weekday masses have only two readings, on a separate two-year cycle independent of the Sunday cycle. The first reading is taken from the Hebrew Scriptures or from an apostle (Letters and Revelation), or from Acts during Easter. The principle is generally one of continuous reading through a biblical book, according to the liturgical season, arranged over two years. The gospel readings for Advent, Christmas, Easter and Ordinary Time are arranged in a single cycle repeated every year (with the principle of harmony relating the first reading and gospel used more closely during Lent).

Gilles Mongeau, SJ
Contributing Editor, Living with Christ

PRAYER IN THE MORNING

INVITATION TO PRAYER

Lord, open our lips.
And we shall proclaim your praise.
Glory to God in the highest.
And peace to God's people on earth.

HYMN OF PRAISE *(Optional)*

PSALM OF PRAISE

Psalm 63 and/or another psalm of praise, followed by a moment of silence.

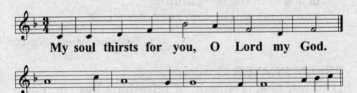

My soul thirsts for you, O Lord my God.

R. **My soul thirsts for you, O Lord my God.**

O God, you are my God, I · **seek_you**,
my soul · **thirsts_for_you;**
my flesh · **faints_for_you,**
as in a dry and weary land
    where there · **is** no water. R.

So I have looked upon you in the · **sanctuary,**
beholding your power and · **glory.**
Because your steadfast love is better than · **life,**
my · **lips** will praise_you. R.

So I will bless you as long as I · **live;**
I will lift up my hands and call on your · **name.**
My soul is satisfied as with a rich · **feast,**
and my mouth praises you
    with · **joy**-ful lips. ℟.

For you have been my · **help,**
and in the shadow of your wings I sing for · **joy.**
My soul · **clings_to_you;**
your right · **hand** up-holds_me. ℟.

Glory to the Father, and to the · **Son,**
and to the Holy · **Spirit.**
As it was in the be-·**ginning,**
is now and will be for · **ever.** A-men. ℟.

PSALM PRAYER *(Optional)*

Lord our God, Fountain of refreshing love, in morning light we seek your presence and strength, for your love is better than life itself. Accept our prayers with uplifted hands as we proclaim your praise in songs of joy. Satisfy our longing hearts and renew our thirsting spirits that our worship may give you glory and our lives be poured out in loving service.

    Glory and praise to you, loving God, through our Lord Jesus Christ, your Son, who lives and reigns with you in the unity of the Holy Spirit, God for ever and ever. **Amen.**

WORD OF GOD

Appropriate verse(s) selected beforehand from the readings of the day, followed by a moment of silence.

CANTICLE OF ZECHARIAH

1. Blessed be the God of Israel,
   Who comes to set us free,
   Who visits and redeems us,
   And grants us liberty.
   The prophets spoke of mercy,
   Of freedom and release;
   God shall fulfill the promise
   To bring our people peace.

2. Now from the house of David
   A child of grace is giv'n;
   A Saviour comes among us
   To raise us up to heaven.
   Before him goes the herald,
   Forerunner in the way:
   The prophet of salvation,
   The messenger of Day.

3. Where once were fear and darkness
   The sun begins to rise,
   The dawning of forgiveness
   Upon the sinners' eyes,
   To guide the feet of pilgrims
   Along the paths of peace:
   O bless our God and Saviour
   With songs that never cease!

Text: Michael Perry, ©1973 Hope Publishing Co.
Tune: MERLE'S TUNE, 76.76.D.; ©1983 Hope Publishing Co. Used with permission. All rights reserved. **Music:** *CBW III* 13E

PETITIONS

These reflect the needs of the Church, the world, the suffering, and the local community. Weekly suggestions are available at www.livingwithchrist.ca.

OUR FATHER...

CONCLUDING PRAYER

God of glory and compassion, at your touch the wilderness blossoms, broken lives are made whole, and fearful hearts grow strong in faith. Open our eyes to your presence and awaken our hearts to sing your praise. To all who long for your Son's return grant perseverance and patience, that we may announce in word and deed the good news of the kingdom.

We ask this through our Lord Jesus Christ, your Son, who lives and reigns with you in the unity of the Holy Spirit, God for ever and ever. **Amen.**

BLESSING

May the Lord almighty order our days and our deeds in lasting peace. **Amen.**

Let us offer each other a sign of Christ's peace.

The celebration ends with the exchange of peace.

* * *

For a fuller version of the Liturgy of the Hours, consult the Living with Christ *missalette.*

PRAYER IN THE EVENING

The paschal candle is lit and carried in procession. During Advent, the Advent wreath may be lit instead. If you plan to use Psalm 141, prepare the thurible beforehand so that incense may be burned during the singing of the psalm.

INVITATION TO PRAYER

God, come to our assistance.
Lord, make haste to help us.
Glory to the Father, and to the Son,
and to the Holy Spirit.
**As it was in the beginning, is now,
and will be forever. Amen.**

HYMN OF PRAISE *(Optional)*

PSALM OF PRAISE

Psalm 141 and/or another psalm of praise, followed by a moment of silence.

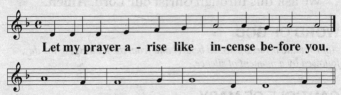

Let my prayer a - rise like   in-cense be-fore you.

R. **Let my prayer arise like incense before you.**

I call upon you, O Lord: come quickly to · **me;**
give ear to my voice when I call to · **you.**
Let my prayer be counted as incense be-·**fore you.**
and the lifting up of my hands as
    an eve-·**ning** sacrifice. R.

Set a guard over my mouth, O · **Lord;**
keep watch over the door of my · **lips.**
But my eyes are turned toward you,
    O God, my · **Lord;**
in you I seek refuge; do not leave me
    · **de**-fenceless. R.

Glory to the Father, and to the · **Son,**
and to the Holy · **Spirit.**
As it was in the be-·**ginning,**
is now and will be for ever. · **A**-men. R.

PSALM PRAYER *(Optional)*
Loving God, creator of light and life, may our prayers
ascend to you like the fragrance of incense. Purify
our hearts to sing your praise in the company of your
saints in glory.
    We ask this through Christ our Lord. **Amen.**

WORD OF GOD
*Appropriate verse(s) selected beforehand from the readings of the day,
followed by a moment of silence.*

CANTICLE OF MARY
1. My soul proclaims the Lord my God.
    My spirit sings God's praise,
    Who looks on me and lifts me up,
    That gladness fill my days.

2. All nations now will share my joy,
   For gifts God has outpoured.
   This lowly one has been made great
   I magnify the Lord.

3. For those who fear the Holy One,
   God's mercy will not die,
   Whose strong right arm puts down the proud,
   And lifts the lowly high.

4. God fills the hungry with good things,
   And sends the rich away.
   The promise made to Abraham,
   Is filled to endless day.

5. Then let all nations praise our God,
   The Father and the Son,
   The Spirit blest who lives in us,
   While endless ages run.

Text: Anne Carter, ©1988 *Religious of the Sacred Heart.*
Tune: HEATHER DEW **Music:** *CBW III* 592, 617; *CBW II* 74, **589**

PETITIONS

*These reflect the needs of the Church, the world, the suffering,
and the local community. Weekly suggestions are available at
www.livingwithchrist.ca.*

OUR FATHER...

CONCLUDING PRAYER

Creator of the universe, watch over us and keep us in the light of your presence. May our praise continually blend with that of all creation, until we come together to the eternal joys which you promise in your love.

We ask this through our Lord Jesus Christ, your Son, who lives and reigns with you in the unity of the Holy Spirit, God for ever and ever. **Amen.**

BLESSING

May God the Father almighty bless and keep us. **Amen.**

May Jesus Christ, his only Son, our Lord, graciously smile upon us. **Amen.**

May the Holy Spirit, the Lord and giver of life, grant us peace. **Amen.**

Let us offer each other a sign of Christ's peace.

The celebration ends with the exchange of peace.

* * *

For a fuller version of the Liturgy of the Hours, consult the Living with Christ *missalette.*

CELEBRATING THE SACRAMENT OF RECONCILIATION

When ready to celebrate the sacrament of Reconciliation (Confession), the following steps are involved.

BEFOREHAND

Examination of Conscience (p. 622):

Pray to the Holy Spirit for light and strength, examine your conscience in the light of the Scriptures and the Commandments since your last confession and become truly sorry for your sins.

GOING TO CONFESSION

Welcome:

The priest welcomes you, the penitent. It is helpful if you indicate the time of your last Confession and anything else that will help the priest hearing your confession.

Scripture:

A short passage of Scripture may be read.

Confession:

Confess your sins and listen to the advice of the priest.

Penance:

The priest proposes a good action or prayer to help make up for sin and deepen virtue.

Prayer of Sorrow (Act of Contrition – p. 624):

Pray expressing personal sorrow and asking for forgiveness.

Absolution:
The priest grants absolution in the name of God and the Church.

Praise of God and Dismissal:
The priest invites you to praise God and dismisses you to go in peace.

AFTERWARD
Spend some time in thanking God for forgiving us and restoring us to full life in Christ.

EXAMINATION OF CONSCIENCE

Do I centre my life on God, on fidelity to the Gospel and the Commandments? Do I set aside time for personal prayer? Am I open to the guidance of the Holy Spirit, to personal growth and change? Do I place more value on my desires for success, public recognition and personal comfort than on living my God-given mission?

Do I keep Sunday by participating in the Eucharist?

Is Sunday a day of prayer and rest? Do I observe the penitential practices of the Church? Do I keep Lent as a time of prayer and sacrifice?

Do I behave as a Christian in daily and public life? Am I charitable in my interactions with others, whether in person or online? Is my faith reflected in my employment?

Have I taken property of others, including that of my employer? As an employer, have I treated my employees with respect, paying a just wage with appropriate benefits?

Am I envious of what others have? Do I share my goods and time with those in need? Do I respect the inherent dignity of every person?

Do I care for my family? Do I try to live the Christian life within my family — towards my parents, spouse, children? Do I set aside distractions to give quality time to my family? Am I passing on the faith to my children?

Do I exercise authority with genuine concern and responsibility? Do I give others the same respect that I expect for myself?

Have I dishonoured my body by thoughts or actions incompatible with Christian life? Am I faithful to my marriage? Do I set an example of committed single living?

Do I live out my responsibility for God's creation? Do I live wastefully? Are there changes I can make in my daily living — at home, school, work, community — to conserve the earth's resources for future generations?

How do I deal with the difficulties, failures and disappointments of life? Do I reach out to help family members or friends who are suffering? Do I recognize the face of Christ in each person, regardless of their race, class, age, ability, gender or sexuality?

Do I tend to the spiritual, physical and medical needs of my body? Can others see the grace of Baptism at work in my life?

ACT OF CONTRITION

My God,
I am sorry for my sins with all my heart.
In choosing to do wrong
and failing to do good,
I have sinned against you
whom I should love above all things.
I firmly intend, with your help,
to do penance,
to sin no more,
and to avoid whatever leads me to sin.
Our Saviour Jesus Christ
suffered and died for us.
In his name, my God, have mercy.

Excerpted from *Celebrating Reconciliation*
(Ottawa: Concacan Inc., 2006).

PRAYERS FOR ADORATION

Loving Jesus,

I am filled with gratitude for the privilege of this
quiet time in your Presence.

Grant me strength to go out from this place of
sacred silence into the busy world.

May my experience of your Presence here
help me to see your Presence there –

in the faces of the lonely and seeking souls I meet,
in the outstretched hands of the poor and needy,
in the hearts of my family and my dearest friends,
in the eyes of those who are most difficult
and hard for me to bear.

As I experience your Presence in your beloved ones,
may I act with love and generosity so that they may
also experience it in me. Amen.

Christine Way Skinner

Dear Jesus,

here present in the Blessed Sacrament,
I know you are always with me throughout the day
and night,
but in this special time, help me to turn my mind
and heart to you.

As I pray, first of all I want to offer you praise and
glory
for inviting me to be a member of your family
through Baptism

and for enabling me to grow in your love
by receiving your Body and Blood in the Holy
    Eucharist.

Secondly, I wish to thank you for watching over me
    and guiding me
as I go about my daily activities.

Thirdly, I ask for forgiveness for the many times
when I fail to accept and follow your guidance –
the times when my weak human nature yields
    to temptation.

Fourthly, I petition and ask for your special help
in the numerous difficult situations and problems
that I seem to encounter so often.

Without you I can do nothing.
I'm sure that not long after I leave you
    here in this Eucharistic presence,
I will be calling on your special help again.
Please listen to my petitions
and grant those which will help me become more
    pleasing in your sight.

I offer this prayer to you, Our Lord Jesus,
who live and reign with the Father and the Holy
    Spirit forever and ever.

Amen.

Norbert Oberle

Excerpted from *Prayers and Devotions for Eucharistic
Adoration* (Toronto: Novalis, 2016), pp. 66, 69-70.

KYRIE – PENITENTIAL ACT, FORM 1

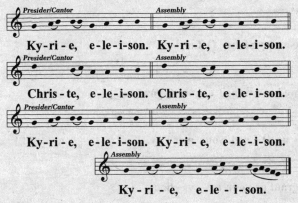

Presider/Cantor — Assembly
Ky-ri-e, e-le-i-son. Ky-ri-e, e-le-i-son.

Presider/Cantor — Assembly
Chris-te, e-le-i-son. Chris-te, e-le-i-son.

Presider/Cantor — Assembly
Ky-ri-e, e-le-i-son. Ky-ri-e, e-le-i-son.

Assembly
Ky-ri-e, e-le-i-son.

or

Presider/Cantor — Assembly
Lord, have mer-cy. Lord, have mer-cy.

Presider/Cantor — Assembly
Christ, have mer-cy. Christ, have mer-cy.

Presider/Cantor — Assembly
Lord, have mer-cy. Lord, have mer-cy.

KYRIE – PENITENTIAL ACT, FORM 2

Presider/Cantor

Have mercy on us, O Lord.

Assembly

For we have sinned a-gainst you.

Presider/Cantor

Show us, O Lord, your mer - cy.

Assembly

And grant us your sal - va - tion.

Text and setting: *Excerpts from Chants of the Roman Missal*
© 2010 ICEL. Used with permission.

KYRIE – PENITENTIAL ACT, FORM 3

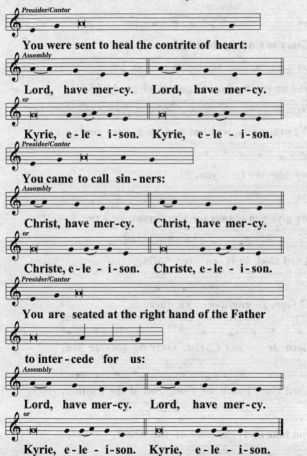

Presider/Cantor

You were sent to heal the contrite of heart:

Assembly

Lord, have mer-cy. Lord, have mer-cy.

or

Kyrie, e-le-i-son. Kyrie, e-le-i-son.

Presider/Cantor

You came to call sin-ners:

Assembly

Christ, have mer-cy. Christ, have mer-cy.

or

Christe, e-le-i-son. Christe, e-le-i-son.

Presider/Cantor

You are seated at the right hand of the Father

to inter-cede for us:

Assembly

Lord, have mer-cy. Lord, have mer-cy.

or

Kyrie, e-le-i-son. Kyrie, e-le-i-son.

Text and setting: *Excerpts from Chants of the Roman Missal*
© 2010 ICEL. Used with permission.

GLORIA

Glory to God in the high - est,

and on earth peace to people of good will.

We praise you, we bless you, we a - dore you,

we glo - ri - fy   you,

we give you thanks for your great glo - ry,

Lord God, heav - en - ly   King,

O God, al - might - y   Fa - ther.

Lord Je - sus Christ, Only Be - got - ten Son,

Lord God, Lamb of God, Son of the Fa - ther,

you take away the sins of the world,

have mer - cy   on us;

GLORIA *(continue)*

you take away the sins of the world,

re - ceive our prayer;

you are seated at the right hand of the Fa-ther,

have mer - cy on us.

For you alone are the Ho - ly One,

you a - lone are the Lord,

you alone are the Most High, Je - sus Christ,

with the Ho - ly Spir - it,

in the glory of God the Fa-ther. A - men.

Music: *Anonymous.* **Text:** *Excerpts from Chants of the Roman Missal* © 2010 ICEL. Used with permission.

HOLY, HOLY, HOLY

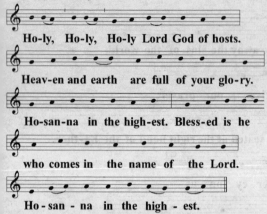

Ho-ly, Ho-ly, Ho-ly Lord God of hosts.

Heav-en and earth are full of your glo-ry.

Ho-san-na in the high-est. Bless-ed is he

who comes in the name of the Lord.

Ho - san - na in the high - est.

Text and setting: *Excerpts from Chants of the Roman Missal*
© 2010 ICEL. Used with permission.

SANCTUS, SANCTUS, SANCTUS

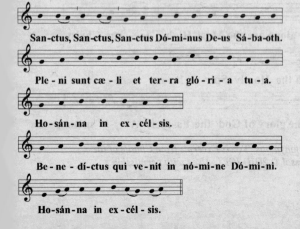

San-ctus, San-ctus, San-ctus Dó-mi-nus De-us Sá-ba-oth.

Ple - ni sunt cæ - li et ter - ra gló - ri - a tu - a.

Ho - sán - na in ex - cél - sis.

Be - ne - dí-ctus qui ve - nit in nó-mi-ne Dó-mi-ni.

Ho - sán - na in ex - cél - sis.

MEMORIAL ACCLAMATIONS

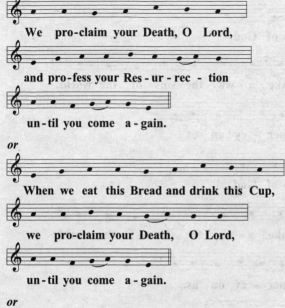

We pro-claim your Death, O Lord,

and pro-fess your Res - ur - rec - tion

un - til you come a - gain.

or

When we eat this Bread and drink this Cup,

we pro-claim your Death, O Lord,

un - til you come a - gain.

or

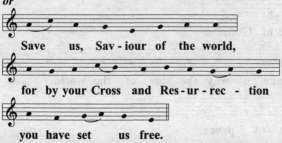

Save us, Sav - iour of the world,

for by your Cross and Res - ur - rec - tion

you have set us free.

Text and setting: *Excerpts from Chants of the Roman Missal*
© 2010 ICEL. Used with permission.

LAMB OF GOD

Lamb of God,

you take a - way the sins of the world,

have mer - cy on us.

Lamb of God,

you take a - way the sins of the world,

have mer - cy on us.

Lamb of God,

you take a - way the sins of the world,

Grant us peace.

Text and setting: *Excerpts from Chants of the Roman Missal*
© 2010, ICEL. Used with permission.

AGNUS DEI

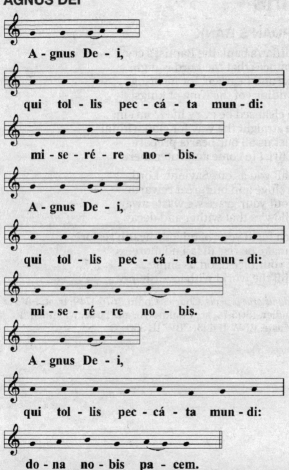

A - gnus De - i,

qui tol - lis pec - cá - ta mun - di:

mi - se - ré - re no - bis.

A - gnus De - i,

qui tol - lis pec - cá - ta mun - di:

mi - se - ré - re no - bis.

A - gnus De - i,

qui tol - lis pec - cá - ta mun - di:

do - na no - bis pa - cem.

Text and setting: *Excerpts from Chants of the Roman Missal*

Hymns

ON JORDAN'S BANK

1. On Jordan's bank the Baptist's cry
   Announces that the Lord is nigh;
   Awake and hearken, for he brings
   Glad tidings of the King of kings!

2. Then cleansed be ev'ry life from sin;
   Make straight the way for God within;
   And let us all our hearts prepare
   For Christ to come and enter there.

3. We hail you as our Saviour, Lord,
   Our refuge and our great reward;
   Without your grace we waste away
   Like flow'rs that wither and decay.

4. Stretch forth your hand, our health restore,
   And make us rise to fall no more;
   O, let your face upon us shine
   And fill the world with love divine.

Text: *Jordanis oras praevis*, Charles Coffin, 1676-1749; tr. st. 1-3
John Chandler, 1806-76; st. 4 unknown; alt. **Tune:** WINCHESTER
NEW, LM **Music:** CBW II 443; CBW III 350

O COME, O COME EMMANUEL

1. O come, O come, Emmanuel,
   And ransom captive Israel
   That mourns in lonely exile here
   Until the Son of God appear.

Ref: Rejoice! Rejoice! Emmanuel shall come to you, O Israel.

2. O come, O Wisdom from on high,
   Who order all things mightily;
   To us the path of knowledge show,
   And teach us in your ways to go.

3. O come, O come, great Lord of might,
   Who to your tribes on Sinai's height
   In ancient times once gave the law,
   In cloud, and majesty, and awe.

4. O come, O rod of Jesse's stem,
   From ev'ry foe deliver them
   That trust your mighty pow'r to save,
   and give them vict'ry o'er the grave.

5. O come, O key of David, come
   And open wide our heav'nly home;
   Make safe the way that leads on high,
   And close the path to misery.

6. O come, O Dayspring from on high,
   And cheer us by your drawing nigh;
   Disperse the gloomy clouds of night,
   And death's dark shadow put to flight.

7. O come, Desire of nations, bind
   In one the hearts of humankind;
   O bid our sad divisions cease,
   And be for us our king of peace.

Text: *Veni, veni Emmanuel;* Latin 9th c.; tr. by John Mason Neale, 1818-1866, alt. **Tune:** VENI, VENI EMMANUEL **Music:** CBW II 440; CBW III 312

O COME, DIVINE MESSIAH!

1. O come, divine Messiah!
   The world in silence waits the day
   When hope shall sing its triumph,
   And sadness flee away.

Ref: Sweet Saviour, haste;
   Come, come to earth:
   Dispel the night, and show thy face,
   And bid us hail the dawn of grace.
   O come, divine Messiah,
   The world in silence waits the day
   When hope shall sing its triumph,
   And sadness flee away.

2. O thou, whom nations sighed for,
   Whom priests and prophets long foretold,
   Wilt break the captive fetters,
   Redeem the long-lost fold.

3. Shalt come in peace and meekness,
   And lowly will your cradle be:
   All clothed in human weakness
   Shall we thy God-head see.

Text: Abbé Pellegrin, 1663-1745; tr. Sr. Mary of St. Philip
Tune: VENEZ DIVIN MESSIE, 78.76.888 **Music:** CBW II 441;
CBW III 310

WHAT CHILD IS THIS

1. What Child is this, who laid to rest,
   On Mary's lap is sleeping?
   Whom angels greet with anthems sweet,
   While shepherds watch are keeping?

Ref: This, this is Christ the King,
   Whom shepherds guard and angels sing:
   Haste, haste to bring him laud,
   The babe, the son of Mary.

2. Why lies he in such mean estate
   Where ox and ass are feeding?
   Good Christian, fear: for sinners here
   The silent Word is pleading.

3. So bring him incense, gold, and myrrh,
   Come, peasant, king to own him,
   The King of kings salvation brings,
   Let loving hearts enthrone him.

Text: William Chatterton Dix, 1837-1898 **Tune:** GREENSLEEVES, 87 87 with refrain **Music:** CBW II 461; CBW III 338

GOOD CHRISTIAN FRIENDS, REJOICE

Good Christian friends, rejoice
With heart and soul and voice;

1. O give heed to what we say:
    Jesus Christ was born today!
    Ox and ass before him bow,
    and he is in the manger now.
    Christ is born today!
    Christ is born today!

2. Now you hear of endless bliss:
    Jesus Christ was born for this!
    He has opened heaven's door,
    And we are blest for ever more.
    Christ was born for this!
    Christ was born for this!

3. Now you need not fear the grave:
    Jesus Christ was born to save!
    Calls you one and calls you all
    To gain his everlasting hall.
    Christ was born to save!
    Christ was born to save!

Text: *In dulci jubilo;* Latin and German, 14th c., tr. John Mason
Neale, 1818-1866, alt. **Tune:** IN DULCI JUBILO; 66 77 77 55
Music: *CBW II 465; CBW III 322*

O COME, ALL YE FAITHFUL

1. O come, all ye faithful, joyful and triumphant,
   O come ye, o come ye to Bethlehem;
   Come and behold him, born the king of angels.

Ref: O come, let us adore him,
   O come, let us adore him,
   O come, let us adore him, Christ, the Lord!

2. Sing, choirs of angels, sing in exultation,
   Sing, all ye citizens of heav'n above!
   Glory to God in the highest.

3. Yea, Lord, we greet thee, born this happy morning,
   Jesus, to thee be glory giv'n;
   Word of the Father, now in flesh appearing.

Text: *Adeste, fideles;* John F. Wade, c. 1711-1786; tr. Frederick Oakley, 1802-80, alt. **Tune:** ADESTE, FIDELES, Irregular with refrain; John F. Wade, c. 1711-1786 **Music:** CBW II 458; CBW III 329

THE FIRST NOWELL

1. The first Nowell the angel did say
   Was to certain poor shepherds in fields as they lay;
   In fields where they lay, keeping their sheep,
   On a cold winter's night that was so deep.

Ref: Nowell, Nowell, Nowell, Nowell,
   born is the King of Israel.

2. They lookéd up and saw a star
   Shining in the east, beyond them far,
   And to the earth it gave great light
   And so it continued both day and night.

3. And by the light of that same star
   Three wise men came from country far;
   To seek for a king was their intent,
   And to follow the star wherever it went.

4. This star drew nigh to the northwest,
   O'er Bethlehem it took its rest,
   And there it did both stop and stay
   Right over the place where Jesus lay.

5. Then entered in those wise men three,
   Full reverently upon their knee,
   And offered there in his presence,
   Their gold and myrrh and frankincense.

6. Then let us all with one accord
   Sing praises to our heav'nly Lord:
   Who with the Father we adore
   And Spirit blest for evermore.

Text: English Carol, 17th c. **Tune:** THE FIRST NOWELL, Irregular
Music: CBW II 460; CBW III 344

TAKE UP YOUR CROSS

1. Take up your cross, the Saviour said,
   If you would my disciple be;
   Take up your cross with willing heart,
   And humbly follow after me.

2. Take up your cross, let not its weight
   Fill your weak spirit with alarm;
   His strength shall bear your spirit up,
   And brace your heart and nerve your arm.

3. Take up your cross, heed not the shame,
   And let your foolish heart be still;
   The Lord for you accepted death
   Upon a cross, on Calvary's hill.

4. Take up your cross, then, in his strength,
   And calmly every danger brave:
   It guides you to abundant life,
   And leads to vict'ry o'er the grave.

5. Take up your cross, and follow Christ,
   Nor think till death to lay it down;
   For only those who bear the cross
   May hope to wear the glorious crown.

Text: Charles W. Everest, 1814-1877, alt. **Tune:** ERHALT UNS, HERR, LM **Music:** CBW II 481; CBW III 352

O SACRED HEAD SURROUNDED

1. O sacred head surrounded
   By crown of piercing thorn.
   O bleeding head, so wounded
   Reviled and put to scorn.
   The pow'r of death comes o'er you,
   The glow of life decays,
   Yet angel hosts adore you,
   And tremble as they gaze.

2. In this your bitter passion,
   Good Shepherd, think of me
   With your most sweet compassion,
   Unworthy though I be:
   Beneath your cross abiding
   For ever would I rest,
   In your dear love confiding,
   And with your presence blest.

3. Christ Jesus, we adore you,
   Our thorn-crowned Lord and King.
   We bow our heads before you,
   And to your cross we cling.
   Lord, give us strength to bear it
   With patience and with love,
   That we may truly merit
   A glorious crown above.

Text: Bernard of Clairvaux, v. 1, tr. Henry W. Baker, 1821-77; v. 2 & 3, tr. Arthur T. Russell, 1806-74, alt. **Tune:** PASSION CHORALE; 76 76 D; Hans Leo Hassler, 1564-1612 **Music:** CBW II 491; CBW III 377

LORD, WHO THROUGHOUT THESE FORTY DAYS

1. Lord, who throughout these forty days
   For us did fast and pray,
   Teach us to overcome our sins
   And close by you to stay.

2. As you with Satan did contend
   And did the vict'ry win,
   O give us strength in you to fight,
   In you to conquer sin.

3. As you did hunger and did thirst,
   So teach us, gracious Lord,
   To die to self and so to live
   By your most holy word.

4. And through these days of penitence,
   and through your passion-tide,
   For evermore, in life and death,
   O Lord, with us abide.

5. Abide with us, that through this life
   Of doubts and hopes and pain
   An Easter of unending joy
   We may at last attain.

Text: Claudia F. Hernaman, 1838-98, in her *A Child's Book of Praise*, 1873, alt. **Tune:** ST. FLAVIAN, CM; adapted from Day's Psalter, 1562 **Music:** CBW II 482; CBW III 367

JESUS CHRIST IS RIS'N TODAY

1. Jesus Christ is ris'n today, Alleluia!
   Our triumphant holy day, Alleluia!
   Who did once upon the cross, Alleluia!
   Suffer to redeem our loss. Alleluia!

2. Hymns of praise then let us sing, Alleluia!
   Unto Christ our heav'nly king, Alleluia!
   Who endured the cross and grave, Alleluia!
   Sinners to redeem and save. Alleluia!

3. But the pains which he endured, Alleluia!
   Our salvation have procured; Alleluia!
   Now above the sky he's king, Alleluia!
   Where the angels ever sing. Alleluia!

4. Sing we to our God above, Alleluia!
   Praise eternal as his love, Alleluia!
   Praise him, now his might confess, Alleluia!
   Father, Son and Spirit bless. Alleluia!

Text: Lyra Davidica, 1708, alt. & others **Tune:** EASTER HYMN; 77
77 with Alleluias **Music:** CBW II 500; CBW III 389

O SONS AND DAUGHTERS

Ref: Alleluia, alleluia, alleluia!

1. O sons and daughters, let us sing!
   The king of heav'n, our glorious king,
   From death today rose triumphing. Alleluia!

2. That Easter morn, at break of day,
   The faithful women went their way,
   To seek the tomb where Jesus lay. Alleluia!

3. An angel clothed in white they see,
   Who sat and spoke unto the three,
   "Your Lord has gone to Galilee." Alleluia!

4. That night th'apostles met in fear;
   And Christ did in their midst appear,
   And said, "My peace be with you here." Alleluia!

5. How blest are they who have not seen,
   And yet whose faith has constant been,
   For they eternal life shall win. Alleluia!

6. On this most holy day of days,
   To God your hearts and voices raise,
   In laud and jubilee and praise. Alleluia!

Text: Jean Tisserand, †1494; tr. John Mason Neale, 1818-66, alt.
Tune: O FILII ET FILIAE 8 8 8 4 with Alleluias
Music: CBW II 506; CBW III 404

THE STRIFE IS O'ER

Ref: Alleluia, alleluia, alleluia!

1. The strife is o'er, the battle done;
   Now is the victor's triumph won;
   O let the song of praise be sung! Alleluia!

2. The pow'rs of sin have done their worst;
   But Jesus has his foes dispersed;
   Let shouts of joy and praise out-burst! Alleluia!

3. Lord, by the stripes which wounded you,
   From death's sting free your servants too,
   That we may live and sing to you. Alleluia!

4. On the third morn you rose again,
   Glorious in majesty to reign;
   O let us swell the joyful strain! Alleluia!

Text: *Finita iam sunt praelia*, Latin 12th c.; *Symphonia Sirenum Selectarum*, Cologne, 1695; tr. Francis Pott, 1832-1909, alt. **Tune:** VICTORY, 8 8 8 with Alleluias **Music:** CBW II 503; CBW III 395

THAT EASTER DAY WITH JOY WAS BRIGHT

1. That Easter day with joy was bright,
   The sun shone out with fairer light,
   Alleluia, alleluia!
   When to their longing eyes restored,
   The glad apostles saw their Lord.

Ref: Alleluia, alleluia, alleluia, alleluia, alleluia!

2. His risen flesh with radiance glowed;
   His wounded hands and feet he showed;
   Alleluia, alleluia!
   Those scars their solemn witness gave
   That Christ was risen from the grave.

3. O Jesus, in your gentleness,
   With constant love our hearts possess;
   Alleluia, alleluia!
   To you our lips will ever raise
   The tribute of our grateful praise.

4. O Lord of all, with us abide
   In this our joyful Eastertide;
   Alleluia, alleluia!
   From ev'ry weapon death can wield
   Your own redeemed for ever shield.

5. All praise to you, O risen Lord,
   Now by both heav'n and earth adored;
   Alleluia, alleluia!
   To God the Father equal praise,
   And Spirit blest our songs we raise.

Text: *Claro paschali gaudio;* Latin 5th c; tr. By John Mason Neal, 1818-1866; alt. **Tune:** LASST UNS ERFREUEN, LM with Alleluias
Music: CBW II 507; CBW III 392

HAIL, HOLY QUEEN, ENTHRONED ABOVE

1. Hail, holy Queen, enthroned above, O Maria!
    Hail, Queen of mercy and of love, O Maria!

Ref: Triumph, all you cherubim,
    sing with us, you seraphim,
    Heav'n and earth resound the hymn:
    Salve, salve, salve, Regina!

2. Our life, our sweetness here below, O Maria!
    Our hope in sorrow and in woe, O Maria!

3. We honour you for Christ, your son, O Maria!
    Who has for us redemption won, O Maria!

Text: *Salve, Regina, mater misericordiae*, c. 1080; tr. from the
Roman Hymnal, 1884 **Tune:** SALVE, REGINA COELITUM, 84 84 with
refrain **Music:** CBW II 610; CBW III 457

IMMACULATE MARY

1. Immaculate Mary, your praises we sing,
   You reign now in heaven with Jesus our king.

Ref: Ave, Ave, Ave, Maria!
   Ave, Ave, Ave, Maria!

2. In heaven, the blessed your glory proclaim;
   On earth, we your children invoke your fair name.

3. Your name is our power, your virtues our light;
   Your love is our comfort, your pleading our might.

4. We pray for our mother the Church upon earth,
   And bless, dearest lady, the land of our birth.

Text: Anon., in *Parochial Hymn Book*, Boston, 1897, rev. version of
"Hail, Virgin of Virgins," by Jeremiah Cummings, 1814-1866, in
his *Songs for Catholic Schools*, 1860, alt. **Tune:** LOURDES HYMN, 11 11
Music: CBW II 611: CBW III 463A

HOLY GOD, WE PRAISE YOUR NAME

1. Holy God, we praise your name;
   Lord of all, we bow before you.
   All on earth your sceptre claim;
   All in heav'n above adore you.
   Infinite your vast domain;
   Everlasting is your reign.

2. Hark, the glad celestial hymn
   Angel choirs above are raising:
   Cherubim and seraphim,
   In unceasing chorus praising,
   Fill the heav'ns with sweet accord:
   "Holy, holy, holy Lord!"

3. Lo, the apostolic train
   Joins your sacred name to hallow;
   Prophets swell the glad refrain,
   And the white-robed martyrs follow;
   And from morn to set of sun,
   Through the church the song goes on.

4. Holy Father, holy Son,
   Holy Spirit, three we name you,
   Though in essence only one;
   Undivided God, we claim you,
   And, adoring, bend the knee
   While we own the mystery.

Text: *Te Deum laudamus; tr.* Clarence Walworth, 1820-1900, in
Catholic Psalmist, 1858, alt. **Tune:** GROSSER GOTT, 7 8 7 8 77
Music: CBW II 631; CBW III 555

ALL PEOPLE THAT ON EARTH DO DWELL

1. All people that on earth do dwell,
   Sing to the Lord with cheerful voice;
   Him serve with mirth, his praise forth tell,
   Come we before him and rejoice.

2. Know that the Lord is God indeed;
   Without our aid he did us make;
   We are his folk, he does us feed,
   And for his sheep he does us take.

3. O enter then his gates with praise;
   Approach with joy his courts unto;
   Praise, laud, and bless his name always,
   For it is seemly so to do.

4. For why? The Lord our God is good:
   His mercy is for ever sure;
   His truth at all times firmly stood,
   And shall from age to age endure.

5. To Father, Son, and Holy Ghost,
   The God whom heav'n and earth adore,
   From us and from the angel host
   Be praise and glory evermore.

6. Praise God, from whom all blessings flow,
   Praise him, all creatures here below;
   Praise him above, you heav'nly host;
   Praise Father, Son, and Holy Ghost.

Text: Psalm 100; William Kethe, d. c. 1594; v. 6: Thomas Ken, 1637-1711 **Tune:** OLD HUNDREDTH, LM 8 8 8 8 **Music:** CBW II 621; CBW III 578

COME, HOLY SPIRIT

1. Come, Holy Spirit, Creator blest,
   And in our hearts take up your rest;
   Come with your grace and heav'nly aid
   To fill the hearts which you have made.

2. O Comforter, to you we cry,
   The heav'nly gift of God most high;
   The fount of life and fire of love,
   And sweet anointing from above.

3. To ev'ry sense your light impart,
   And shed your love in ev'ry heart.
   To our weak flesh your strength supply:
   Unfailing courage from on high.

4. O grant that we through you may come
   To know the Father and the Son,
   And hold with firm, unchanging faith
   That you are Spirit of them both.

5. Now let us praise Father and Son,
   And Holy Spirit, with them one;
   And may the Son on us bestow
   The gifts that from the Spirit flow.

Text: *Veni, Creator Spiritus*, anon., 9th c.; tr. by Edward
Caswall, 1814-1878, et al.; alt. **Tune:** LAMBILOTTE, LM
Music: CBW II 516; CBW III 416

FOR ALL THE SAINTS

1. For all the saints,
   Who from their labours rest,
   Who their great faith
   To all the world confessed,
   Your name, O Jesus,
   Be forever blest. Alleluia, alleluia.

2. You were their rock,
   Their fortress and their might,
   Their strength and solace
   In the well-fought fight,
   And in the darkness
   their unfailing light. Alleluia, alleluia.

3. O blest communion,
   Family divine,
   We live and struggle,
   You in glory shine;
   Yet all are one
   within God's great design. Alleluia, alleluia.

4. And when the strife
   Is fierce, the conflict long,
   Then from the distance
   Sounds the trumpet song,
   And hearts are bold again,
   And courage strong. Alleluia, alleluia.

Text: William How, 1823-1897 **Tune:** SINE NOMINE, 10 10 10 with
Alleluias **Music:** CBW II 617; CBW III 449. SERVICE MUSIC

Music Index

SERVICE MUSIC

Eucharistic Chants   627

HYMNS

All People That on Earth Do Dwell   653

Come, Holy Spirit   654

For All the Saints   655

Good Christian Friends, Rejoice   640

Hail Holy Queen, Enthroned Above   650

Hail Our Saviour's Glorious Body   270

Holy God, We Praise Your Name   652

Immaculate Mary   651

Jesus Christ Is Ris'n Today   646

Lord, Who Throughout These Forty Days   645

O Come, All Ye Faithful   641

O Come, Divine Messiah   638

O Come, O Come Emmanuel   637

O Sacred Head Surrounded   644

O Sons and Daughters   647

On Jordan's Bank   636

Pange Lingua / Tantum Ergo   270

Take Up Your Cross   643

That Easter Day with Joy Was Bright   649

The First Nowell   642

The Strife Is O'er   648

What Child Is This   639